P9-BJW-357

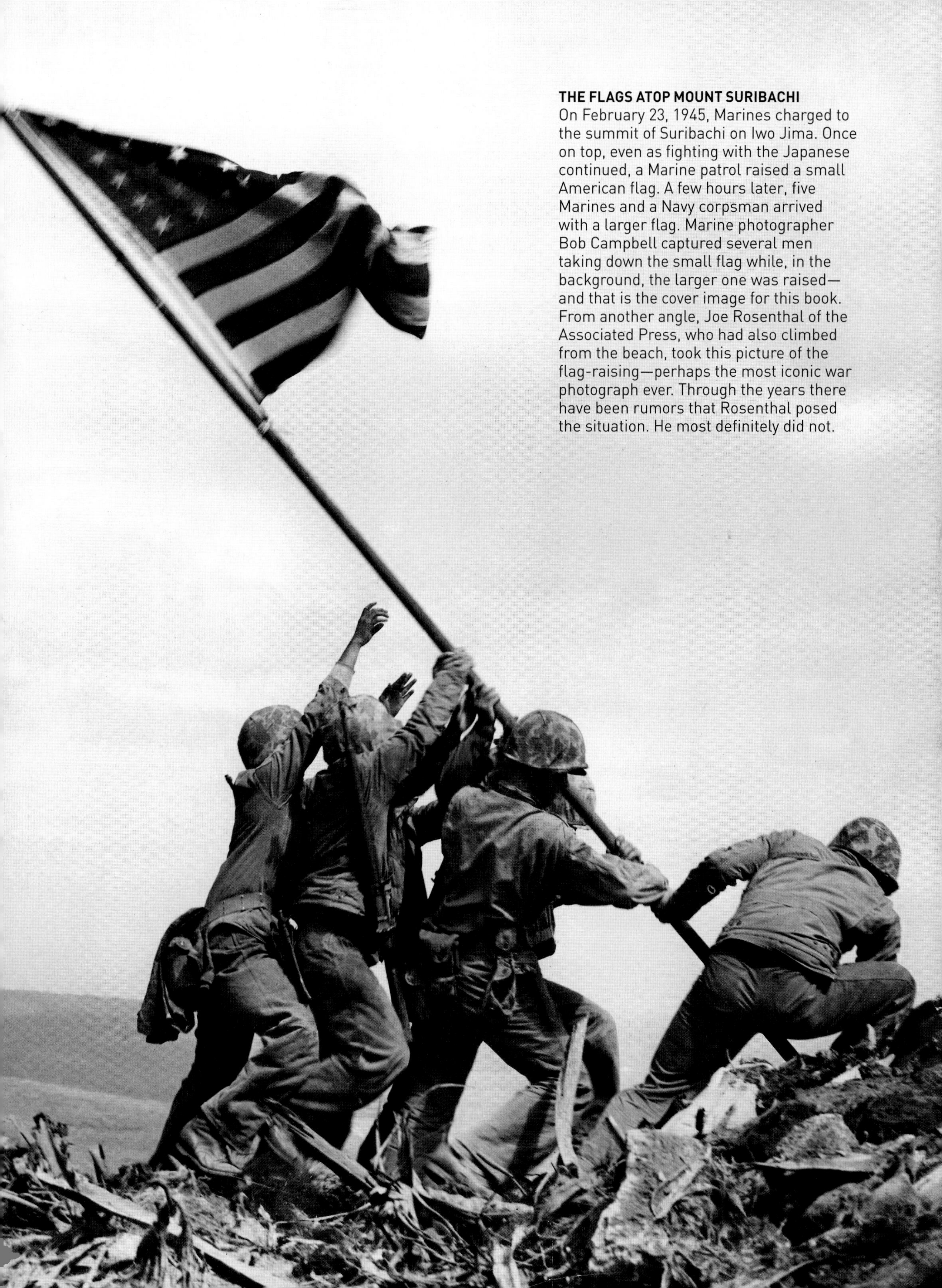

THE FLAGS ATOP MOUNT SURIBACHI
On February 23, 1945, Marines charged to the summit of Suribachi on Iwo Jima. Once on top, even as fighting with the Japanese continued, a Marine patrol raised a small American flag. A few hours later, five Marines and a Navy corpsman arrived with a larger flag. Marine photographer Bob Campbell captured several men taking down the small flag while, in the background, the larger one was raised—and that is the cover image for this book. From another angle, Joe Rosenthal of the Associated Press, who had also climbed from the beach, took this picture of the flag-raising—perhaps the most iconic war photograph ever. Through the years there have been rumors that Rosenthal posed the situation. He most definitely did not.

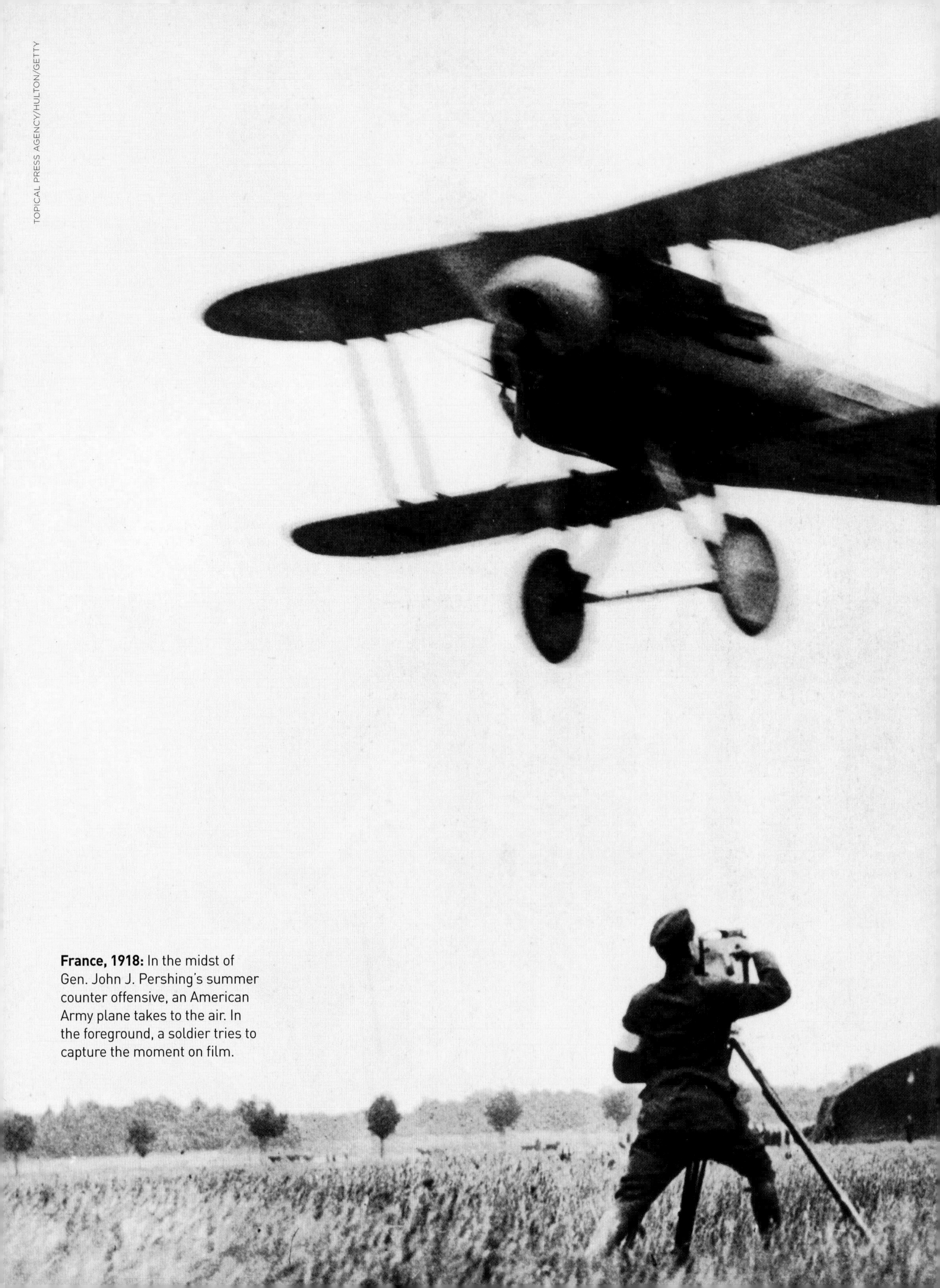

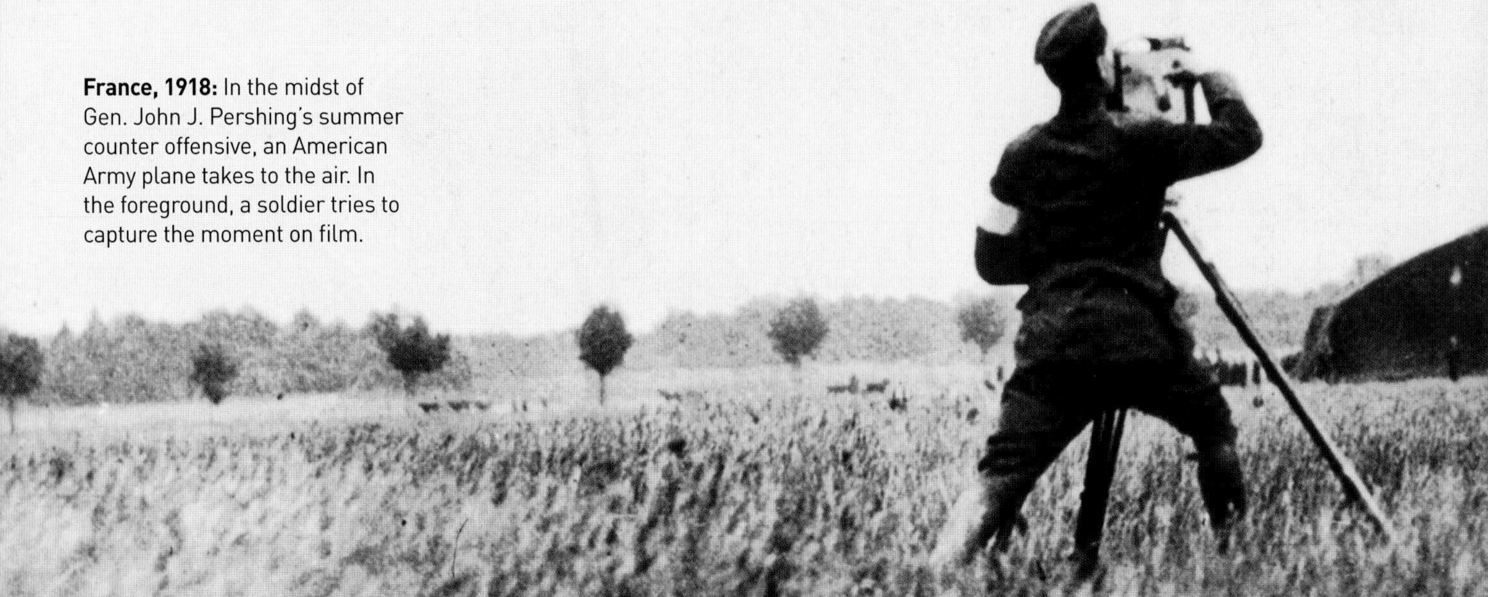

France, 1918: In the midst of Gen. John J. Pershing's summer counter offensive, an American Army plane takes to the air. In the foreground, a soldier tries to capture the moment on film.

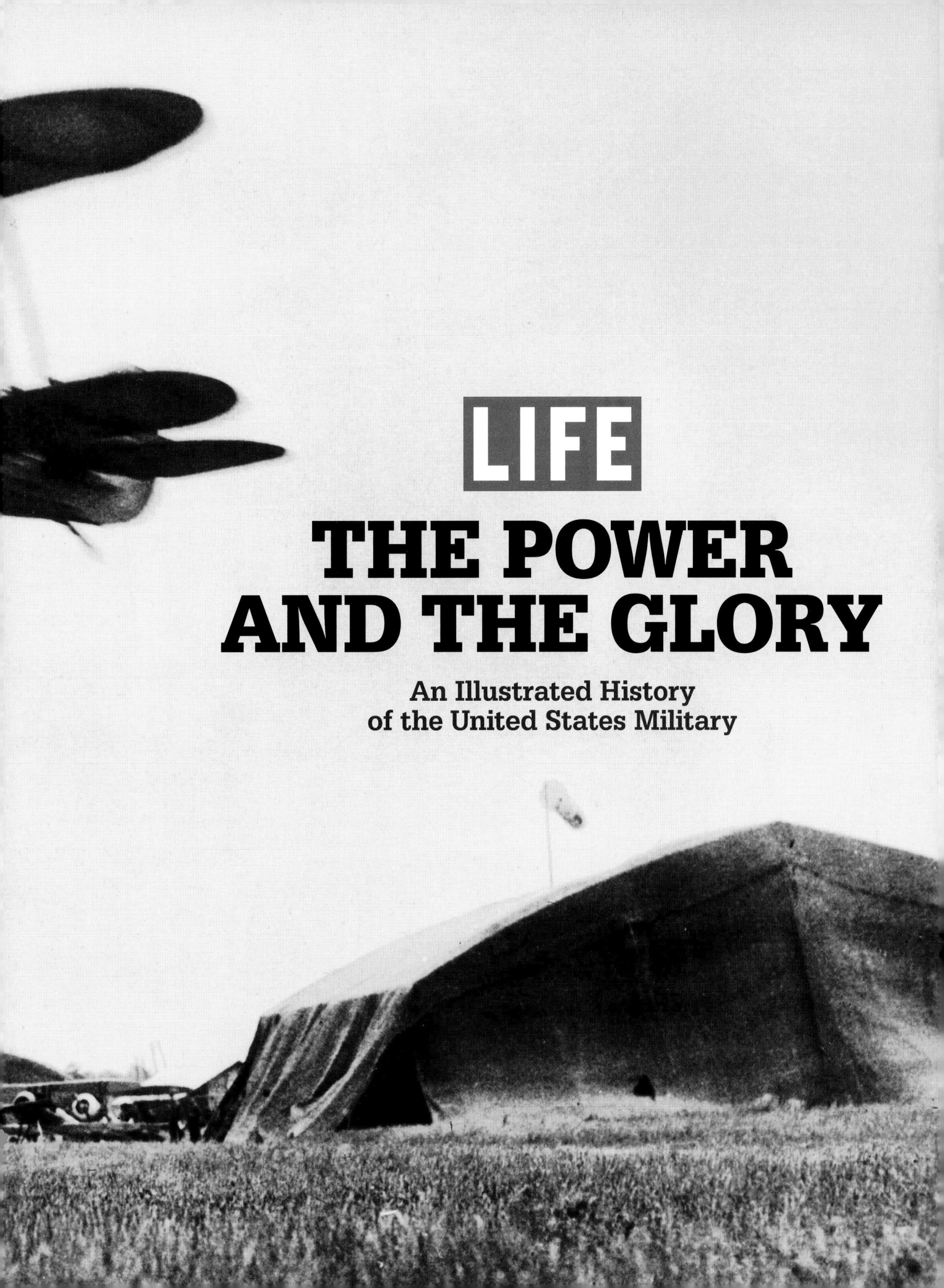

LIFE

THE POWER AND THE GLORY

An Illustrated History of the United States Military

Managing Editor Robert Sullivan
Creative Director Ian Denning
Director of Photography Barbara Baker Burrows
Deputy Picture Editor Christina Lieberman
Senior Editor Robert Andreas
Senior Reporter Hildegard Anderson
Copy Editors J.C. Choi, Barbara Gogan, Parlan McGaw, Pam Warren
Photo Associate Sarah Cates
Senior Contributing Writers Robert H. Boyle, David M. Shribman

Editorial Director Stephen Koepp

Editorial Operations
Richard K. Prue (Director), Brian Fellows (Manager), Richard Shaffer (Production), Keith Aurelio, Charlotte Coco, Tracey Eure, Kevin Hart, Mert Kerimoglu, Rosalie Khan, Patricia Koh, Marco Lau, Brian Mai, Po Fung Ng, Rudi Papiri, Robert Pizarro, Barry Pribula, Clara Renauro, Katy Saunders, Hia Tan, Vaune Trachtman

Time Home Entertainment
Publisher Jim Childs
Vice President, Brand & Digital Strategy Steven Sandonato
Executive Director, Marketing Services Carol Pittard
Executive Director, Retail & Special Sales Tom Mifsud
Executive Publishing Director Joy Butts
Director, Bookazine Development & Marketing Laura Adam
Finance Director Glenn Buonocore
Associate Publishing Director Megan Pearlman
Assistant General Counsel Helen Wan
Assistant Director, Special Sales Ilene Schreider
Senior Book Production Manager Susan Chodakiewicz
Design & Prepress Manager Anne-Michelle Gallero
Brand Manager Roshni Patel
Associate Prepress Manager Alex Voznesenskiy
Assistant Brand Manager Stephanie Braga

Special thanks:
Katherine Barnet, Jeremy Biloon, Rose Cirrincione, Jacqueline Fitzgerald, Christine Font, Jenna Goldberg, Hillary Hirsch, David Kahn, Amy Mangus, Kimberly Marshall, Amy Migliaccio, Nina Mistry, Dave Rozzelle, Ricardo Santiago, Adriana Tierno, Vanessa Wu

We relied on numerous written sources and would especially like to acknowledge our debt to: *The Army*, by Brig. Gen. Harold W. Nelson, USA (Ret), Maj. Gen. Bruce Jacobs, AUS (Ret) and Col. Raymond K. Bluhm Jr., USA (Ret), editors; *The Navy,* by Rear Adm. W.J. Holland Jr., USN (Ret), editor; *Pete Ellis: An Amphibious Warfare Prophet, 1880-1923*, by Dirk Anthony Ballendorf and Merrill Lewis Bartlett; *Semper Fidelis: The History of the United States Marine Corps*, by Allan R. Millett; *West Point: The First 200 Years,* by John Grant, James M. Lynch and Ronald H. Bailey.

Published by
LIFE Books
an imprint of
Time Home Entertainment Inc.
135 West 50th Street
New York, New York 10020

ISBN 10: 1-61893-061-3
ISBN 13: 978-1-61893-061-3
Library of Congress Control No.: 2012955017

Revised edition produced in association with
KENSINGTON MEDIA GROUP
Editorial Director Morin Bishop
Designer Barbara Chilenskas
Fact Checker Ward Calhoun

We welcome your comments and suggestions about LIFE Books. Please write to us at:
LIFE Books
Attention: Book Editors
PO Box 11016
Des Moines, IA 50336-1016

If you would like to order any of our hardcover Collector's Edition books, please call us at 1-800-327-6388. (Monday through Friday, 7:00 a.m.— 8:00 p.m. or Saturday, 7:00 a.m.— 6:00 p.m. Central Time).

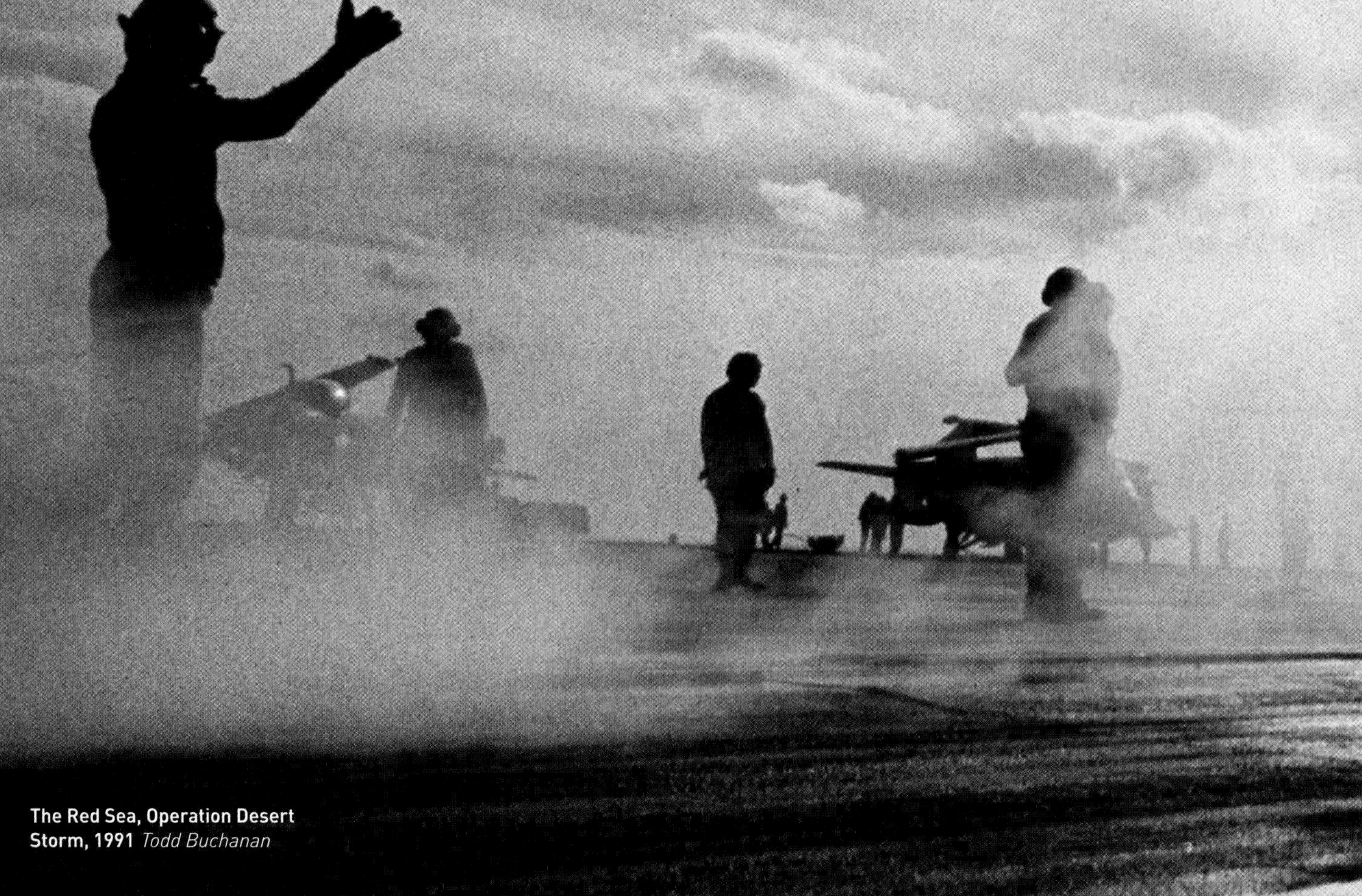

The Red Sea, Operation Desert Storm, 1991 *Todd Buchanan*

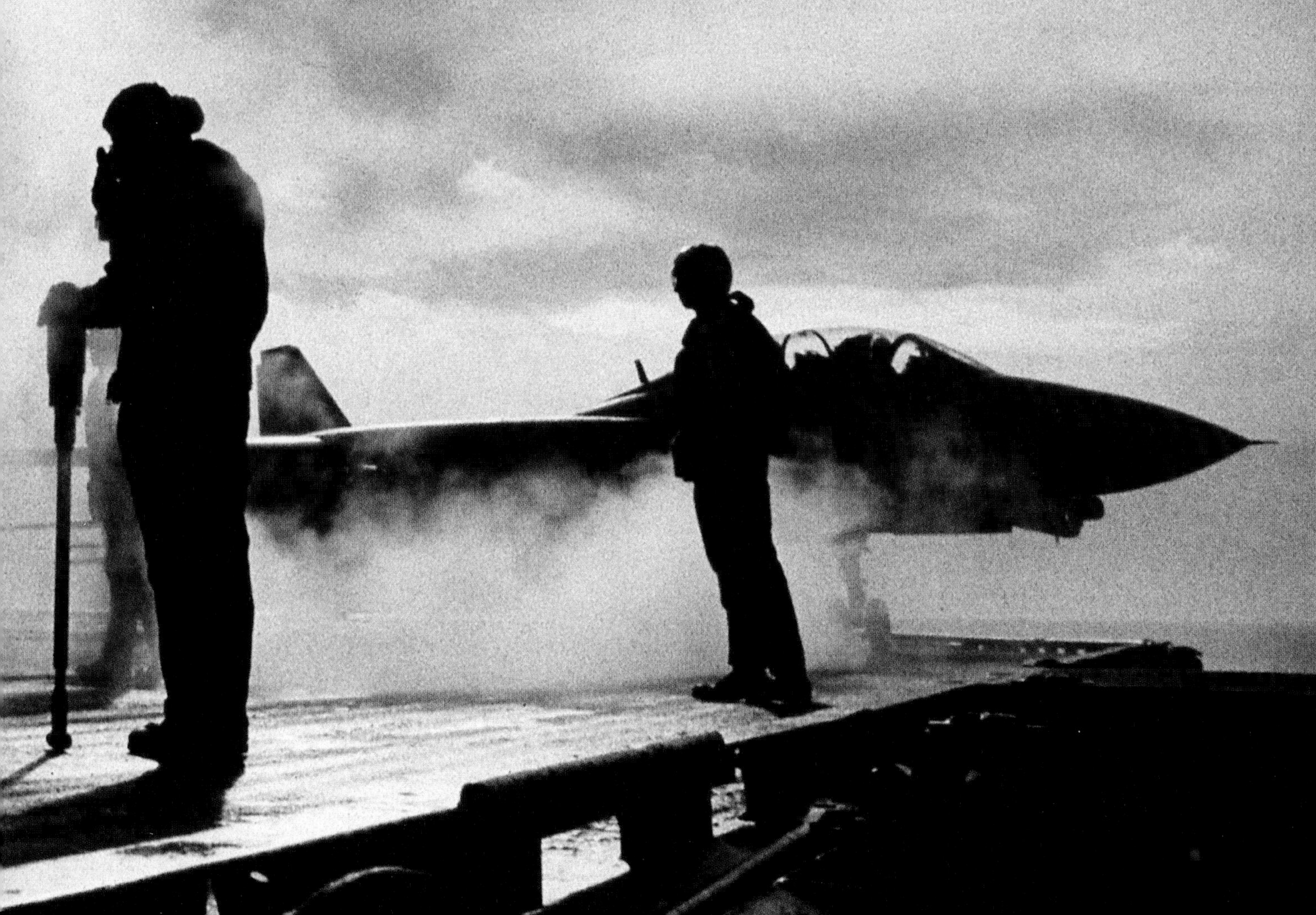

DUTY, HONOR, COUNTRY

Introduction by Bob Dole, *Platoon Leader, 10th Mountain Division, World War II*

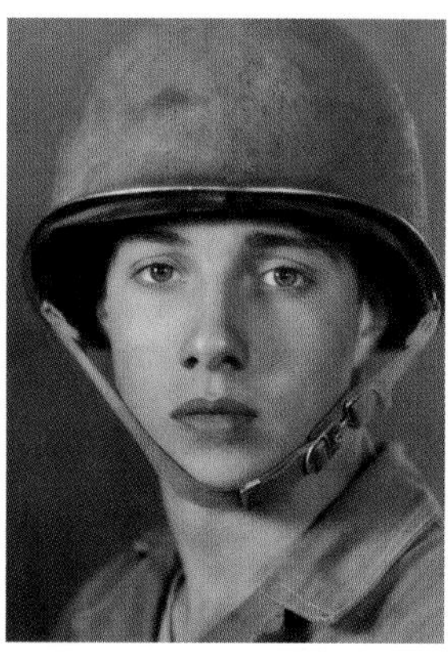

The 19-year-old Dole withdrew from the University of Kansas on December 14, 1942, and joined the Army. In 1945 he was a member of the 10th Mountain Division, an alpine organization that entered into action on January 28 of that year and saw fierce fighting in the mountains of Italy. In 114 days of combat, the 10th suffered 5,146 casualties. One of them was 2nd Lt. Bob Dole. Opposite: On the presidential campaign trail in 1995, he poses with the same exercise setup at his Russell, Kans., house that he used after the war.

IT IS ONE of the great, unforgettable scenes of movie, and military, history: George C. Scott, in a take-no-prisoners mode, expounding the warmaking theories of Gen. George S. Patton while standing before a gigantic American flag. As the camera lovingly pans from his riding crop and four-star helmet to the famous pearl-handled revolvers, an indignant Scott/Patton decries "all this stuff you've heard about America not wanting to fight . . . Americans traditionally love to fight. All real Americans love the sting of battle. When you were kids, you all admired the champion marble-shooter, the fastest runner, big league ballplayers, the toughest boxers. Americans love a winner, and will not tolerate a loser."

Whatever one thinks of Patton's motivational techniques, the fact is that his countrymen have elected too many generals, awarded too many medals, toured too many battlefields, purchased too many books by Stephen E. Ambrose, and experienced too many lumps in the throat to dismiss such appeals out of hand. Imagine American history books without Paul Revere, Molly Pitcher or Sergeant York. Erase Bunker, San Juan and Pork Chop hills from the collective memory. Likewise Belleau Wood, Midway, Omaha Beach, Khe Sanh, Kuwait and Kandahar. Pretend that Washington never crossed the Delaware, that Pickett never charged at Gettysburg, that the Tuskegee Airmen never took to the skies, that John F. Kennedy never captained *PT-109*, and that John McCain never languished in the Hanoi Hilton.

Military prowess, however, is not to be confused with militarism. The United States is as peace-loving as it is patriotic. Theodore Roosevelt said it best, a century ago, when he declared, "The American people are slow to wrath, but when their wrath is kindled it burns like a consuming flame." Roosevelt himself, who never lost his Patton-like ability to romanticize the brutality of conflict, loved nothing better than a good fight. Yet he was also the first American to win the Nobel Peace Prize. Early in his presidency, TR paid a visit to the military academy at West Point. Those assembled in June of 1902 to celebrate the academy's centenary were pointedly reminded that they belonged to "a real American aristocracy—an aristocracy of character."

Such boasts said more about school pride than about the challenge of reconciling elite training with democratic values. Long before the first plebes fell out to reveille on the plain high above the Hudson, West Point was synonymous with the defense of America. During the Revolution, George Washington's army stretched a giant iron link chain across the river—a cork in the bottle thwarting British invaders who hoped to detach New England from her rebellious sisters. Over time the west bank of the Hudson had been converted into a natural fortress whose steep ramparts bristled with Yankee cannon.

But as armies have known since the siege of Troy, what cannot be taken by frontal assault can sometimes be won through treachery. For Washington, September 25, 1780, represented the low point in a war filled with disappointments. In exchange for 20,000 pounds sterling and the status he felt unjustly withheld from him in the continental army, Gen. Benedict Arnold intended to hand the weakened garrison at West Point over to his British paymasters. Only the timely capture of a British spy enabled

HARRY BENSON

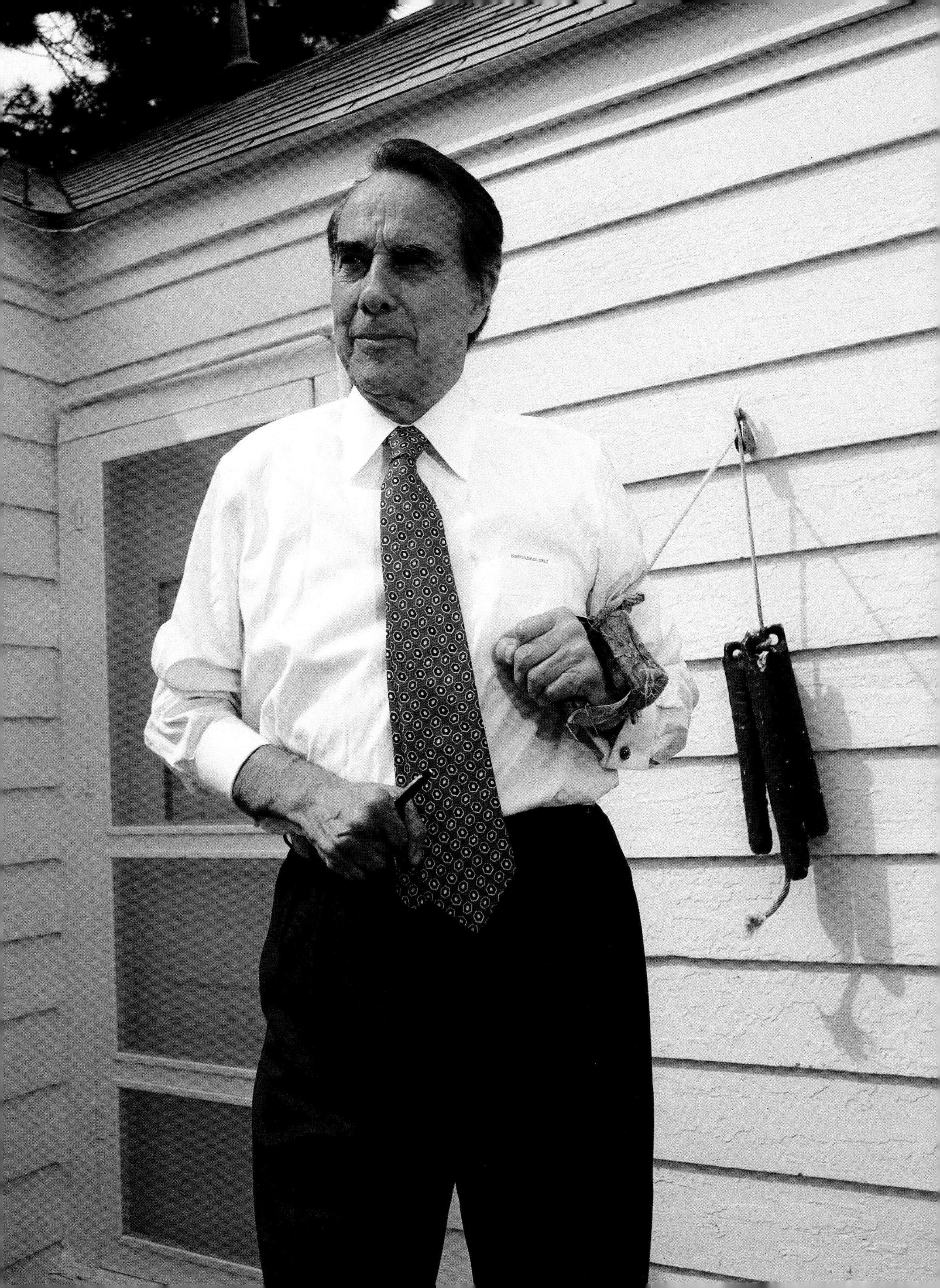

Washington to avert Arnold's stab in the back. Nevertheless, the impact was shattering. "Arnold has betrayed us," muttered the American commander. "Whom can we trust now?"

Washington's question answered itself, as it has for every warrior who grapples with doubts, or fear, in the three words reverently adopted as West Point's motto: Duty, Honor, Country. Which makes it all the more ironic that today's hallowed symbol of American arms should also be the site of the single most traitorous act in American history. The struggle for independence was largely entrusted to citizen soldiers, of whom Washington himself was the personification. Even so, no one more fully appreciated the value of professional soldiery than did the Father of His Country.

At the Constitutional Convention in Philadelphia, Washington as presiding officer kept a majestic silence throughout the proceedings. Only once, it is said, did he come down from his lofty perch to engage in verbal swordplay. According to legend, one delegate imbued with the popular distrust of military establishments—after all, hadn't the Revolution been fought in part to prevent such governmental abuses as the quartering of troops in private homes?—proposed that any future American force be strictly limited to 5,000 soldiers. In response Washington offered an amendment facetiously restricting any foreign invading army to the same arbitrary number.

In 1802, professionalism won out. That year the United States Military Academy received its charter from Thomas Jefferson, a President less committed to standing armies than to government-sponsored education. Originally conceived as a school for military engineers, the academy in its early years reflected prevailing concepts of warfare waged by small, professional armies. Plucked from the flower of American youth, drilled to within an inch of its regimented life, the Long Gray Line occupied a parallel universe. Cadets spoke their own language: Milk was "cow," the towering full dress hat worn on parade a "tarbucket," and demerits "quills," for the ancient writing instruments once used to record infractions. When Robert E. Lee finished second in his class of 1829, not a single demerit marred his almost eerie perfection (in stark contrast to his Confederate superior, Jefferson Davis, who racked up 132 in his final year alone, not including his role in the notorious Christmas Day Eggnog Riot of 1826).

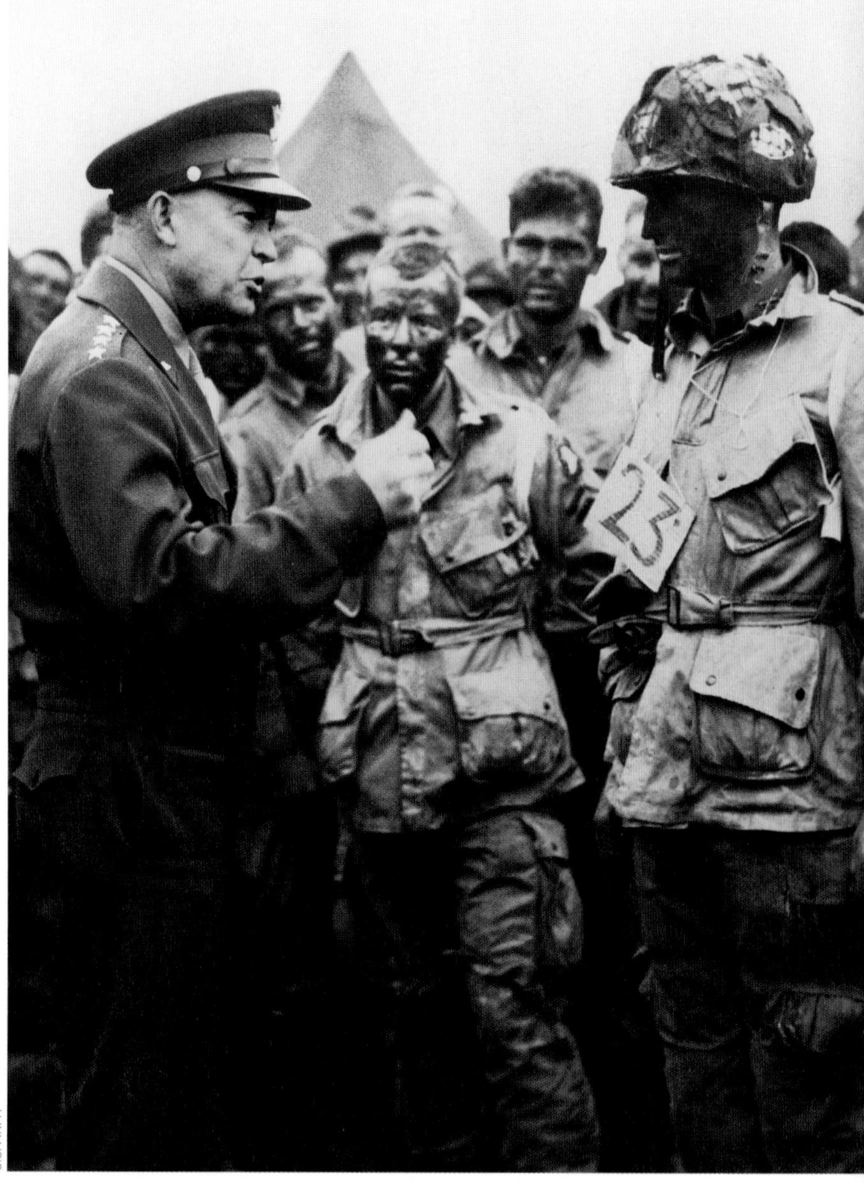

U.S. ARMY

On June 5, 1944, one day before D-Day, Supreme Allied Commander Dwight D. Eisenhower exhorts troops from the 101st Airborne. Ike—soldier, President—is a hero to Dole.

Somehow, the idea of armed elites survived the Civil War, whose massed forces of eager volunteers and reluctant conscripts were led into battle by West Point graduates sworn to defend or destroy the government that educated them. As the army withered in postwar neglect, West Point earned notoriety for a series of hazing scandals and incidents of racial ostracism. A disgruntled general named John A. Logan, resentful of the academy's privileged status in the military hierarchy, wrote a book calling for its abolition as a threat to democratic government. Certainly America's prospective

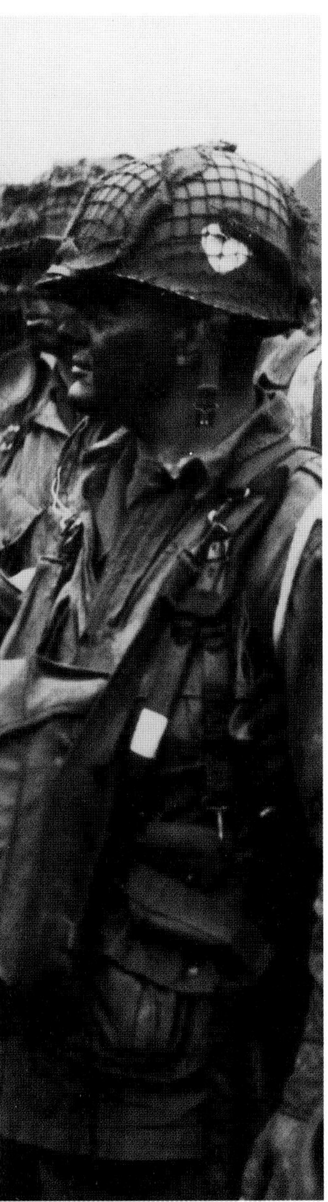

"Whether you are a West Point blueblood or the lowliest draftee—in battle, men share everything as if their lives depend on it."

defenders in their remote "monastery on the Hudson" experienced little of the freedom they were preparing to defend.

"The cadets enter from nineteen to twenty-two and stay four years," wrote an appalled English visitor, Winston Churchill, at the end of the 19th century. "They are not allowed to smoke. In fact they have far less liberty than any public schoolboys in our country . . . Young men of 24 or 25 who would resign their personal liberty to such an extent can never make good citizens or fine soldiers." Churchill would have cause to reassess his harsh judgment. What Henry Luce famously labeled The American Century, and Henry Wallace called The Century of the Common Man, was, in truth, both—nowhere more than on the field of battle. The sheer numbers involved in global combat had a democratizing influence on armies and their training. Inevitably, West Point came to more nearly reflect the nation, a welcome trend that has only accelerated in the years since World War II.

"As you get older it is harder to have heroes, but it is sort of necessary," wrote Ernest Hemingway. My hero is Dwight D. Eisenhower. No one did more to eliminate the gap between the warrior caste and the democratic armies called upon to fight America's 20th century wars. His pacifist mother may have wept when Ike joined the Corps of Cadets in 1911, but Ida Stover Eisenhower's son never forgot where he came from. "I hate war as only a soldier who has lived it can, only as one who has seen its brutality, its stupidity," said Eisenhower. This concern for the lives of his men, coupled with an evident disdain for brass hats, established a bond between Eisenhower and ordinary GIs that would have been unimaginable for the flamboyant MacArthur or the strutting Patton, of whom it was said that he would march his Third Army 50 miles for a headline and twice as far for a press conference.

War changes much more than frontiers on a map. Indeed, if it obeys any rule, it is the law of unintended consequences. World War I toppled European thrones and introduced the virus of bolshevism to a weakened continent. Its sequel redefined the role of women as it undermined the hateful regime of Jim Crow. World War II transformed America, one life at a time. I know. On December 7, 1941, I was a first-term student at the University of Kansas in Lawrence, with dreams of a medical career. Like most of my contemporaries I had taken refuge behind two oceans divinely placed, like some medieval moat, to shelter the United States in splendid isolation. I was too busy waiting on tables in the Kappa Sigma fraternity house—for which I received $12.50 a month plus all I could eat—to pay much attention to geopolitics. The siege of Leningrad mattered less than getting through Rush Week.

The idea that the Class of 1945 might someday be rechristened part of the greatest generation would have seemed as foreign to my frat brothers as Pearl Harbor itself. Nevertheless, we grew up fast in the aftermath of the Japanese attack. Exactly a quarter century after my father fibbed about his age in an attempt to go Over There, I joined the Army's Enlisted Reserve Corps. At the time, I had never flown in an airplane or ridden in a bus. I had never been farther east than Kansas City. Now, assigned to an engineering class at New York's Brooklyn College, I first encountered black and Jewish families in significant numbers. Exposed to a rich mix of cultures, accents and traditions, I got a crash course in the diversity that was, and is, America's greatest strength.

In February 1945, I left Georgia's Fort Benning Officer Candidate School for the 10th Mountain Division, a crack outfit of Ivy Leaguers and world class skiers spearheading a bloody assault against heavily fortified German positions in Italy's Apennine Mountains between Florence and Bologna. Kansans, needless to say, don't get much practice on the ski slopes, but any unease I felt was quickly dissolved in a comradeship reminiscent of my earlier experience on the football field and basketball court. It doesn't matter whether you are a West Point blueblood or the lowliest draftee—in battle, men share everything as if their lives depend on it. Survival requires unwavering trust in comrades who a few days earlier were total strangers. There is no margin for error, and no allowance for selfishness, much less prejudice. The blood spilled in battle is all the same color, whether from the sons of immigrants or the grandsons of slaves.

As a platoon leader, I was responsible for three rifle squads and a machine-gun unit.

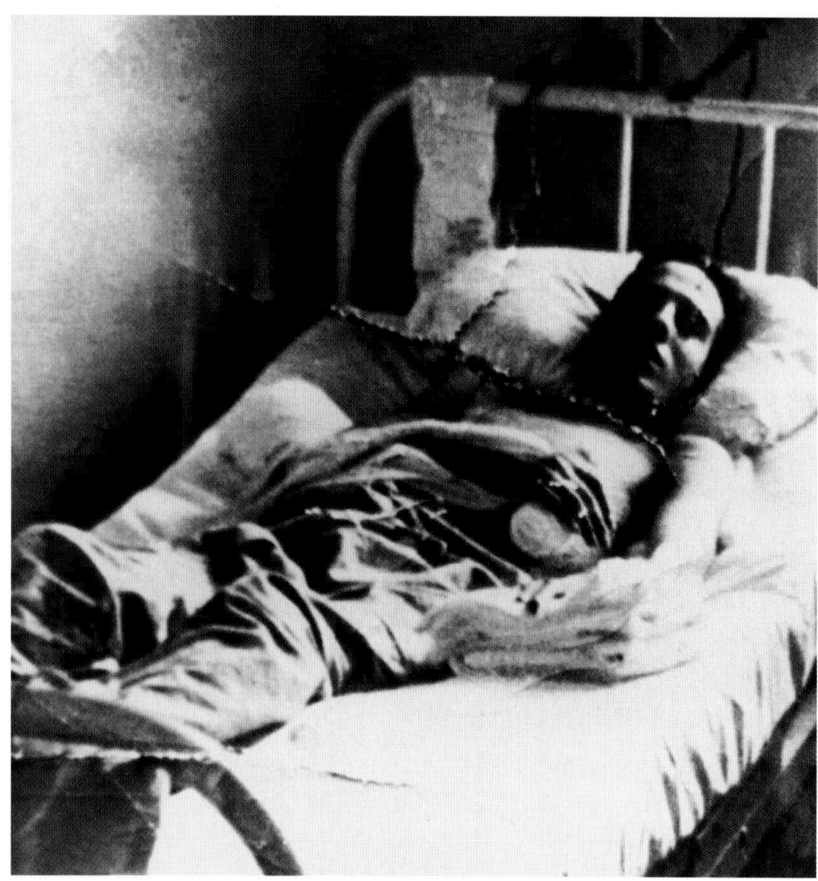

In 1945, having been moved from the field hospital, Dole lies in a hospital bed in Pistoia, Italy, not far from Florence. Treatment for his shrapnel wound would keep him in one hospital or another for three years, a transforming experience.

On the morning of April 14, we were part of a major assault along the flank of Monte Della Spe. Pinned down by sniper and small-arms fire, I chose a small squad to help me find a safer route up the slope. We ran into a hail of German machine-gun fire. I tossed a grenade at a farmhouse from which the bullets were spraying, then pulled the lifeless form of my platoon's radioman into a foxhole. Scrambling back out again, I felt a sharp sting in my back. Most likely it was an exploding shell that smashed my right shoulder, scattering metal fragments along its path.

I lay facedown in the dirt, paralyzed from the neck down, until Tech. Sgt. Frank Carafa dragged me to safety. My second in command, Sgt. Stan Kuschik, gave me a shot of morphine. With my own blood Stan made a cross on my forehead, a precaution to warn any medics who might happen by against administering a second, fatal dose of the powerful drug. Nine hours later I was at the Fifteenth Evacuation Hospital. My war ended there. Or so I thought. Actually, my war, and my education, were only beginning.

Don't believe that wars are concluded by treaties signed by diplomats beneath gilded chandeliers. Each veteran has his own war, which lives on, not just in scrapbooks or at reunions where old stories get retold, but in midnight memories and sudden flashbacks. For me, it all comes back each morning getting dressed, tying a tie or even looking in the mirror. On April 14, I had weighed 194 pounds. That autumn I was down to 122. For nearly a year I couldn't feed myself. On the other hand, one of war's perversely beneficial side effects is the acceleration of medical science. Fighting a potentially lethal pulmonary embolism, I was given a miracle drug called streptomycin. I was told it saved my life.

Moreover, if it hadn't been for the war, I never would have met Phil Hart or Dan Inouye, fellow patients at the Percy Jones Army Medical Center in Battle Creek, Mich., and, much later, cherished colleagues in the United States Senate. War teaches patience. It also teaches perspective. One morning I found myself sitting in a hospital parking lot, waiting to be shuttled to another part of the complex. Striking up a conversation with the patient beside me, I asked him if his feet got cold in the winter air. He looked down and tapped his artificial legs with a cane.

From my father I inherited a gift for wisecracking. Pretty soon they started wheeling me around to wards where the morale was low. Better to do something useful than complain about needles and bedsores. Eventually I met Hampar Kelikian, Dr. K to his friends, and as great a war hero as ever wore the Purple Heart. An Armenian immigrant, Kelikian was a pioneer in the surgical restoration of otherwise useless limbs. Promising to do everything in his power to restore the use of my shattered right arm and hand, Dr. K was frank to say that after that, it would be up to me to make the most of what I had. There would be no miracles, he added.

But he was wrong. Dr. K himself was a miracle. So were the friends back home in Russell who started the Bob Dole Fund to pay for the half dozen operations that followed. It began with a few paper bills tossed into an old cigar box. Eventually the box overflowed with $1,800. For me the spring of 2002 had special meaning. It was exactly 50 years since Dwight Eisenhower came home to Abilene to launch his campaign for the White House. Lost in the huge rain-drenched crowd that turned out for

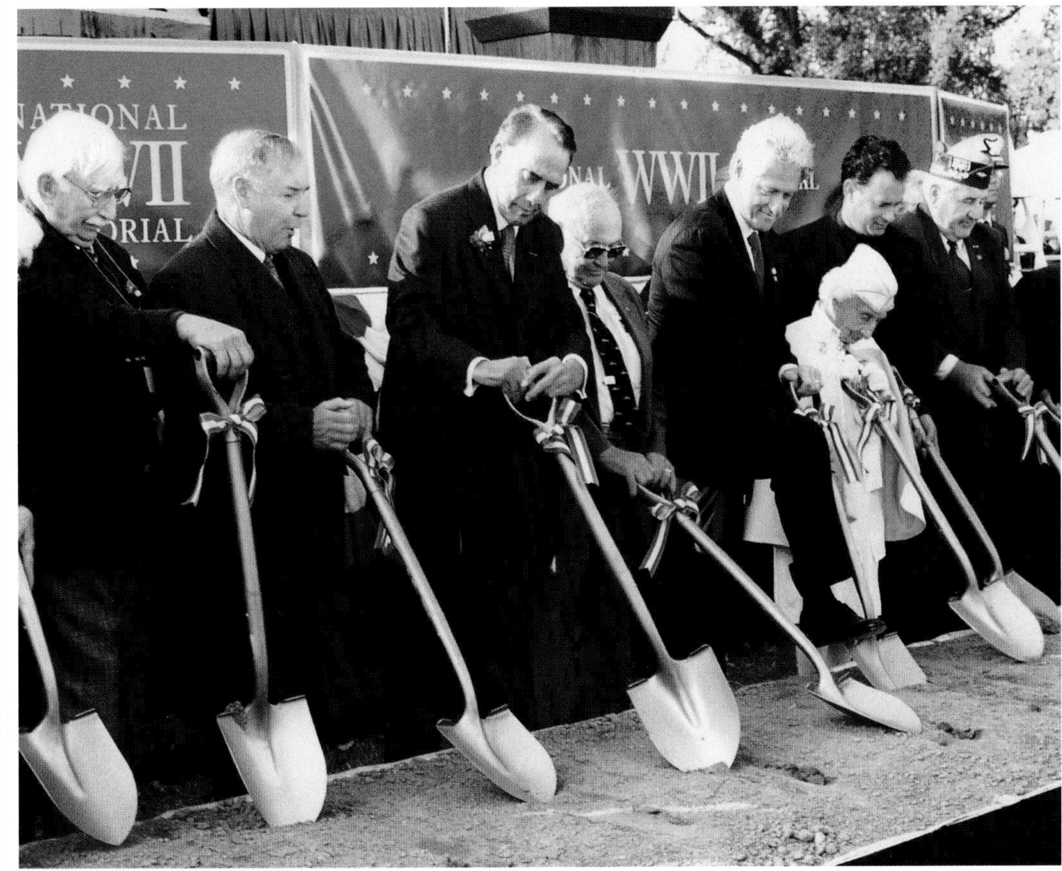

> "Each veteran has his own war, which lives on in midnight memories and flashbacks."

On November 11, 2000, a row of determined excavationists attends to the ground breaking for Washington's World War II Memorial. Among them are Dole, President Bill Clinton and actor Tom Hanks.

his homecoming was a young veteran, scarred by battle and looking to find his place in postwar America. What I heard that day confirmed what I had long suspected—that my commanding general was also my political hero. Professional dreams of operating rooms gave way to legislative chambers, first in Topeka, and then in Washington.

When, 17 years later, I was called upon to give my first floor speech as a United States Senator, it came two weeks after we buried Ike in his $80 regulation army casket in Abilene, Kans. On that day, I spoke about the challenges faced by disabled Americans. And I thought of Dan Inouye, and Phil Hart, who once defined politics as "an opportunity to make a more humane life for everybody." Here was yet another wartime lesson with peacetime applications.

Finally, on Veterans Day 2000, I joined President Clinton, Tom Hanks (whose father was a veteran of the naval war), Fred Smith, CEO of FedEx and a decorated Vietnam veteran, along with thousands of men and women from the dwindling ranks of World War II veterans in breaking ground for a World War II Memorial on Washington, D.C.'s Mall. We build memorials to remember, and as mirrors reflecting the intensely personal memories of each combatant. That afternoon I remembered Frank Carafa and Stan Kuschik, and countless others in the hospitals where my own war raged on long after V-E Day. I thought of everyone, plain GIs and the armed services' finest—from all the branches—who died assaulting Hitler's Fortress Europe, or in the jungles of Borneo, or in ships entombed beneath the glassy turquoise waters of the South Pacific. In the fraternity of heroes they are as one.

Little could we imagine on that crisp November afternoon that America would so soon find itself again at war, this time with a shadowy enemy, harnessing medieval concepts to sophisticated technology and pure evil. Under the circumstances, one recalls the haunting farewell Douglas MacArthur paid to West Point, his spiritual home and refuge, in 1962. "The Long Gray Line has never failed us. Were you to do so, a million ghosts in olive drab, in brown khaki, in blue and gray, would rise from their white crosses, thundering those magic words: Duty-Honor-Country."

After 200 years and more, the words have lost none of their magic. God Bless America.

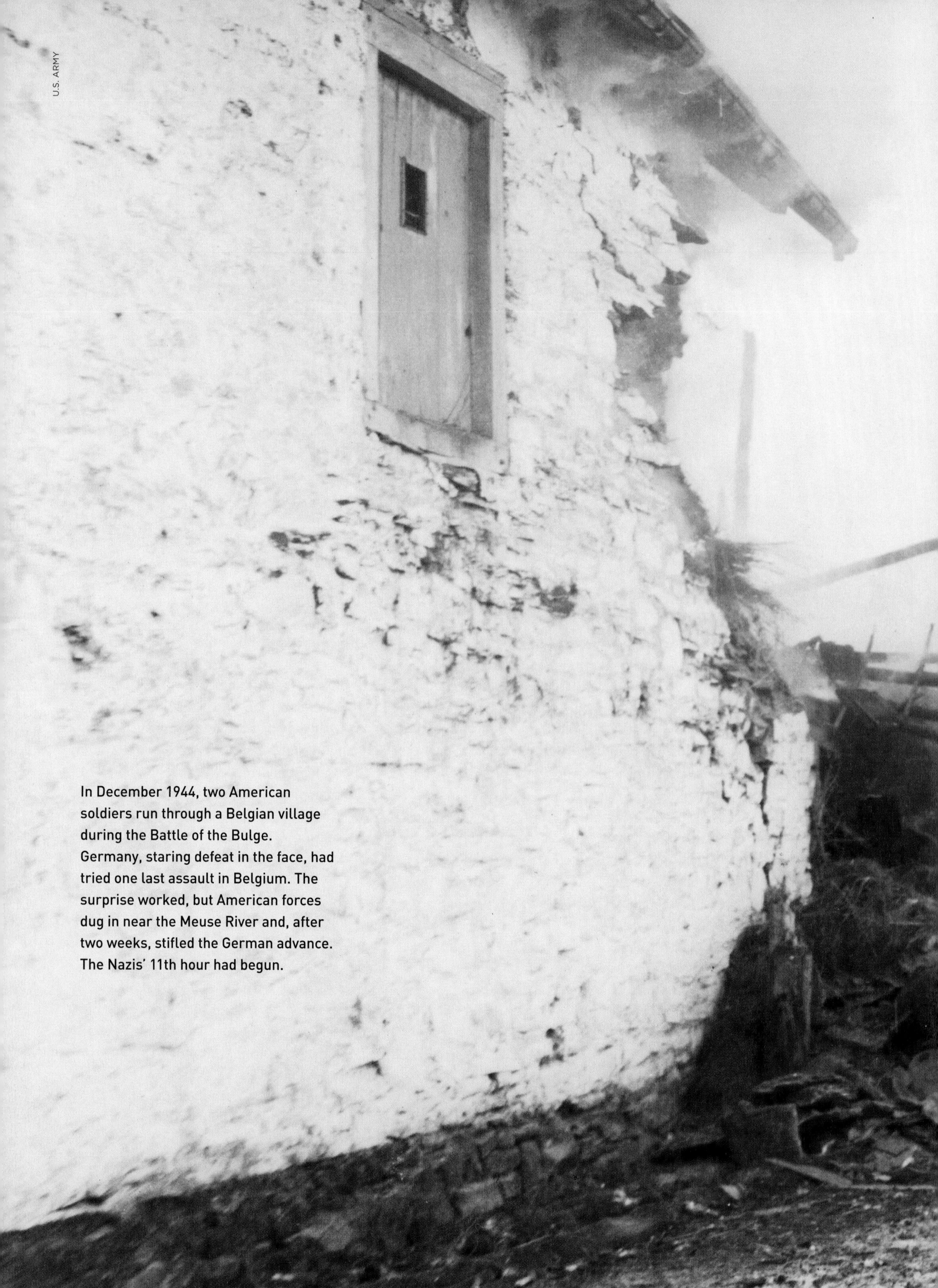

U.S. ARMY

In December 1944, two American soldiers run through a Belgian village during the Battle of the Bulge. Germany, staring defeat in the face, had tried one last assault in Belgium. The surprise worked, but American forces dug in near the Meuse River and, after two weeks, stifled the German advance. The Nazis' 11th hour had begun.

THE ARMY

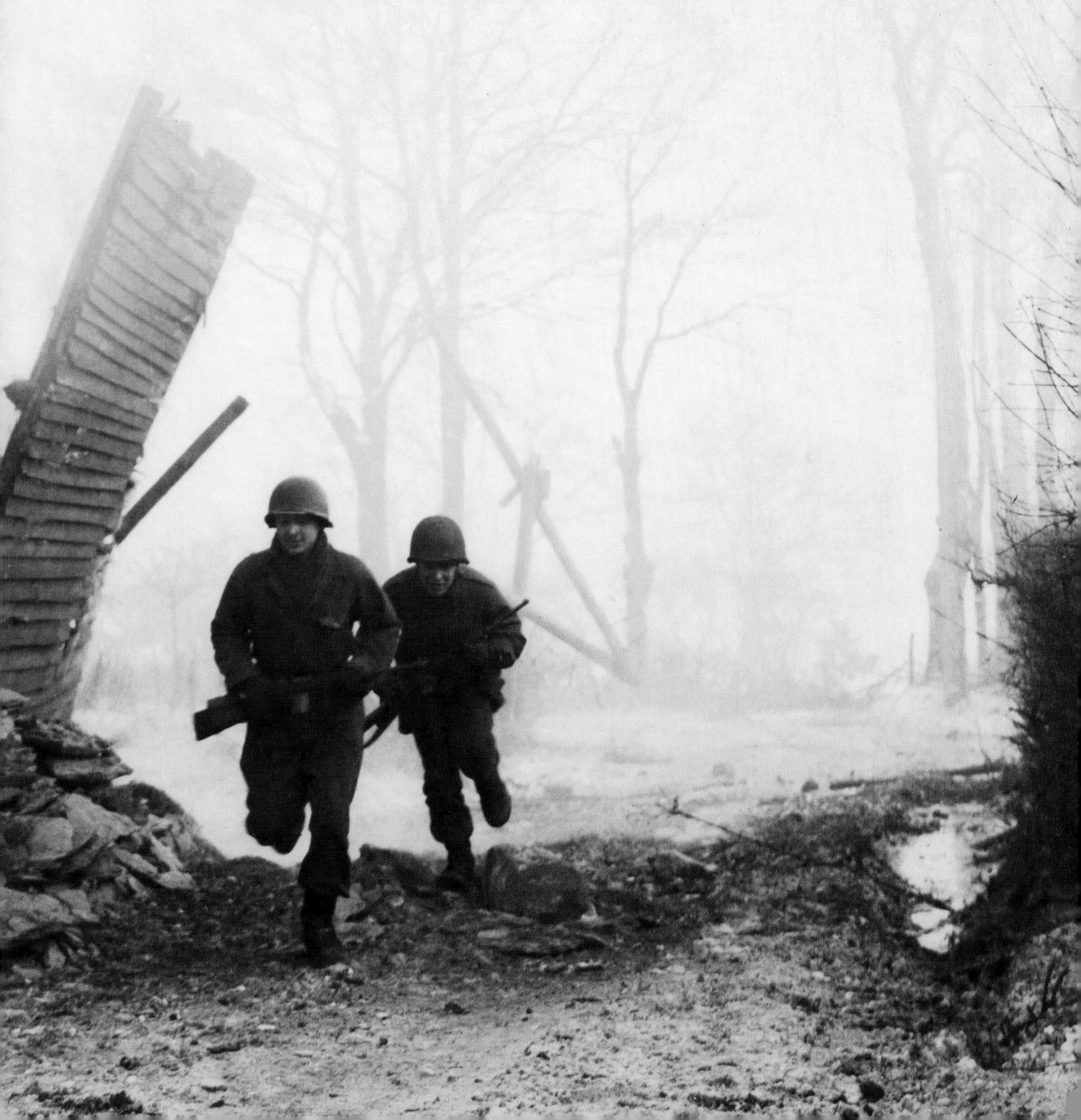

THE ARMY

" Every citizen [should] be a soldier. This was the case with the Greeks and the Romans and must be that of every free state. **"**

— Thomas Jefferson, 1813

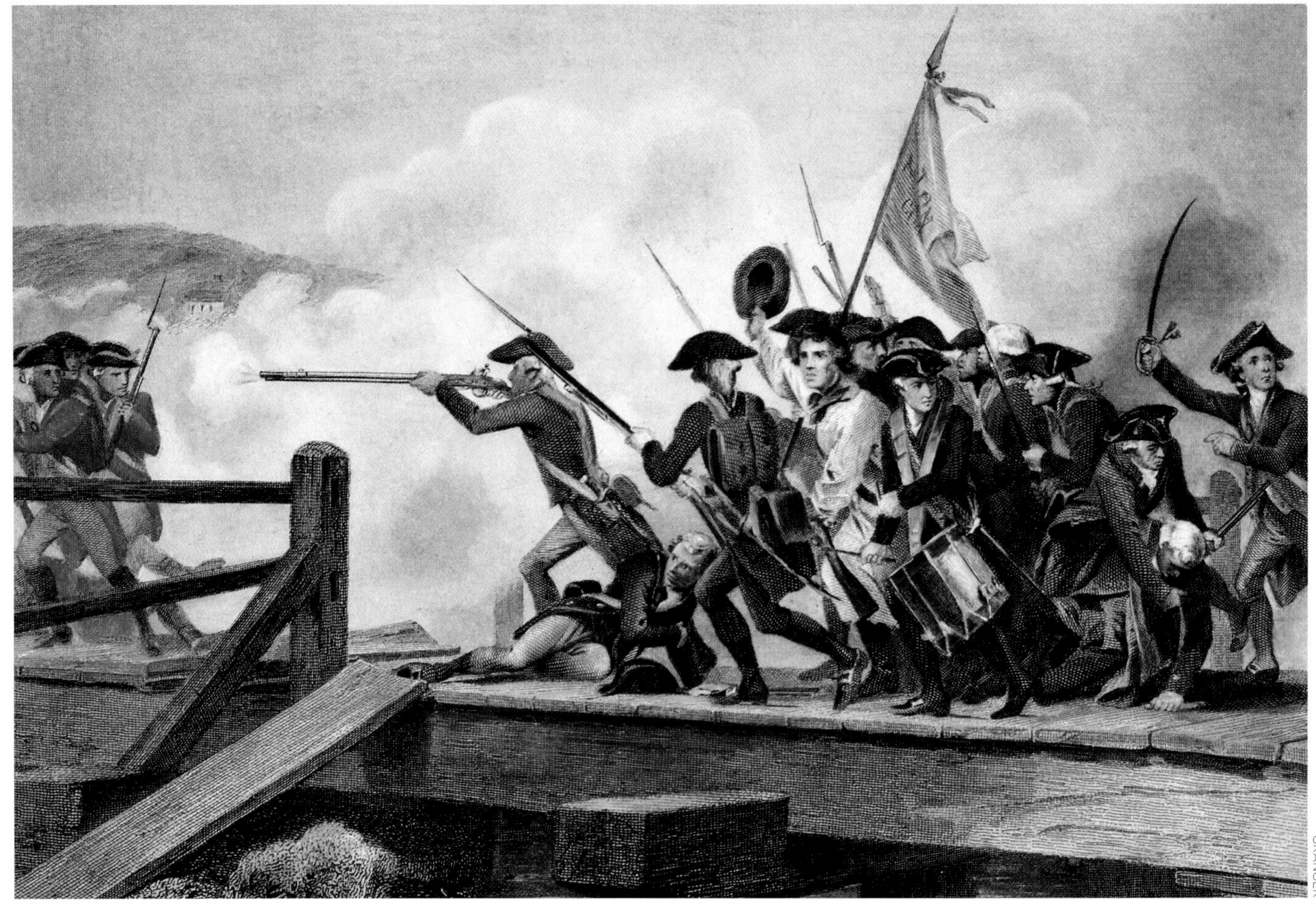

GRANGER

IN THE U.S. ARMY'S prehistory there were formed, in 1636, the three militias of Massachusetts Bay Colony. (One of them is the forebear of the 182nd Infantry Regiment, which is the oldest unit in the Army National Guard—and so the legacy lives today.) They fought Indians, sometimes forging an alliance with one tribe against another, as did militias subsequently organized in neighboring colonies. They also, in the 18th century, supported the British in trying to drive the French from Canada.

In time, this support of colonial militias for England waned, and radicalized "minutemen," politically opposed to what they saw as British brutishness toward its own subjects, stood ready to oppose the crown on a moment's notice. Sensing that push would soon come to shove, several of these formerly loyalist units began stashing arms out of sight. The most militant of the rebel farmers and tradesmen were in Massachusetts, where uprisings and engagements—the Boston Tea Party, the Boston Massacre—had already taken place. At dawn on April 19, 1775, 12 miles northwest of Boston in the town of

On the morning of April 19, 1775, the British moved on from Lexington to Concord, where, at the North Bridge, the embattled farmers stood and, in Emerson's immortal words, fired the shot heard round the world. It can be said that the opening salvo at Concord, which fatally felled three redcoats, signaled the birth of the American Army.

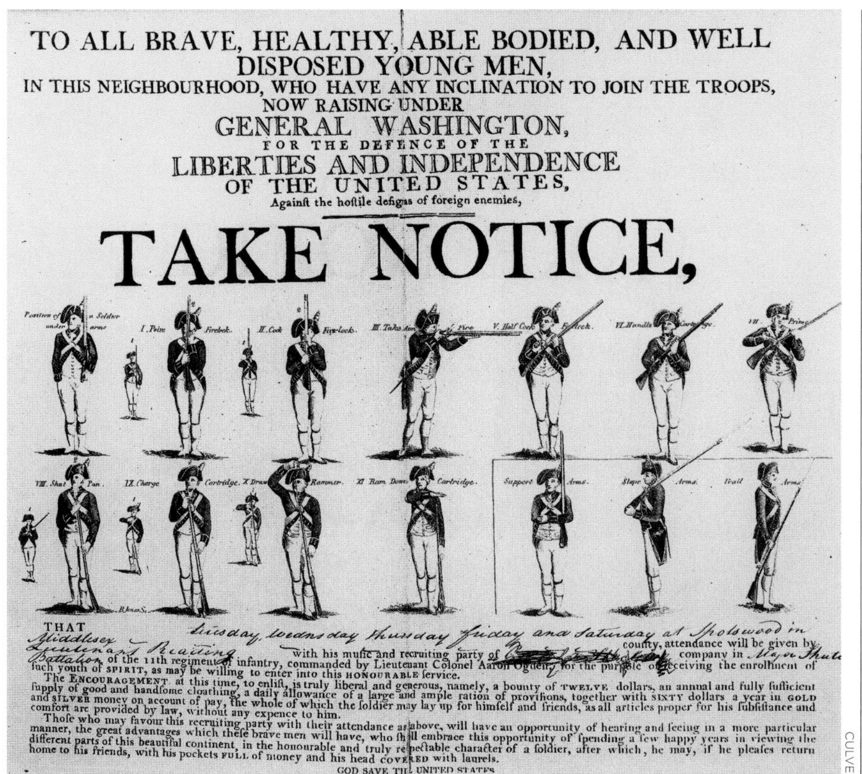

CULVER

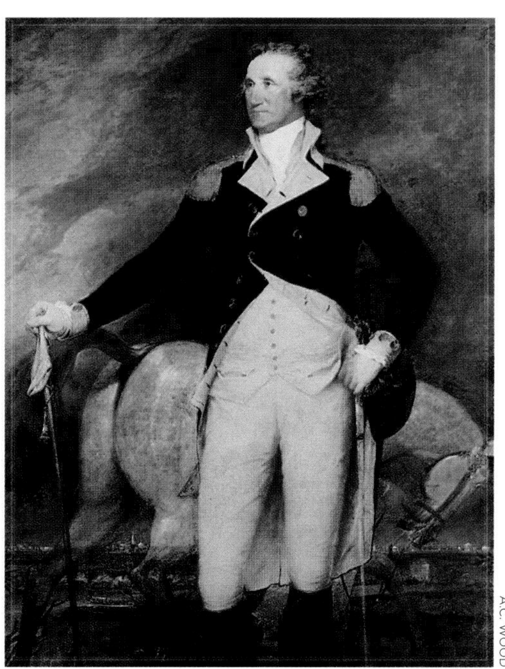

A.C. WOOD

In the aftermath of April 19, recruiting posters urged "the enrollment of such youth of spirit, as may be willing to enter into this honourable service"—to wit, Gen. George Washington's Continental Army. Also in the fine print, recruits were promised a "supply of good and handsome cloathing," ample rations, an annual salary of $60 "in gold and silver money" and the "opportunity of spending a few happy years in viewing the different parts of this beautiful continent." Then the soldier would return home "with his pockets full of money and his head covered with laurels."

Lexington, a shot rang out. No one knows who pulled the trigger, redcoat or minuteman. What *is* known is that the British killed eight colonials on Lexington green, then marched on to neighboring Concord, where it was suspected, correctly, that munitions were hidden. In a battle at the North Bridge three members of the King's Army were shot dead, and as the British marched in retreat to Boston throughout the remainder of that bloody day, the militias of several towns, heeding the call, scurried over fields and through forests to fight, guerrilla-style, from behind stone walls and embankments. Soon these ragtag troops bearing flintlock and powder, who killed 273 British that day, would be calling themselves not just patriots but Americans. Soon these freedom fighters would be calling themselves, under General Washington, the Continental Army. And when the smoke finally cleared from the American Revolution and independence had been won, the next generation of soldiers would, in 1784, be declared the United States Army.

So we arrive, finally, at the beginning. The Army existed as an idea before it was a thing. The idea was that it was the defending force for our thoughts and ideals, our democracy. It has ever been thus, performing with extraordinary nobility in times of peace and war, erring sometimes, as is human, but often and characteristically going beyond the call.

Washington's notion was that the "Peace Establishment" would encompass both a standing military and a supporting, well-organized militia. Despite the high regard in which the former general was held by his countrymen, the toddling United States government did not heed his advice for a strong defense, and in the very year of its authorization the Army saw its manpower cut to 80 men, stationed at two forts. It did increase in size somewhat during Washington's two terms, but in its earliest years was rightly seen as suspect. It was regularly challenged, even from within the nation. In 1794, when farmers in western Pennsylvania staged an armed uprising in protest against a tax on whiskey, the President himself, as Commander in Chief, led the Army into battle. Washington and his men were able to put down the Whiskey Rebellion, thereby establishing the right of the U.S. military to protect the Constitution against anyone. Anyone.

The Army grew smarter; in 1802 Congress established the United States Military Academy at West Point, N.Y. The Army grew adventurous: Meriwether Lewis was a captain and William Clark was a lieutenant when, responding to Thomas Jefferson's entreaty, they set out with 40 soldiers on their mission of discovery in 1804. But the Army didn't grow large. By 1812 there were barely 3,000 soldiers and only 172 officers in the entire force. And, that year, war was again joined with Britain.

Volunteers and militiamen enlisted in the defense against the allied English and Indians, and while there were setbacks—Gen. William Hull surrendered his fort in Detroit without a fight and was later court-martialed; Gen. James Wilkinson retreated from an advanced position in Canada and was also court-martialed; British troops invaded and burned much of Washington, D.C., in the summer of 1814—there was ultimate victory. Great Britain signed the Treaty of Ghent on Christmas Eve, 1814, and America's many years of warring with the crown were ended. Still the Army's credibility was doubted. Mexico, with a larger military, was supremely confident that it would win its war with the United States in 1846, and it was the inventive and inspirational leadership of Gen. Winfield Scott that turned the tide for America. The Mexican War is when the Army itself turned a corner, and began to be perceived as a strong, even fearsome force.

The crucible that might confront any military—and which did confront America's—is to be split asunder, then to face off, brother against brother. If it will surely never happen again, it did happen, formally and with atrocious consequences, on December 20, 1860, when South Carolina seceded from the Union and approximately one third of the Regular Army officers resigned to join the Confederacy. Four months later, the Civil War was begun in earnest when a 34-hour bombardment by Confederate artillery forced the surrender of the Union's Fort Sumter in Charleston, S.C. The Rebel army fought fiercely and bravely under the great generals Thomas "Stonewall" Jackson, J.E.B. Stuart and particularly Robert E. Lee (who, as a U.S. Army lieutenant colonel in 1859, had led the detachment of Marines that captured the radical abolitionist John Brown at Harper's Ferry, Va.). Despite the Union's greater manpower—an advantage that was strengthened in August 1862 when the War Department authorized the enlistment of America's first black soldiers, whose number would swell during the campaign to approximately 178,000—the Confederacy scored a series of early victories in Virginia and Missouri.

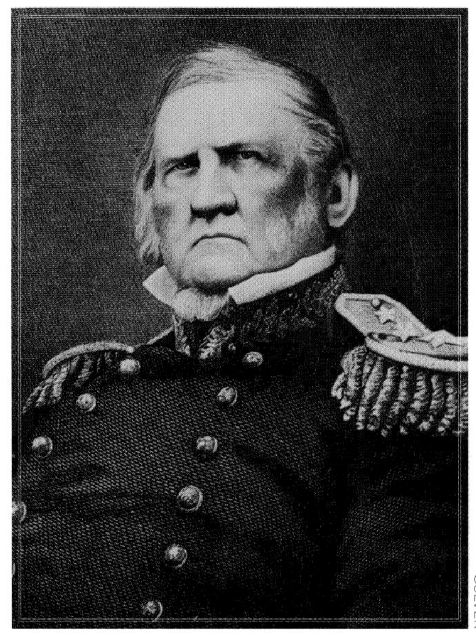
CULVER

Winfield Scott gave up the law in 1808 to join the Army; four years later, in the War of 1812, he proved himself an intrepid leader, fighting on at Lundy's Lane after two horses had been shot from under him. In 1825, Scott wrote the Army's first tactics manual, and the strategies therein informed his triumphant Mexican War campaign. When the Civil War began, the Virginian, who revered the idea of union, refused to join the Confederacy.

In 1863 the Union's fortunes improved, and the South's last vestige of hope for an eventual victory was dashed in early July when Union Gen. George Meade's Army of the Potomac defeated Lee's Army of Northern Virginia in a three-day battle at Gettysburg, Pa. Lee and his confederates fought on for nearly two more years, but finally were forced to surrender.

The reunified Army spent the remainder of the 19th century in near constant battle with Mexican raiders and in attacking Indians throughout the West. William "Buffalo Bill" Cody was an Army scout for the 5th Cavalry in its battles with the Cheyenne, and Lt. Aldolphus W. Greely, who would later gain fame by leading Army scientific missions to the Arctic and for heading the Army's relief effort following the 1906 San Francisco earthquake, was in charge of a 4th Infantry detachment that in 1875 laid the first telegraph line in Oklahoma Indian Territory. But certainly the most storied of the Indian fighters was West Pointer and Civil War veteran Lt. Col. George Armstrong Custer, whose 7th Cavalry was involved in several clashes in the western territories before being surrounded by Sioux at the Little Big Horn River in Montana Territory in 1876. The general and five of his companies were wiped out, while seven other companies escaped.

The war with Spain began in 1898 and can now be seen as heralding the Army's role in the century to come, for suddenly the fighting wasn't being done here, but over there—not in Europe, yet, but against Spanish forces in Cuba and Puerto Rico. In 1900 the American Expeditionary Force joined in putting down the Boxer Rebellion in China; in that and subsequent years the Army was involved in quelling insurrections in the Philippines. Even as the Army was adapting to a less isolationist domestic policy, it was refining and modernizing its methodology. The Army Signal Corps began playing around with balloons and dirigibles, and in 1909 the Army signed up a Wright brothers' Flyer as its first aircraft. Two years later, in a trial, the Army dropped a bomb from 1,500 feet. The Army Nurse Corps was

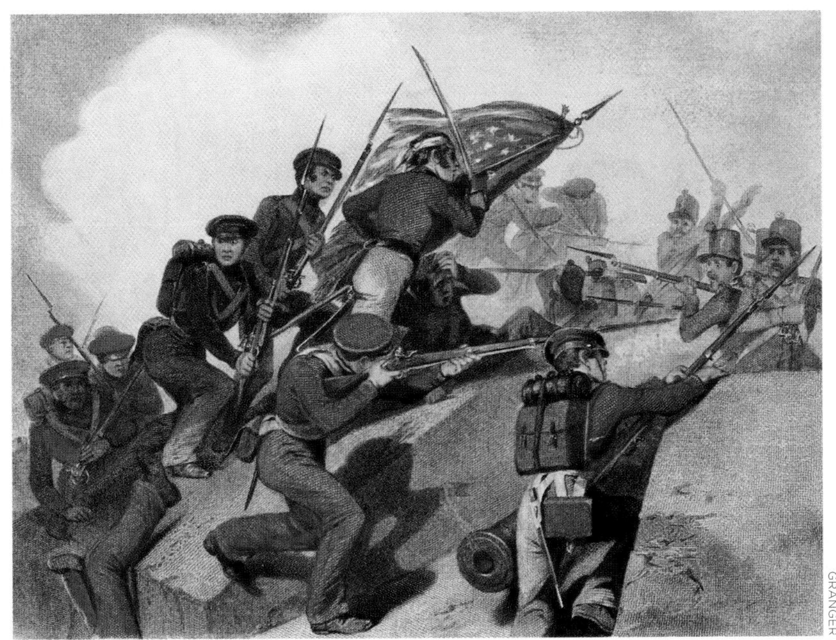

In 1847, in a defining moment for the Army, Scott's forces pushed into Mexico to confront the larger foe. They won battles at Veracruz, Cerro Gordo, Contreras, Churubusco (above, on August 20), Molino del Rey and Chapultepec. Then they captured Mexico City. "We conquered a great country," Scott reported succinctly, "without the loss of a single battle or skirmish."

established in 1901, and in 1907, after more than one civilian effort—by the U.S. and others—had failed, the Army Corps of Engineers was assigned the task of building the Panama Canal. In this period the Army adopted olive drab as its color, metal dog tags as its form of identification, the Model 1903 Springfield as its favorite rifle and the .45-caliber M1911 as its pistol. By the time the United States finally entered the First World War by declaring against Germany on April 6, 1917, its Army was a force that could make a difference.

Under Gen. John J. Pershing, it did, and quickly. Fighting alongside the British in Belgium, taking over for French units in France and bringing down German planes on high—Army Signal Corps Capt. Edward V. Rickenbacker registered 26 kills—the Army was crucial in breaking the enemy lines and forcing an armistice by November 11, 1918. In a year and a week of combat, the U.S. suffered 50,510 battle deaths, but proved for the first time that it possessed the world's greatest military.

It would be forced to prove it another time in another global war. In July 1924, Army Brig. Gen. William "Billy" Mitchell visited the naval installation at Pearl Harbor, Hawaii, and famously predicted that the expansionist Japanese might one day launch an early morning air attack against American materiel there. Seventeen years later he was proved only too correct, and while Army pilots shot down a Japanese plane on the infamous date, the attack on Pearl represented one of the darkest episodes in U.S. history. And one of the most catalytic, as the country leapt into a world war that it had been eyeing warily from afar.

With Gen. Douglas MacArthur as Allied Supreme Commander in the Southwest Pacific, Gen. George S. Patton fighting in Africa and then in Europe, Gen. Dwight D. Eisenhower directing the June 6, 1944, D-Day invasion of France, and the atomic bomb being dropped upon Hiroshima from the bay of the Army Air Force B-29 *Enola Gay*, the Army's contribution to the winning of World War II was everywhere, in all theaters, in each and every manner of fighting. It was a frighteningly awesome display.

And then, in the confusing conflicts in Korea and especially Vietnam: shocking difficulty, irresolution, even failure. In the 1960s and into the '70s the Army fought seven years, eight months in Vietnam, and at the end not only had much human life been lost, but also the notion that the U.S. was invincible. It would take a new kind of warfare, as practiced in the overwhelming military actions in Grenada (1983), the Persian Gulf (1991) and, finally, Afghanistan to restore the military's confidence and, indeed, its stature. It is supposed that Osama bin Laden presumed the ferocity and dedication of his followers would confound and frustrate U.S. forces just as they had the Russians a decade earlier. The remarkably fast liberation of Afghanistan showed off, to stunning effect, the current status of American might.

Today the Army stands tall. All races and classes play a part as do, finally, women—everyone contributing to the nation's security. Its affiliated militias are intact in the National Guard and Army Reserve, each of them brimful with citizen-soldiers who are just as dedicated and patriotic as the founding fathers (78,000 of the 306,730 U.S. soldiers deployed to the Gulf War were reservists or guardsmen). The Army's weaponry is ultra sophisticated, its training methods modern and adaptive to the new realities of terrorism, biochemical warfare and whatever might come next. West Point, now more than 200 years old, is teaching cadets that a brave, sometimes scary new world awaits.

UNITED STATES MILITARY ACADEMY

At 211 years old, the United States Military Academy is venerable, proud and strong.

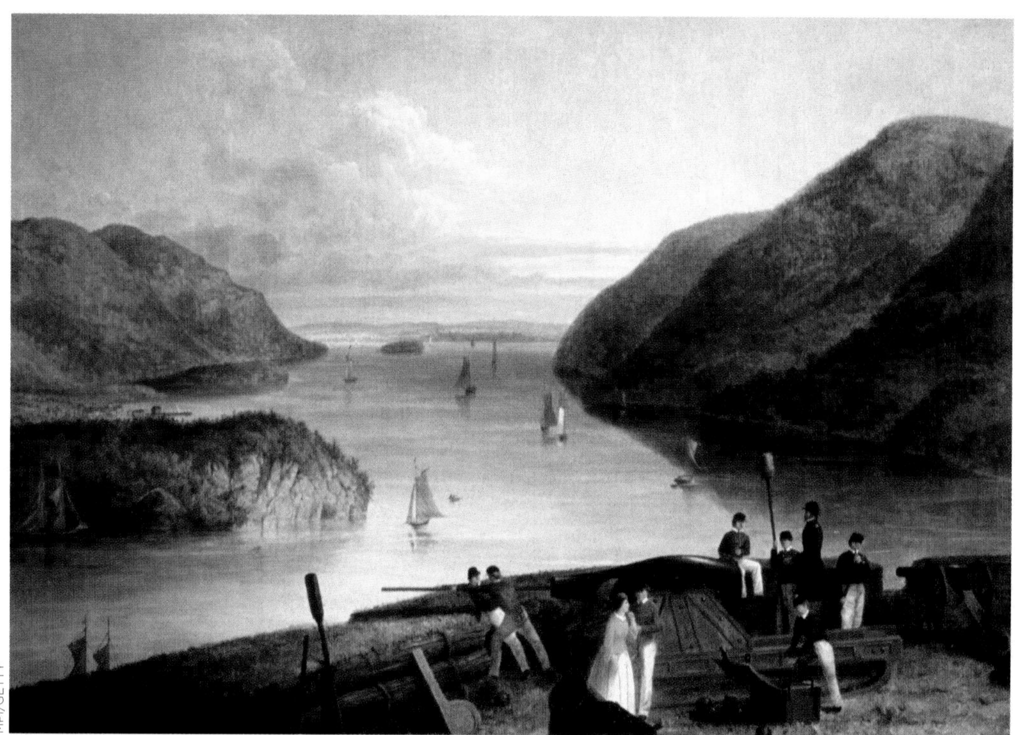
MPI/GETTY

ON THE MIGHTY HUDSON
The Academy had an immediate impact. General Winfield Scott observed in the mid-1800s, "[B]ut for our graduated cadets the war between the United States and Mexico might . . . have lasted some four or five years, with, in its first half, more defeats than victories." In 1957 a plebe "braces" before a cadet officer, a required act. Bracing, judged by the number of wrinkles in the neck, has been abolished.

BEFORE IT WAS a school, it was already a fort, looming stoically atop a cliff that plunged to the Hudson River in a serenely beautiful part of New York state. Now, 211 years after Congress authorized the U.S. Military Academy, which opened its doors in July of 1802, "West Point," along with the surrounding Army post (16,000 acres in all), represents a powerful symbol of American honor and might. Cadets in the Corps, each of whom is working toward a bachelor's degree and an Army commission, live by a strict but simple code, which asserts that a cadet will never lie, cheat, steal nor tolerate a classmate who does. Violation is cause for dismissal. Four years of rigorous academic and physical training, covering everything from math to maneuvers, leads to a career as an officer and, perhaps, history. Grant and Lee were educated at West Point. Stonewall Jackson received his training there as well. Pershing. Patton. MacArthur. Eisenhower. Schwarzkopf. When we consider those names, notions of strength, dignity, loyalty and pride come immediately to mind. The Academy is legendary not only for schooling leaders but also for instilling in them a sense of what it means to be of America, of the Army and—not least—of West Point. Cadets and alumni are their own band of brothers, and never was this more apparent than when West Pointers fought against one another during the Civil War. At Fair Oaks, Gen. George Custer's Union troops took one of Custer's West Point mates prisoner. When the general learned of

PIERRE BOULAT

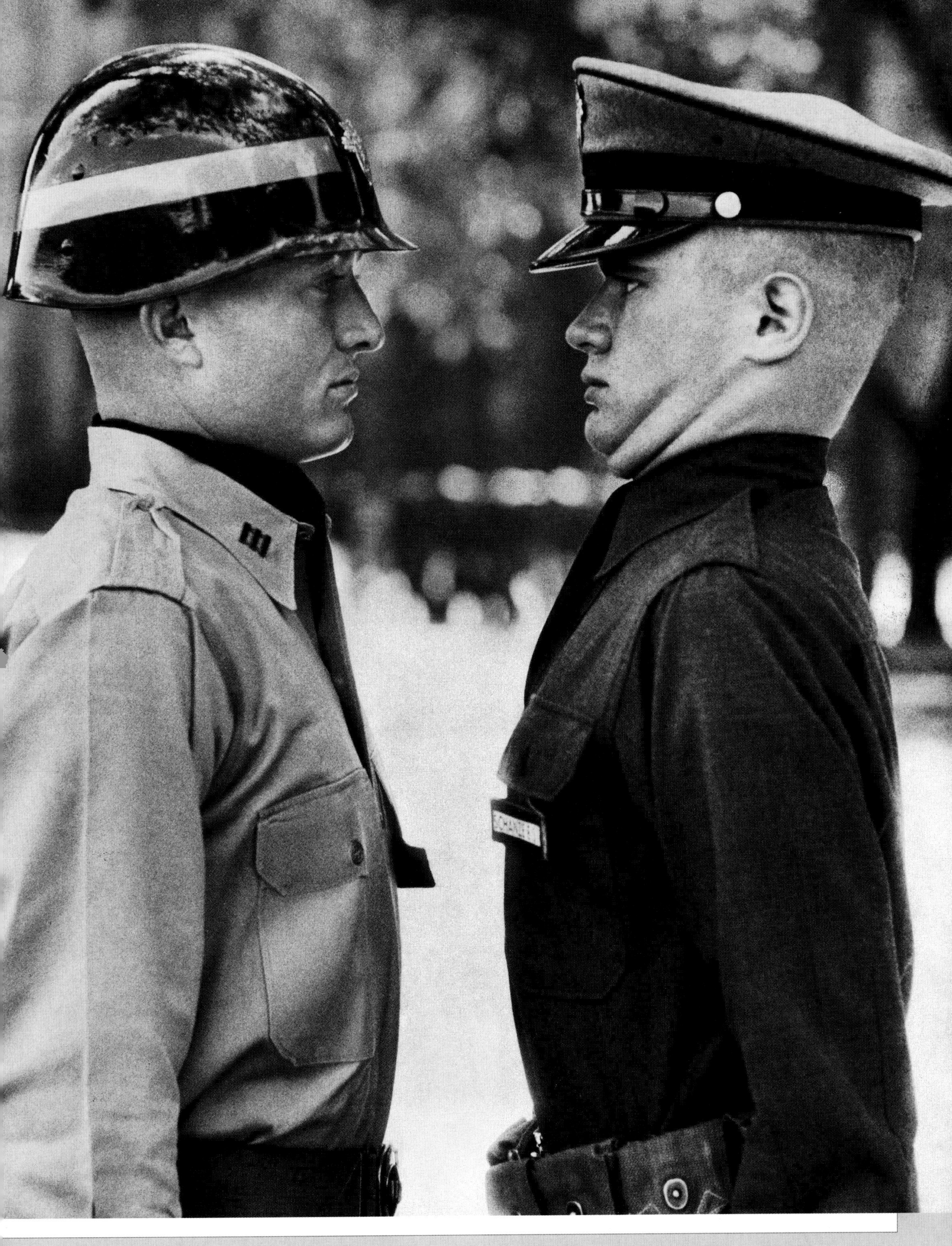

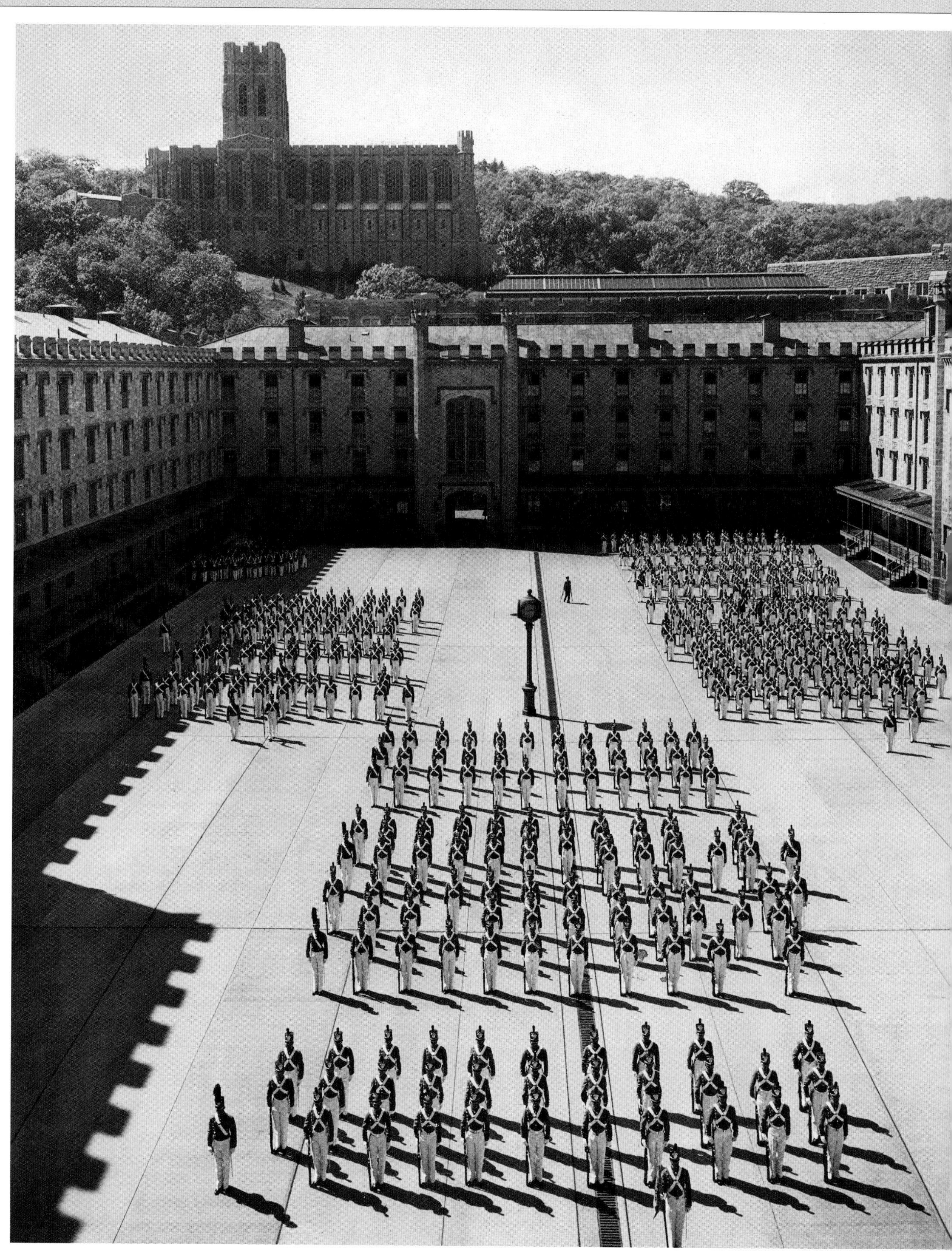

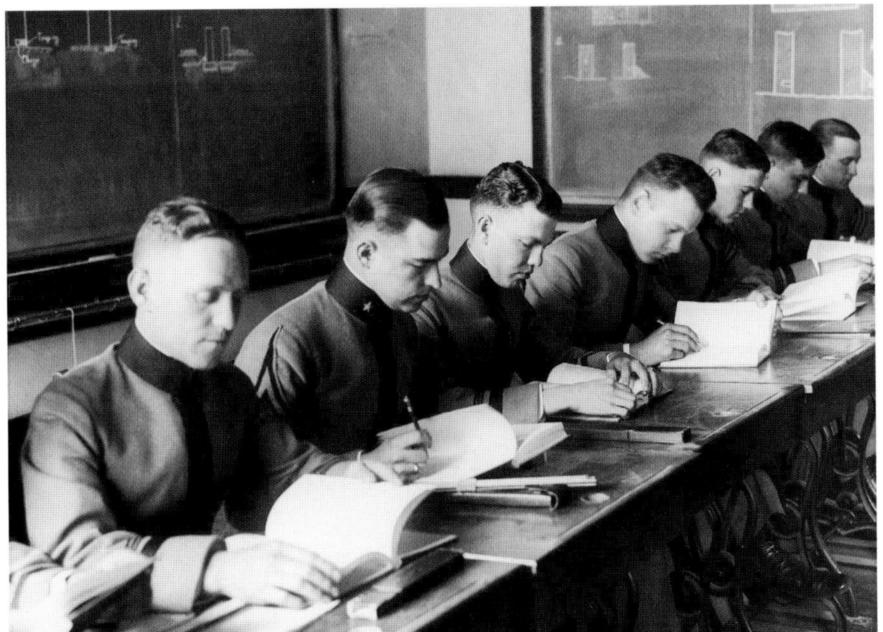

A DAY IN THE LIFE, THEN AS NOW
Whether drilling on the parade ground or studying up to nine hours a day, a cadet leads a highly disciplined existence. For its second issue, November 30, 1936, LIFE sent staff photographer Alfred Eisenstaedt up the river to capture the essence of life at West Point. A simple, evocative shot of a young man in the dining hall made the cover, while inside was a photo of cadets being taught how to handle a French 75 field gun. The twin forces that powered a cadet, said LIFE, were "competition and coercion."

ALFRED EISENSTAEDT (2)

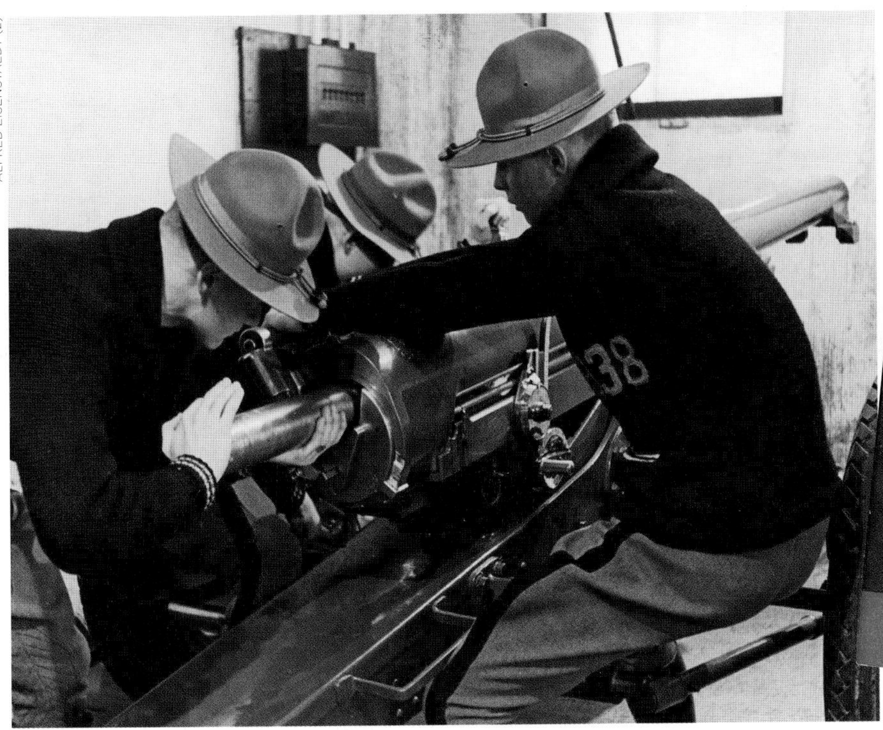

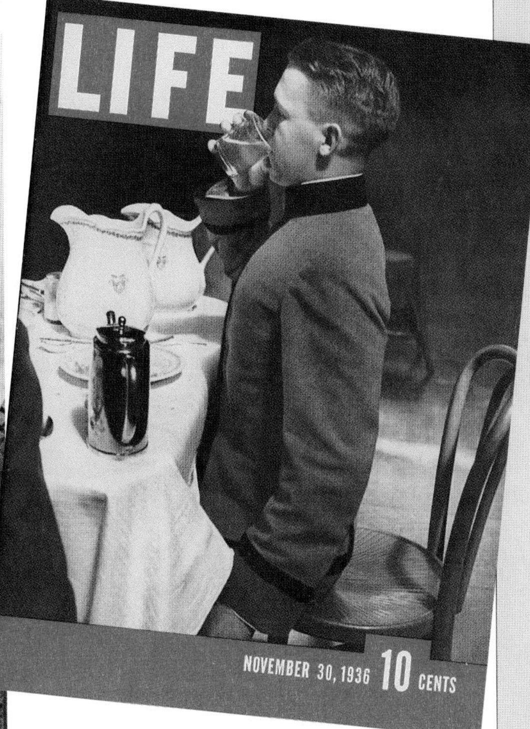

this, he posed for a picture with the man. After the wife of Confederate Gen. George Pickett gave birth to a boy, other alums who were fighting for the North, Gen. Ulysses S. Grant principal among them, bought a baby's silver tea set as a present, then had it smuggled through enemy lines. Some things have changed at West Point—technology, football versus Navy, the admission of women in 1976—but much has remained essentially the same since Custer and Pickett's day. The cadets live in barracks, just as they did back then. They drill and parade as they did back then. Taps sounds at 11:30, and a new day begins with first call for reveille at 6:15 sharp. There is a sense of permanence and hard-earned confidence about West Point. As Gen. Douglas MacArthur, who once served as superintendent of the Academy, observed, "The Long Gray Line has never failed us."

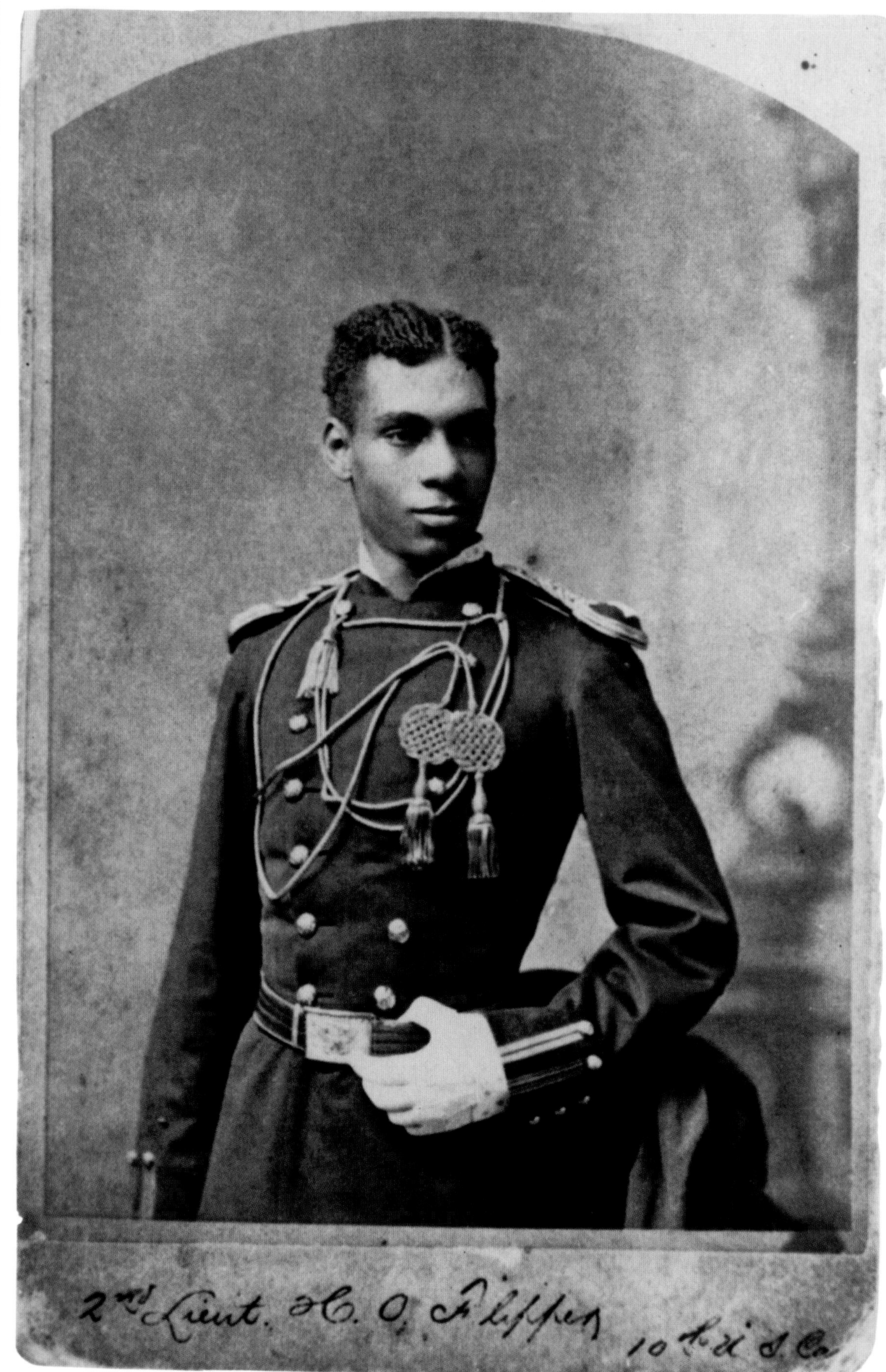

NATIONAL ARCHIVES

BREAKING BARRIERS, PART ONE Henry Ossian Flipper, a former slave from Georgia, was shunned and ostracized after he joined the Corps. He persevered, however, and in 1877 became the first black to graduate from West Point. He joined the famous Buffalo Soldiers regiment in the West, but in Texas ran into trouble when questionable charges against him in a money matter led to his dismissal from the Army in 1882. Flipper went on to a successful career as an engineer, and more than a century after being dishonorably discharged he was pardoned by President Bill Clinton.

LIBRARY OF CONGRESS

FRIENDS AND ENEMIES

Confederate officer James B. Washington (left), West Point class of 1863, was a captive guest of the Union's George Armstrong Custer ('61) during the Civil War. Other notable alums are below.

BROWN BROTHERS

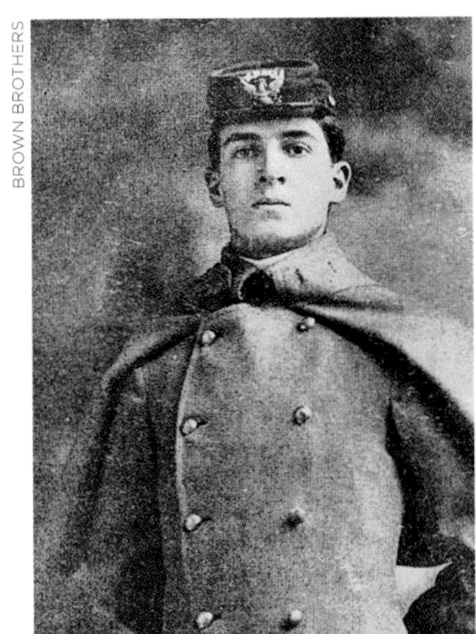

Douglas MacArthur, 1903

HULTON/GETTY

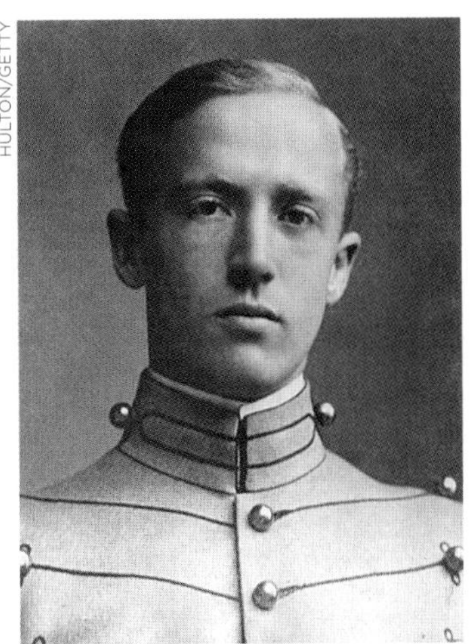

George S. Patton, 1909

BROWN BROTHERS

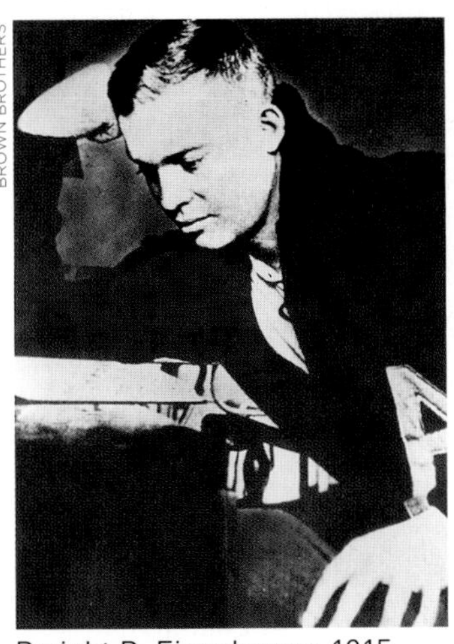

Dwight D. Eisenhower, 1915

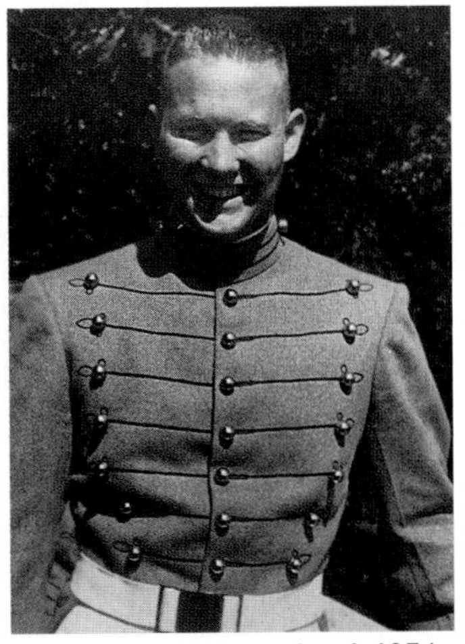

H. Norman Schwarzkopf, 1956

BREAKING BARRIERS, PART TWO

When women were admitted in 1976 (below), they were greeted with derision. Wrote a male cadet: "It is my duty to the alumni and the entire Army to run out as many females as possible." Such hidebound attitudes are no longer acceptable in the Corps.

AP

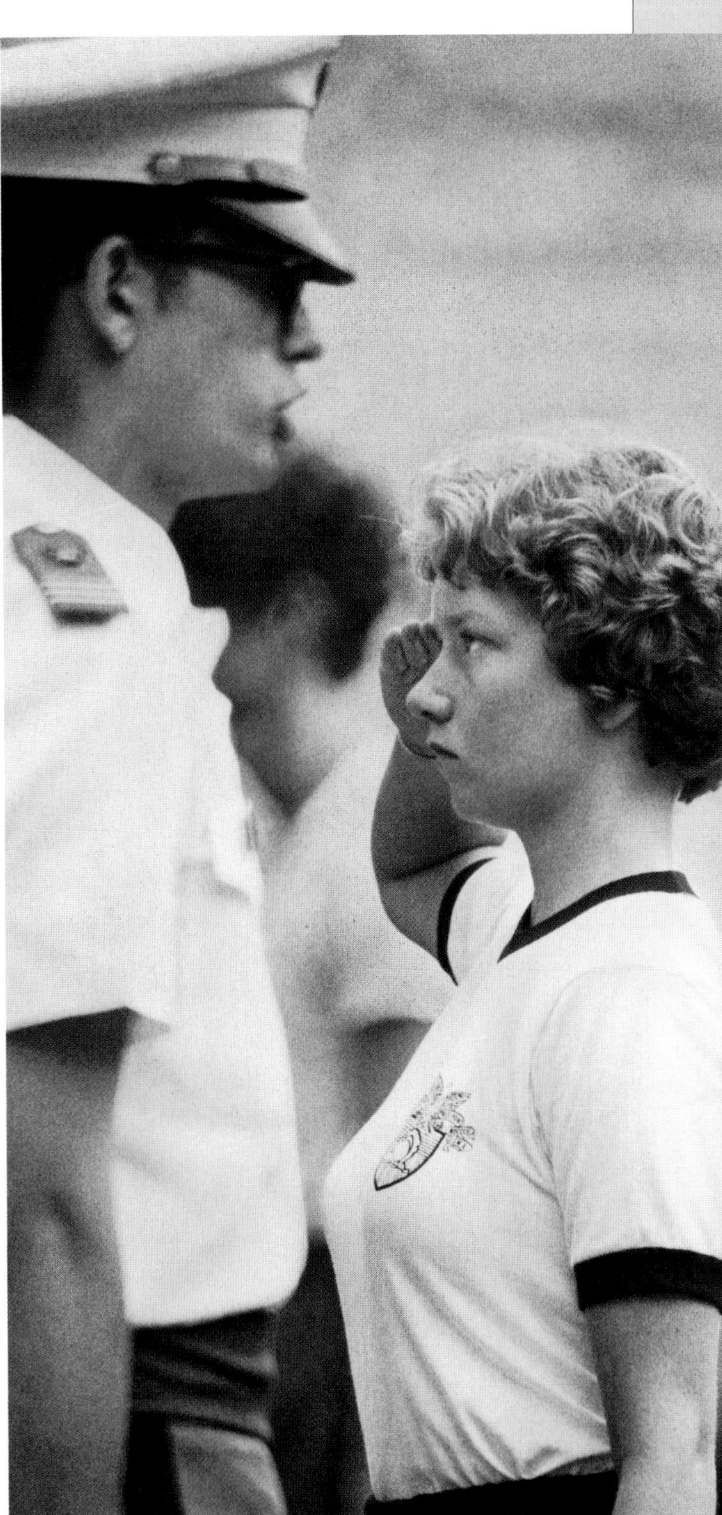

THE ARMY

A NATION—AND A FORCE—DIVIDED

It was the darkest period in American history. From 1861 to 1865, North fought South, and while ordinary citizens became courageous fighting men, the cost was dreadful. More than 600,000 lives were lost, and resentments still fester in some quarters. Here, with 1st New Jersey troops in the foreground, a Union officer surveys the Confederate position outside Fredericksburg, Va. In mid-December 1862, the Union army suffered a demoralizing loss there to Robert E. Lee's forces.

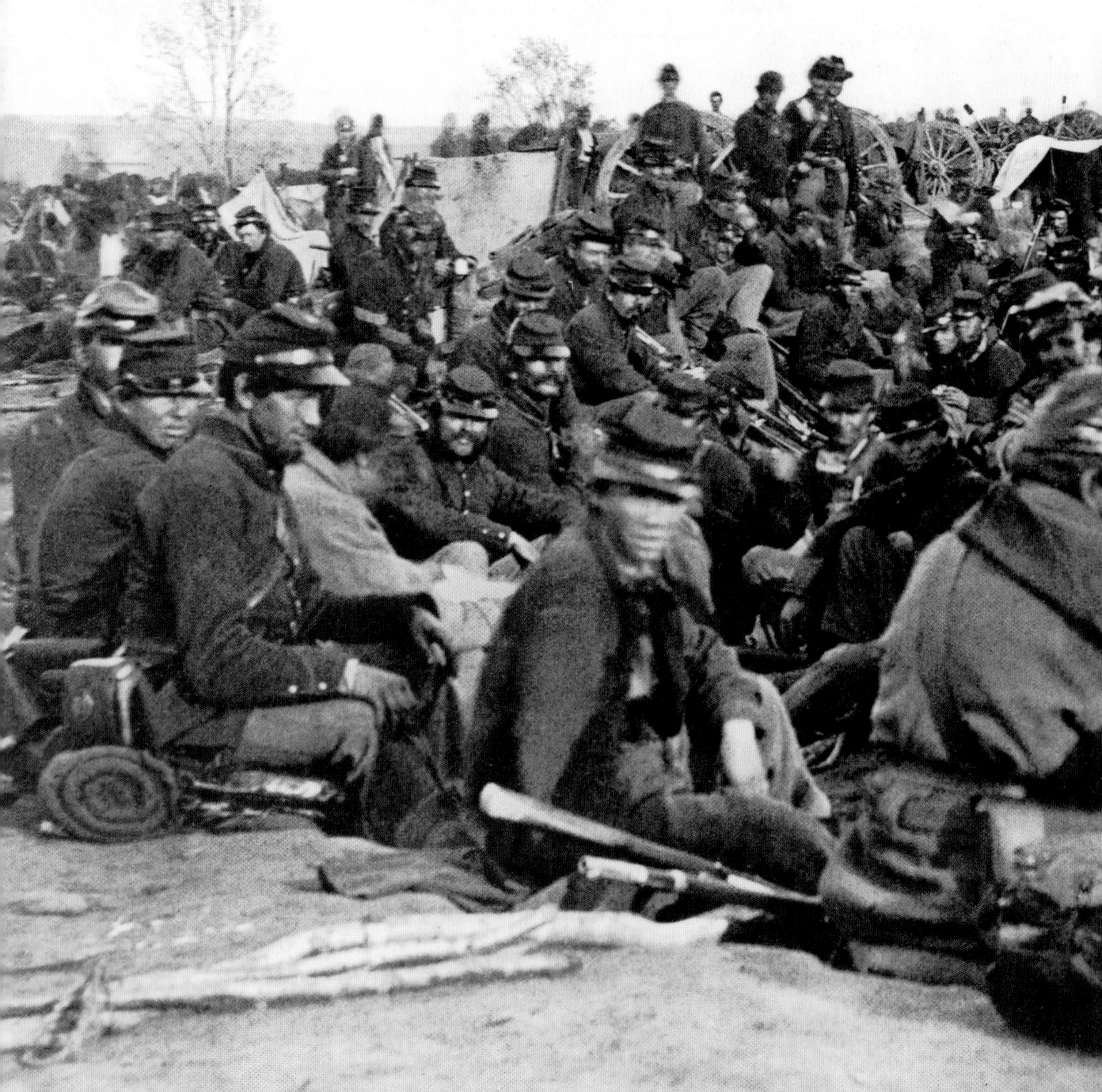

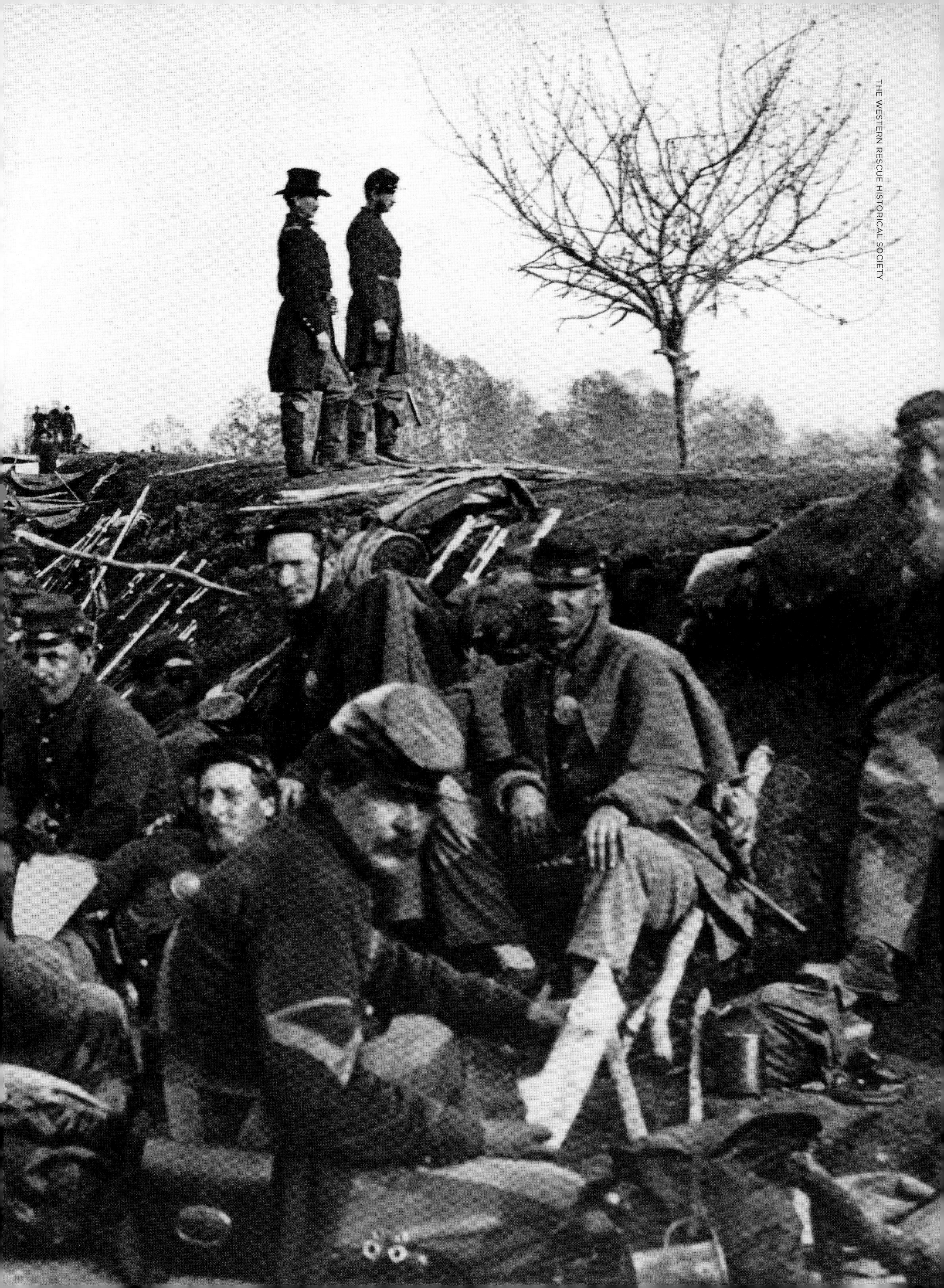

THE WESTERN RESCUE HISTORICAL SOCIETY

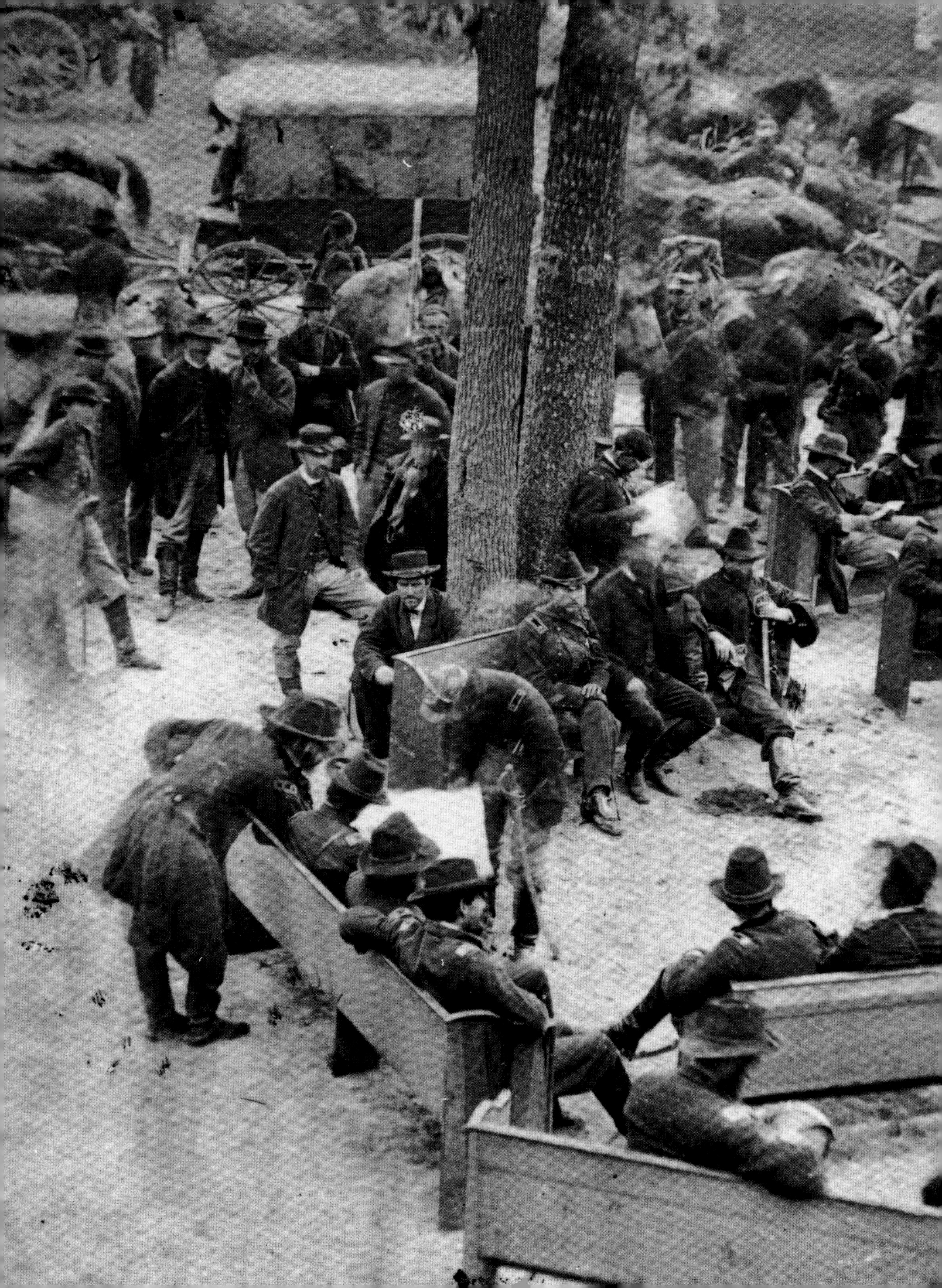

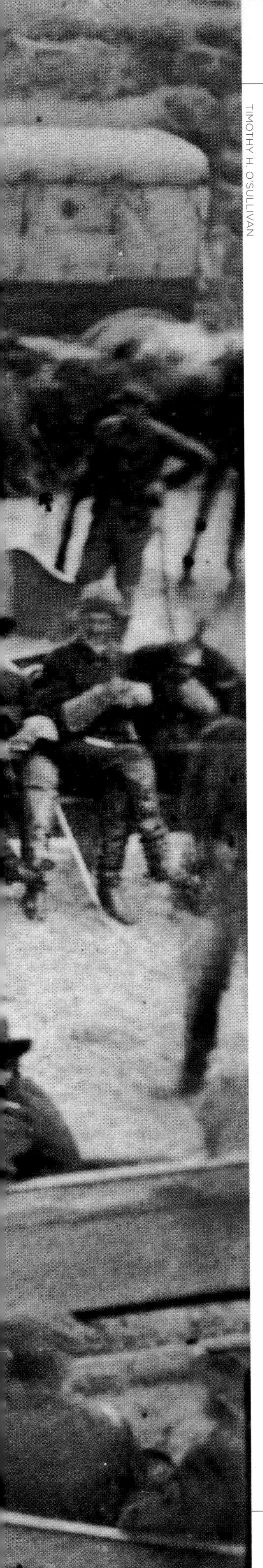

TIMOTHY H. O'SULLIVAN

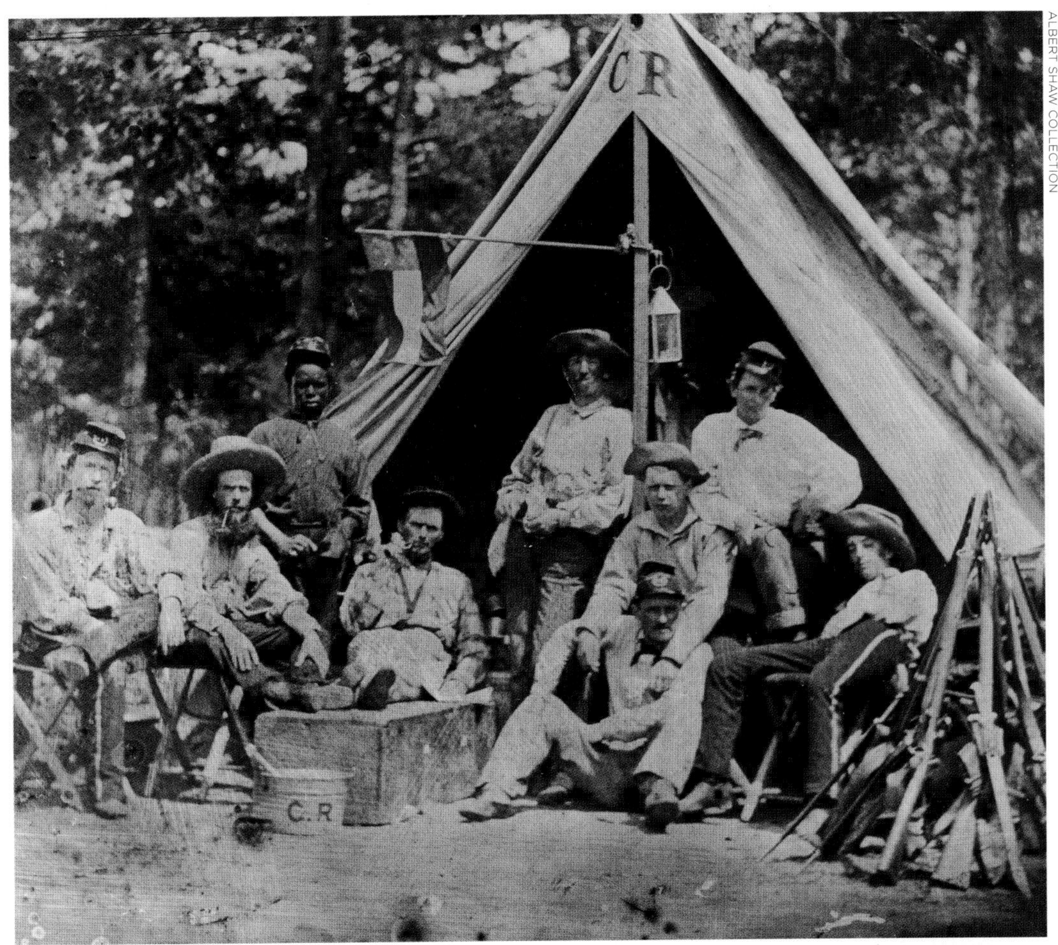

ALBERT SHAW COLLECTION

OFFICERS AND MEN
Above, Confederate soldiers of the 5th Georgia Volunteers take some R&R in 1862. The initials "CR" on the tent stand for their informal name, the Clinch Rifles. Near Washington, D.C., that same year, a Union soldier, probably a butcher, judging by his saw, poses with his family. Wives were sometimes permitted to live in camp and work as laundresses. In May 1864, near Massaponax Church, Va., Gen. Ulysses S. Grant bends over to study a map held by Gen. George Meade.

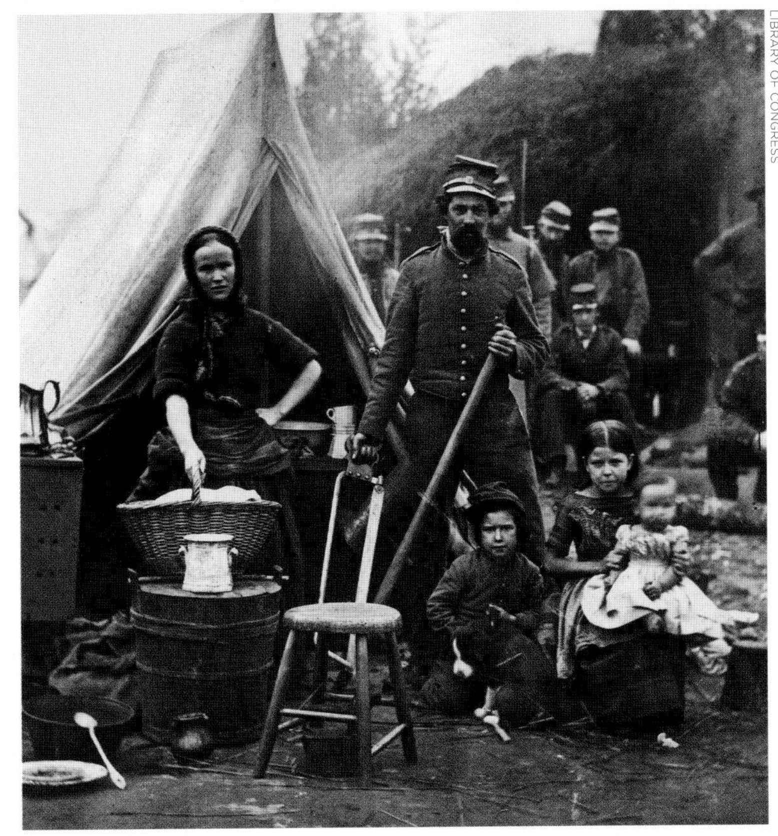

LIBRARY OF CONGRESS

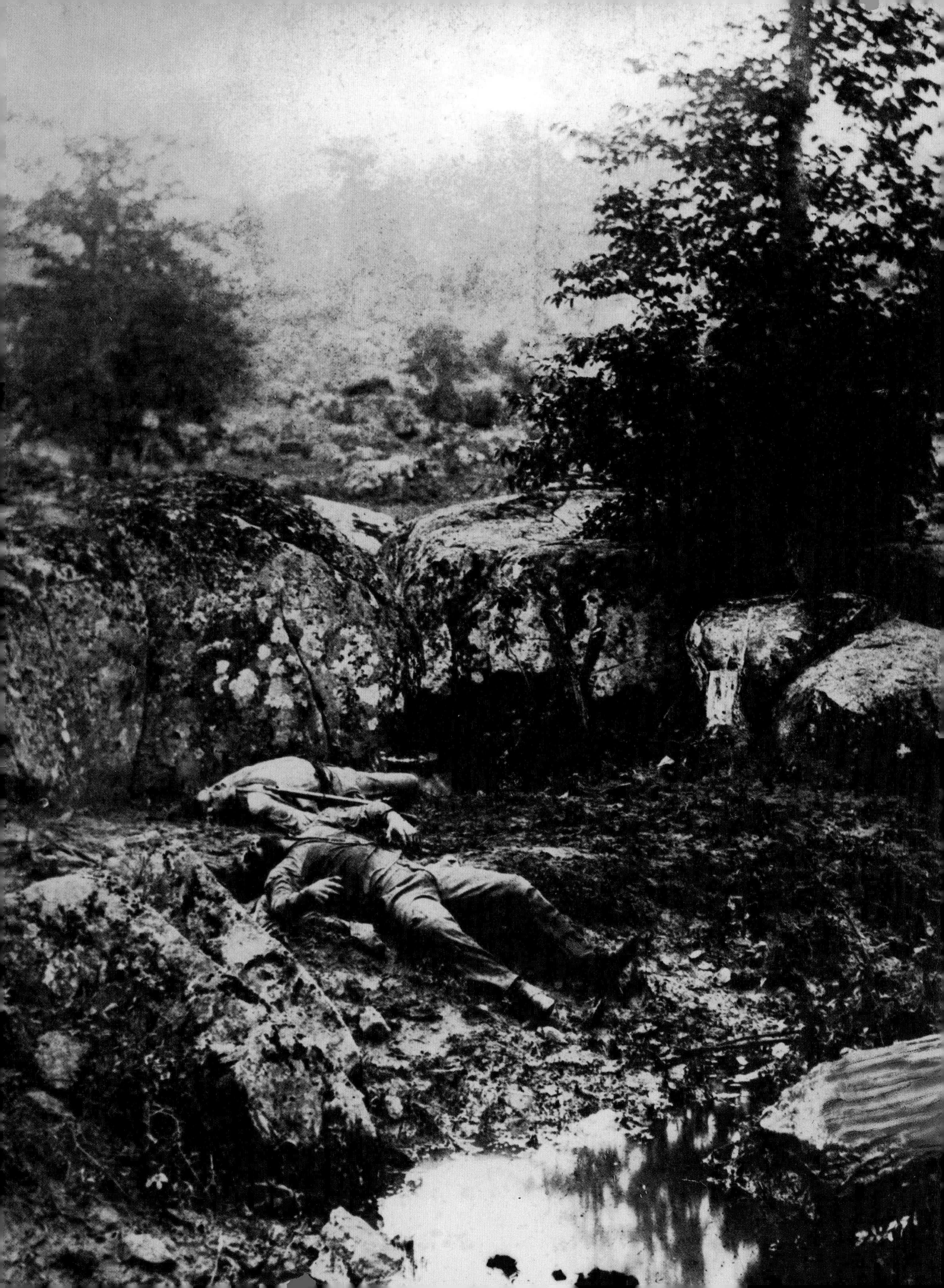

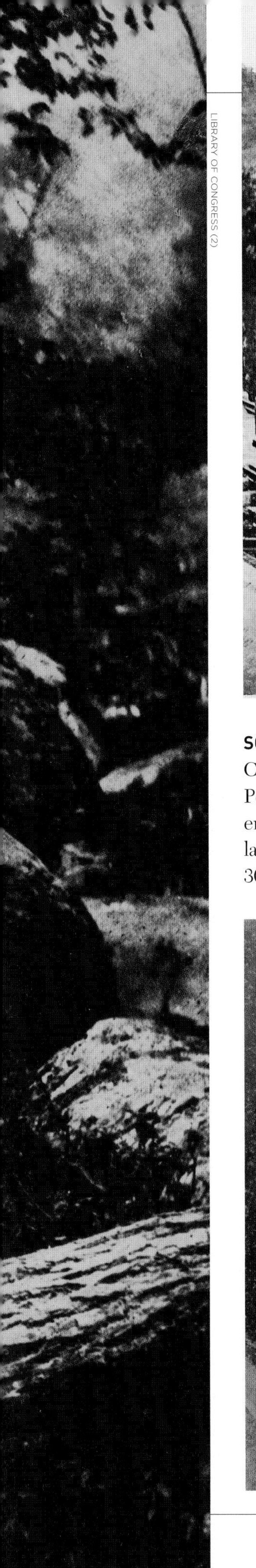

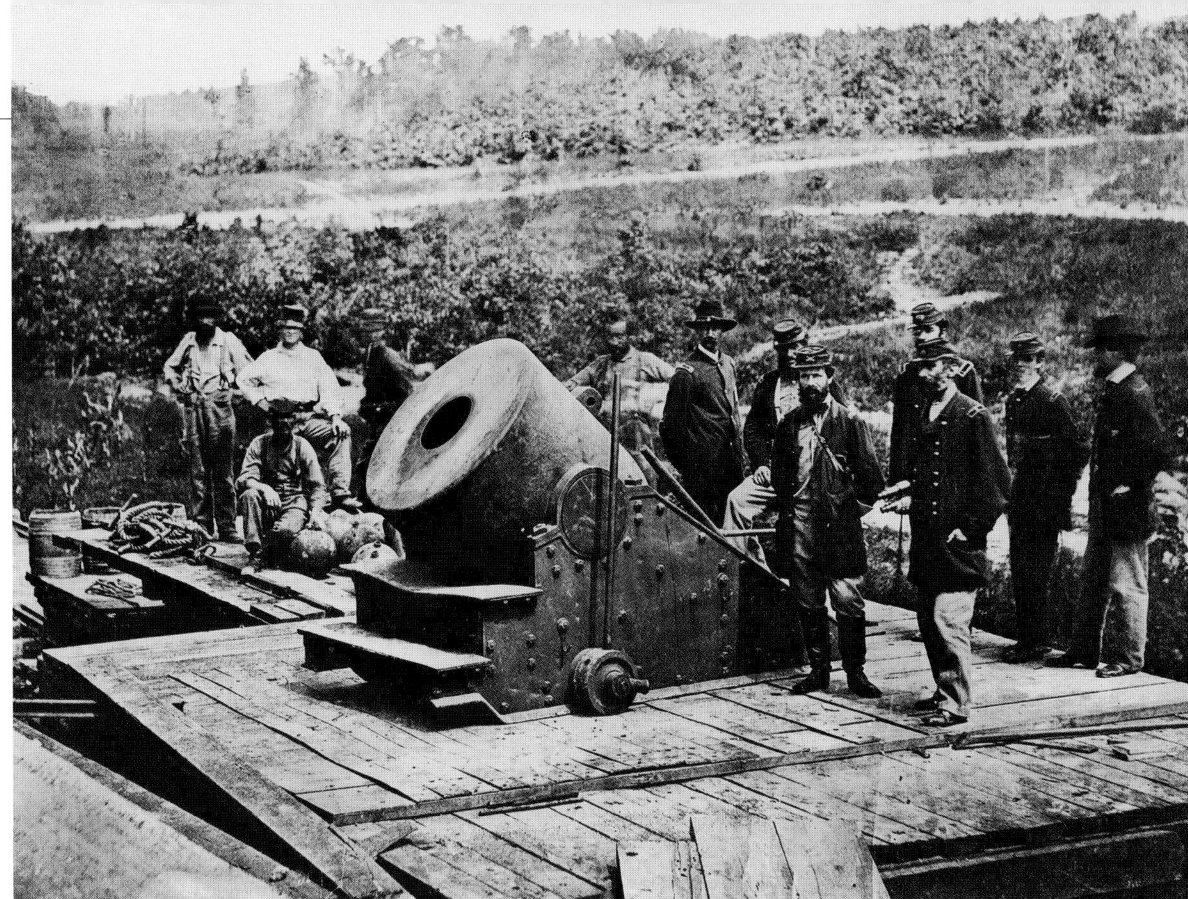

LIBRARY OF CONGRESS (2)

SOLDIERS, VOLUNTEERS, RAIDERS

Confederate dead lie along Plum Run (left), a stream running through an area called the Slaughter Pen at Gettysburg, one of the pivotal battles of the war. Here, the 44th Alabama Volunteer Infantry engaged Union troops in hand-to-hand fighting. The 13-inch mortar "Dictator" (above) was the largest gun in the Union siege of Petersburg, Va. Below: Some of Shannon's Scouts, a hand-picked 30-man Texas outfit that carried out audacious raids on Sherman's foraging parties in Georgia.

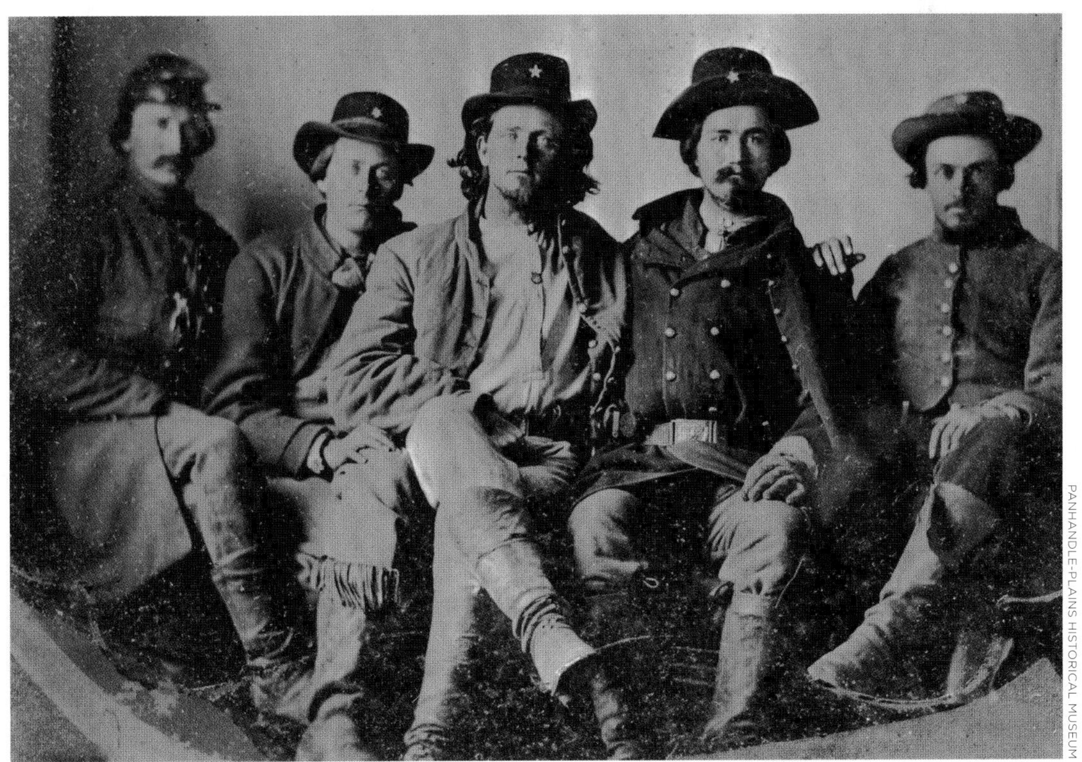

PANHANDLE-PLAINS HISTORICAL MUSEUM

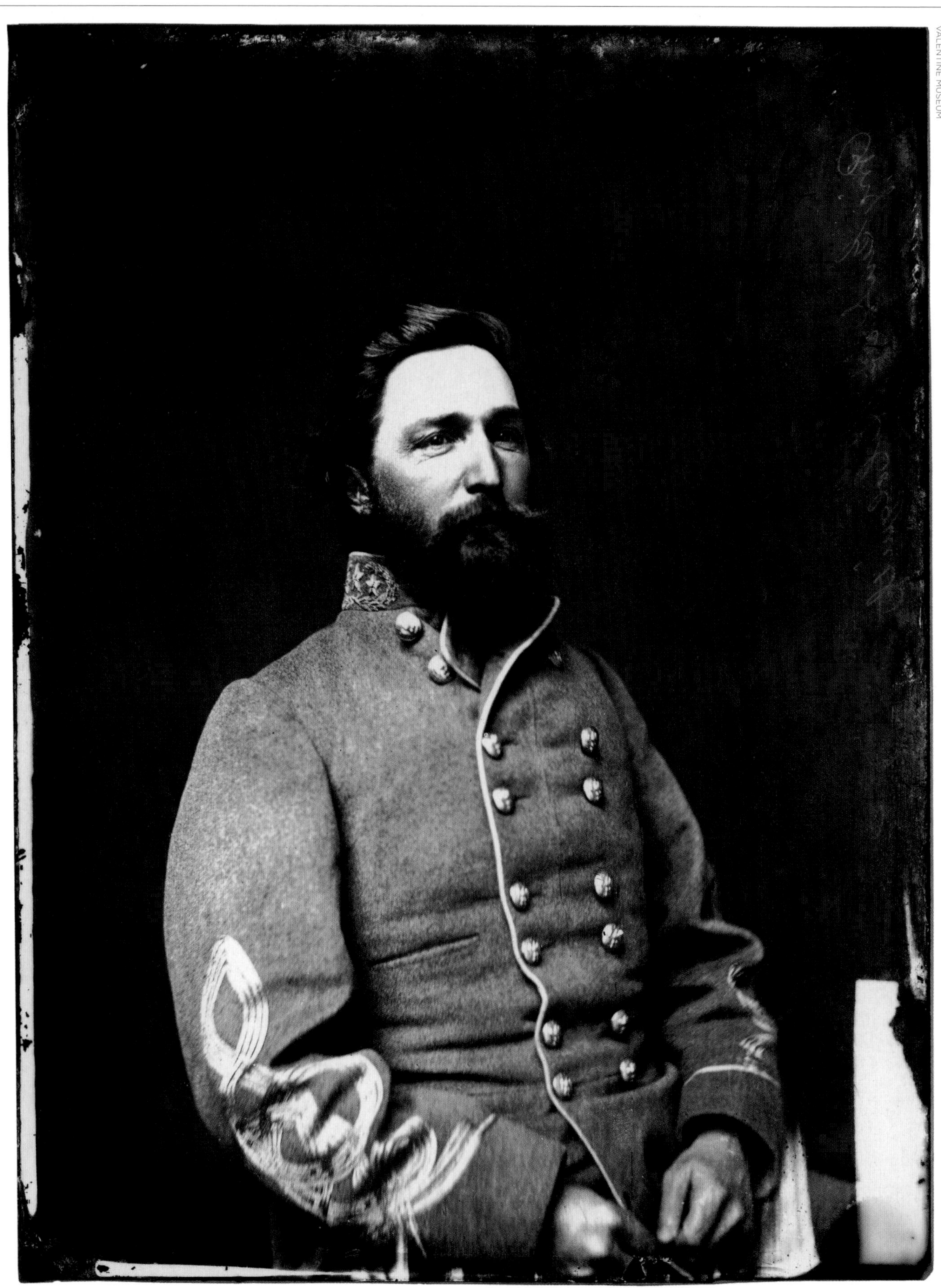

VALENTINE MUSEUM

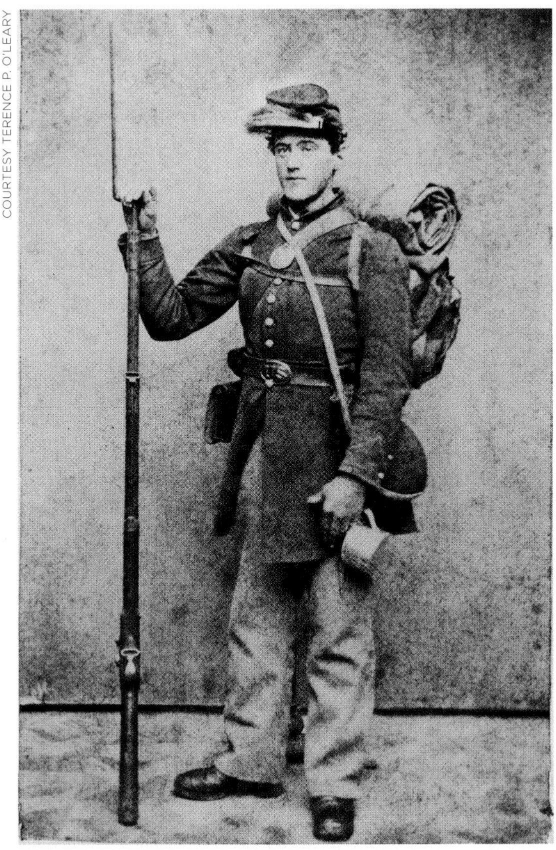

COURTESY TERENCE P. O'LEARY

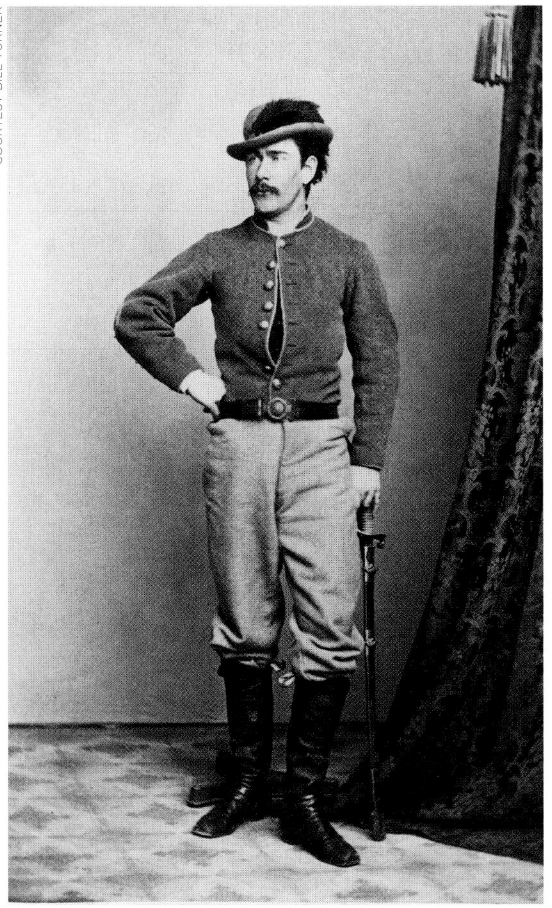

COURTESY BILL TURNER

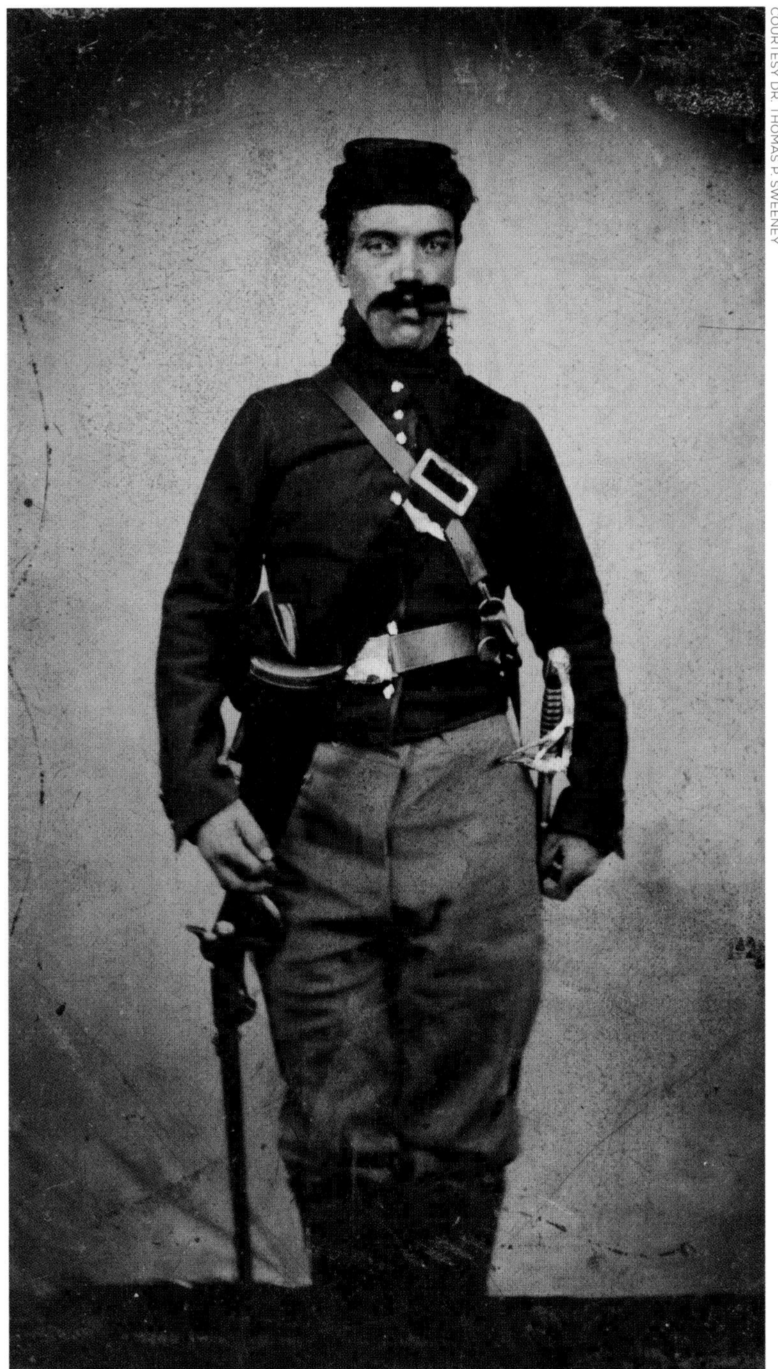

COURTESY DR. THOMAS P. SWEENEY

DRAMATIS PERSONAE

Confederate Brig. Gen. Alfred Holt Colquitt (opposite) was an ardent secessionist from Georgia who commanded under Stonewall Jackson at some of the worst bloodbaths of the war: Antietam, Fredericksburg and Chancellorsville. He later served as governor of his home state and as a member of the U.S. Senate. Clockwise from above: This Union cavalry trooper wears his equipment over a short shell jacket, which was more convenient for riding than a full coat. The dandified Confederate cavalryman had adopted the jaunty style of his leader, Jeb Stuart. Private Samuel Royer of the 149th Pennsylvania, here with rifle and bayonet, was wounded at Gettysburg.

MASS/ MOLLUS/USAMHI

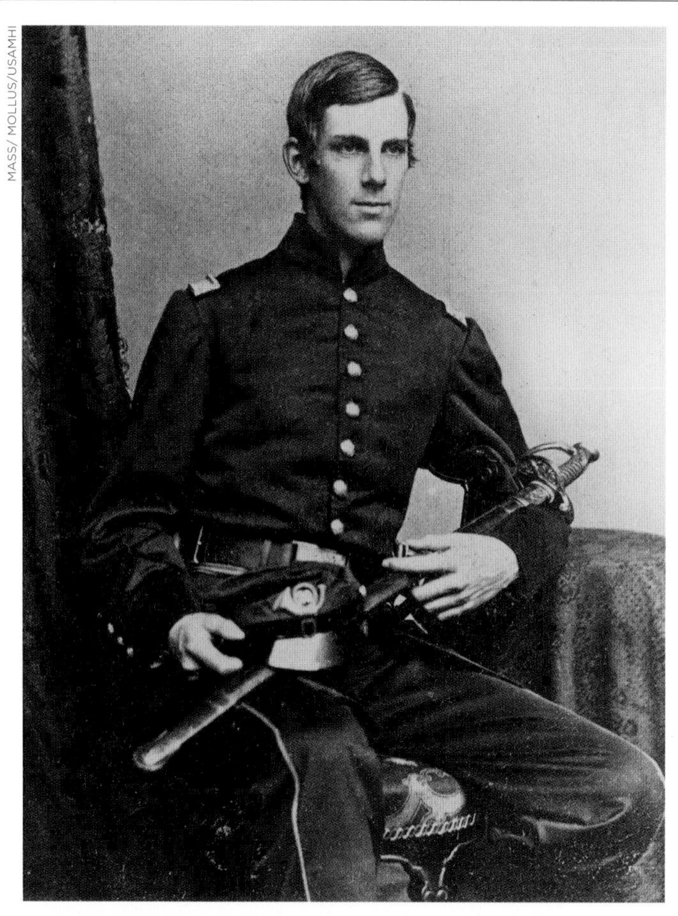

U.S. MILITARY HISTORY INSTITUTE

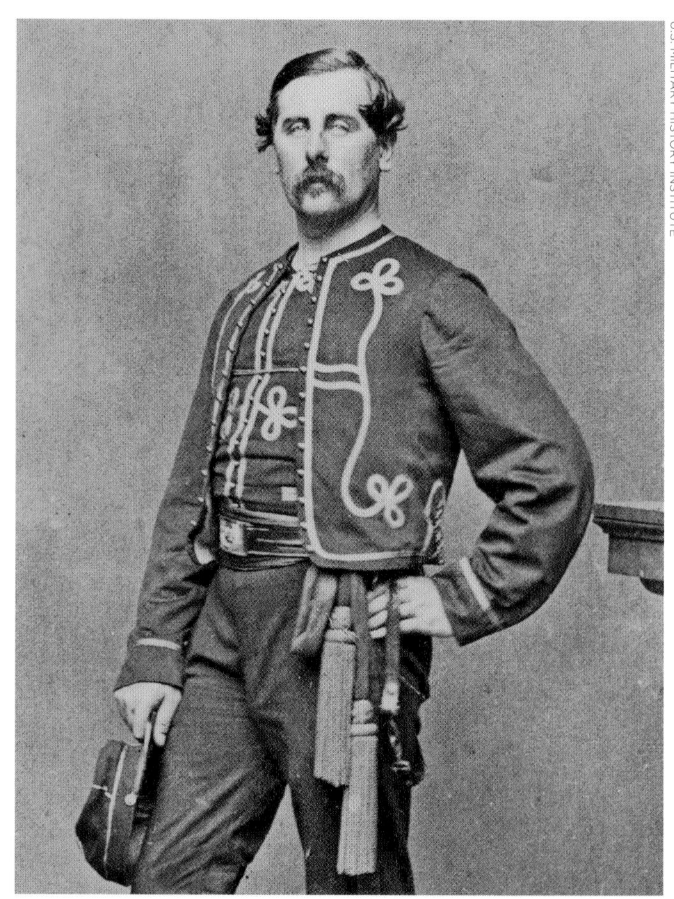

COOK COLLECTION/VALENTINE MUSEUM

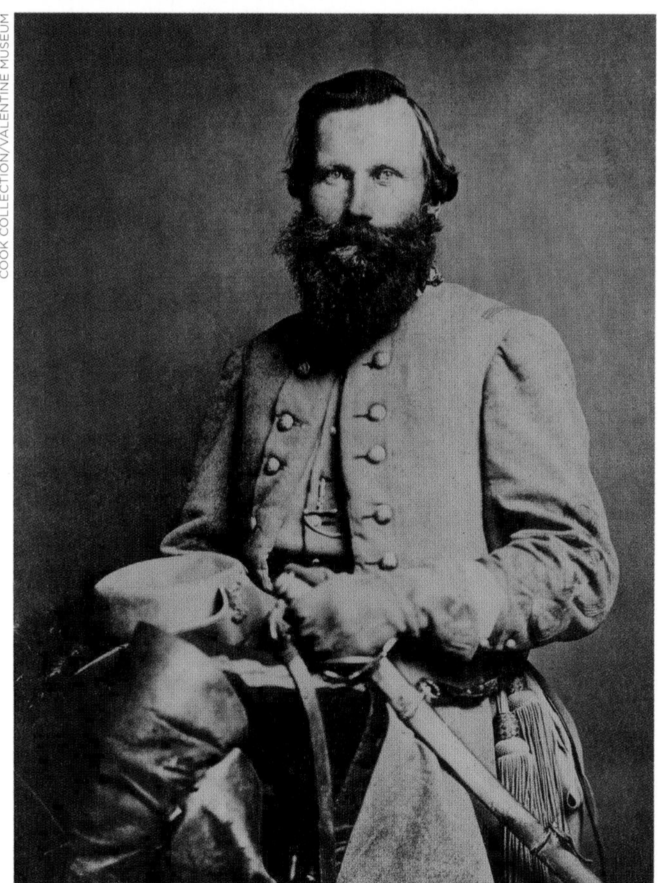

COURTESY MICHAEL J. McAFEE

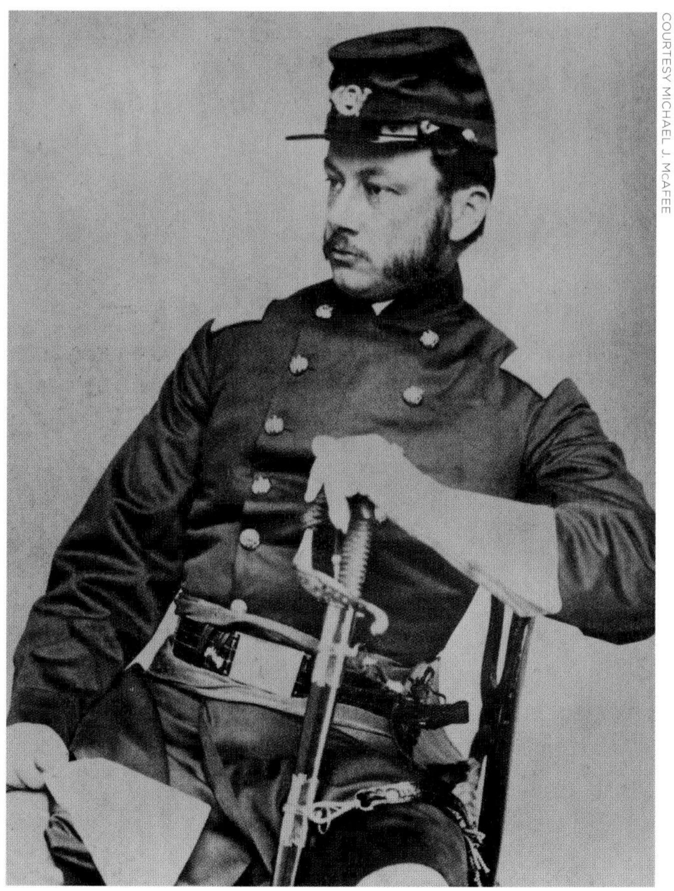

BROWN BROTHERS

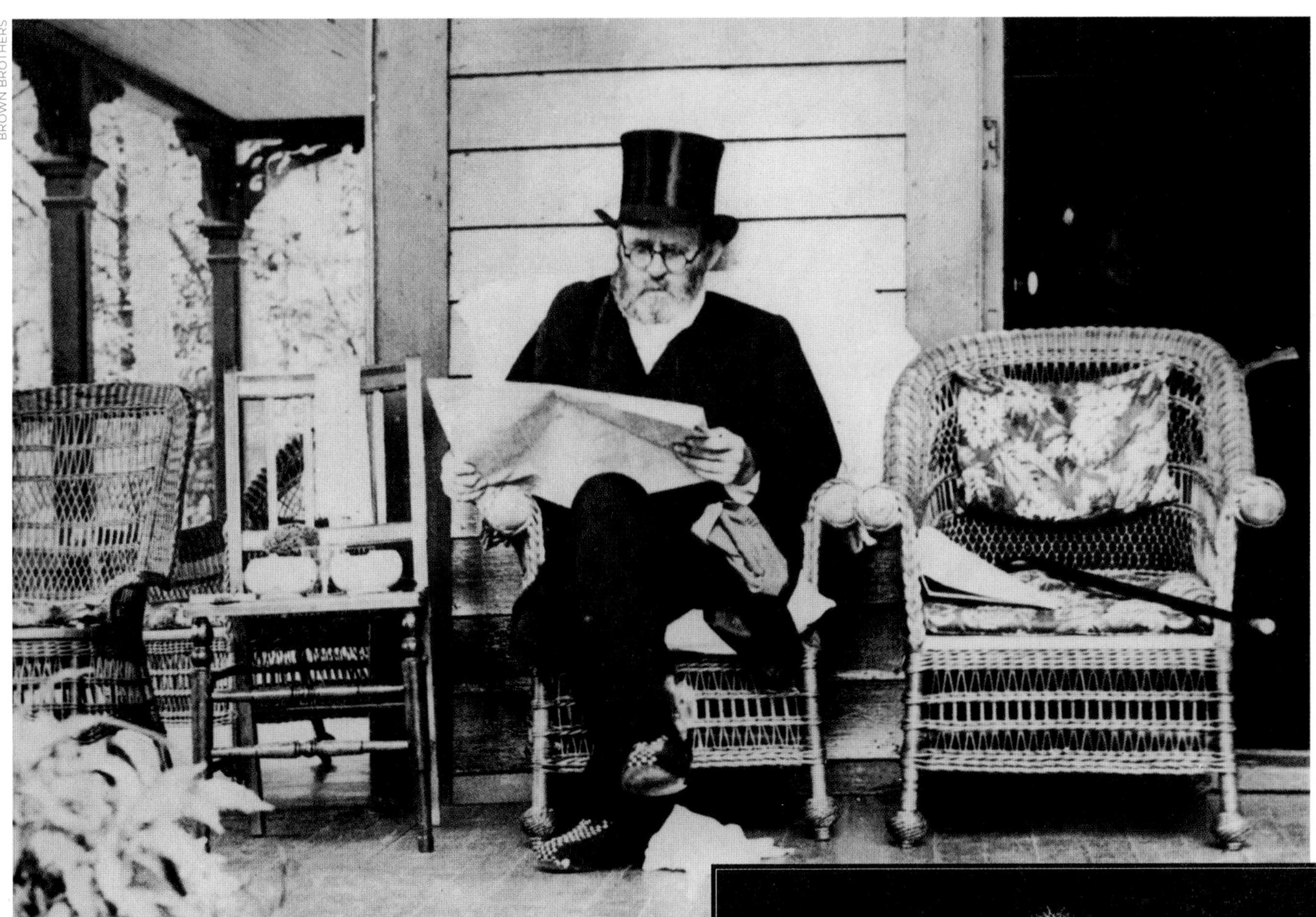

MEN OF WAR

There were countless fascinating participants in the war. Clockwise from near left: Col. Robert Potter of the 51st New York was one of two officers to lead the famed charge over Burnside Bridge, one of the key moments in the Battle of Antietam, the bloodiest single day in the war; Gen. Jeb Stuart, Lee's cavalry chief, was a rakish Virginian who favored hip-length boots, bright yellow gloves and a black ostrich feather in his slouch hat; Capt. Oliver Wendell Holmes of the 20th Massachusetts, who was wounded at Antietam, would be appointed to the Supreme Court in 1902; Gen. Thomas Meagher was an endlessly flamboyant Irish revolutionary who led the Irish Brigade and believed that the experience would help him free his homeland from British rule; Ulysses S. Grant rests at a cottage near Saratoga, N.Y., three days before his death in 1885; Robert E. Lee died five years after the war ended.

MANSELL COLLECTION

LIBRARY OF CONGRESS

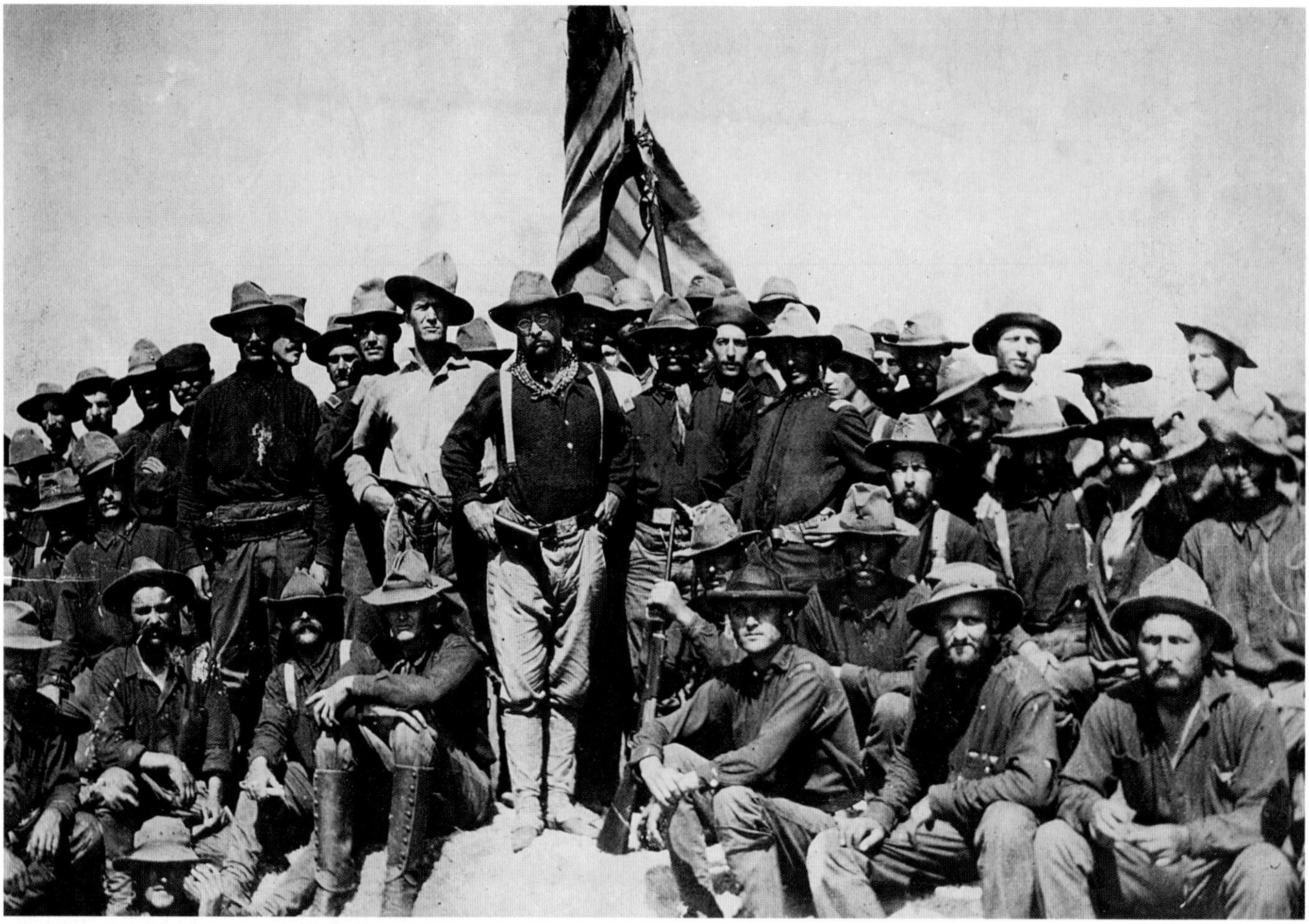

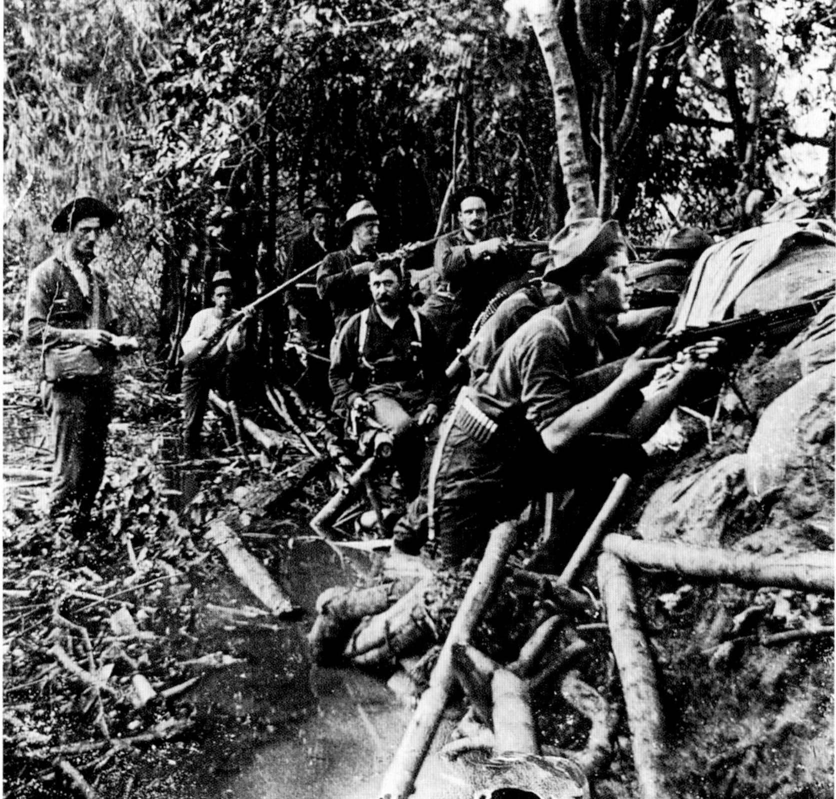

A NATION'S INTERESTS ABROAD

Two months after the battleship *Maine* was sunk, on February 15, 1898, in Havana harbor, the U.S. declared war on Spain. On July 1, American troops in Cuba attacked an area near Santiago. The 1st Volunteer Cavalry, better known as the Rough Riders, were led by Col. Teddy Roosevelt (above, wearing glasses and neckerchief) up Kettle Hill, then up San Juan Hill. He later said, "San Juan was the great day of my life." The Spanish-American War also featured fighting in the Philippines. At left, the 13th Minnesota prepares for action against a Spanish blockhouse defending Manila. Construction of the Panama Canal (opposite) began in 1904 and was completed in 1914. The U.S. Army Corps of Engineers did a sterling job on the project, the largest of its kind at the time. Pictured is the famed Culebra Cut, on October 11, 1913.

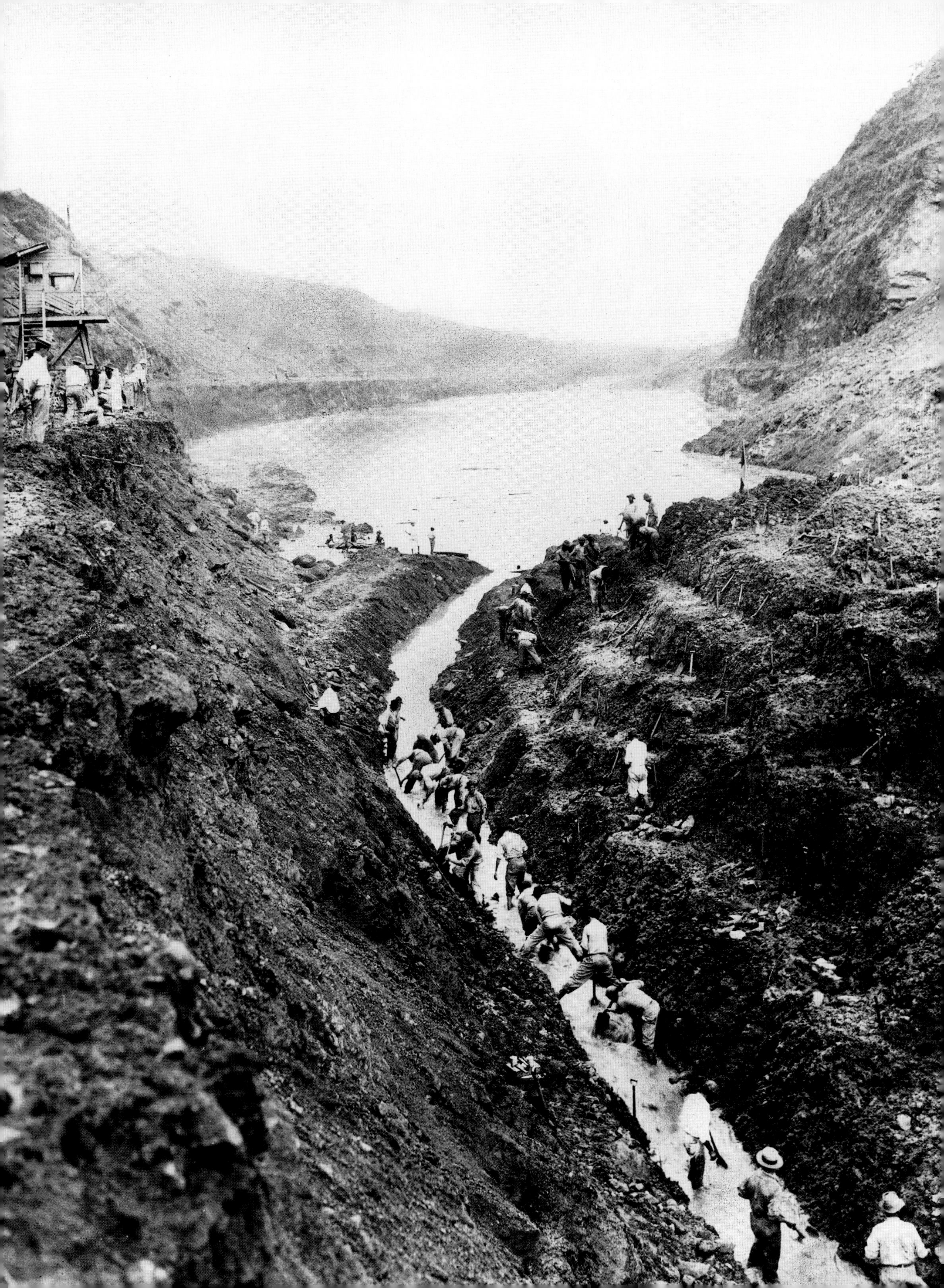

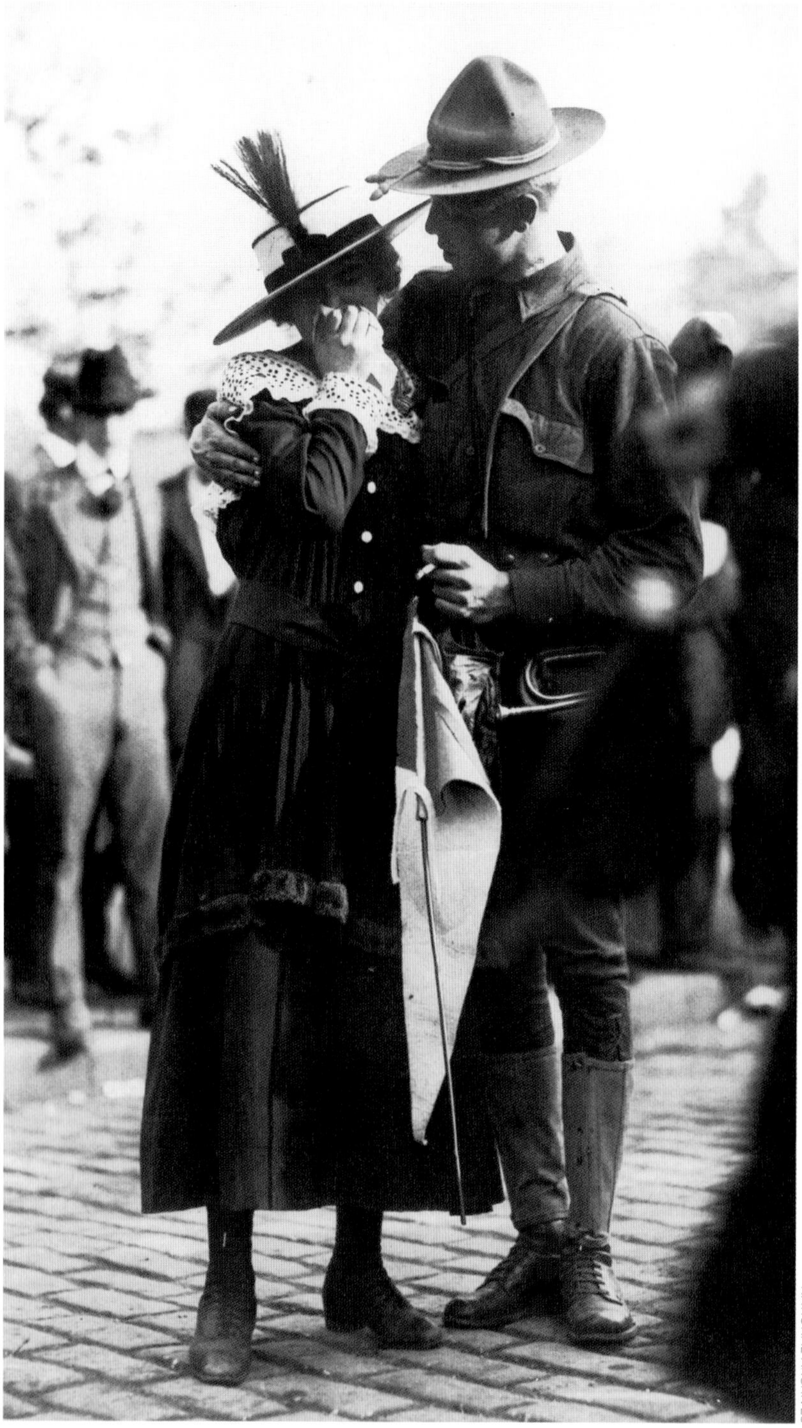

NATIONAL ARCHIVES

OVER THERE . . . "The Great War" was nearly three years old when the U.S. made its formal declaration against Germany on April 6, 1917, and although countless lives had already been sacrificed, there was still plenty of time for blood and glory. Two million doughboys went overseas on transport ships. Above, a member of the 71st Infantry Regiment of the New York National Guard comforts his sweetheart before shoving off for training at Camp Wadsworth in South Carolina.

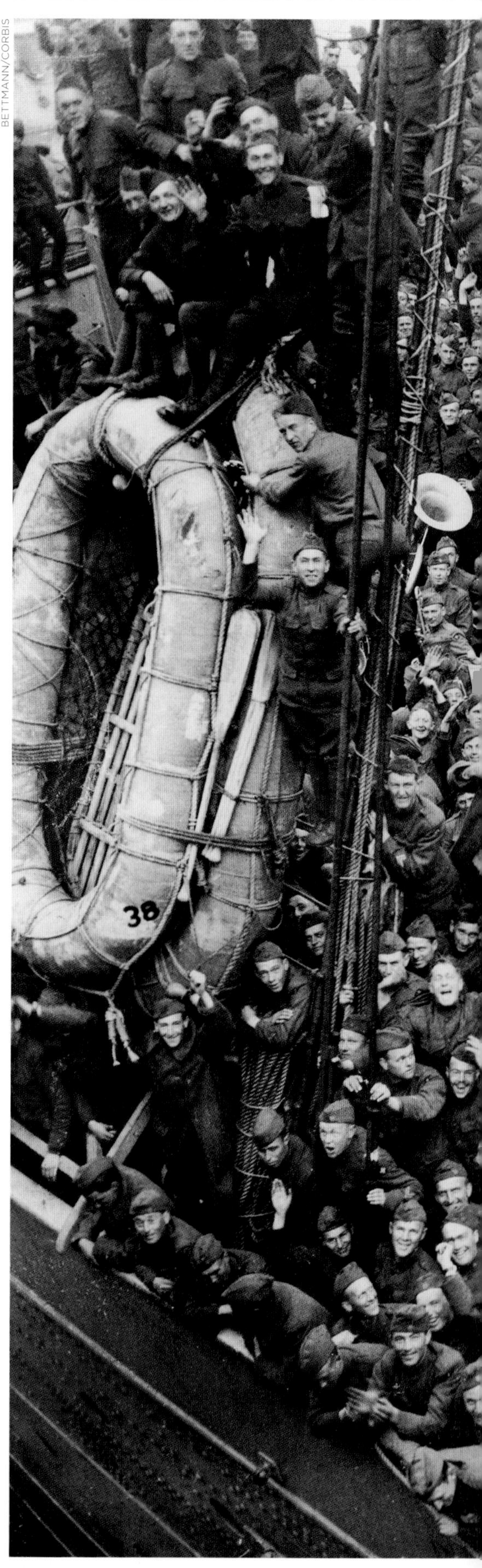

BETTMANN/CORBIS

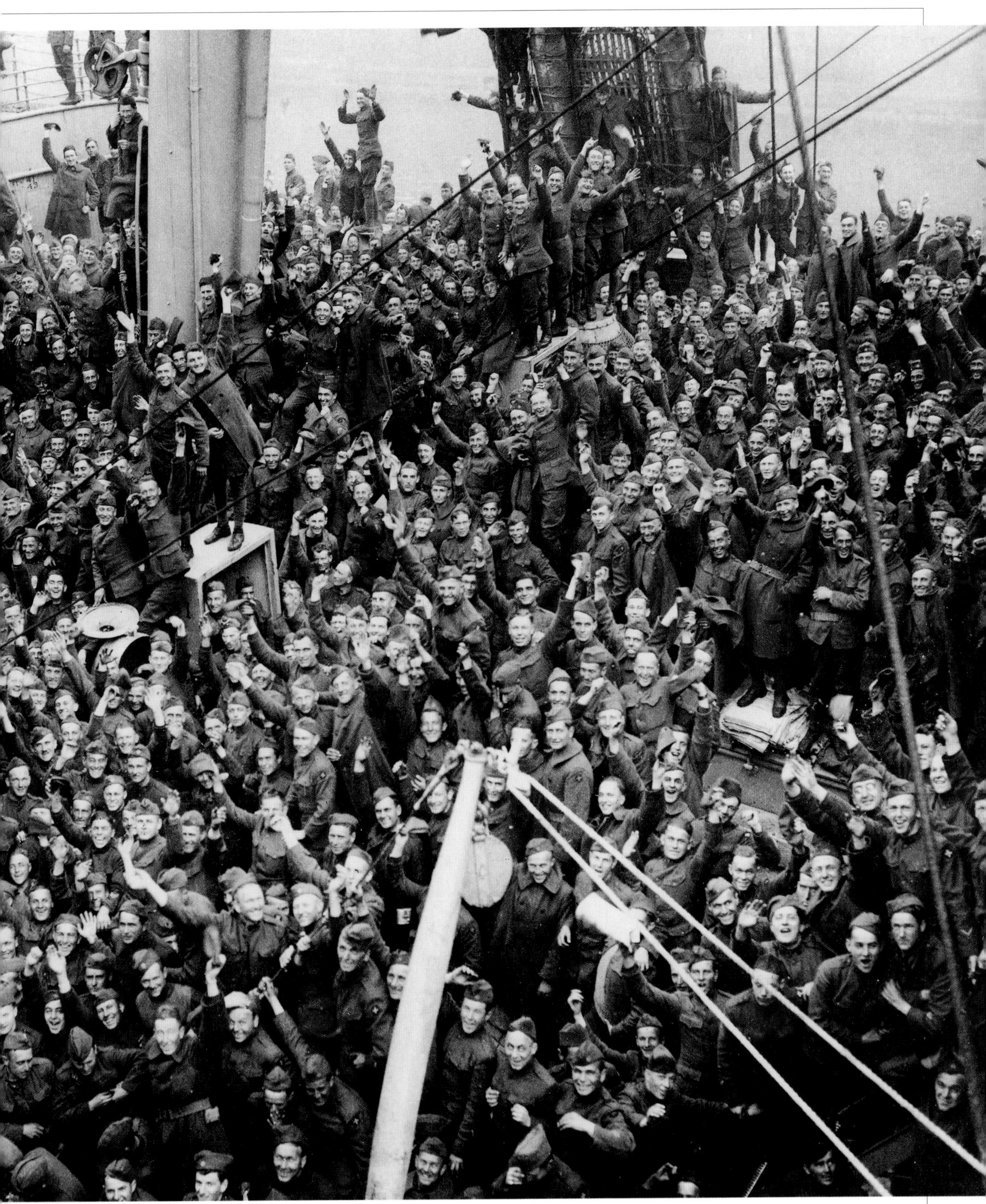

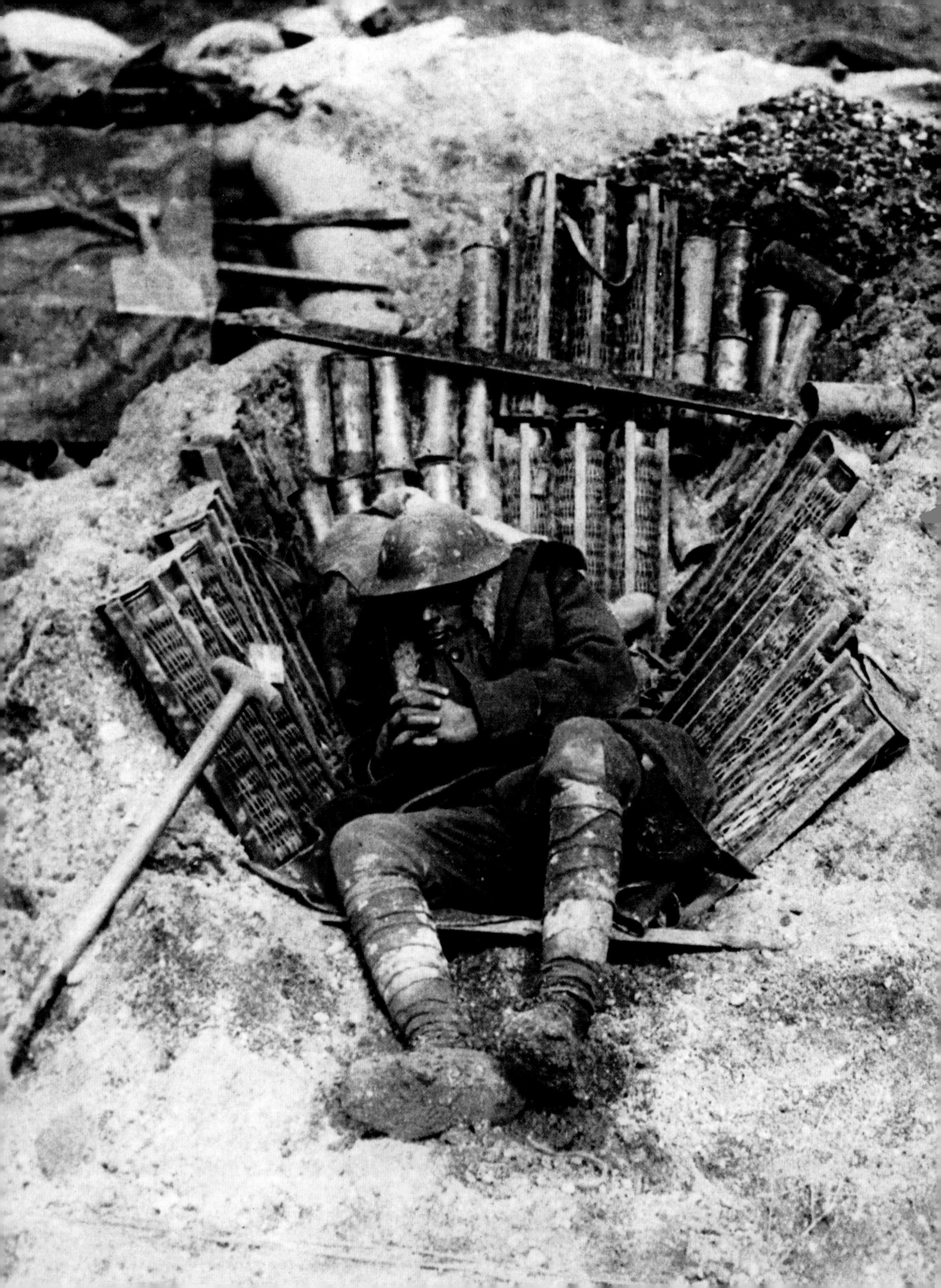

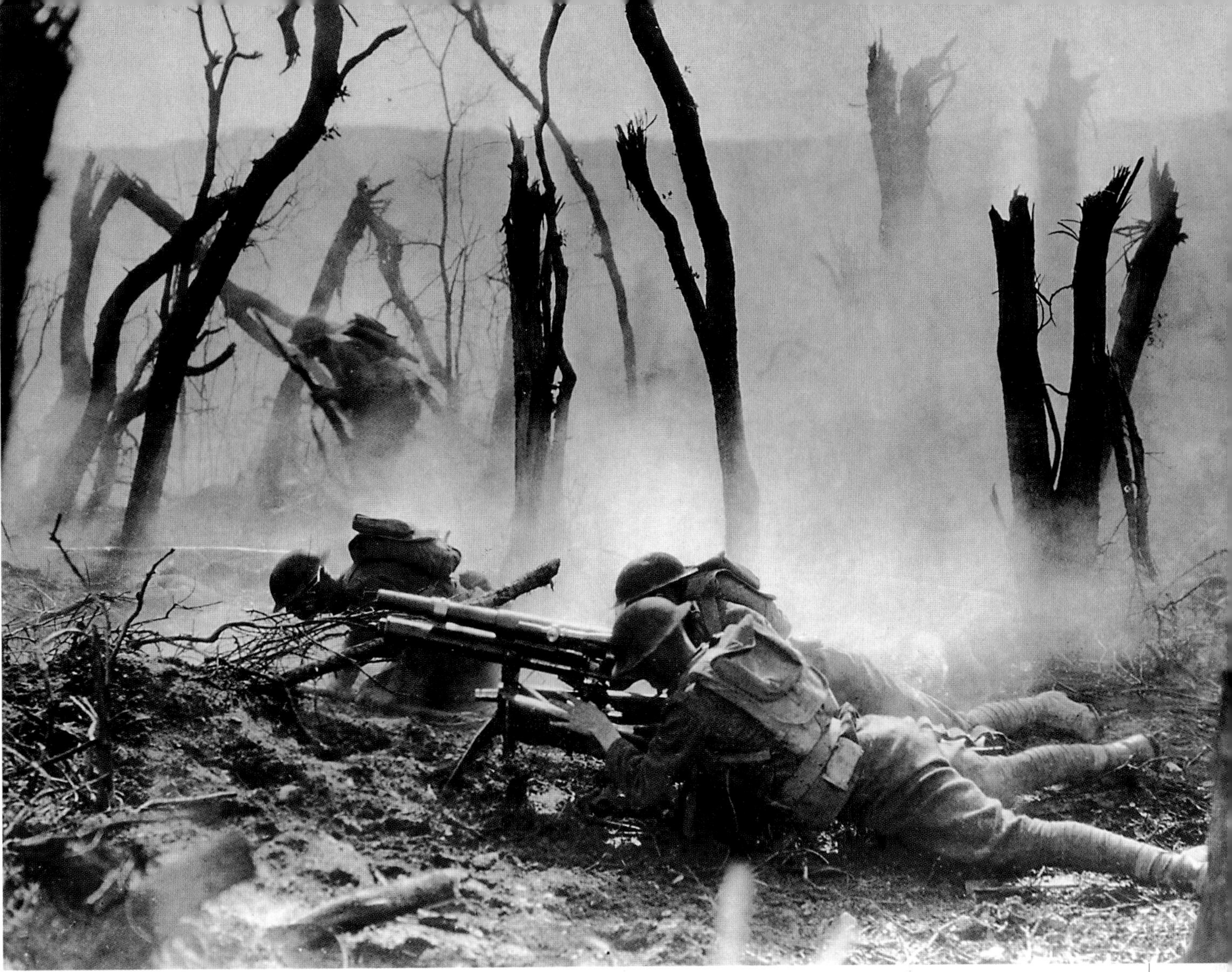

U.S. SIGNAL CORPS/GETTY

EVERYWHERE A NO-MAN'S-LAND

The training at home had been good, but there was no real preparation for war. Right: This modern combat provided a new horror—gas. Here, in the Lorraine region of France, these soldiers from the 1st Division dare not leave their bunker without their masks. An exhausted doughboy (opposite) finds that a bed of captured German ammo is a perfectly fine place to catch some needed shut-eye. The soldiers above, from the 23rd Infantry Regiment, 2nd Division, man a 37mm gun in the ferocious Argonne offensive of 1918, led by "Black Jack" Pershing.

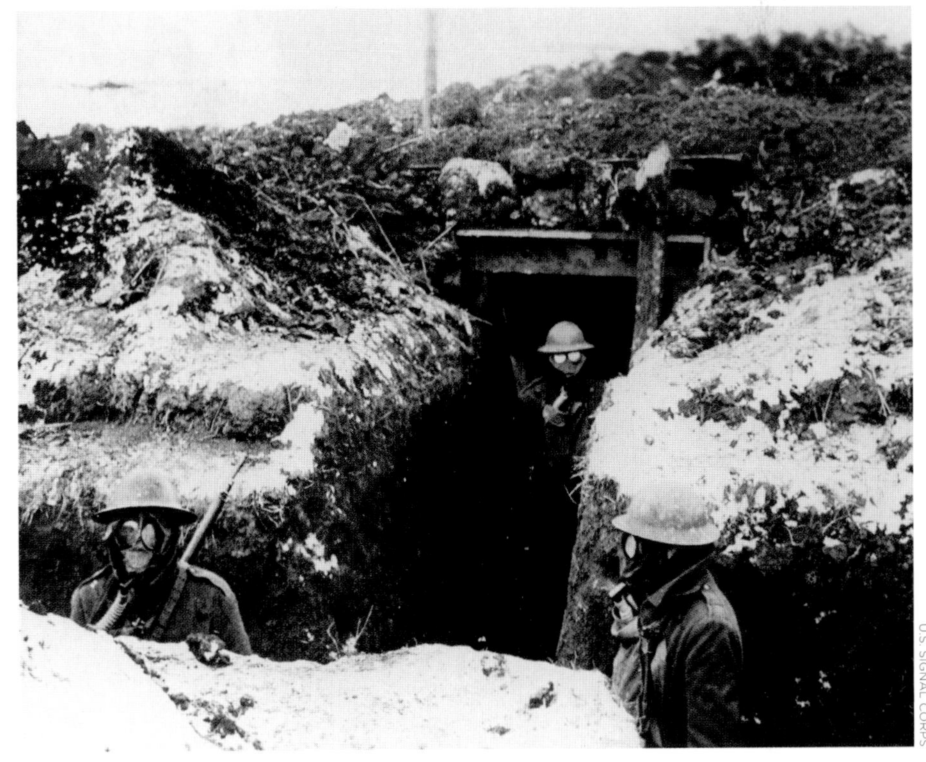

U.S. SIGNAL CORPS

UNDERWOOD

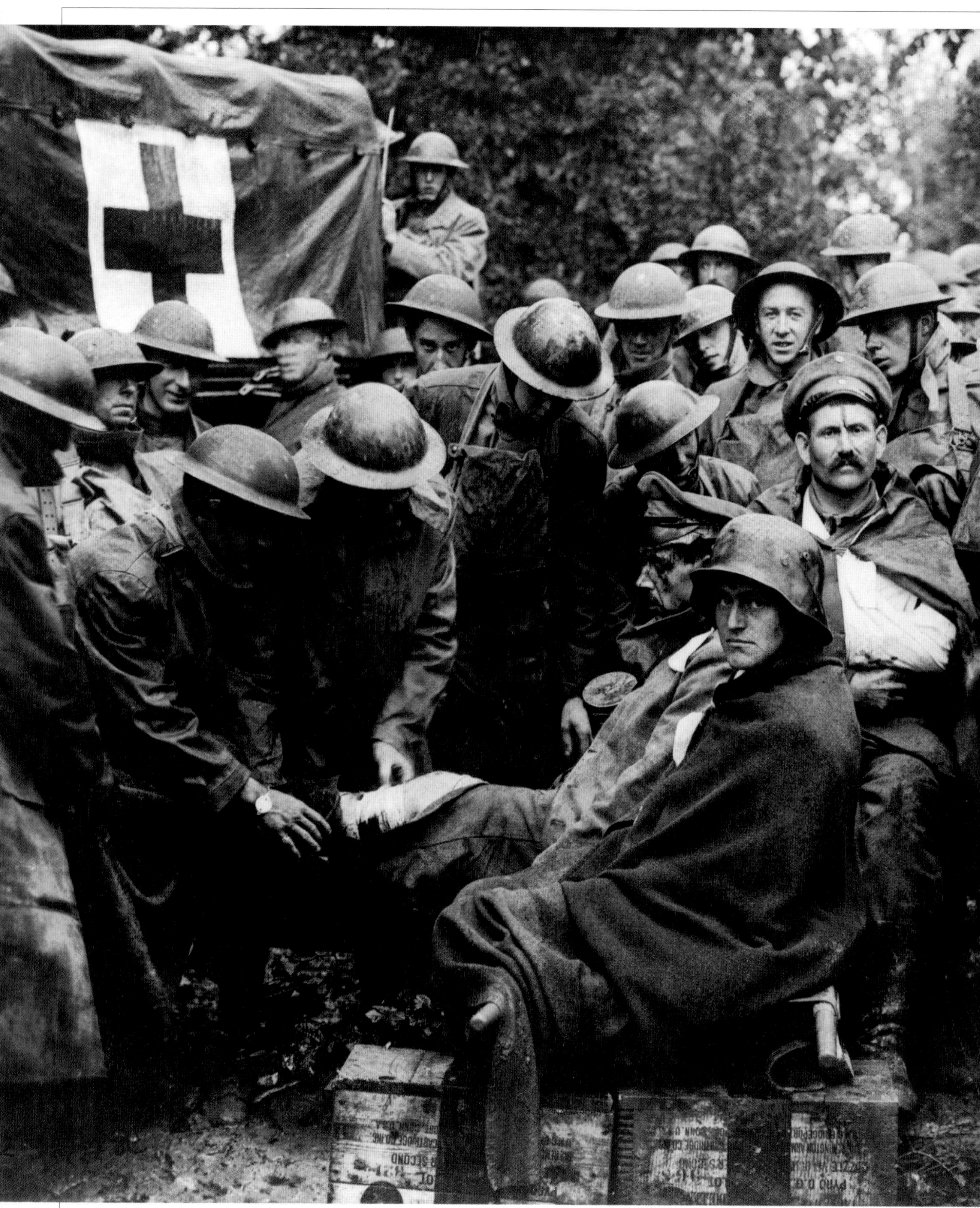

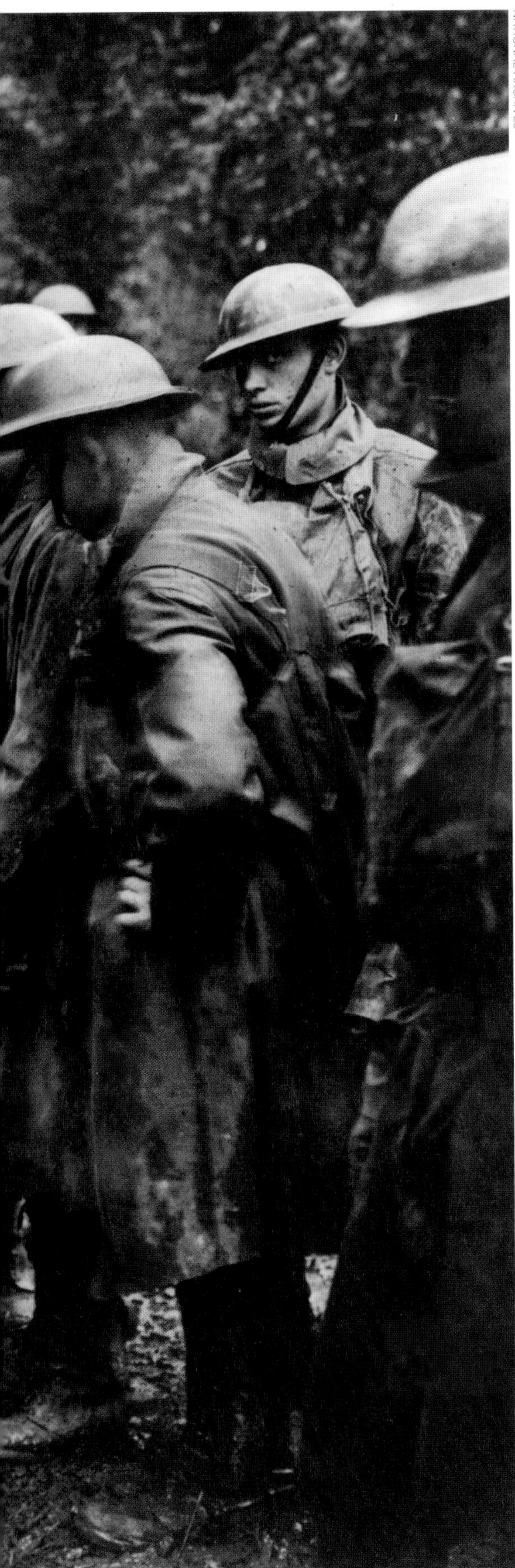

NATIONAL ARCHIVES

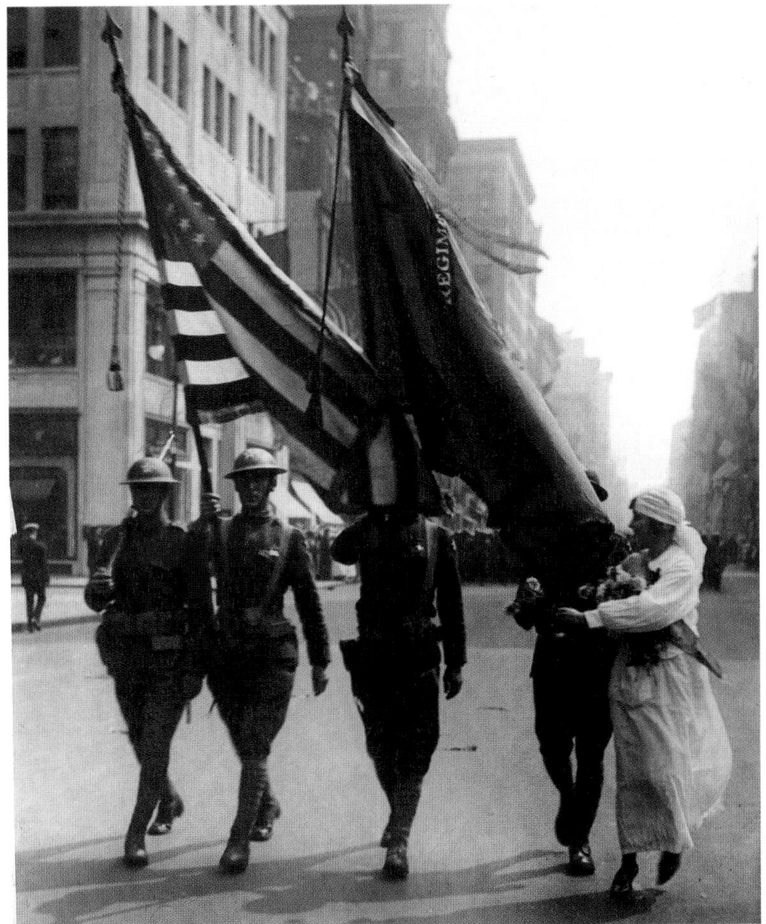

UNDERWOOD

THE WAGES OF WAR

For this German soldier, being treated at the first aid station of the U.S. 103rd and 104th Ambulance Corps, the war is over. American casualties were heavy, totaling a third of a million; the surviving troops came home to great fanfare. A young woman offers flowers in 1919 to these 2nd Division returnees. Below, in Chicago, a sister mourns her lost brother.

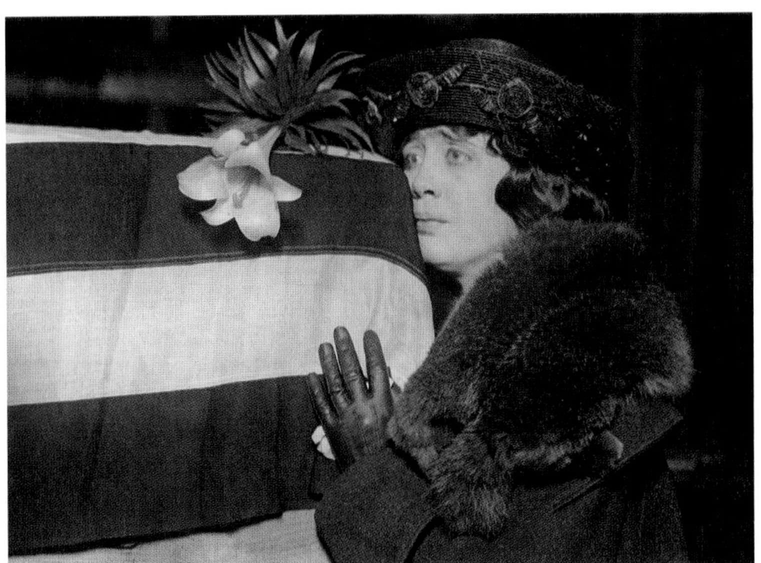

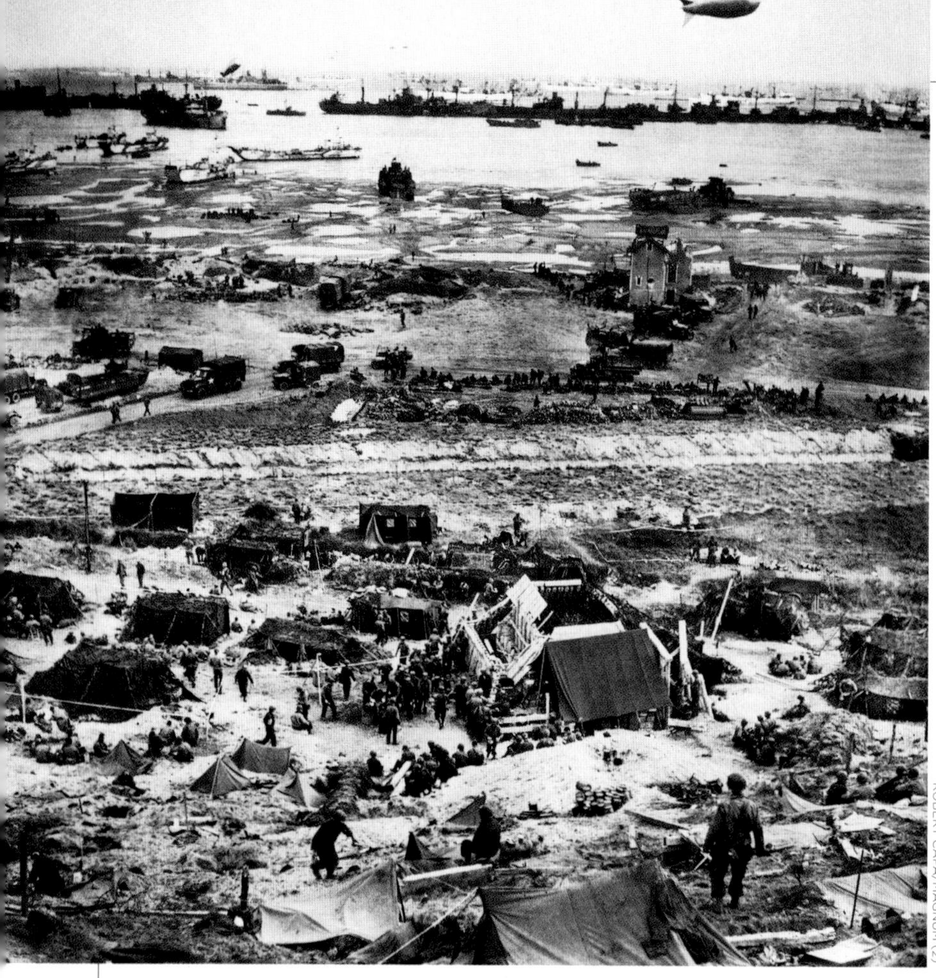

ROBERT CAPA/MAGNUM (2)

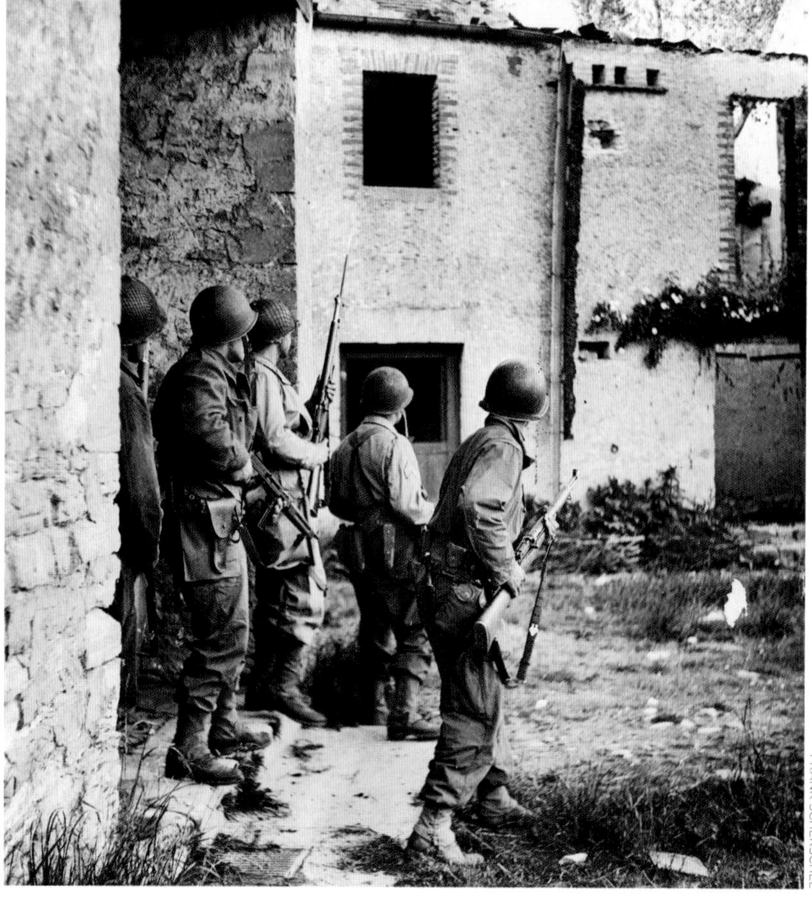

FRANK SCHERSCHEL

THE LONGEST DAY

Rough seas in the English Channel on June 5, 1944, forced postponement of Operation Overlord, an attack on Germany's Atlantic Wall fortifications in France. The next day—the new D-Day, June 6—2,700 ships ferried landing craft and 176,000 soldiers from the U.S., Britain, France and Canada across the channel. As the

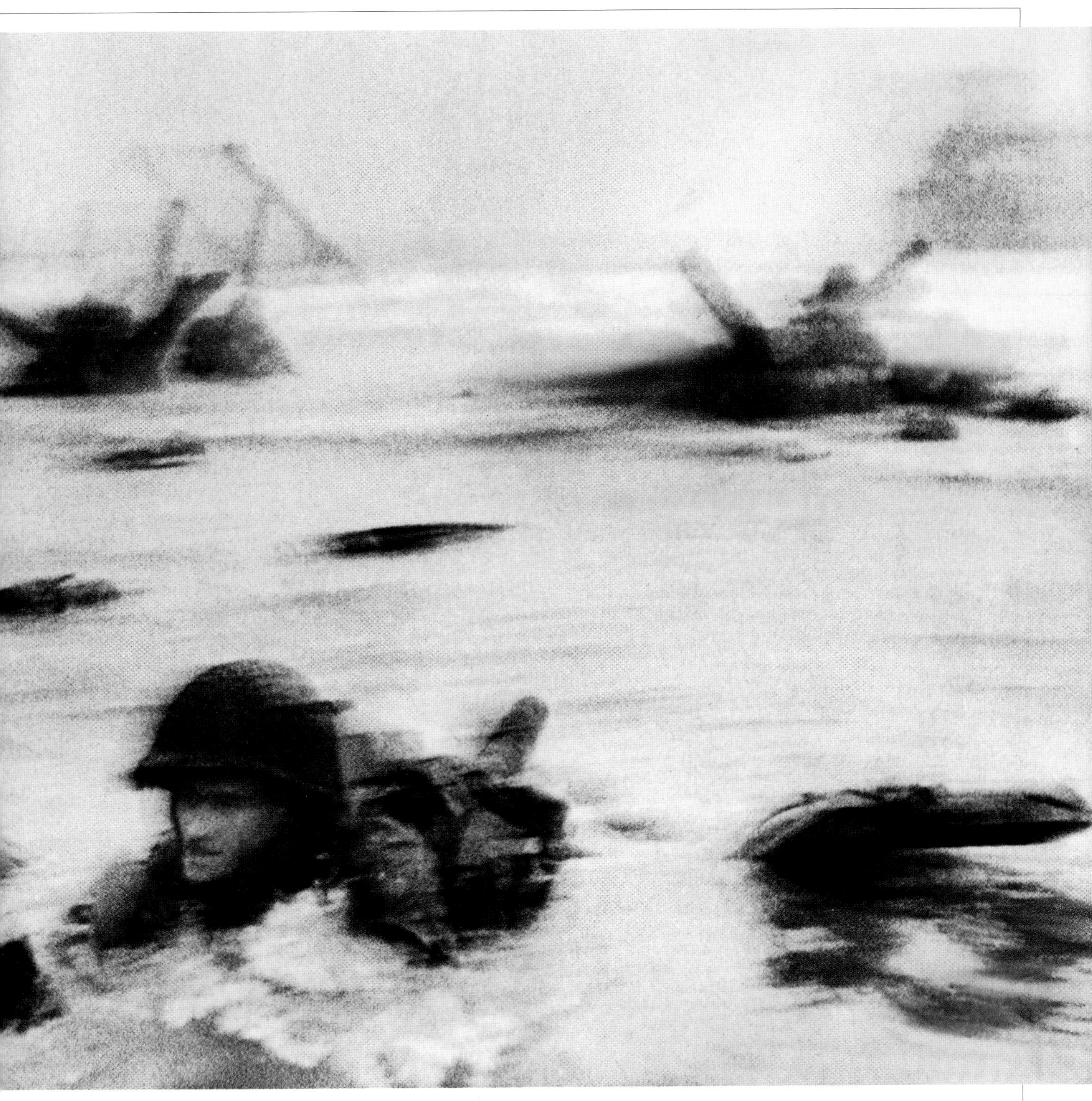

sun rose, German troops felt a battleship bombardment and saw a swarm of transport vessels heading toward them. Five beaches covering 60 miles of the Normandy coast had been targeted for landing, and fighting was fierce along the stretch all day long. War photographer Robert Capa was with the first troops to hit the beaches, and when his riveting pictures, like the one above, appeared in LIFE a week later, the home front got a sense of the drama, perils and bravery of D-Day. By nightfall, all beaches had been taken and thousands of paratroopers had been landed behind enemy lines. Bottom left: In subsequent days, the Allies move inland—always wary of snipers.

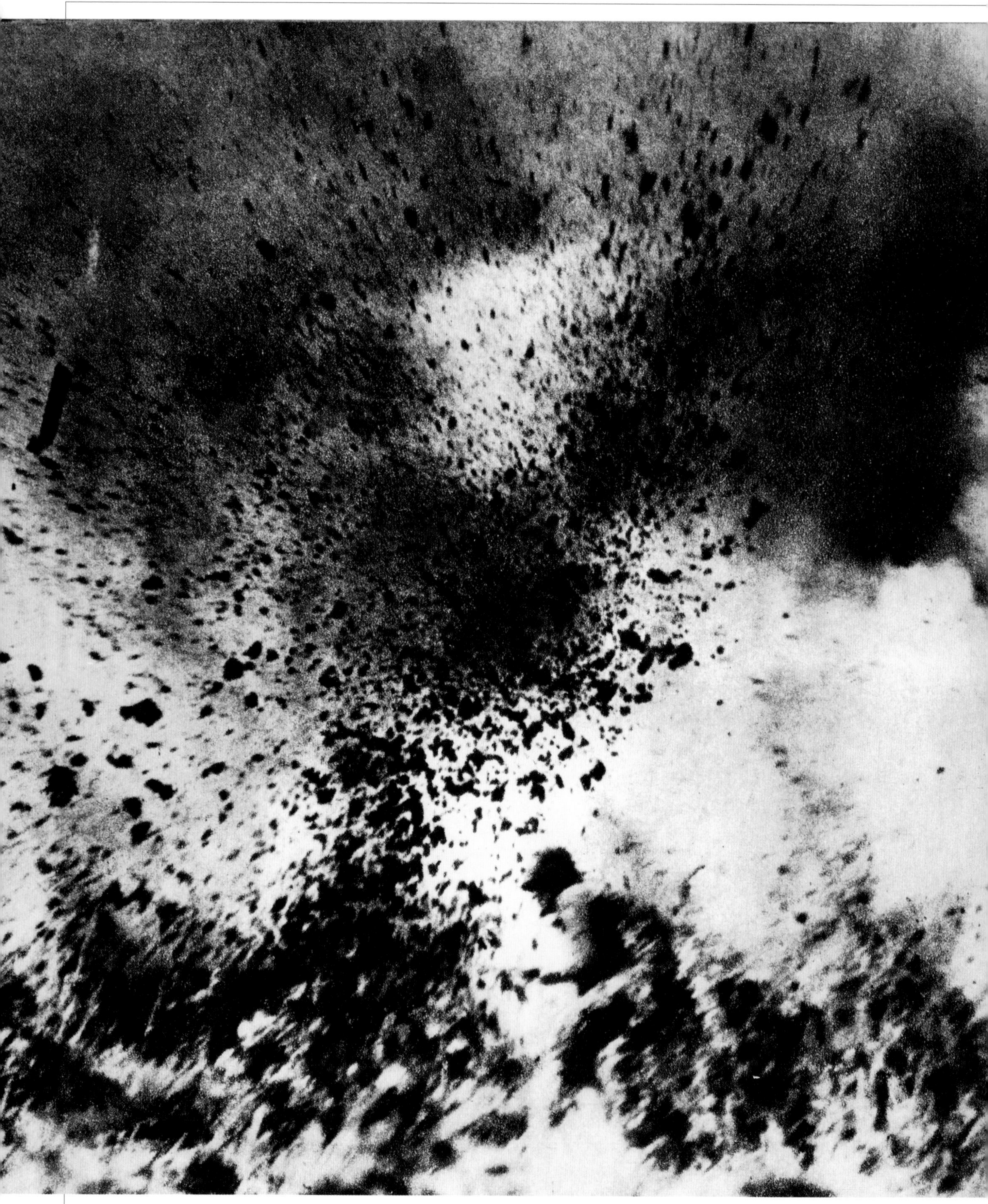

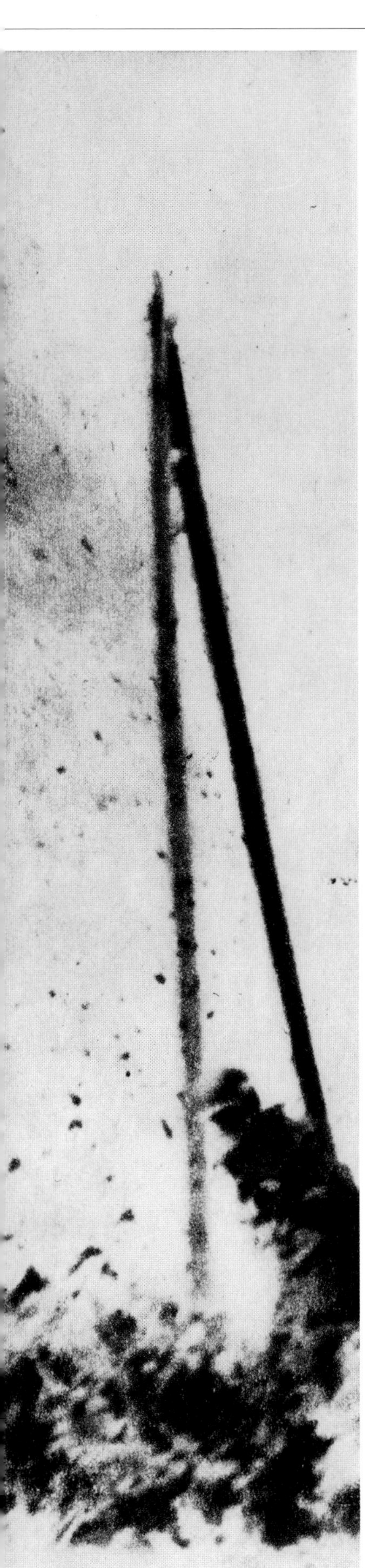

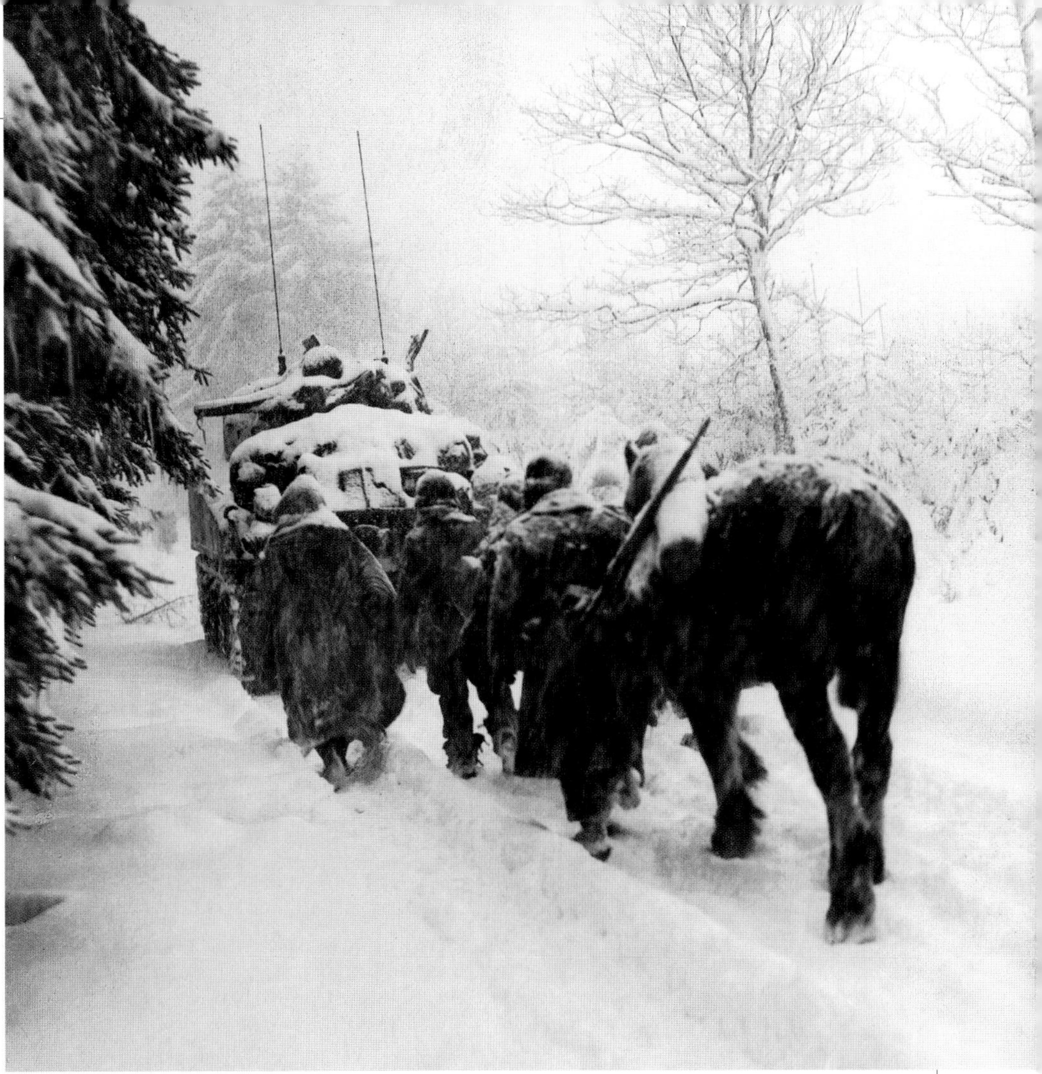

U.S.ARMY

THE BATTLE OF THE BULGE

The Germans were beaten but Hitler refused to accept it and, on December 16, 1944, launched a surprise attack in the Ardennes Forest that stunned American forces. The Nazis didn't have sufficient troops to take advantage of their breakthrough, and the U.S. counterattacked (left). Above: U.S. paratroopers follow the 340th Tank Battalion to Herresbach, Belgium, to meet the foe. Right: Pvt. George Kelly of Philadelphia returns from the front.

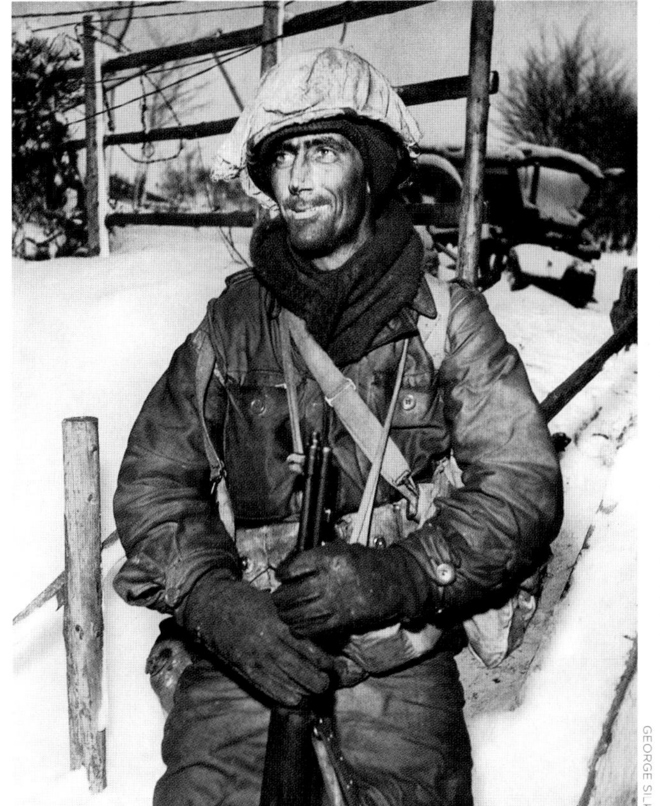

GEORGE SILK

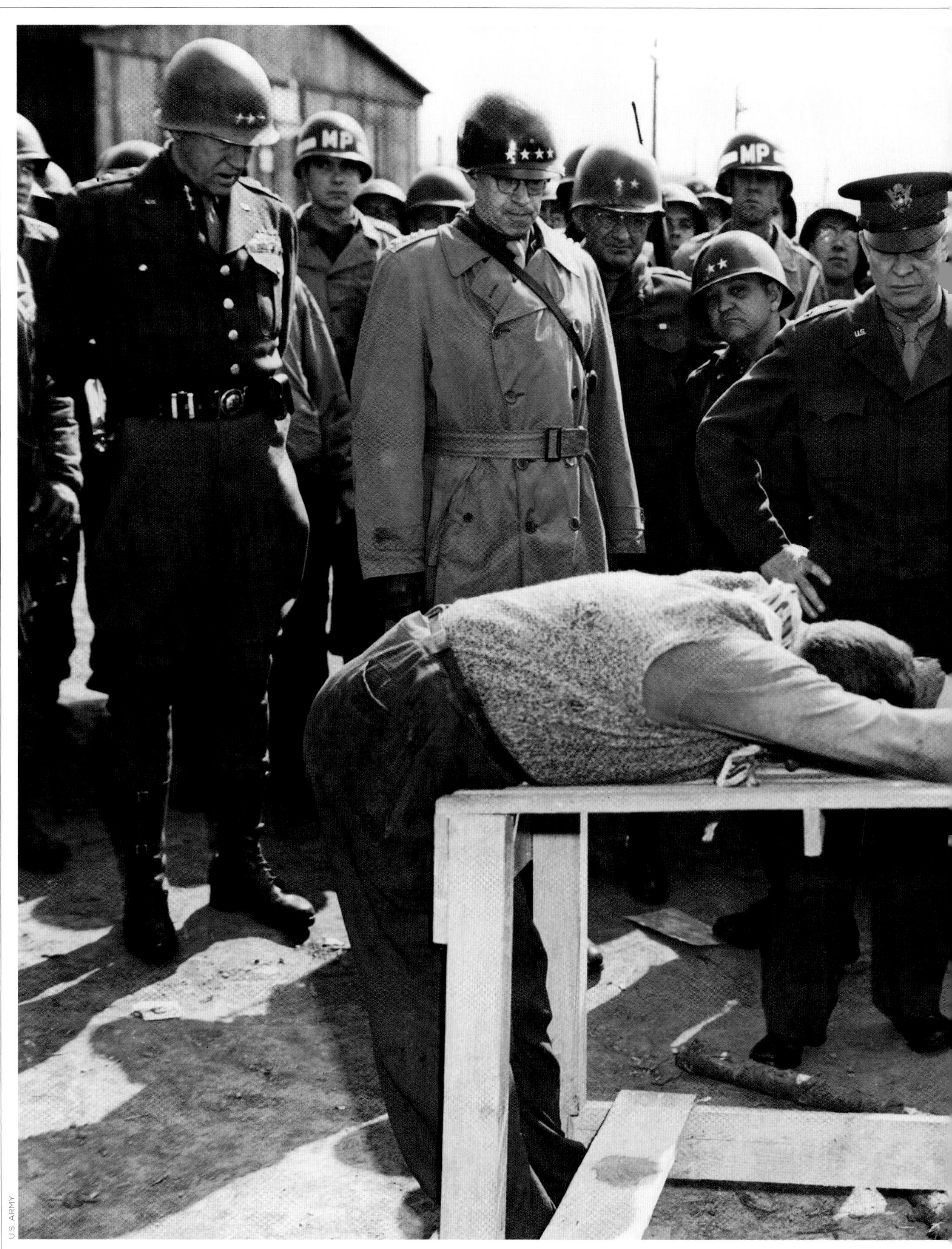

U.S. ARMY

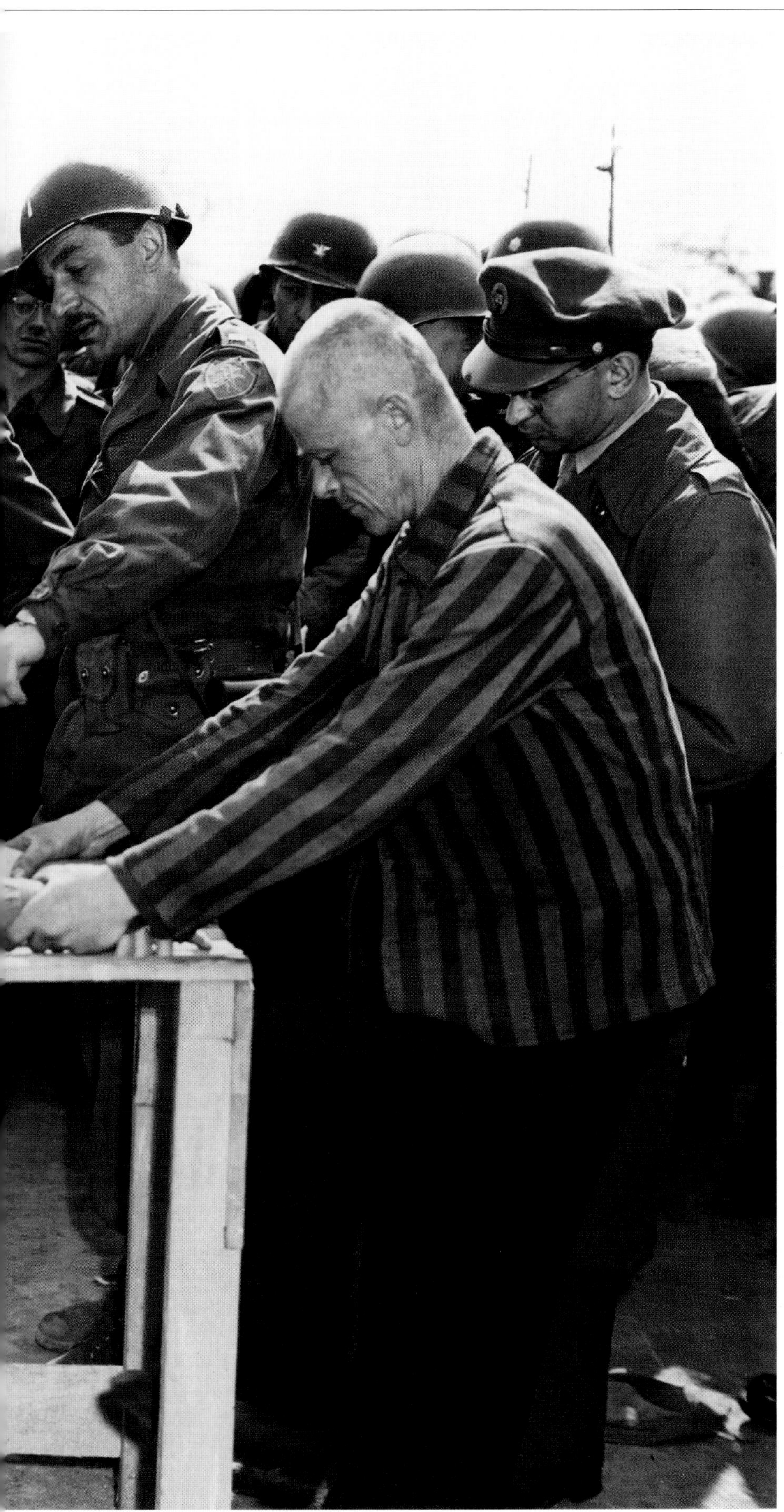

LIBERATION
In April 1945, Gen. George S. Patton (far left), Gen. Omar N. Bradley (next to Patton) and Supreme Allied Commander Gen. Dwight D. Eisenhower look on grimly as a former prisoner at the German concentration camp in Gotha demonstrates one of the tortures to which he had been subjected. Rumors of Nazi atrocities had been circulating among American servicemen for months, but as camps were liberated, the horror was confirmed. On April 30, Adolf Hitler committed suicide in a bunker in Berlin, and a week later Germany surrendered unconditionally at Allied Command headquarters in Reims, France.

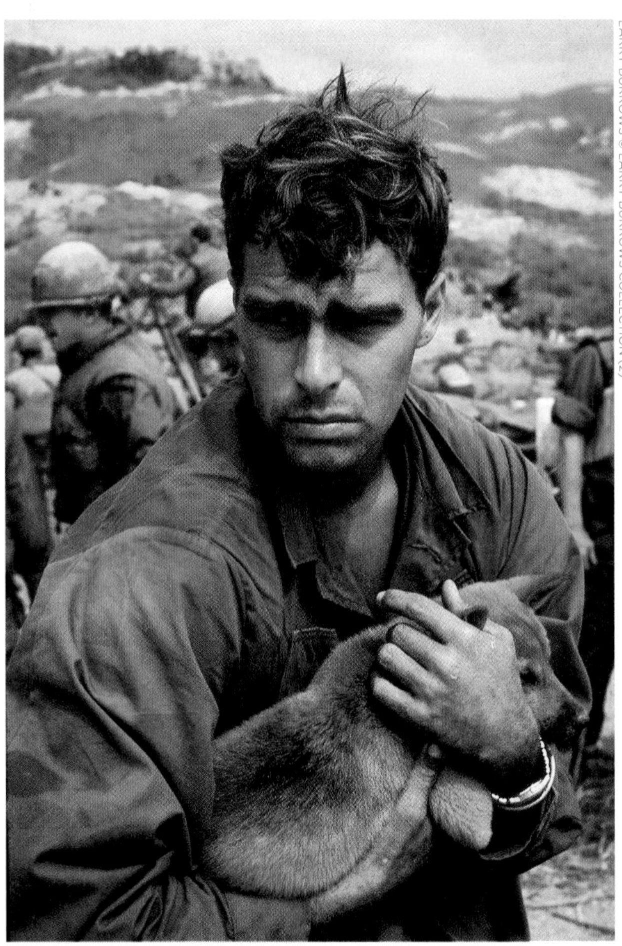

LARRY BURROWS © LARRY BURROWS COLLECTION (2)

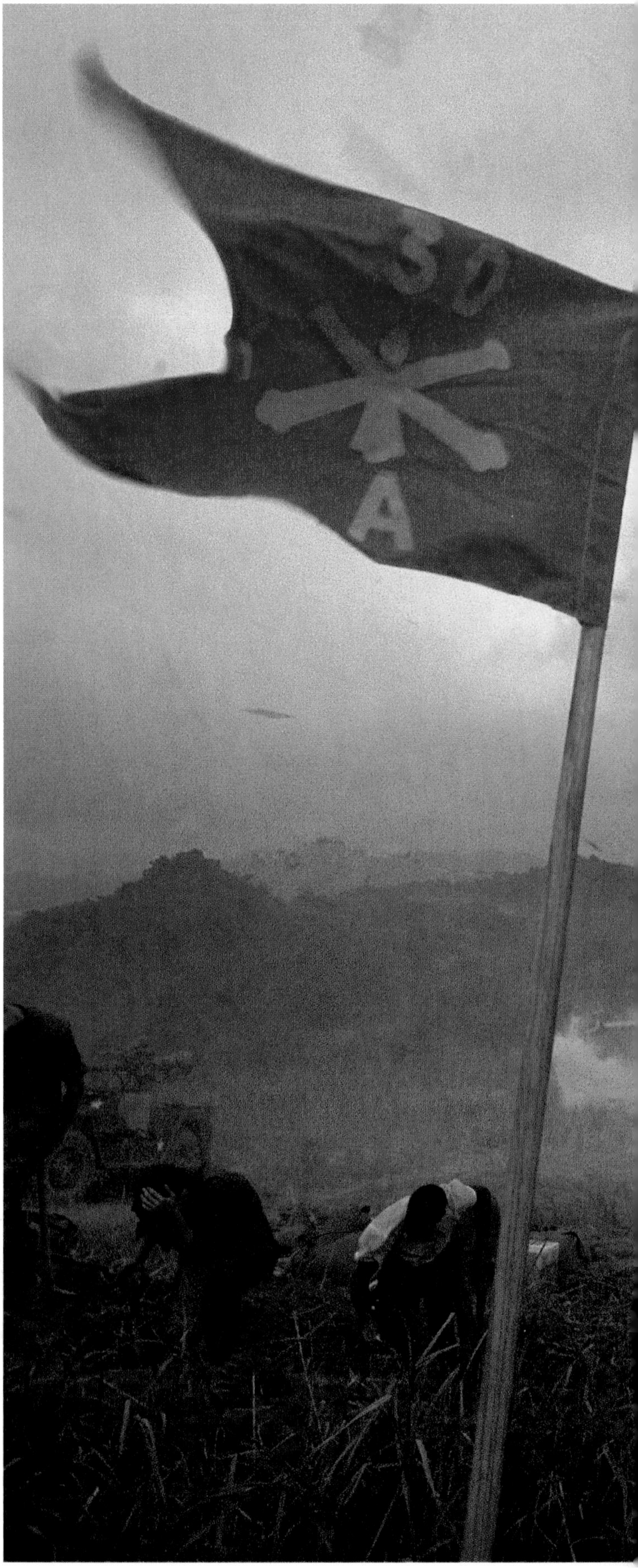

STRANGERS IN A STRANGE LAND

Never before had the U.S. military faced a more frustrating and confusing mission than it did in Vietnam. What started in the late 1950s with a few advisers to the South Vietnamese cause grew into a massive buildup and, finally, an unwinnable war. America's involvement began in response to a theory first put forth by Harry S Truman and then subscribed to by successor Presidents Eisenhower, Kennedy and Johnson: that if a free country fell to communism, neighboring nations would, too. Pursuant to the domino theory, more than a half million U.S. troops were fighting in Vietnam by 1969, and 58,000 ultimately died. Many of the searing images of the war were taken by LIFE's Larry Burrows, who in Khe Sanh recorded an Army 1st Air Cavalry helicopter (right) airlifting ammunition into a Marine outpost that was under attack. In 1971 another copter in which Burrows was traveling was shot down; all aboard were killed. The U.S. finally pulled out of Vietnam in 1973, and the South surrendered in '75. Above: In 1968 in Khe Sanh, a soldier shows some human kindness to a puppy as he grimly surveys the scene around him.

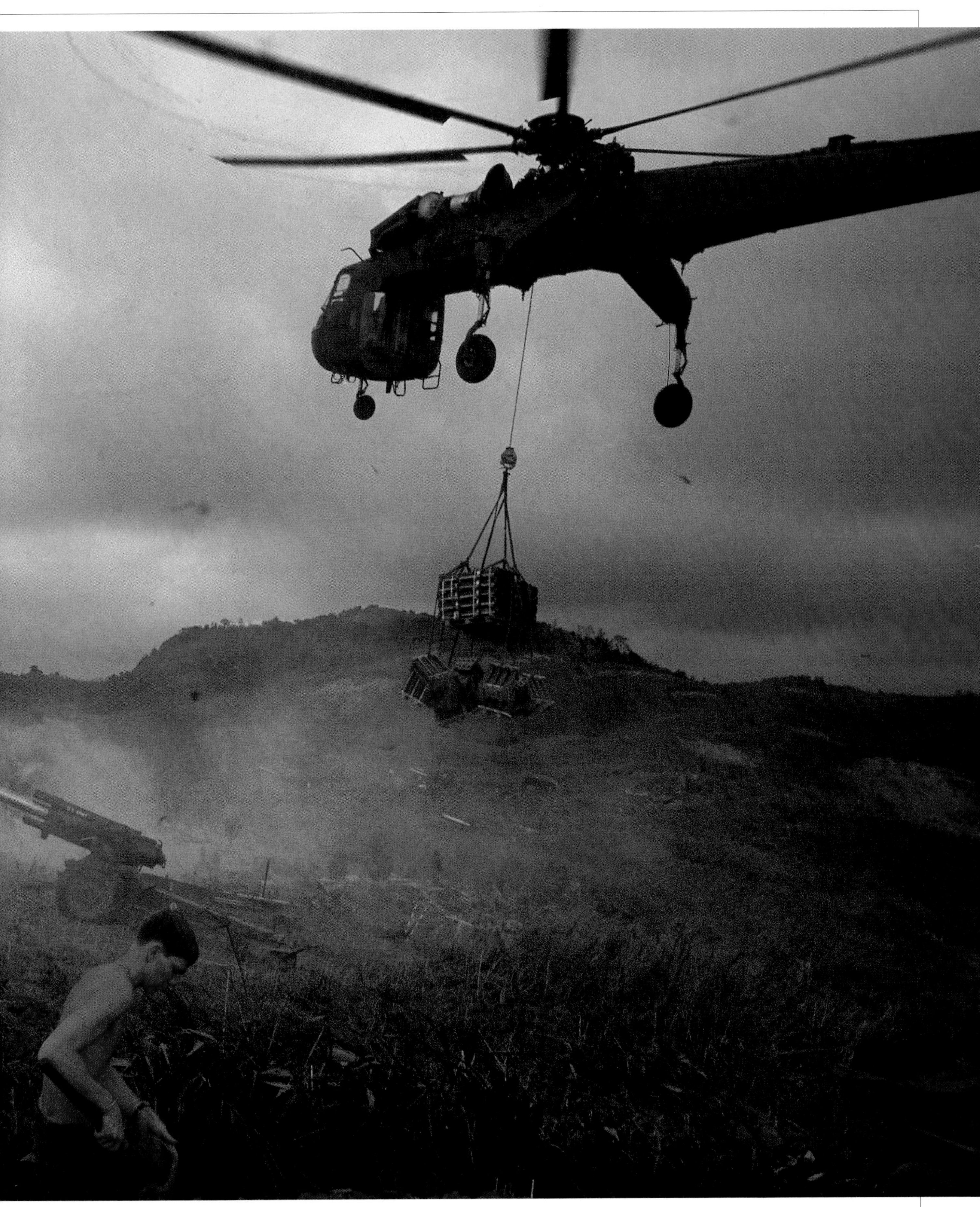

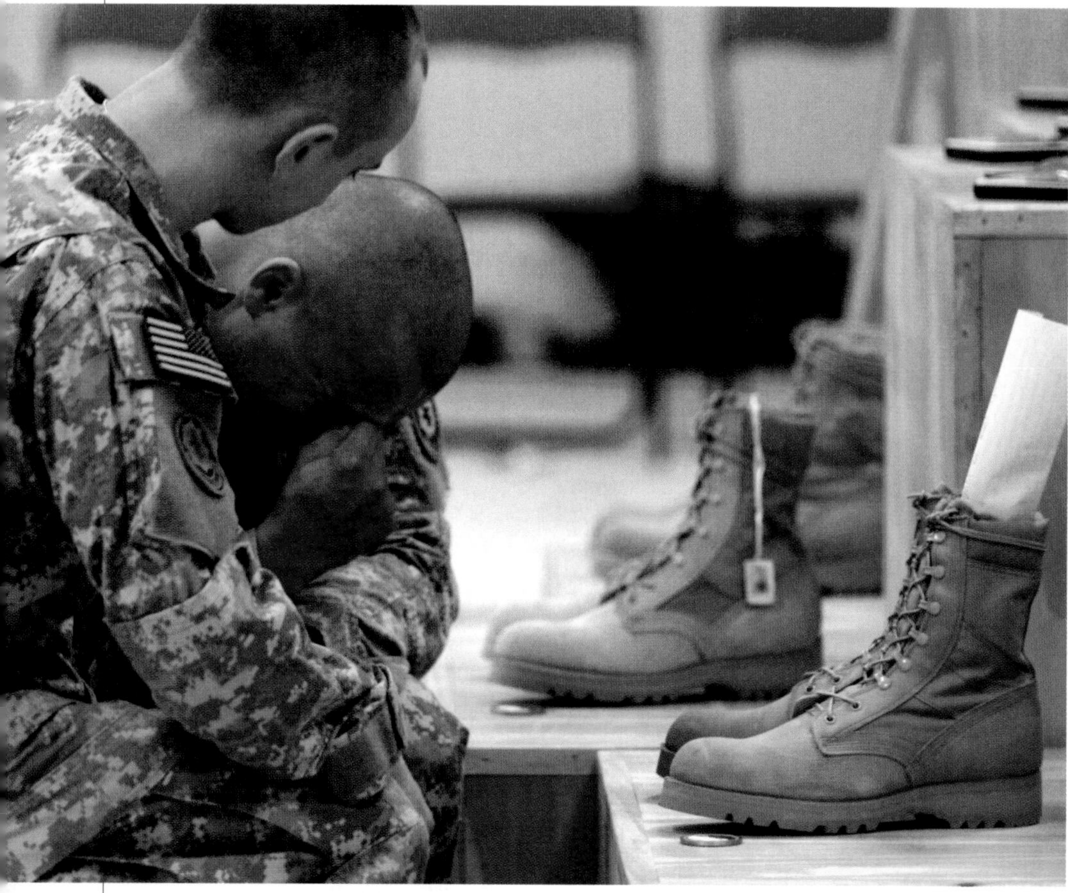

ERIK DE CASTRO/REUTERS

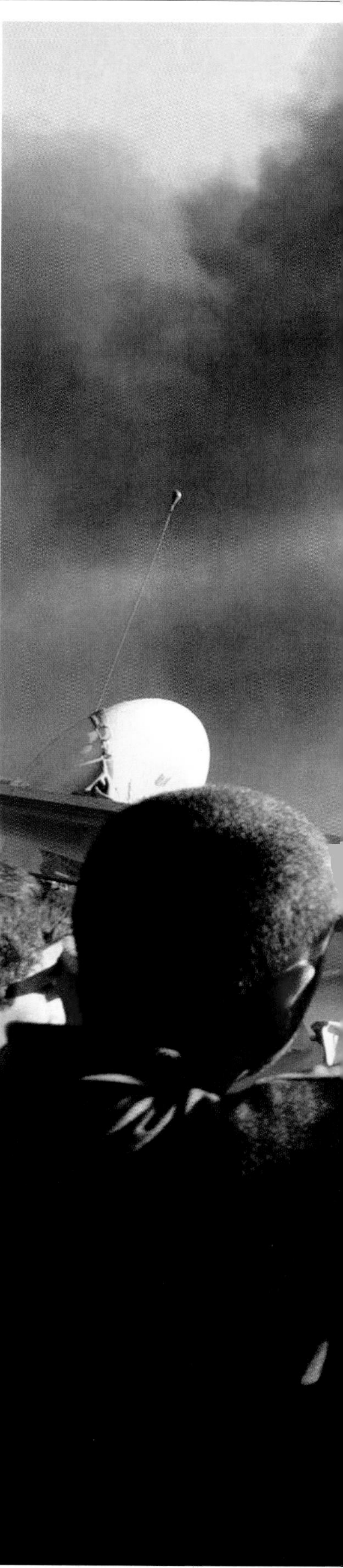

RICHARD PERRY/THE NEW YORK TIMES/REDUX

AT WAR IN THE MIDDLE EAST

When U.S. forces first entered Iraq in 2003, ostensibly to rid President Saddam Hussein of the weapons of mass destruction many believed he possessed, some intelligence experts predicted that American soldiers would be welcomed as liberators and the ensuing military campaign would be swift and decisive, bringing freedom to Iraq and offering hope to pro-democracy movements throughout the Middle East. In the event, while Hussein's brutally repressive regime was toppled, no weapons of mass destruction were ever found and the conflict dragged on, with a determined insurgency fighting American forces for more than eight years before U.S. troops were fully withdrawn at the end of 2011. Right: Early in the conflict, a U.S. soldier warns Iraqi civilians to disperse after a gas station burst into flames in Baghdad. Five years later, a soldier (above) from the 1st Squadron, 2nd Stryker Cavalry Regiment, weeps before the boots of three fellow soldiers killed in combat. A total of 4,486 U.S. soldiers lost their lives in Iraq. After this war, on to another.

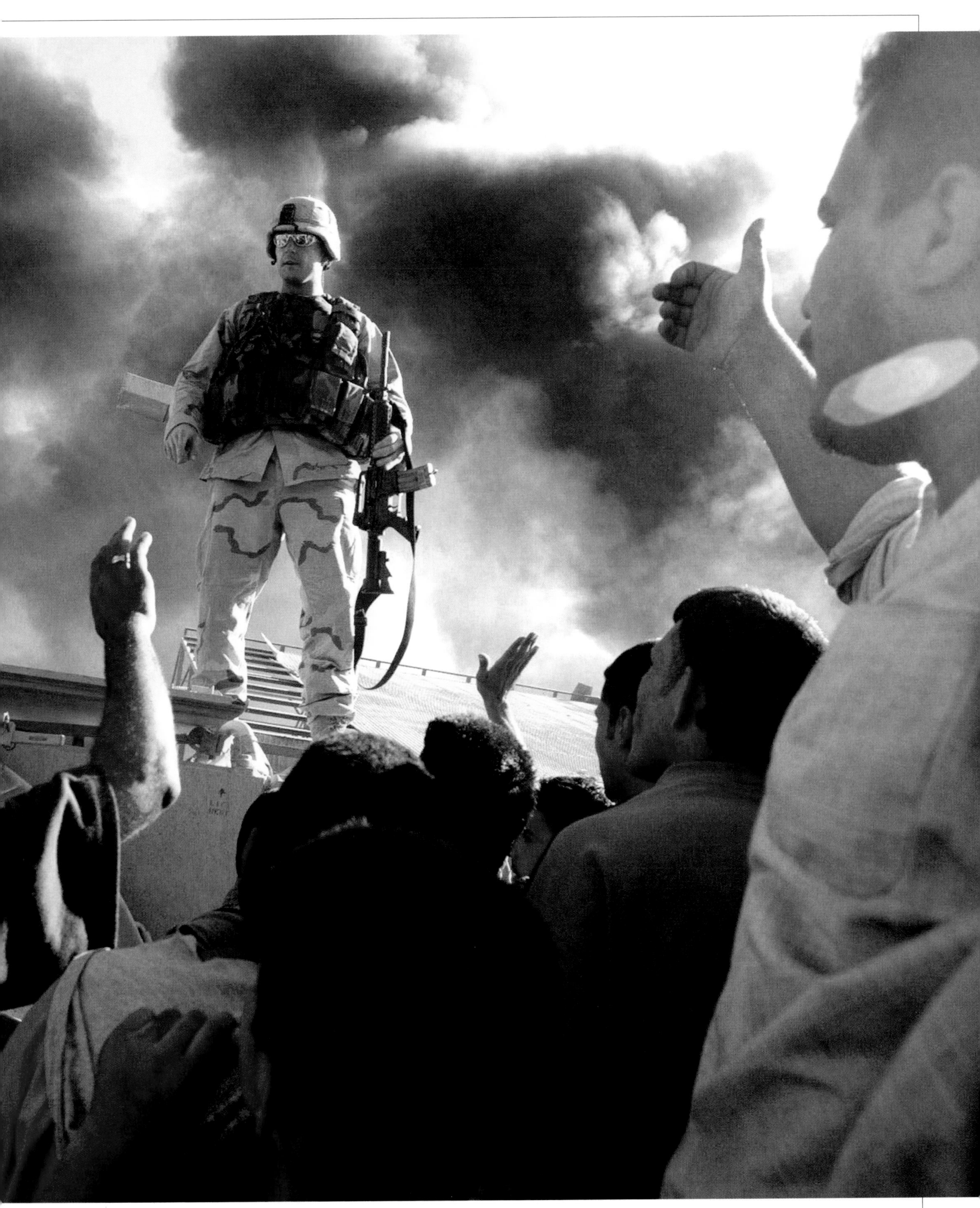

TIM HETHERINGTON/MAGNUM

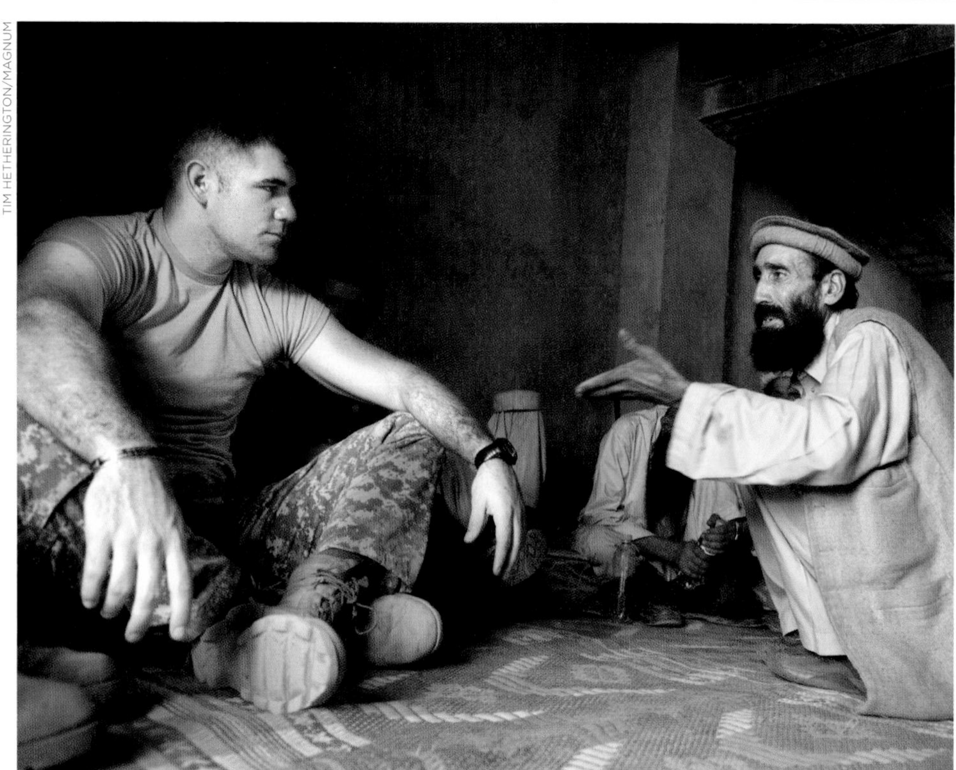

THE FIGHT IN AFGHANISTAN

The conflict in Afghanistan—which moved to center stage as American involvement in Iraq diminished—offered U.S. soldiers yet another set of challenges, including the need to maintain good relations with local villagers, as Capt. Dan Kearney is doing at left, as well as coping with unpredictable threats like the IED (Improvised Explosive Device) that destroyed the M-ATV motorized vehicle of the injured soldier at right. Below: A tired soldier takes a much needed break during a night mission near Kunar Province in northeastern Afghanistan. As a withdrawal of U.S. forces is planned for 2014, the Taliban continues to wage stubborn resistance.

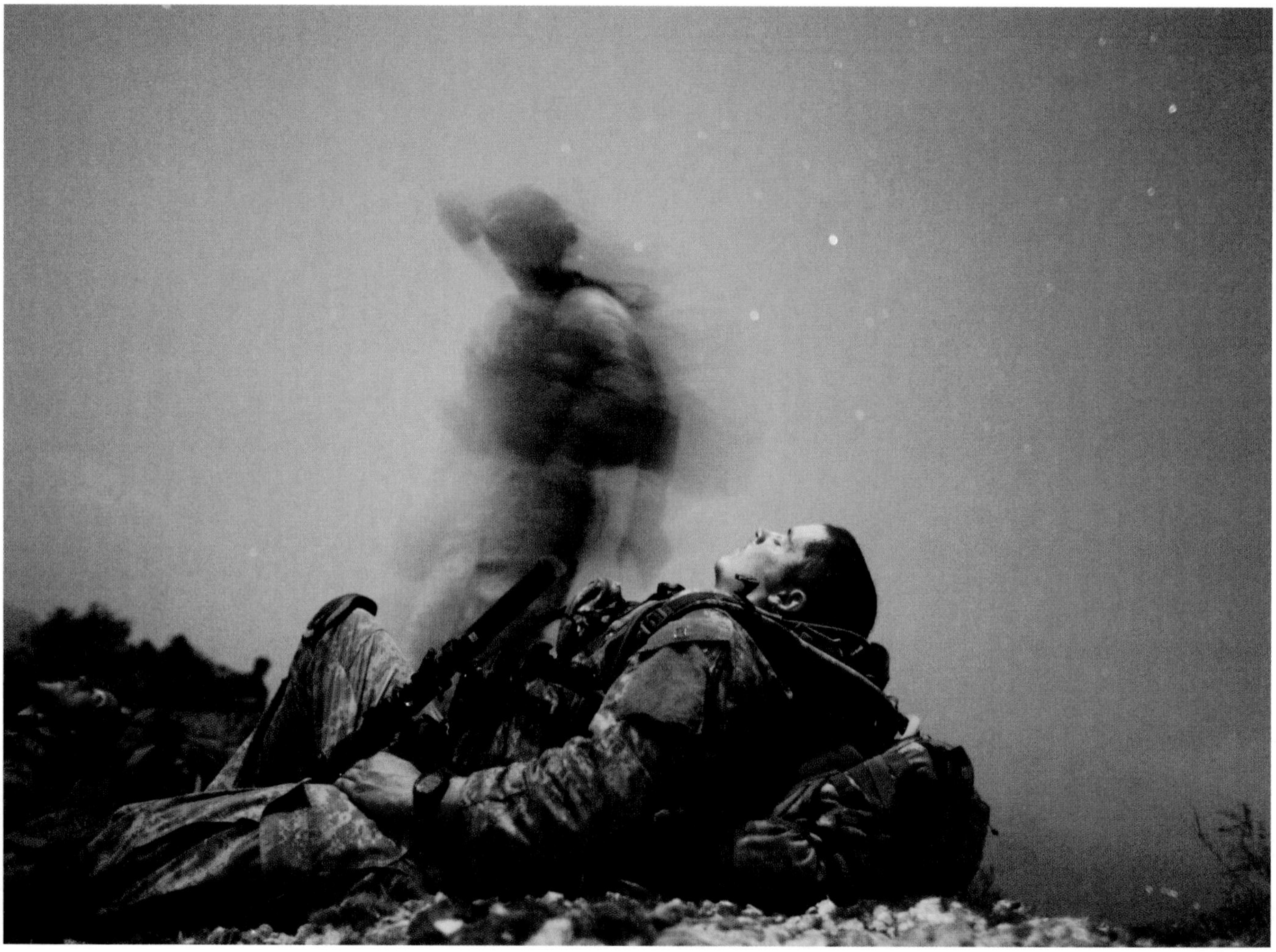

CARLOS BARRIA/REUTERS

BOB STRONG/REUTERS

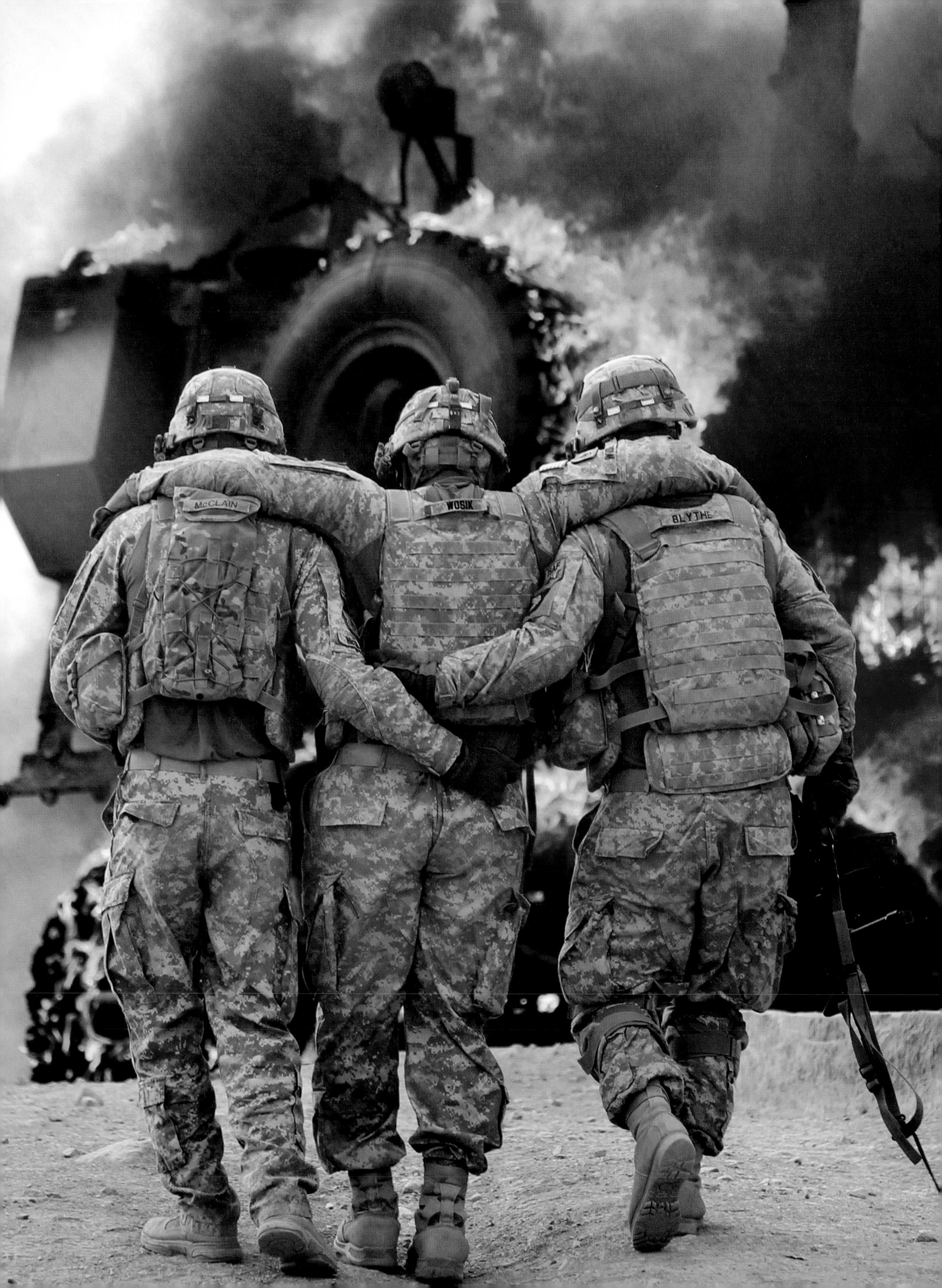
McCLAIN
WOSIK
BLYTHE

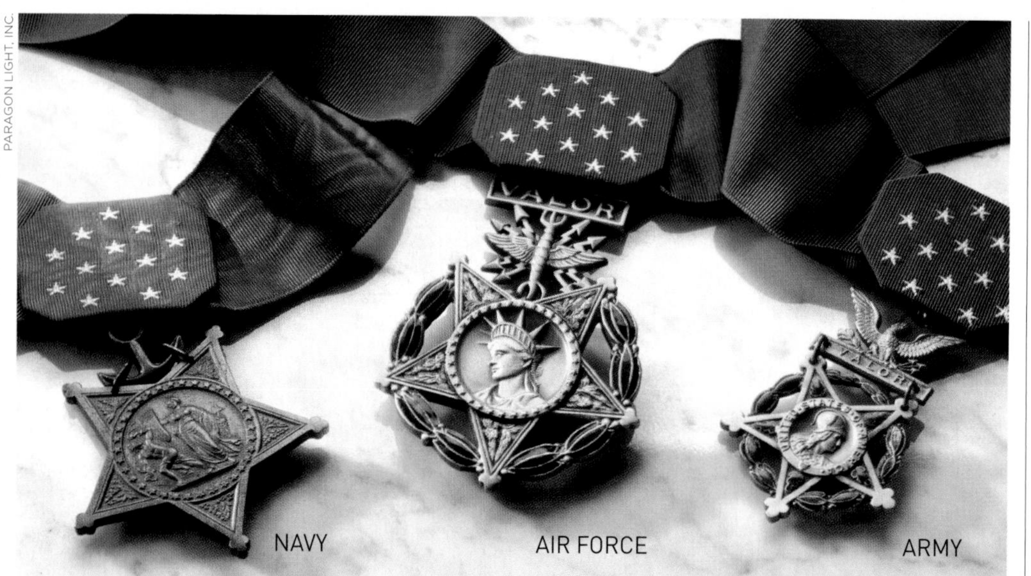

PARAGON LIGHT, INC.

MAJ. GEN. JULIUS STAHEL, DR. MARY E. WALKER The Hungarian-born Stahel was cited for valor shown when he led a U.S. Volunteers attack at Piedmont, Va., was wounded and returned to action despite intense pain. Medals have been awarded to 3,436 men, but only one has gone to a woman. Dr. Walker was a surgeon in the Civil War who showed "earnest and untiring" efforts during the conflict. Because she was a civilian, her Medal was rescinded in 1917, but it was restored in '77.

The Medal of Honor

"For conspicuous gallentry and intrepidity... above and beyond the call of duty..."

SOME CALL IT the Congressional Medal of Honor, because it is "awarded by the President in the name of Congress." Properly, though, it is the Medal of Honor, the highest accolade our country can bestow. Early in the Civil War a medal for individual bravery was proposed to Army General-in-Chief Winfield Scott, but he felt it would smack of European affectation. The Navy, however, liked the idea, and President Lincoln signed a resolution providing for a Navy medal of valor. The Army was soon included, and in 1863, the first Medal of Honor was awarded. There are today three types: the 1861 Naval design, which also covers the Marine Corps and Coast Guard; an Army version from 1904; and an Air Force design, unveiled in 1965. They all mean one thing—this is an extraordinary person, as these two early heroes, plus a representative from each service, attest.

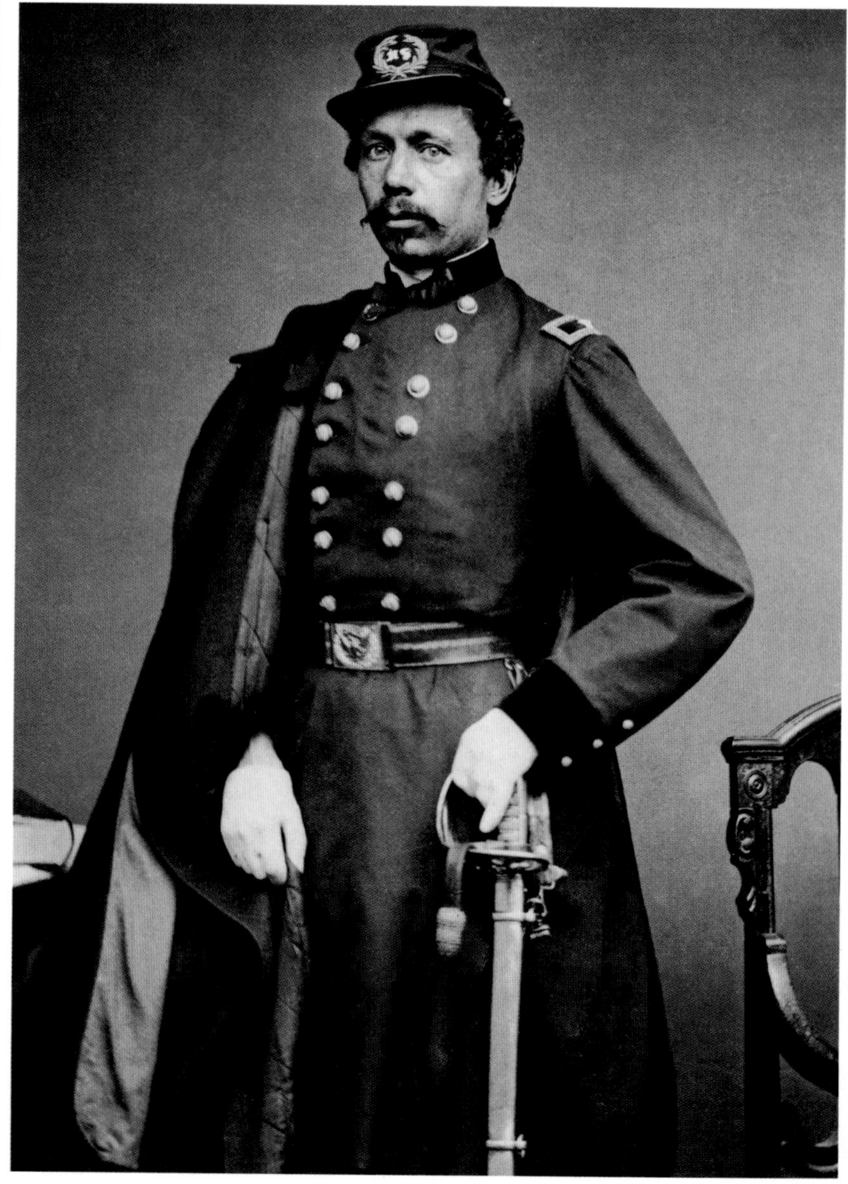

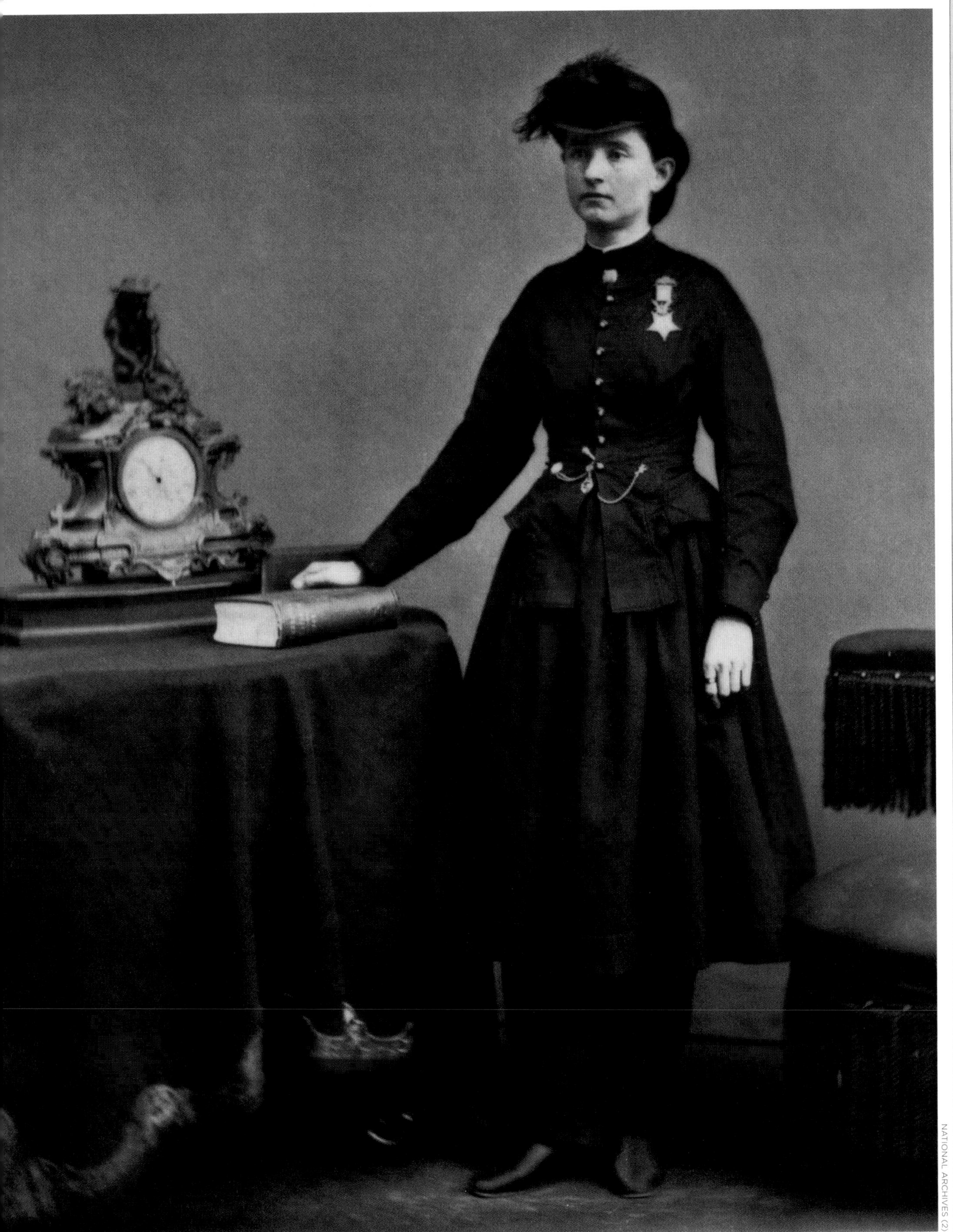

NATIONAL ARCHIVES (2)

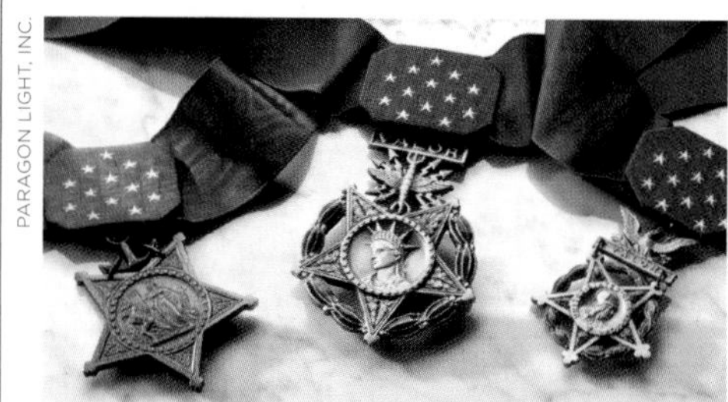

PARAGON LIGHT, INC.

The Medal of Honor

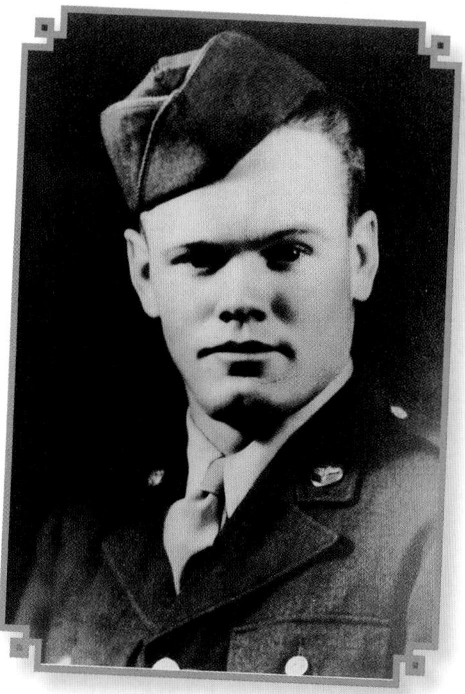

MASTER SGT. HENRY EUGENE "RED" ERWIN SR.
Hailing from Adamsville, Ala., Erwin served in the Army Air Corps in World War II. On April 19, 1945, he was a radio operator aboard a B-29 bomber leading a group formation over Koriyama, Japan. He was also responsible for dropping phosphorus smoke bombs that would help the group assemble at the drop site. Suddenly, one exploded in the launching chute and shot back into the interior of the aircraft, striking him in the face. The burning chemical obliterated his nose and blinded him completely. Realizing the smoke-filled plane would be lost if the bomb wasn't removed, Erwin picked it up and crawled, heading for a window. Hugging the burning bomb between his forearm and body, he struggled through a narrow passage, and groping with his burning hands he found the window and threw the bomb out. Completely aflame, he fell back upon the floor. When the smoke cleared, the pilot pulled the plane out of its dive at 300 feet. Below, Erwin receives the Medal, surrounded by the crew of that plane. He died on January 16, 2002.

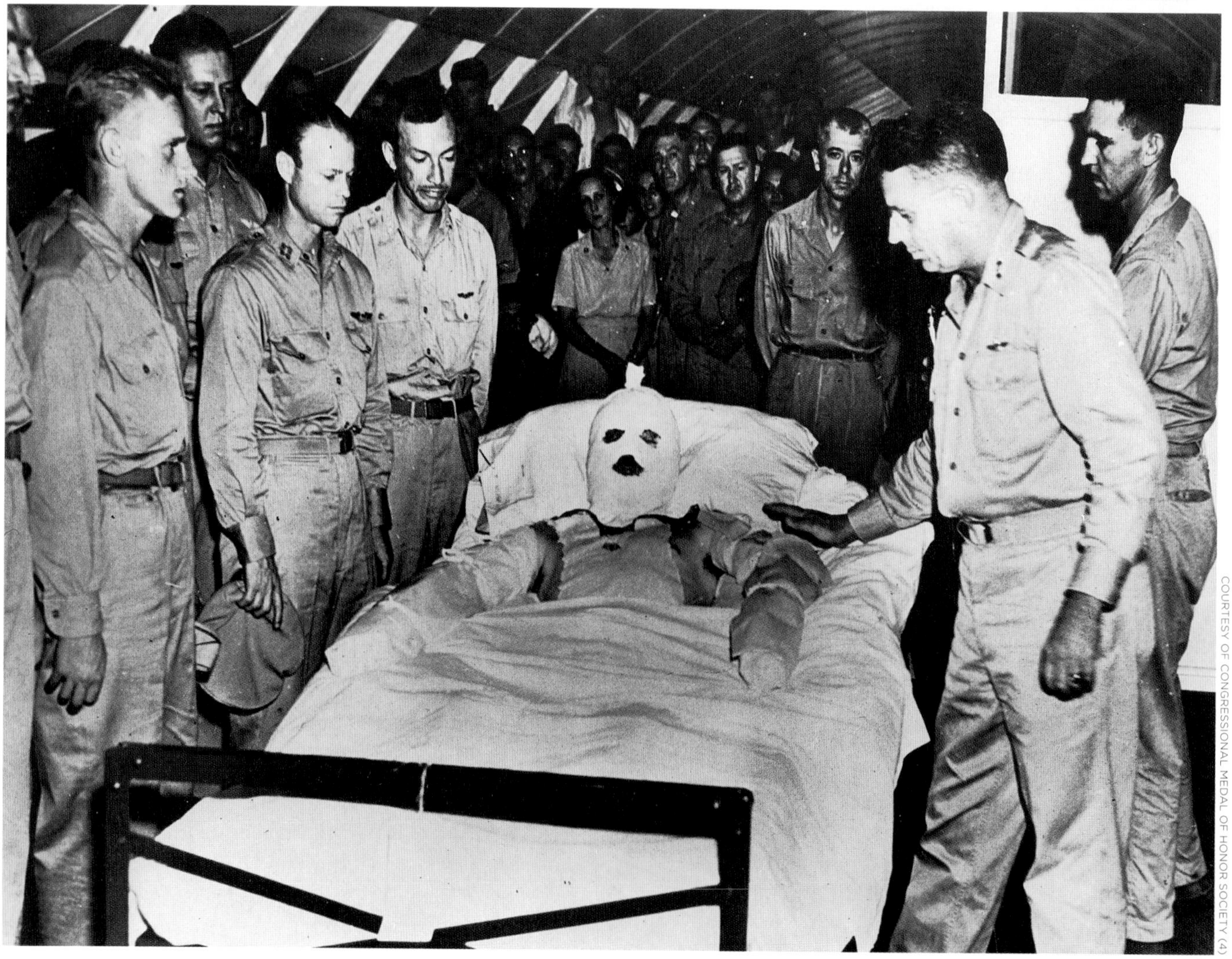

COURTESY OF CONGRESSIONAL MEDAL OF HONOR SOCIETY (4)

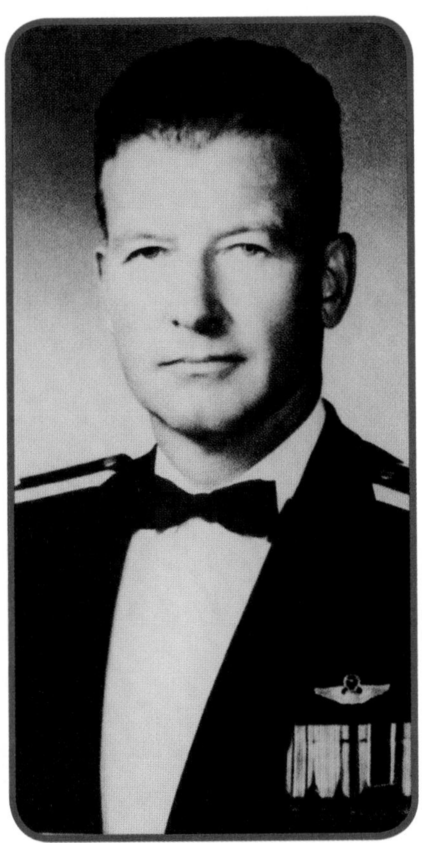

COL. WILLIAM ATKINSON JONES III
On September 1, 1968, this Norfolk, Va., native was flying an Air Force A-1H Skyraider near Dong Hoi, North Vietnam, attempting to rescue a downed pilot. On a low pass, Jones felt an explosion, and his cockpit filled with smoke. Despite the fact that his plane might be on fire, he kept searching. When he sighted the survivor, he also saw a gun position firing at him, but he disregarded that and attacked with cannon and rockets on successive passes. On one pass, antiaircraft fire ignited a rocket mounted behind his headrest, and his fuselage burst into flames, smoke engulfing the cockpit. With the fire worsening, and in pain from severe burns on his face, arms and hands, he tried to transmit the location of the pilot, but the calls were blocked by transmissions telling him to bail out. Instead, he flew his heavily damaged plane back to base and relayed the information while on the operating table. Awarded posthumously.

2D LT. JOHN J.MCGINTY III
A native of Boston, he was a staff sergeant and acting platoon leader in the 3rd Marine Division in Vietnam on July 18, 1966, when his platoon, which was covering a battalion withdrawal, came under heavy fire from small arms, automatic weapons and mortars from an enemy regiment. In one of several attack waves on his platoon, two of the squads became separated. In complete disregard for his safety, he charged through the intense fire to their position. Finding 20 men wounded, and now painfully wounded himself, he reloaded ammunition magazines and weapons and rallied the men. When the enemy tried to outflank them, he killed five of them at point-blank range with his pistol. Then, when they seemed on the verge of overrunning his small force, he radioed for artillery and air strikes within 50 yards of his position, routing the enemy, who left behind some 500 bodies on the battlefield.

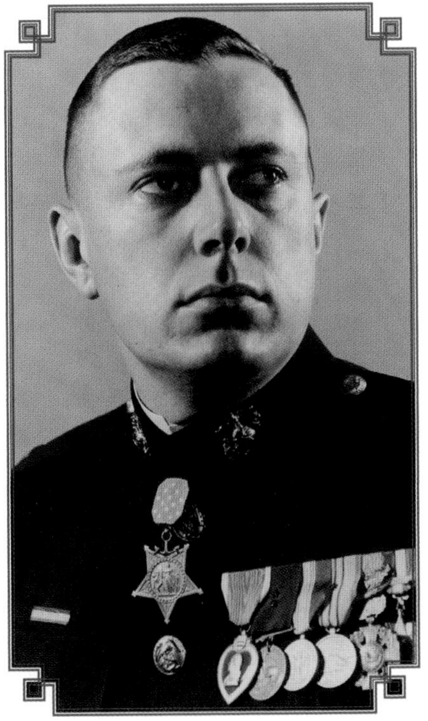

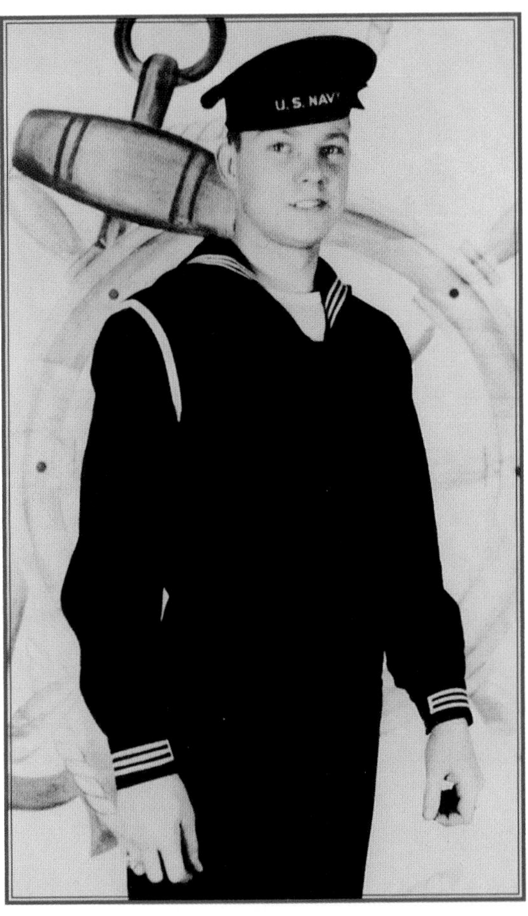

US NAVY

HOSPITAL CORPSMAN RICHARD D. DEWERT
Born in Taunton, Mass., in 1931, he enlisted in the Navy in 1948. On April 5, 1951, he was attached to the 1st Marine Division as they helped drive the enemy beyond Korea's 38th Parallel. When a team from the point platoon of his company was pinned down by automatic-weapons fire, suffering casualties, DeWert rushed to the assistance of one of the more seriously wounded. While dragging the Marine to cover, DeWert was shot in the leg, and although painfully wounded he refused treatment and dashed back through the fire-swept area to carry another man to safety. Despite increasing enemy fire, he went forth a third time and was seriously wounded in the shoulder after discovering that a stricken Marine had already died. Still refusing first aid, he went out a fourth time, to provide medical assistance to a fallen comrade, but was mortally wounded himself. Awarded posthumously.

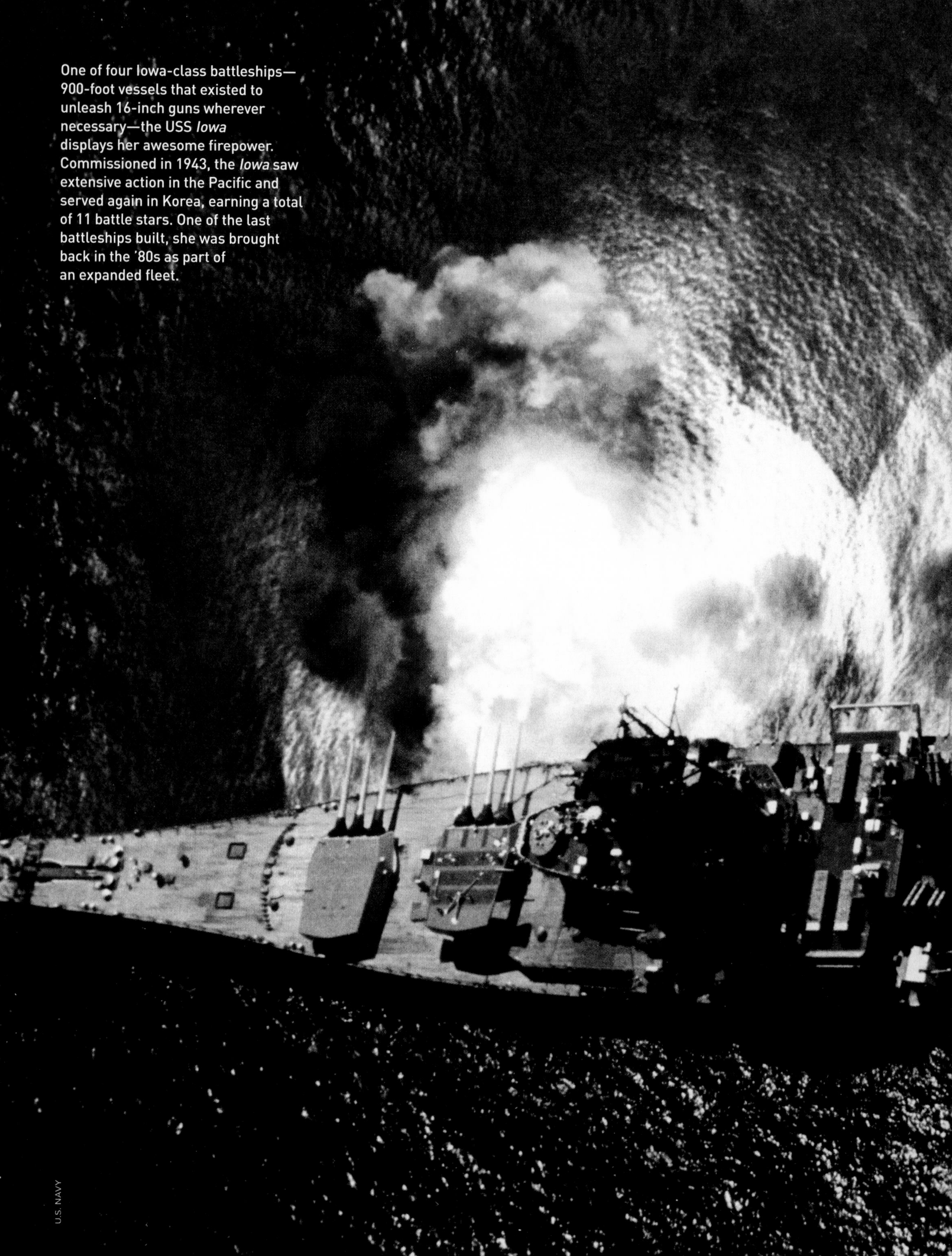

One of four Iowa-class battleships—900-foot vessels that existed to unleash 16-inch guns wherever necessary—the USS *Iowa* displays her awesome firepower. Commissioned in 1943, the *Iowa* saw extensive action in the Pacific and served again in Korea, earning a total of 11 battle stars. One of the last battleships built, she was brought back in the '80s as part of an expanded fleet.

U.S. NAVY

THE NAVY

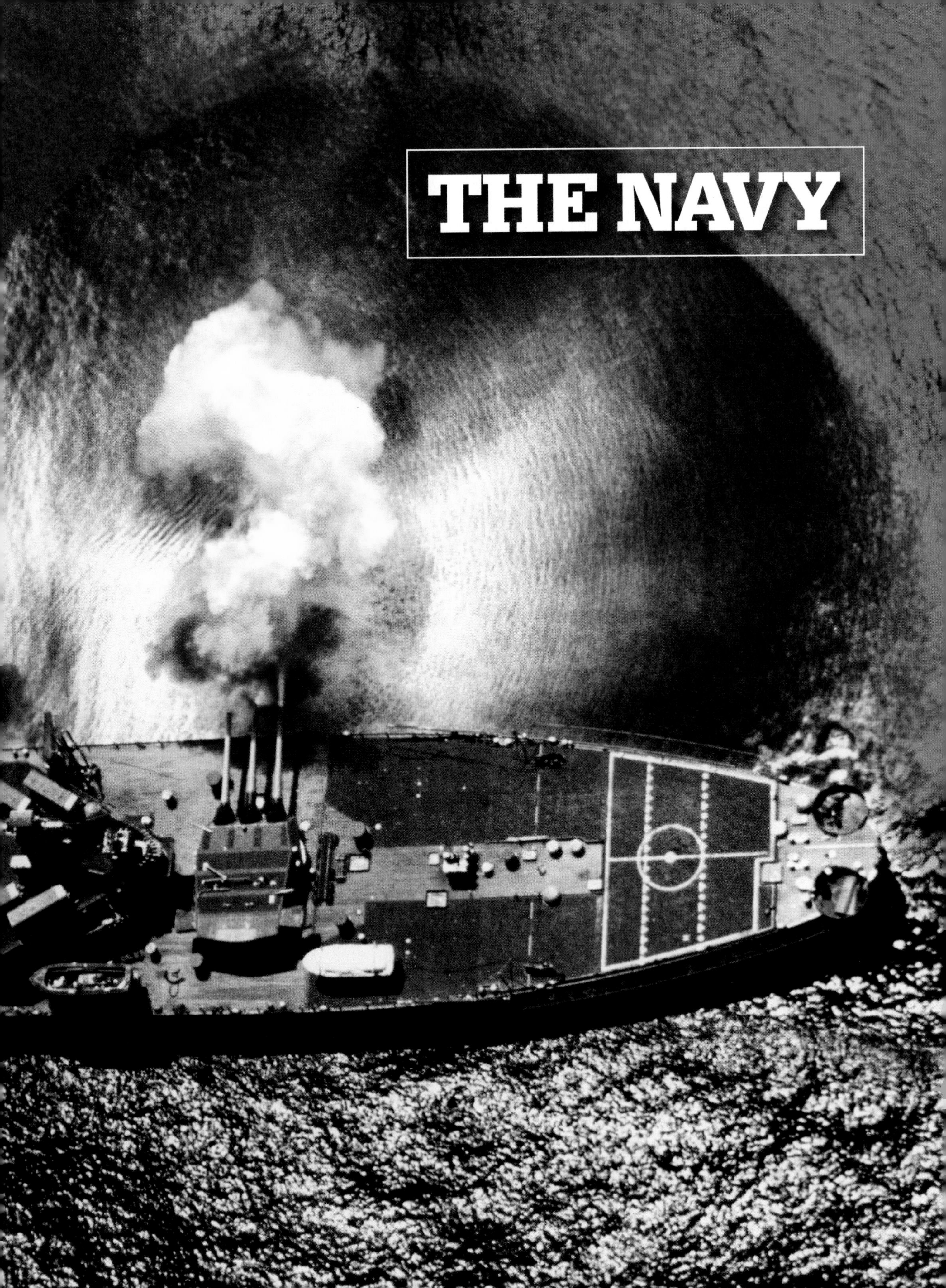

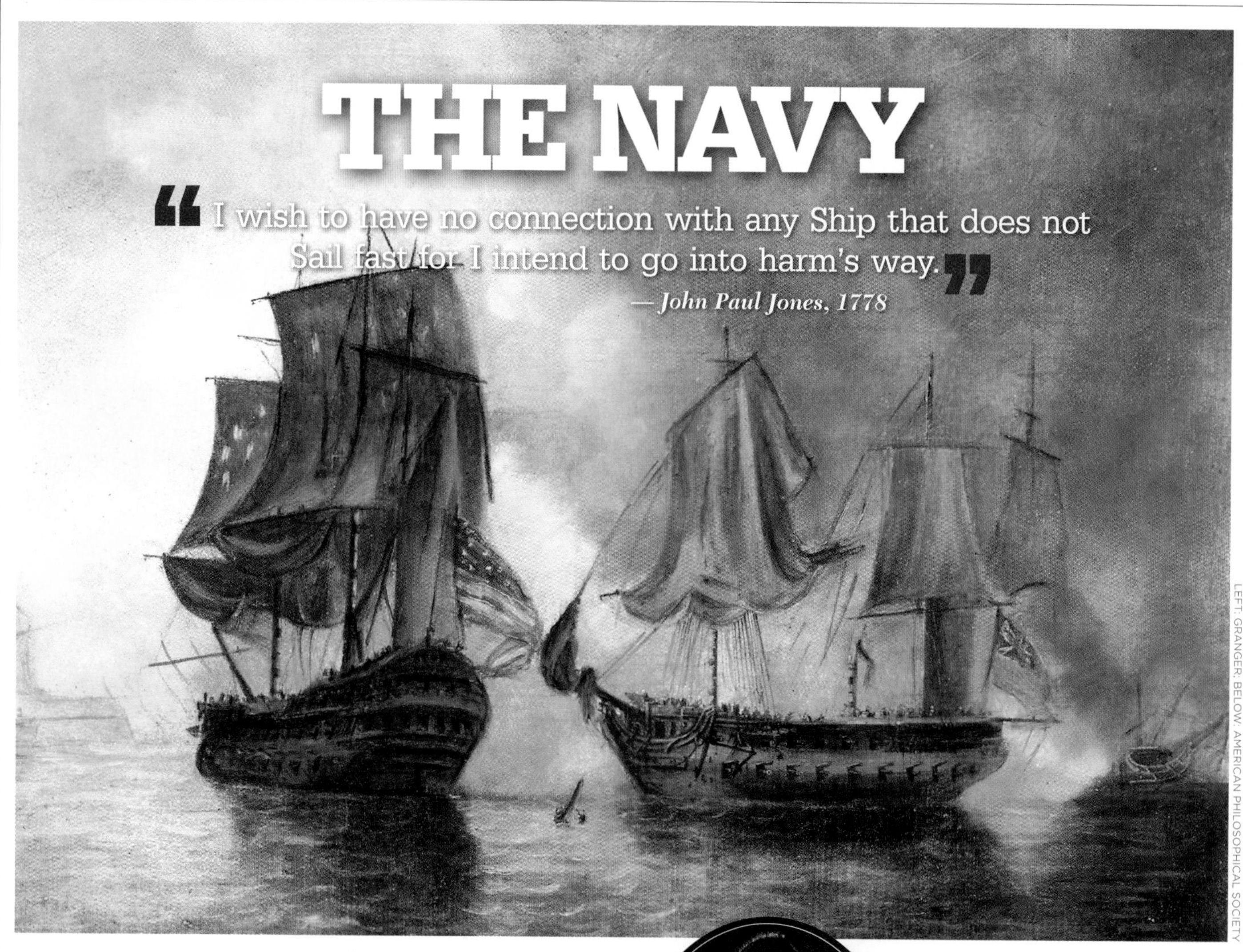

THE NAVY

" I wish to have no connection with any Ship that does not Sail fast for I intend to go into harm's way. **"**

—*John Paul Jones, 1778*

LEFT: GRANGER; BELOW: AMERICAN PHILOSOPHICAL SOCIETY

THE UNITED STATES is a nation founded from the sea, by vessels bearing émigrés from England and other countries. Thus it isn't surprising that, blessed with a magnificent coastline and fruitful waters, Americans have had a long love affair with things nautical, including, of course, the very Navy itself, protector and benefactor.

It is interesting that by the time of the American Revolution, the colonies were producing one third of all the shipping tonnage in the British Empire. So although only an emergent nation, it was certainly capable of assembling its own maritime force. Just a matter of months after independence was declared, the Continental Navy was established, on October 13, 1775, when the Continental Congress authorized the fitting out of two armed craft to confront ships supplying munitions to the British army in America. That number would grow to 20 active warships.

The Continental Navy fared well getting cargo to the Continental Army and was reasonably effective at hectoring British shipping.

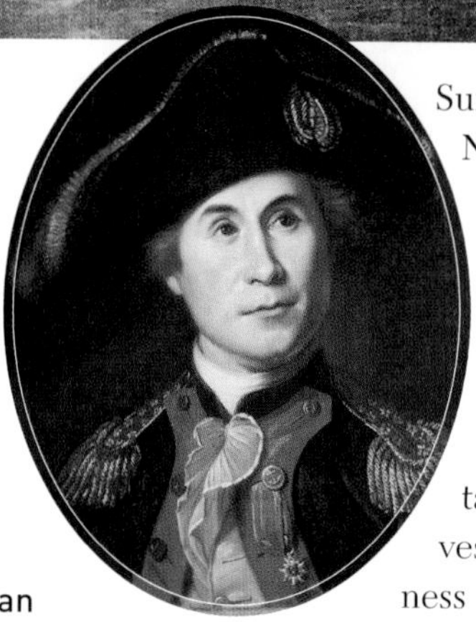

One of the Navy's, and the country's, first and greatest heroes was John Paul Jones. Courageous and fair, he formed the template for the American naval captain. Above, his *Bonhomme Richard* confronts the British frigate *Serapis*.

Surely though, the fledgling Navy's salient moment came when a short, indomitable man painted a timeless scene in American history. Scottish-born John Paul Jones entered the Navy in its first year, and on his maiden voyage as captain he captured 16 British vessels. His reputation for boldness would only grow. In September 1779, off the coast of England, he commanded a small squadron that encountered seven British merchantmen protected by the Royal Navy frigate *Serapis*. Jones's ship, the *Bonhomme Richard*, or "Poor Richard" (he named her for his good friend Benjamin Franklin, the pseudonymous author of *Poor Richard's Almanac*), was slower than *Serapis*, less nimble, and carried considerably less cannon. Still, Jones engaged the enemy. Early in the intense battle, the *Bonhomme Richard* suffered terribly. Then, as Jones wrote in a letter to Franklin, "the English commodore asked me if I demanded quarters, and I having answered him in the most determined negative, they renewed the battle with double fury."

The American's "most determined" response will soar forever: "Sir, I have not yet begun to fight." Buoyed by their captain's words, the American crew fought bravely, and three hours later the British surrendered. Jones and his men would shortly have to repair to the *Serapis*, for their own vessel was fatally damaged. The spirit of John Paul Jones's words will forever inform this country's will, its unyielding spirit.

George Washington certainly recognized the importance of the sea. In 1781 he wrote, "Without a decisive naval force we can do nothing definitive, and with it, everything honorable and glorious." Not all were so prescient: The Continental Navy was dismantled after the war, the ships sold off. But as Barbary pirates increasingly preyed on U.S. shipping, Congress voted in 1794 to build six warships, and four years later established the Department of the Navy.

The undeclared war of the time, against France, was a thundering success for the Navy, which lost one ship to 80 for the French. In ensuing squabbles and through the War of 1812, the American Navy more than held its own against Tripoli and the vaunted British service, as frigates like the *Constitution* and the *United States* repeatedly licked the enemy.

Edward Preble was an early captain of the *Constitution*, a.k.a. "Old Ironsides." His leadership in action at Tripoli was of great value, to be sure; but even more he imbued the officers serving under him with the proper way to do things. The stars among "Preble's Boys" were many—Isaac Hull, William Bainbridge, David Porter, James "Don't Give Up the Ship" Lawrence—but perhaps the brightest was Stephen Decatur, the brilliant officer who first attracted national attention when at the age of 25 he led a raid into Tripoli Harbor to burn the captured, and important, frigate *Philadelphia*. The esteemed British Admiral Lord Nelson called

LEFT: GRANGER; INSET AND BELOW: CULVER

In December 1812, "Old Ironsides" dismasted and sank Britain's *Java* off the coast of Brazil. Edward Preble (left) had an indelible influence on his junior officers, like the glamorous Stephen Decatur.

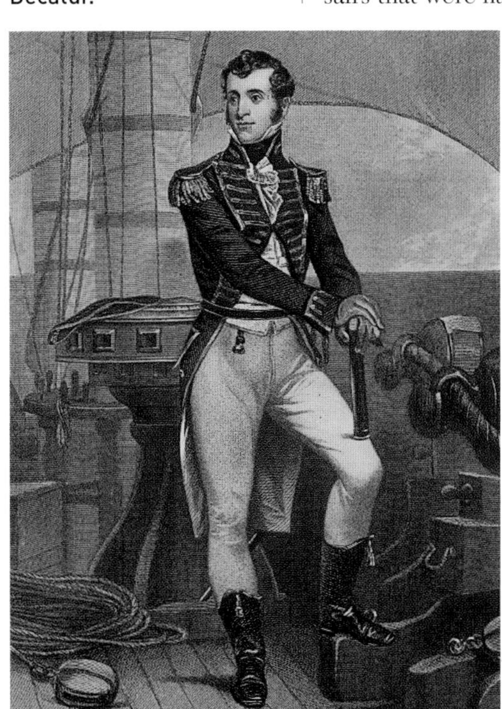

the expedition "the most bold and daring act of the age."

In the War of 1812, Decatur commanded the *United States*. He stunned the British by capturing the frigate *Macedonian*. (They were equally shocked when Hull and the *Constitution* took *Guerrière*; when *Constitution*, with Bainbridge at the helm, took *Java*; and when Porter on the *Essex* destroyed the British whaling fleet in the Pacific.) In 1815, Decatur sailed to the Mediterranean to deal with Algerian corsairs that were having their way with American merchant ships. After a cannon shot cut the captain of an Algerian frigate in half, the ship surrendered, leading to Decatur's securing a treaty. It was after this episode that Decatur observed: "Our country! In her intercourse with foreign nations may she always be right; but our country right or wrong." This, of course, from one of Preble's Boys. For the next century, the United States Navy would have a presence in the Mediterranean, and over the next couple of decades other important squadrons would be established in far-flung waters.

Shortly after Fort Sumter

was fired on, and the Civil War joined, President Lincoln ordered the blockading of the Confederate coast. It was the beginning of a transforming time for the Navy. In a period marked by innovation, the most striking was undoubtedly the unprecedented clash between two ironclad warships in March 1862, the Confederate *Merrimack* and the Union *Monitor*. The fight was a draw, but the Confederacy became mightily impressed with the worth of metal ships, and conventional shipbuilding thereby suffered. The nascent metal-clad craft, in the end, proved ineffectual during the war.

"Uncle Sam's web-feet," however, as Lincoln called the Navy, left their tracks in many venues: bays, rivers and bayous. The blockading was a critical aspect of the Civil War; otherwise the industrial-poor South would have been able to trade its cotton to France and England for munitions. Union vessels, meanwhile, traveled about freely.

At the war's onset, there were 90 ships in the Navy, but only half were active, and a mere eight lay in home waters. By the truce, however, the Navy boasted 670 vessels and 57,000 men. It had become the most powerful navy in the world. Unfortunately, the service was about to slip into its "Dark Ages," when technological advancement—steam and propeller—was shunned while a great deal of money was poorly invested in outmoded wooden cruisers.

With the advent of the 1880s, the Navy got back on course, as Congress voted to halt repairs of ancient ships and moved toward the acquisition of steel vessels. By 1890 that formidable warrior the battleship had become the Navy ship of choice, and would remain so for the next five decades. Another great President, Teddy Roosevelt, also had a keen grasp of naval significance. Speaking in Chicago in 1903, he said, "There is a homely adage which runs, 'Speak softly and carry a big stick; you will go far.' If the American nation will speak softly and yet build and keep at a pitch of the highest training a thoroughly efficient Navy, the Monroe Doctrine will go far." The accruement of battleships would continue for the rest of the decade. Other than a couple of estimable victories in the Spanish-American War, it had been a long, peaceful stint for the service. When the U.S. entered World War I, in 1917, it possessed the third-largest fleet in the world. While the Navy's duties would be considerably less demanding than the Army's, it is impressive that two million American soldiers were transported without the loss of a single man to enemy action. And the Navy laid 56,000 mines in the North Sea, the largest such endeavor in history. In sum, the naval participation was, in the scope of such a titanic encounter, comparatively low-profile, although 431 lives were sacrificed.

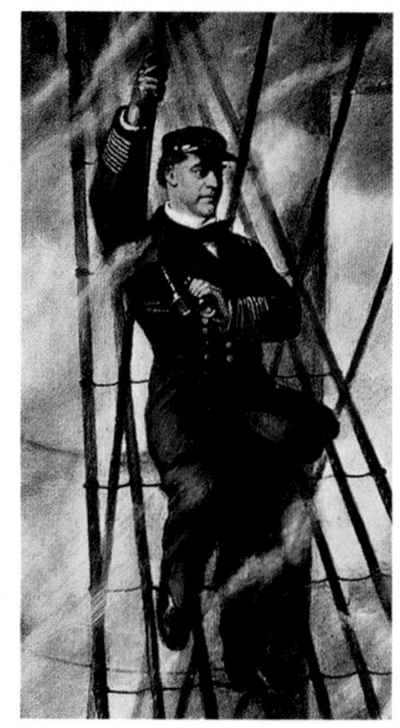

David Farragut was one of the Union's foremost heroes, and his assault on Mobile Bay is naval legend. It was a difficult port to approach, and well defended by forts. His fleet steamed into the harbor on August 5, 1864. Suddenly the lead sloop halted and nearly backed into the flagship. Farragut (above, in the ship's rigging) went to swing past, and when warned that there were "torpedoes" (as mines were called then), he cried out, "Damn the torpedoes! Full speed ahead!" Farragut's ensuing victory was a model of audacity and careful planning.

Following the "War to End All Wars," a lot of ships were scrapped. There followed a fallow period, with the vital exception that in 1922 a collier was converted into the first American aircraft carrier, the *Langley*. That year, Rear Adm. W.A. Moffett, then chief of the Navy Bureau of Aeronautics, said, "The air fleet of an enemy will never get within striking distance of our coast as long as our aircraft carriers are able to carry the preponderance of air power to sea." It was a swift breakthrough for naval aviation, a field in which the U.S. was at the fore. But it was not the only country with a crystal ball. On December 7, 1941, two waves of planes took off from six Japanese aircraft carriers north of Oahu. They would deliver a savage blow to Pearl Harbor, the home of the Pacific Fleet. American casualties totaled 3,581, and 18 ships were sunk or seriously damaged. The importance of naval aviation, however, emerges only after one looks past those terrible numbers and realizes that apart from the attack's galvanizing effect on the nation, the fortuitous absence of carriers from Pearl on that fateful day seriously detracted from the Japanese victory.

After Pearl the Japanese navy spread out in the Pacific. Then in May 1942, the fierce Battle of the Coral Sea marked the first time that a campaign was carried out by opposing fleets that never caught sight of each other. The planes did the fighting. It was the first of six such clashes between carrier forces, and led to the unseating of the battleship as top dog in the naval hierarchy.

One month later the course of events in the Pacific theater was irrevocably altered when Adm. Chester W. Nimitz gathered ships that had survived Pearl Harbor and Coral Sea, and ambushed the Japanese fleet at Midway. One American flat-top was lost, but the Japanese were rocked when four of their carriers, all of which had taken part at Pearl, were suddenly

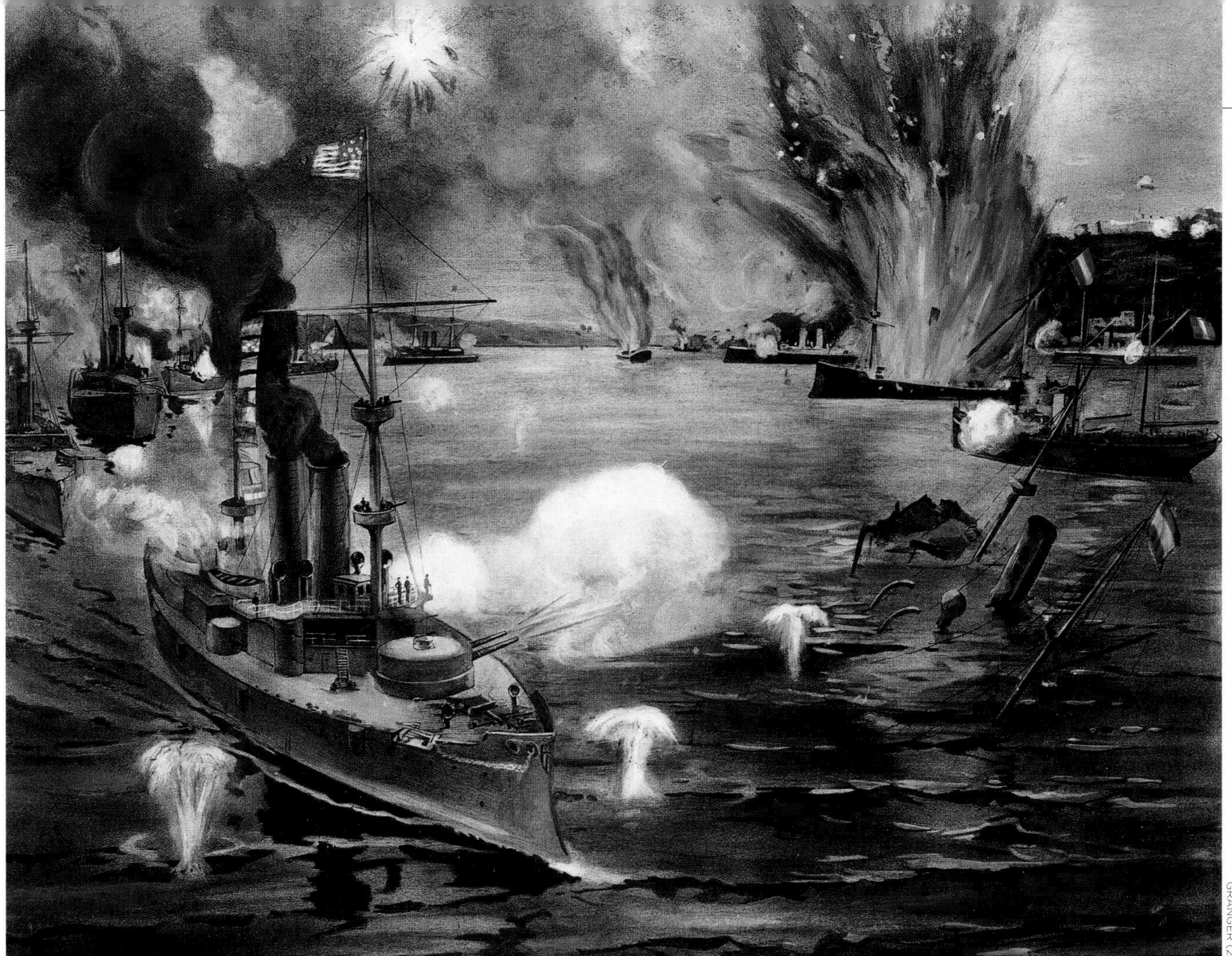
GRANGER (2)

destroyed. Aside from its sensational battles in the Pacific, the Navy in World War II undertook massive troop transport duties and spearheaded amphibious assaults in the Pacific and Atlantic on a hitherto undreamed-of scale. In mid-'41 there were 300,000 officers and men; by the end of the war the Navy had 10 times that many. Its versatility came into play a few years later in the Korean War, at the amphibious landing at Inchon, and in the support provided by naval artillery and aviation. Two years after the Korean armistice, in 1955, there were two important developments. The cruiser *Boston* became the first ship to replace conventional guns with guided missiles, while the submarine *Nautilus* was the first ship of any sort to be powered by nuclear fission rather than oil or coal. Five years hence the *Triton* had the distinction of becoming the first sub to circumnavigate the globe while submerged. Two months later, in July 1960, the *George Washington* became the first to have a submerged launch of the Navy's new Polaris missile.

The Spanish-American War lasted only a few months but hurtled the United States toward becoming a world power. Here, U.S. ships under the command of William T. Sampson and Winfield Scott Schley demolish the Spanish fleet off Santiago, Cuba, on July 3, 1898.

The Navy entered into open combat in Vietnam in 1964, and over the next decade, sorties from carriers and bombardment from offshore destroyers, rocket boats and the battleship *New Jersey*—which could launch one-ton shells 20 miles inland—rained on enemy forces. Surveillance and assault forces actively worked the coast and rivers.

The '70s were also a time of social adjustment in the Navy. With Adm. Elmo R. Zumwalt Jr. at the helm, African Americans were fully integrated into the service. In 1971, Samuel L. Gravely became the first black to achieve flag rank. Zumwalt also was known for his "Z Grams," missives deployed to rid the Navy of red-tape gantlets and to deep-six needless regulation.

In recent years, the Navy has served to forward and defend national interests across the globe, using all manner of patrols, in the Mediterranean, the Persian Gulf, the Red Sea or wherever the situation requires. Names like the *Stark* and the *Cole* have assumed their place in its storied lineage. There is a naval signal, transmittable by flag or radio, that means "Well done." Here then, we shall say to the Navy, "Bravo Zulu."

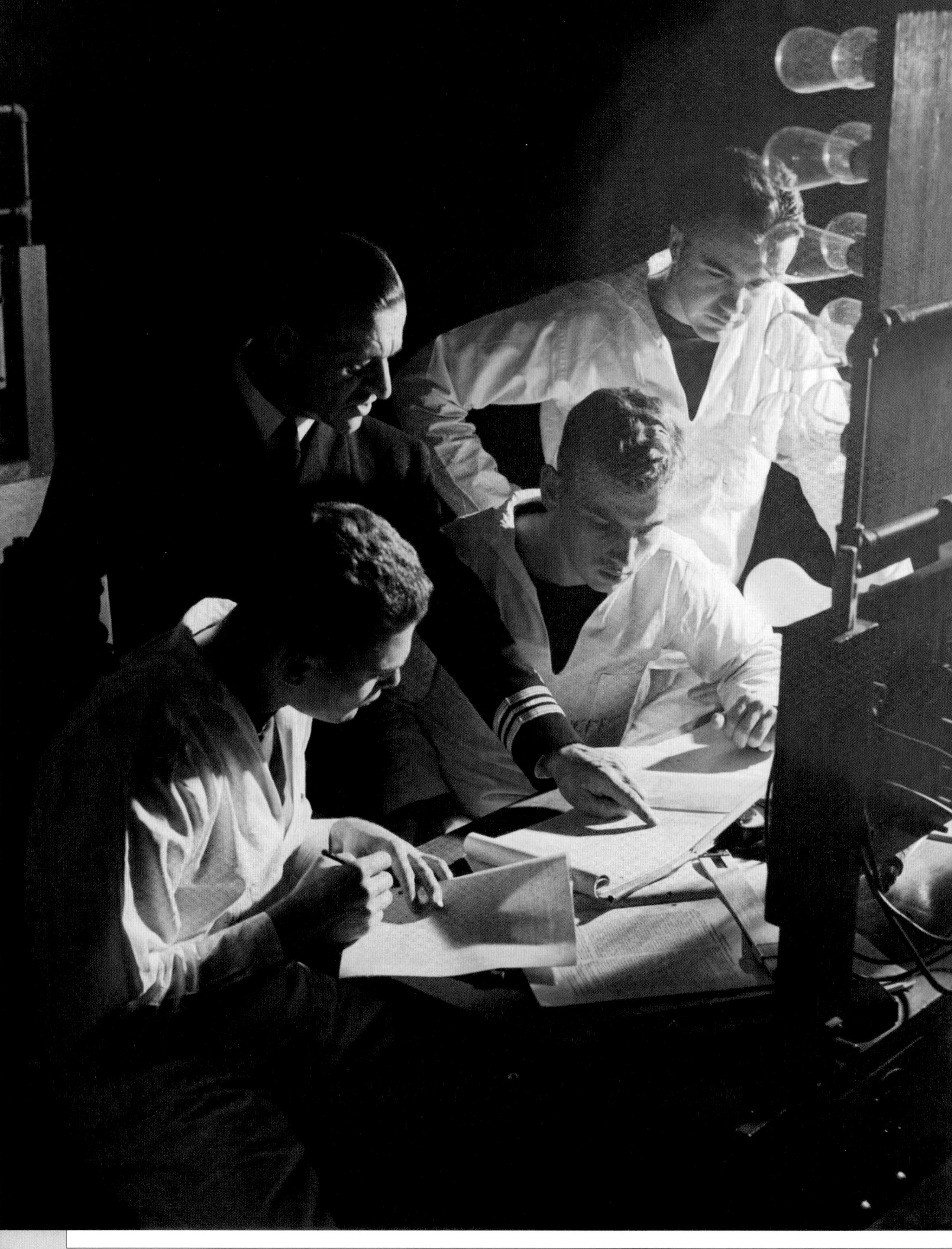

UNITED STATES NAVAL ACADEMY

"To develop midshipmen morally, mentally and physically and to imbue them with the highest ideals of duty, honor and loyalty..." *—The Mission of the USNA*

ON SEPTEMBER 13, 1842, a two-masted vessel called the *Somers* sailed from the Brooklyn Navy Yard as a floating school for teenage apprentice volunteers looking to make a career out of the Navy. This school became instructive in an unexpected manner when discipline disintegrated and three of the lads went mutinous and were later hanged at the yardarm. Three years hence, having seen the error of sending midshipmen directly aboard ship for learning, Secretary of the Navy George Bancroft engineered the opening of the Naval School in Annapolis, Md. The "healthy and secluded" site was designed to rescue young men from the "temptations and distractions" of a large city. There were 50 students and seven teachers, with a curriculum that included math and navigation, natural philosophy and French. In 1850 the name was changed to the United States Naval Academy. Women were admitted in 1976 to a brigade-size student body of 4,000. The institution is now a splendid training ground as well as one of the world's great universities.

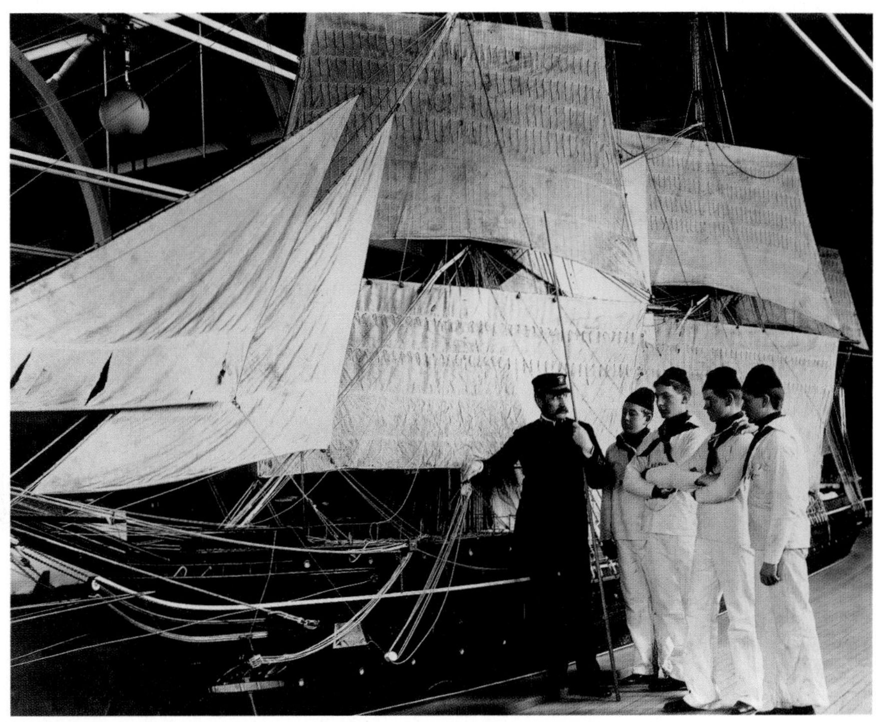

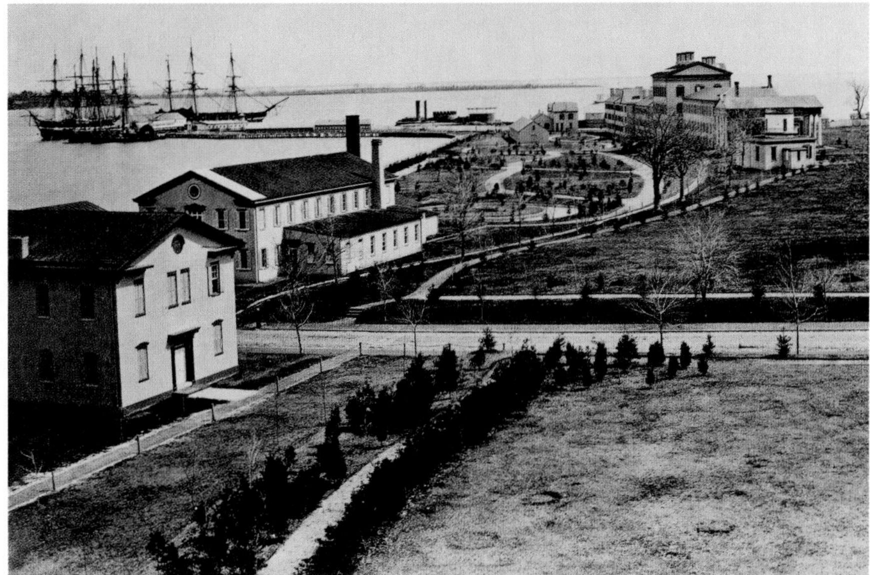

This partial view of the Academy grounds is from 1875, 30 years after the school's founding. Today the USNA sits on 338 acres. Top: Midshipmen at an early Annapolis class get the lowdown on the finer points of sailing. Opposite: A 1940 class in electrical engineering, commonly called Juice.

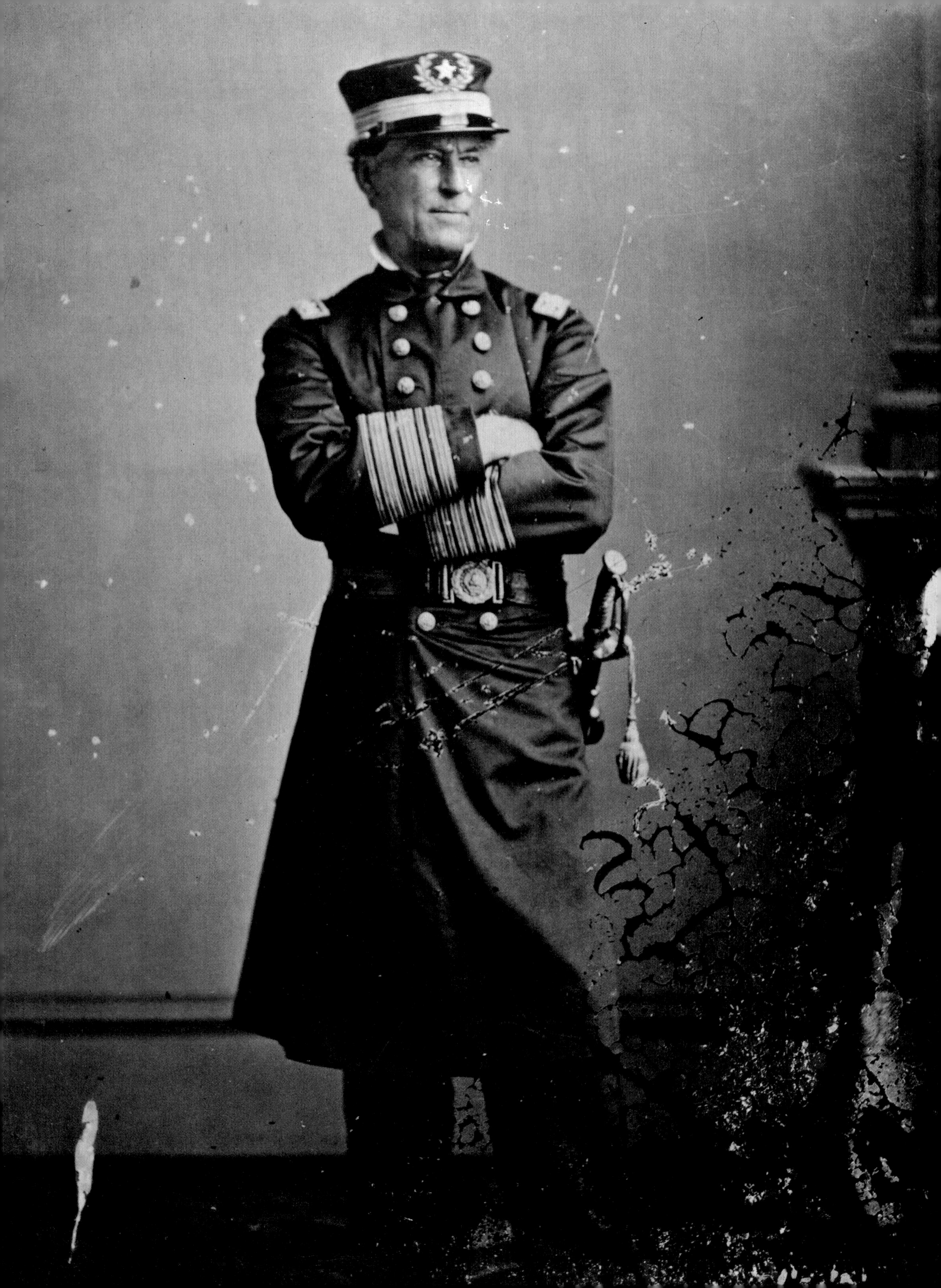

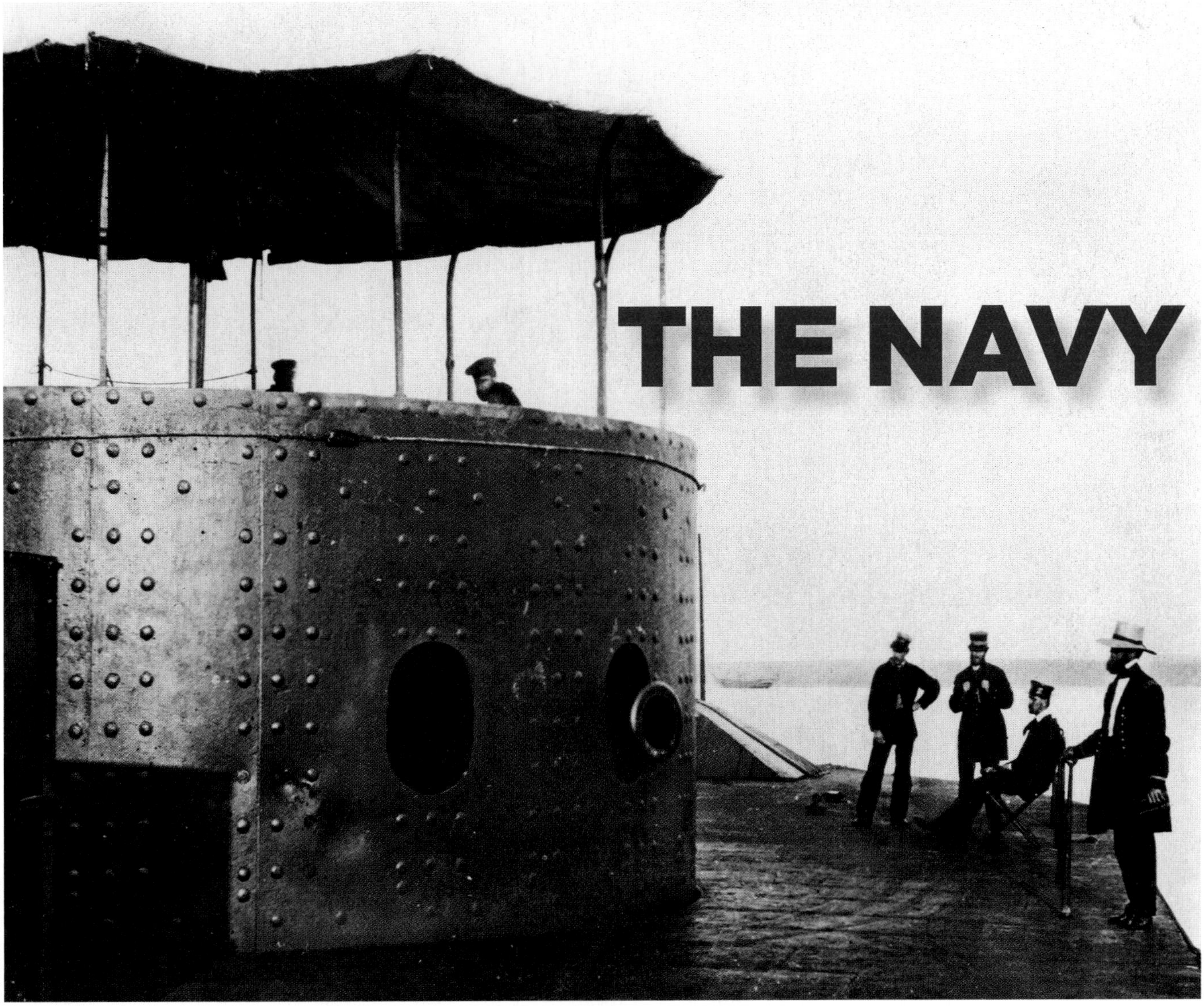

THE NAVY

NATIONAL ARCHIVES

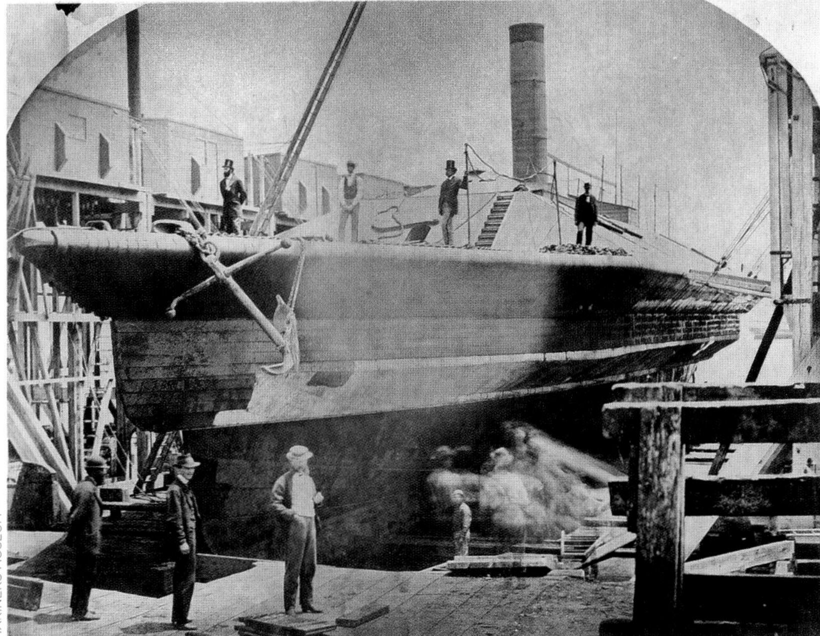

MARINERS MUSEUM

THE CIVIL WAR AT SEA

The clash of the *Monitor* and the *Merrimack* on March 9, 1862, may have lasted for hours, but neither emerged a winner. The view above of the *Monitor* shows the muzzle of one of its guns and dents in the turret from Confederate artillery. The South, for better or worse, became enamored of ironclads. The *Atlanta* ran aground in her first battle under the weight of her armament and was captured. In a Pennsylvania shipyard (left), she is destined for scrap. Opposite: the immortal Adm. David Glasgow Farragut.

CULVER

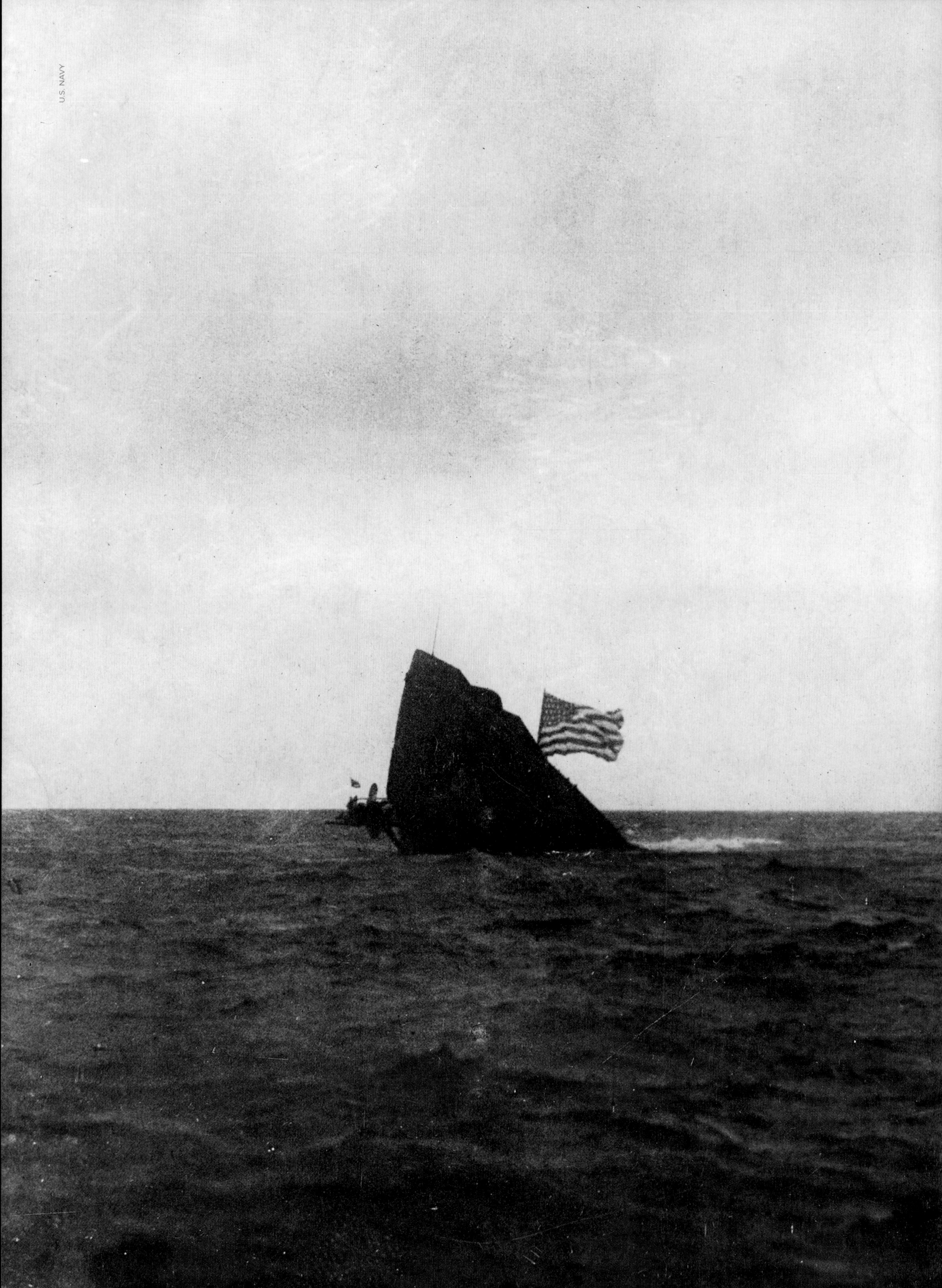

U.S. NAVY

REMEMBER THE *MAINE*!

That slogan resonated during the Spanish-American War, and is familiar even a century later. In January 1898 the battleship entered Havana harbor to protect U.S. interests in a flare-up between Spain and angry colonists. Then on February 15 an explosion savaged the forward third of the vessel, which rapidly sank. An inquiry determined that a mine had detonated under the ship. In 1911 the ship was raised for another inquiry (left), with the same finding. The second inquiry stemmed at least in part from rumors that William Randolph Hearst ("You furnish the pictures and I'll furnish the war"), and his yellow press, may have bombed the ship in order to sell more newspapers. A study by Adm. Hyman G. Rickover published in 1976 said that the damage was inconsistent with a mine; others disagreed. At right, Adm. George Dewey, the "Hero of Manila," was commemorated in 1898 along with an image of the *Maine*.

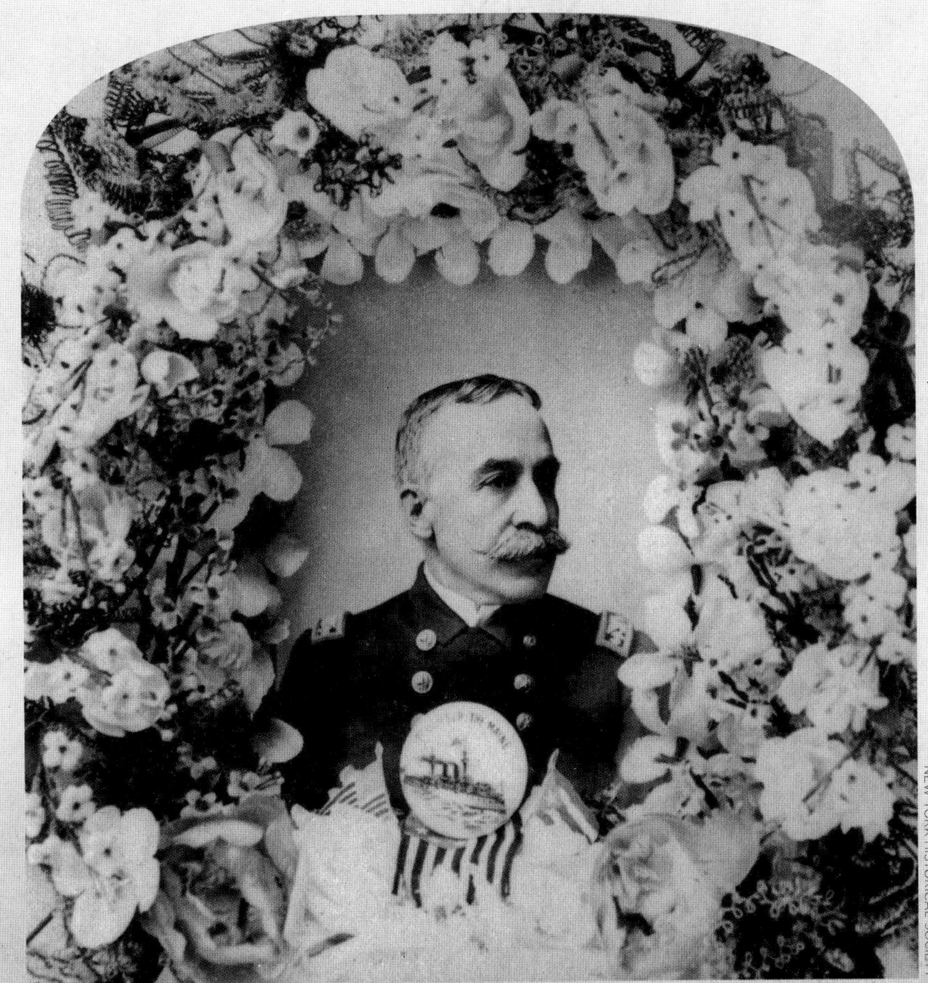

NEW YORK HISTORICAL SOCIETY

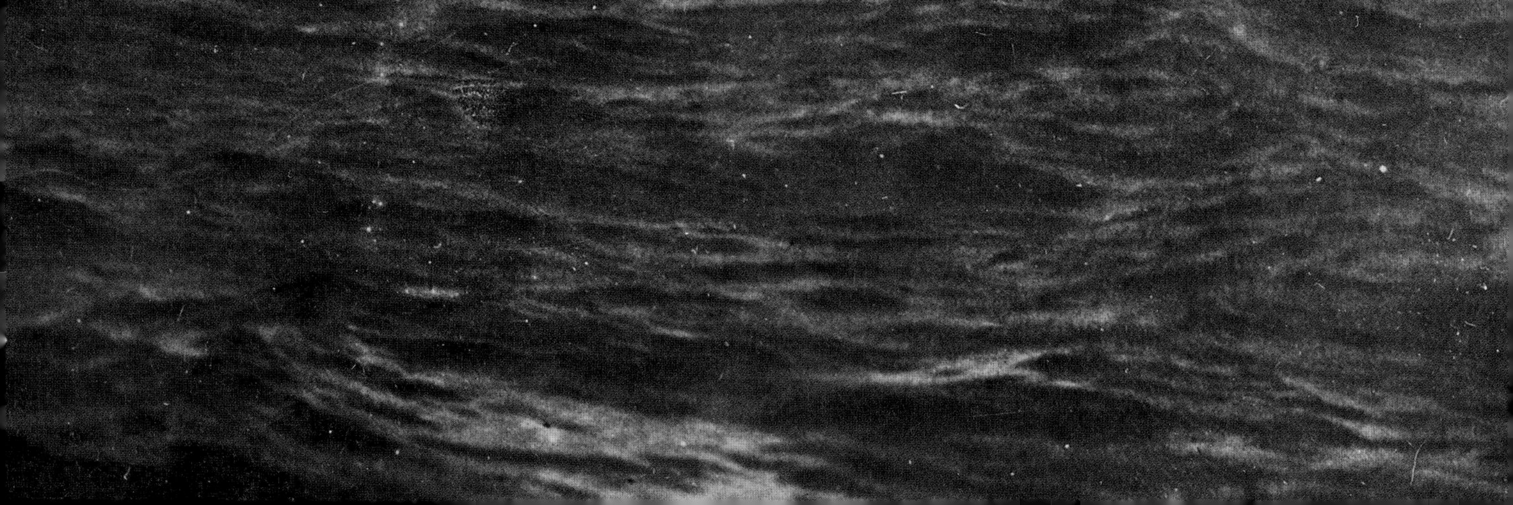

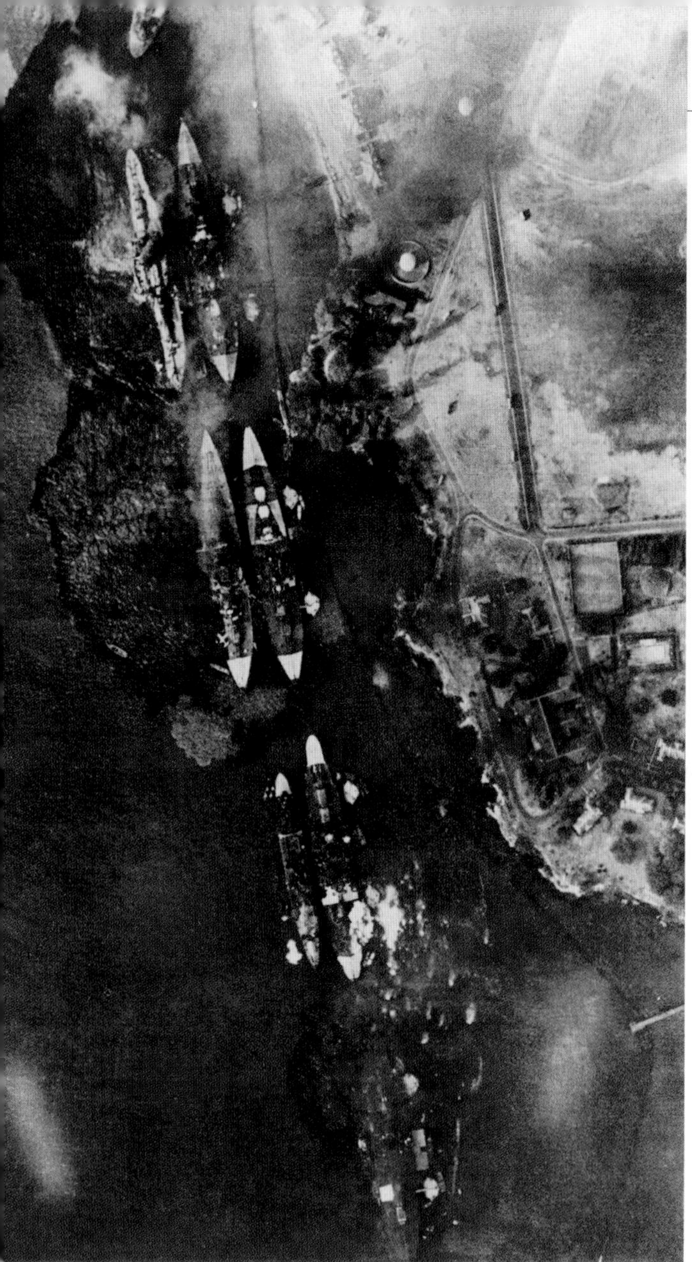

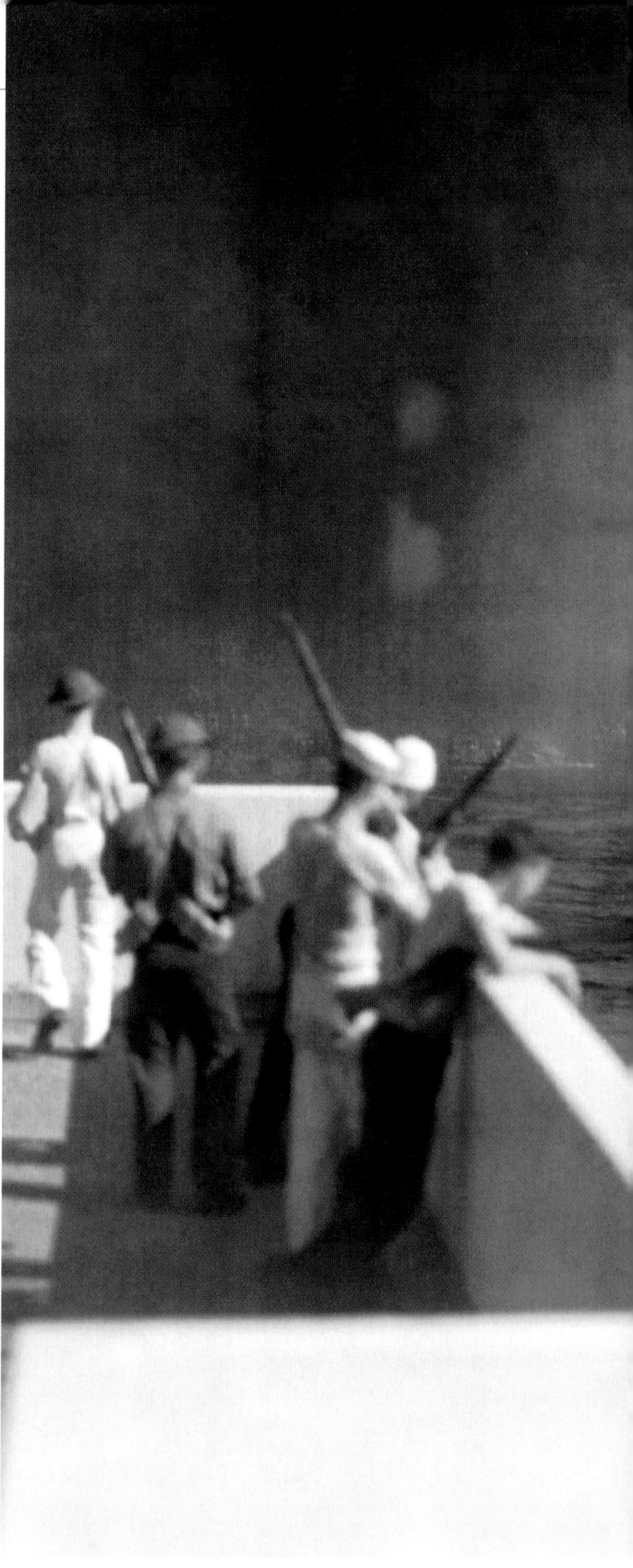

OUR CALL TO ARMS

There was already war in Europe and in the Pacific, but as of December 6, 1941, the U.S. was not a formal participant. The next morning that all changed when the Japanese delivered a surprise attack on Pearl Harbor that took a lot of lives, wrecked a lot of ships—and awakened a sleeping giant. Battleship Row was easy pickings, as shown in the photo above taken early on by a Japanese high-level bomber. From bottom to top: the *Nevada*, torpedoed and smoking; *Vestal*, outside of *Arizona*, which has just been hit; *West Virginia* and *Oklahoma* (outside of *Tennessee* and *Maryland*), listing and spewing oil. At right, sailors on the roof of the Naval Air Station headquarters look on as the flagship *California*, already torpedoed and bombed, is in urgent danger from boiling oil. She sank but was salvaged and returned to fight in the war.

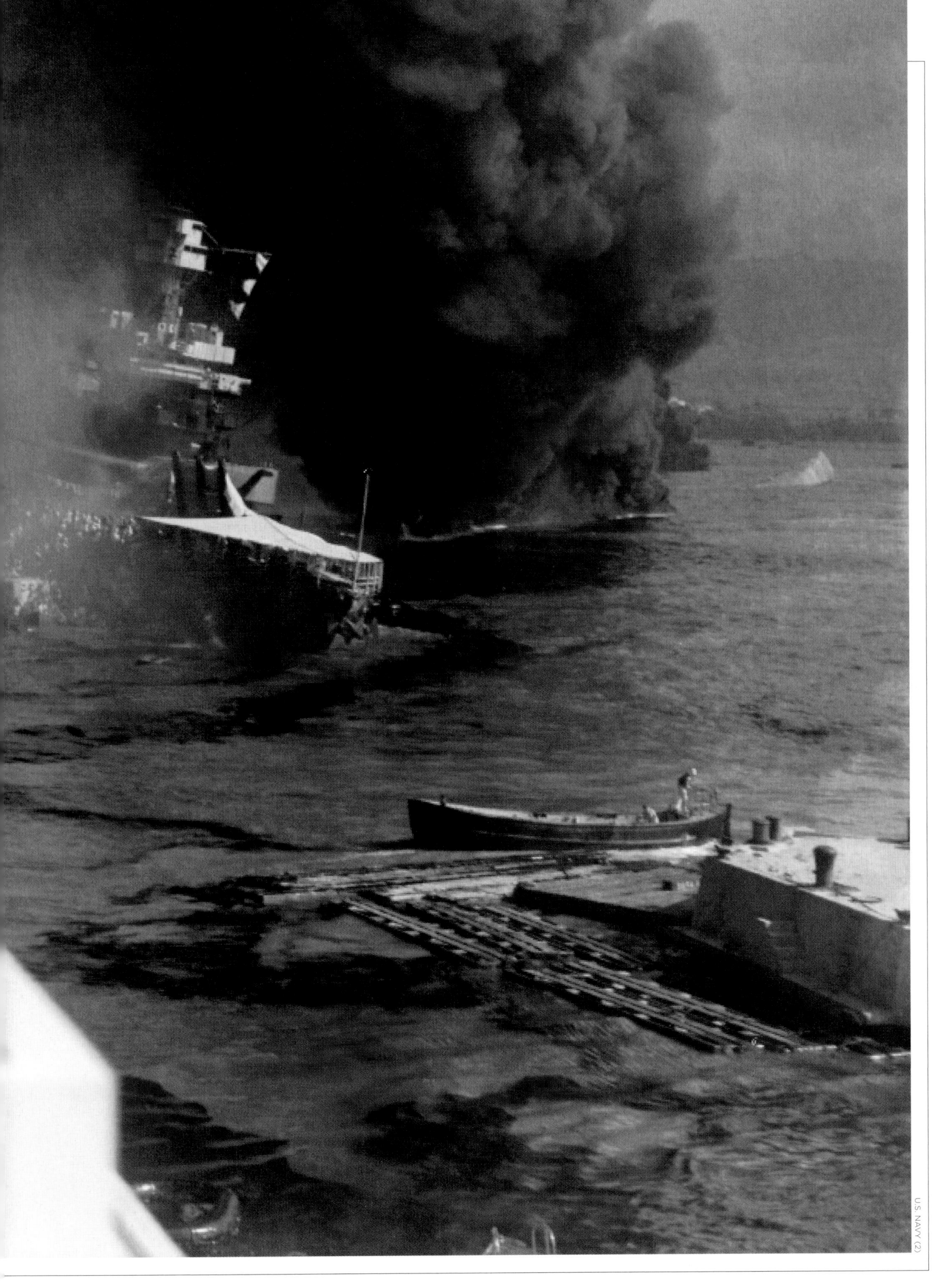

U.S. NAVY (2)

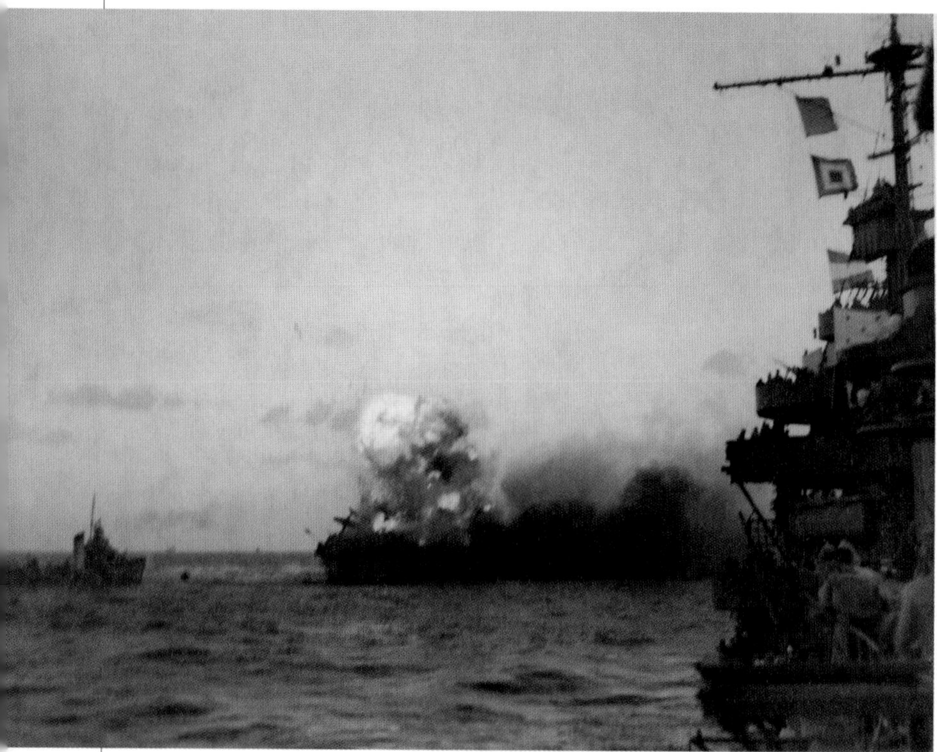

THE BATTLE OF CORAL SEA
Five months after Pearl, the U.S. and Japan engaged in the first sea battle waged entirely from the air. Both sides were hit hard during the momentous all-day affair. In material terms the Japanese came out slightly ahead; the U.S., however, scored a strategic victory in that Japanese expansion had been halted. Below: This antiaircraft battery on the *Enterprise* has just repelled a kamikaze attack. Right: Sailors abandon the doomed *Lexington*. Above: A plane is thrown from the *Lexington* as torpedoes aboard the carrier detonate; the destroyer *Hammann*, at left, backs away with survivors. This photo was taken from the cruiser *Minneapolis*.

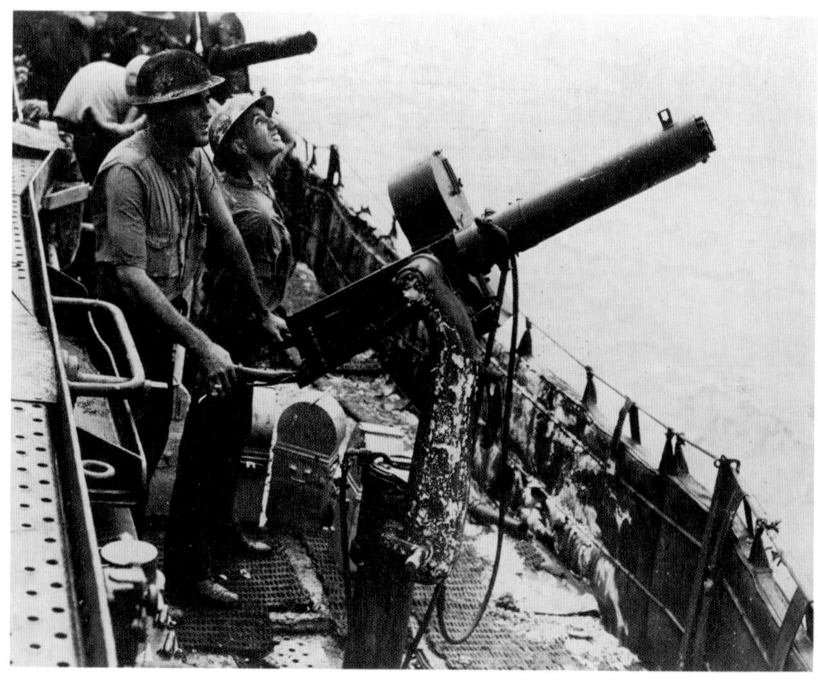

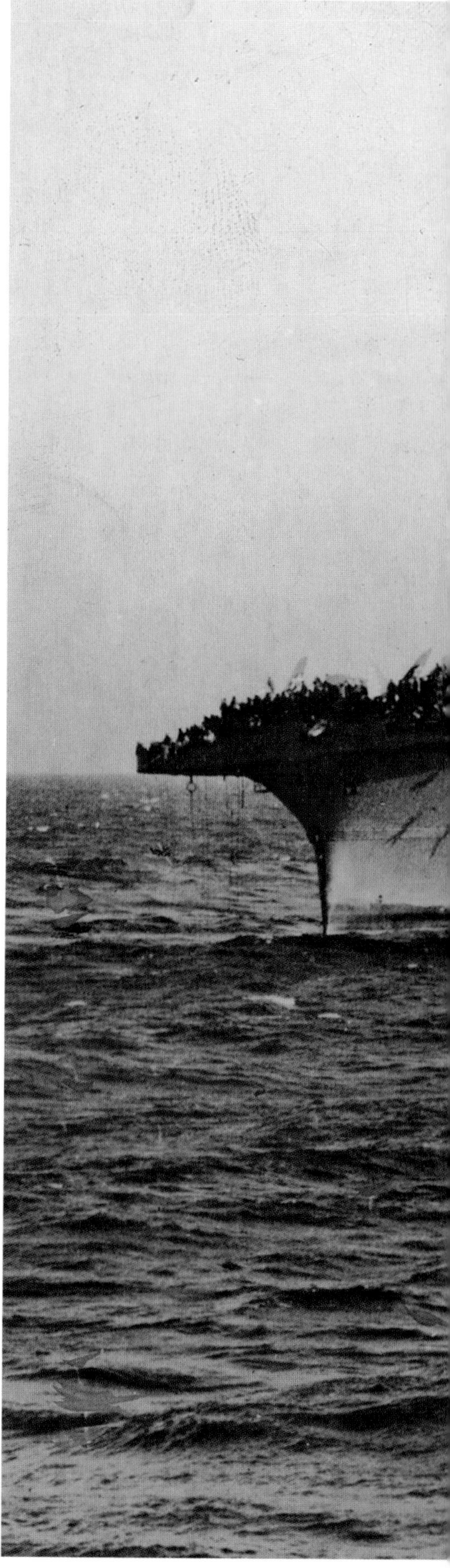

U.S. NAVY (3)

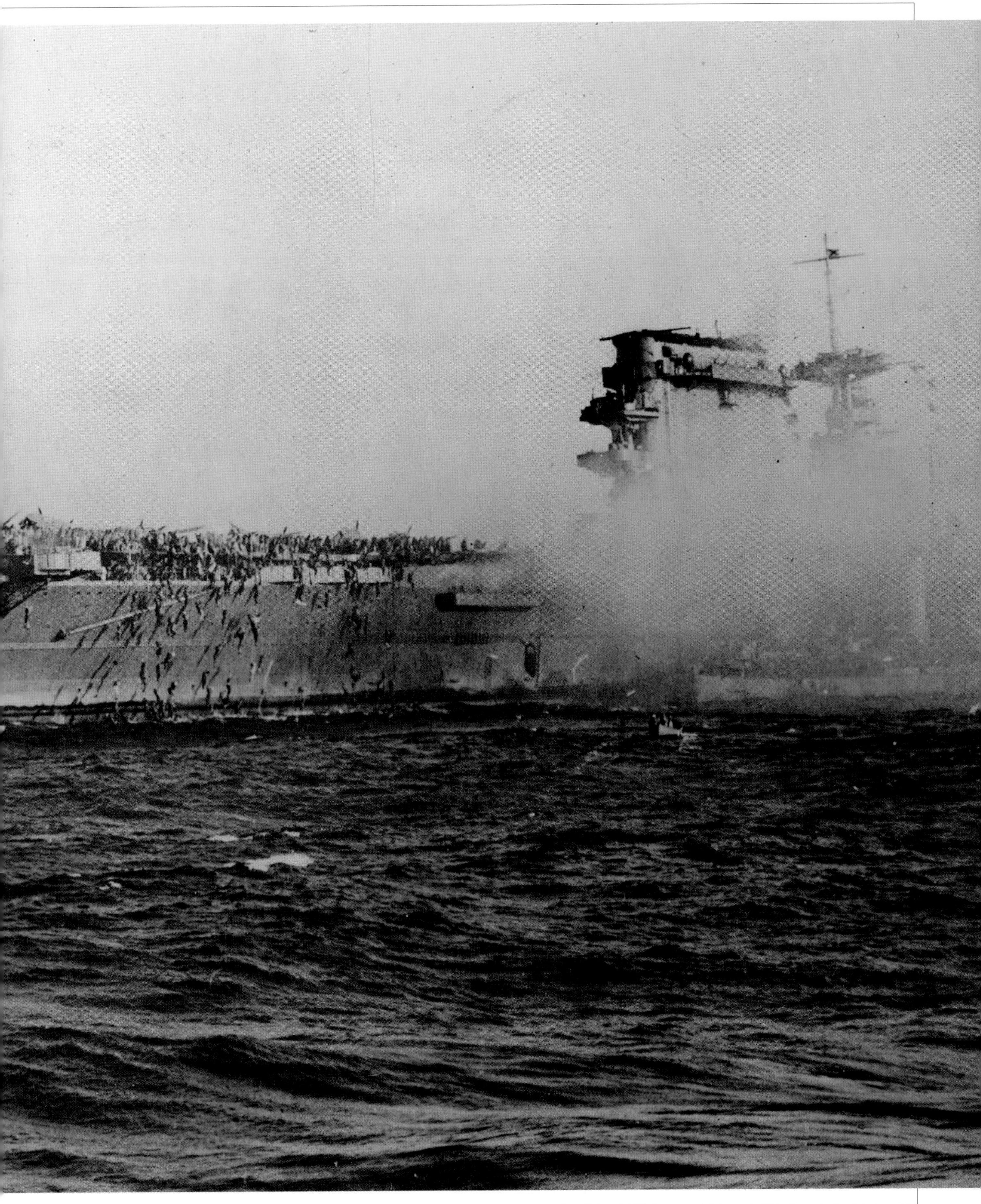

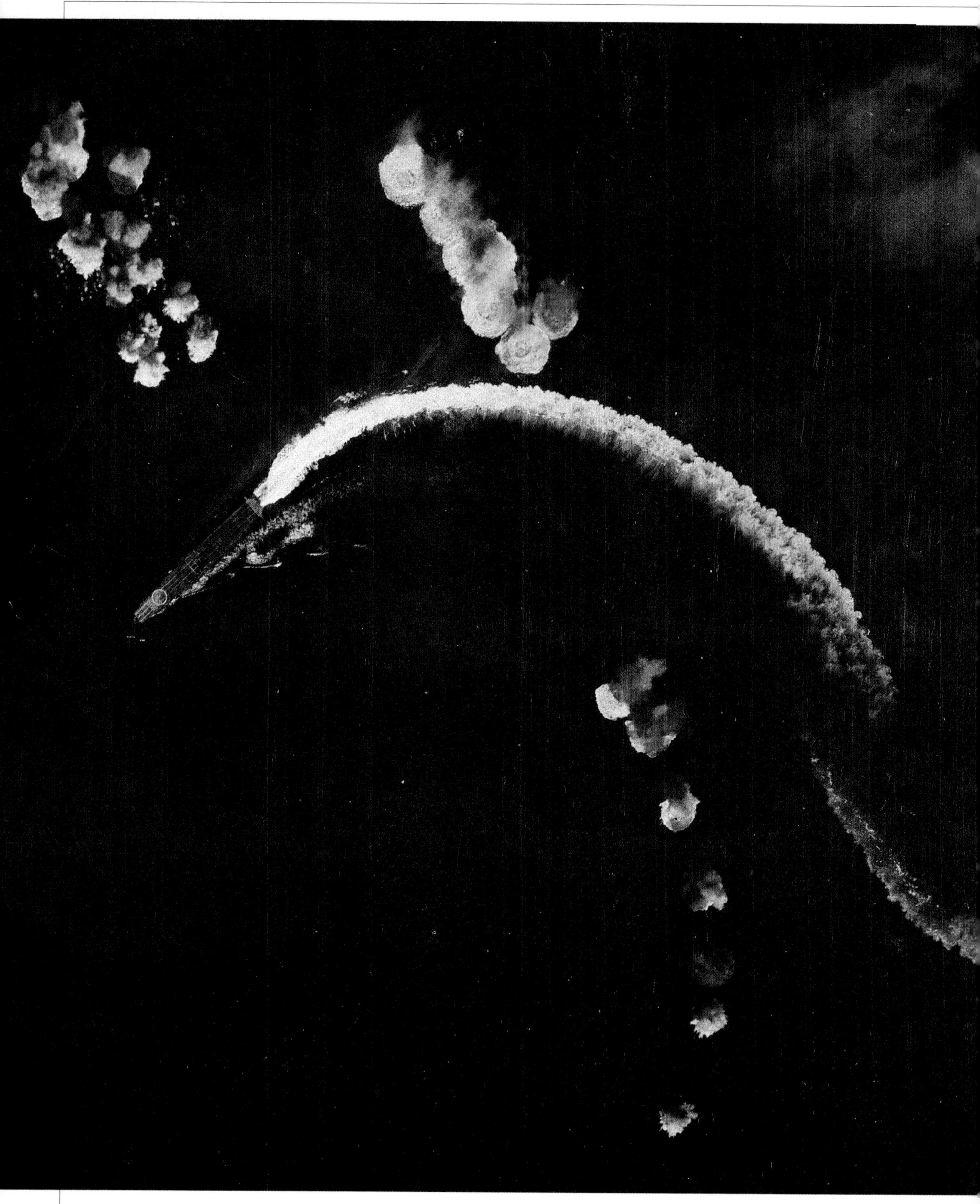

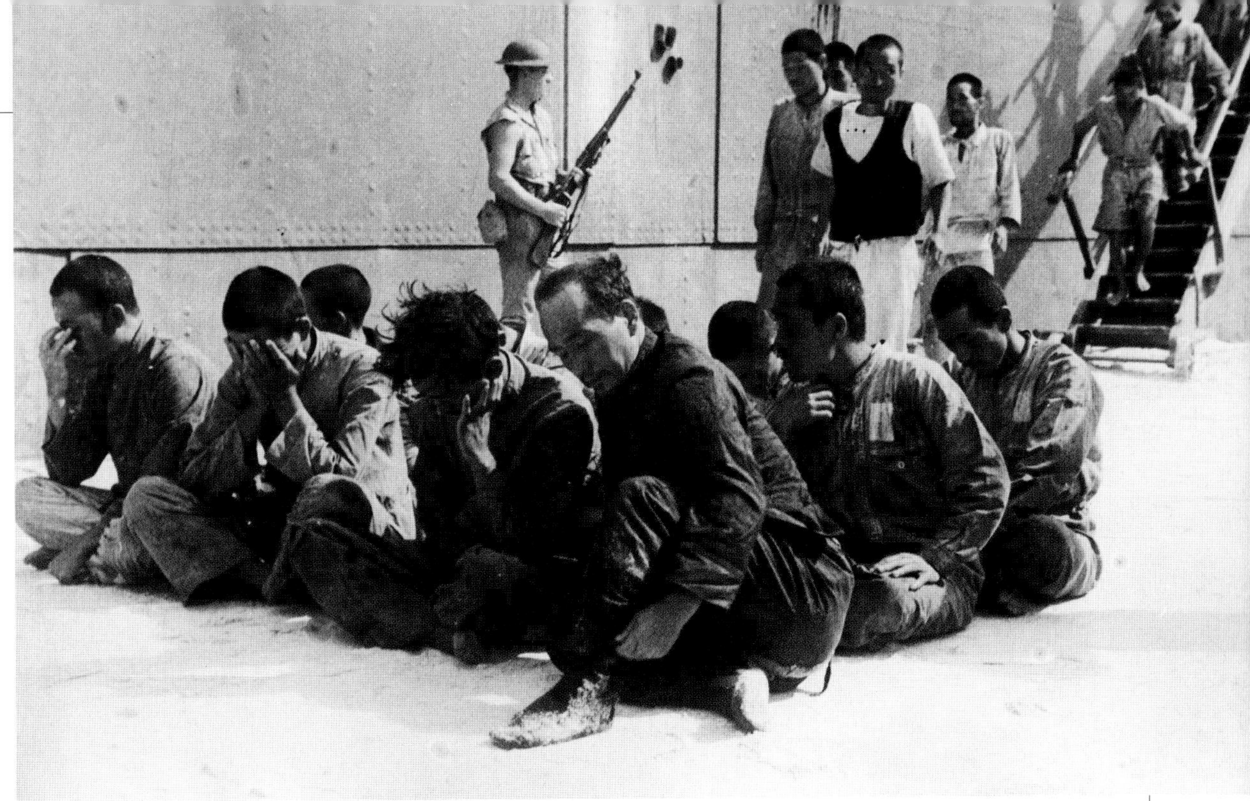

PAYBACK: MIDWAY!
Just one month after Coral Sea, the U.S. and Japan had another huge showdown in the Pacific, this time near Midway, at the western tip of the Hawaiian chain. The Japanese had planned to capture the island and use it as an advance base. Instead, Adm. Chester W. Nimitz, acting on phenomenal intelligence breakthroughs, ambushed the Japanese fleet. At left, the carrier *Hiryu* tries to avoid high-level bombing, in vain, as evidenced by the survivors above, under guard on Midway. Below, the Japanese cruiser *Mikuma*, en route to sinking.

U.S. NAVY (2)

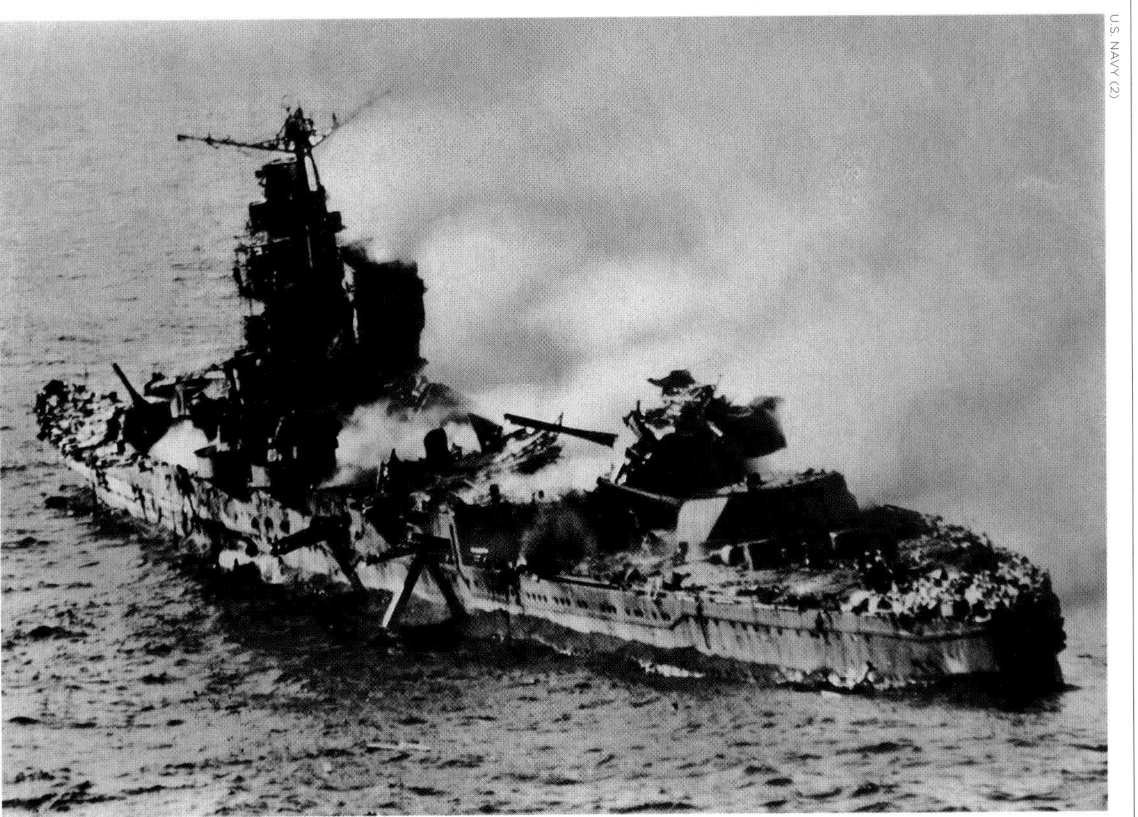

U.S. AIR FORCE

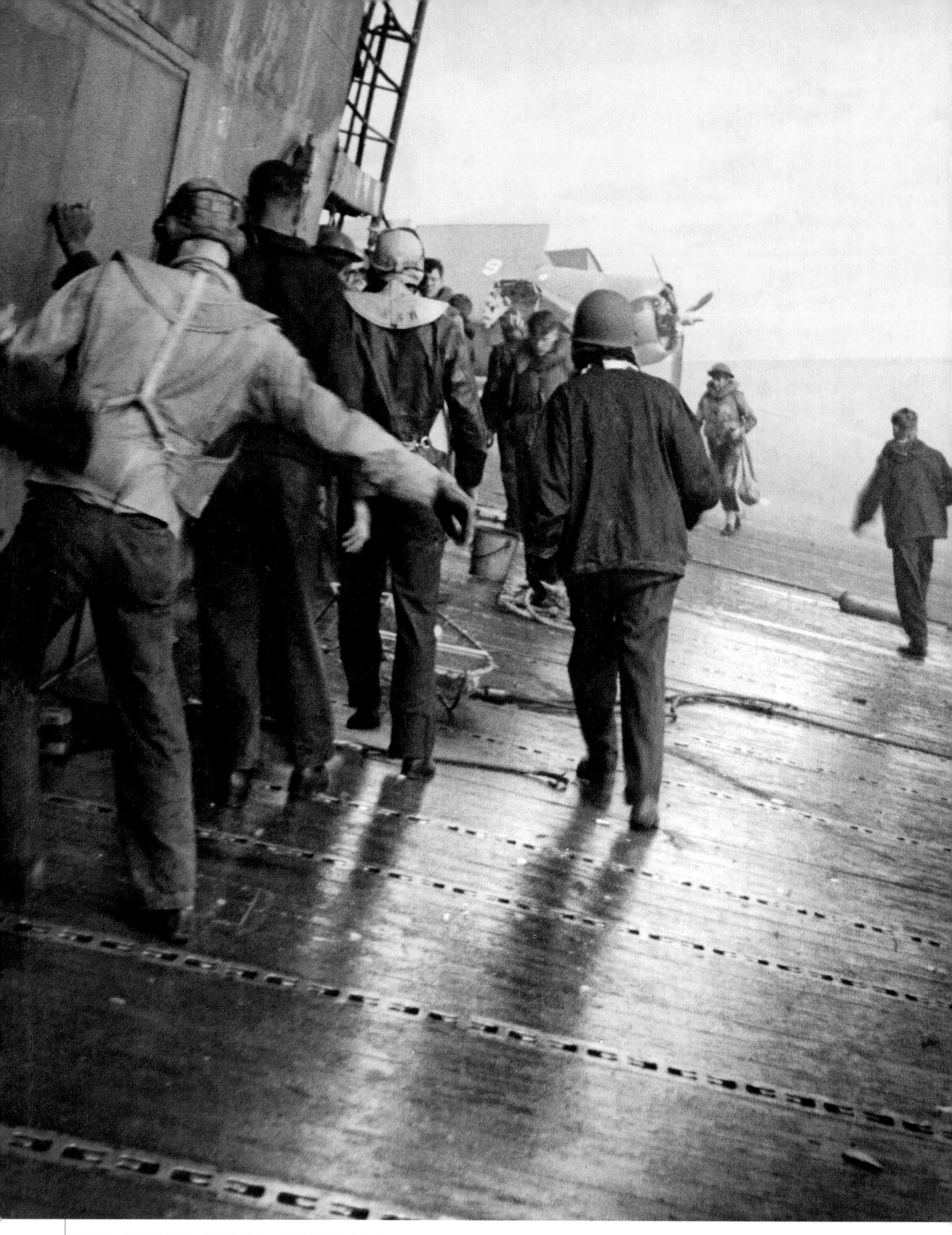

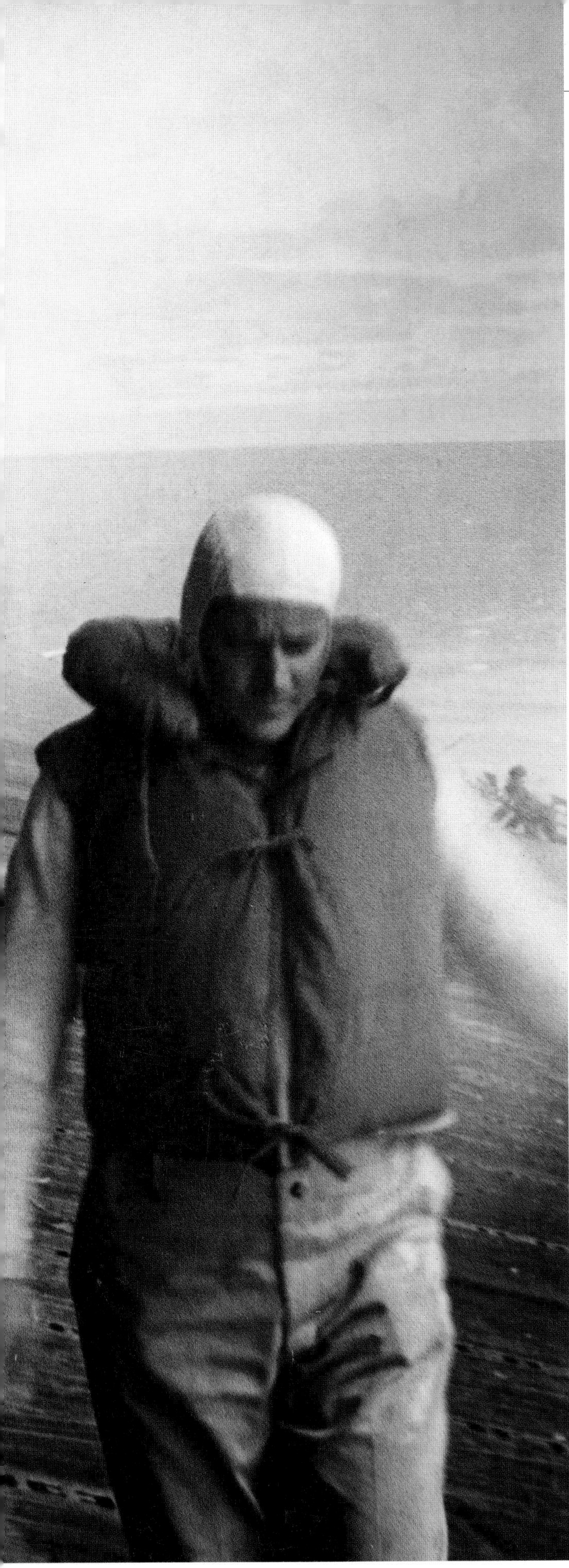

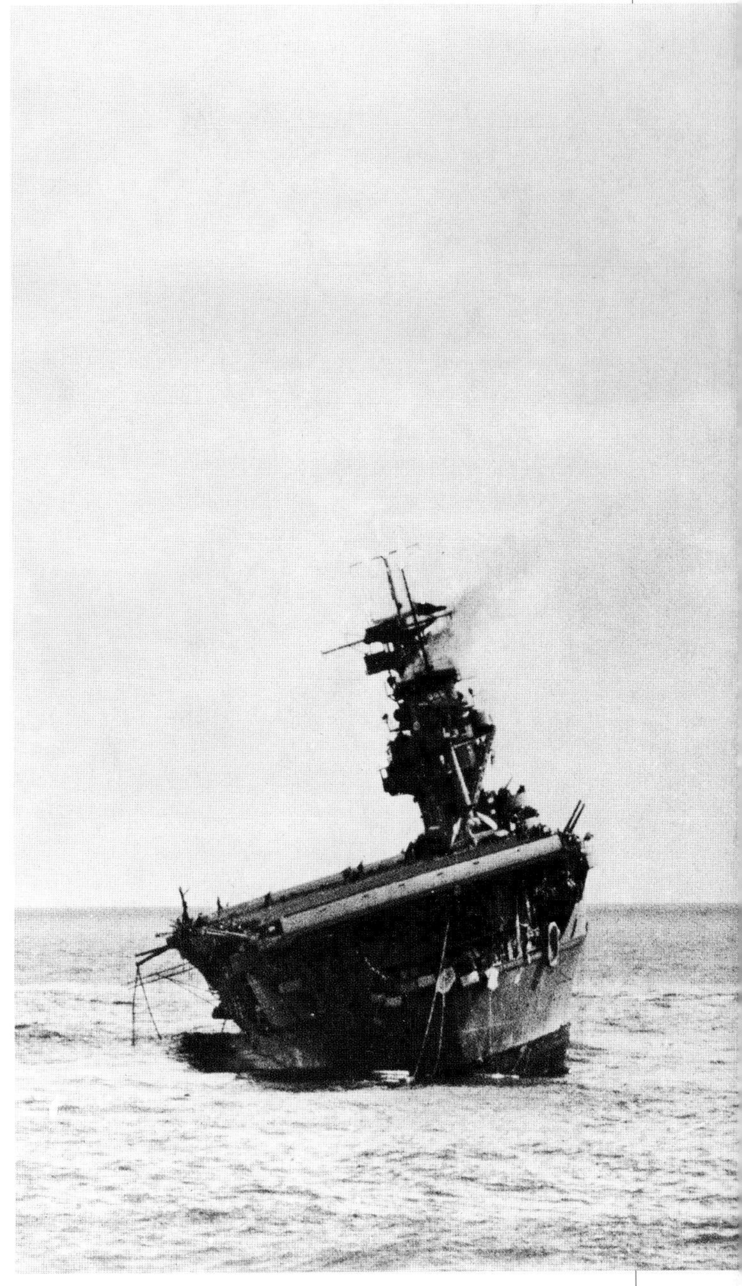

GREAT VICTORY—AT A COST
On June 4, the first day of the Midway battle, the carrier *Yorktown* was hit by a Japanese dive-bomber. The view at left was taken shortly afterward, as men traverse the listing flight deck in preparation for abandoning ship. Above, the *Yorktown*, powerless, surrounded by an oil slick, lists heavily to port. Three days later, a sub torpedoed the ship, sinking her. Still, it was the only flattop the U.S. lost; the Japanese lost a staggering four, and a hundred trained pilots. The Imperial Navy had suffered its worst defeat in 350 years. After Midway—perhaps the greatest naval victory in history—America and her allies had the upper hand in the Pacific.

U.S. NAVY (2)

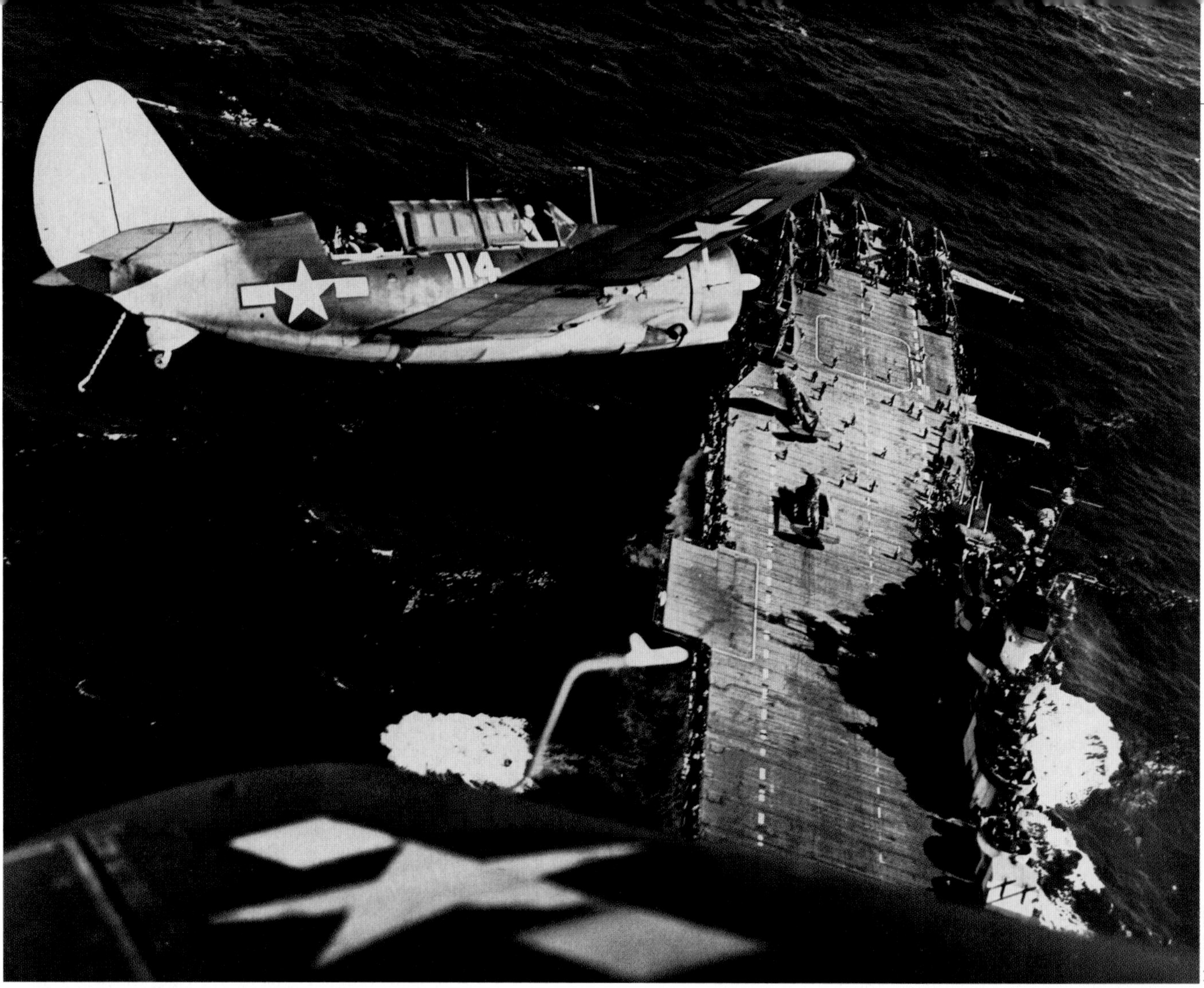

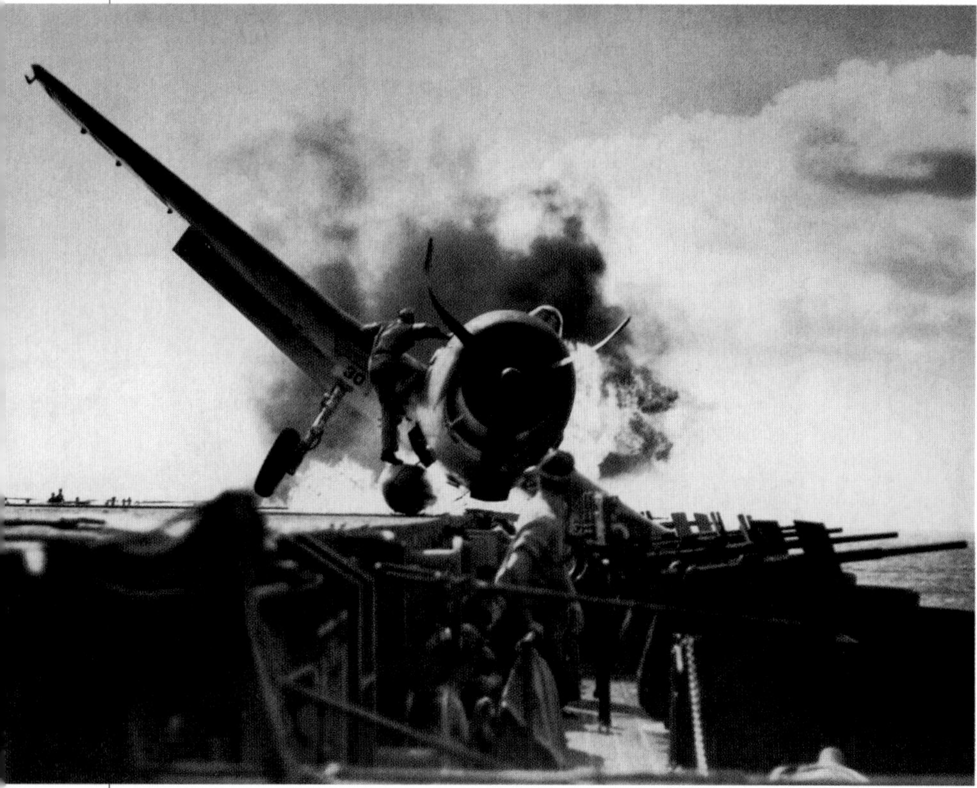

U.S. NAVY (2)

A FIGHT TO THE FINISH

In the wake of Midway, there commenced perhaps the most sustained naval offensive in history. Of course, the litany of victories was not without tears. At left, off the Gilbert Islands in November 1943, a Hellcat fighter was unable to clear the deck of the carrier *Enterprise* after being waved off from landing. Catapult officer Lt. Walter Chewning races up the plane into the flames to free the pilot, Ens. Byron Johnson, from the burning cockpit. The carrier, nicknamed the Big E, was the most decorated ship of World War II. In the photo opposite, a Japanese torpedo plane goes down in flames in 1944 action near Saipan, in the Marianas. Above, Helldivers bank over the *Hornet* in January 1945 after carrying out strikes on Japanese shipping in the China Sea. The plane, which first saw action in November '43, was the last and most advanced of the carrier-based dive-bombers.

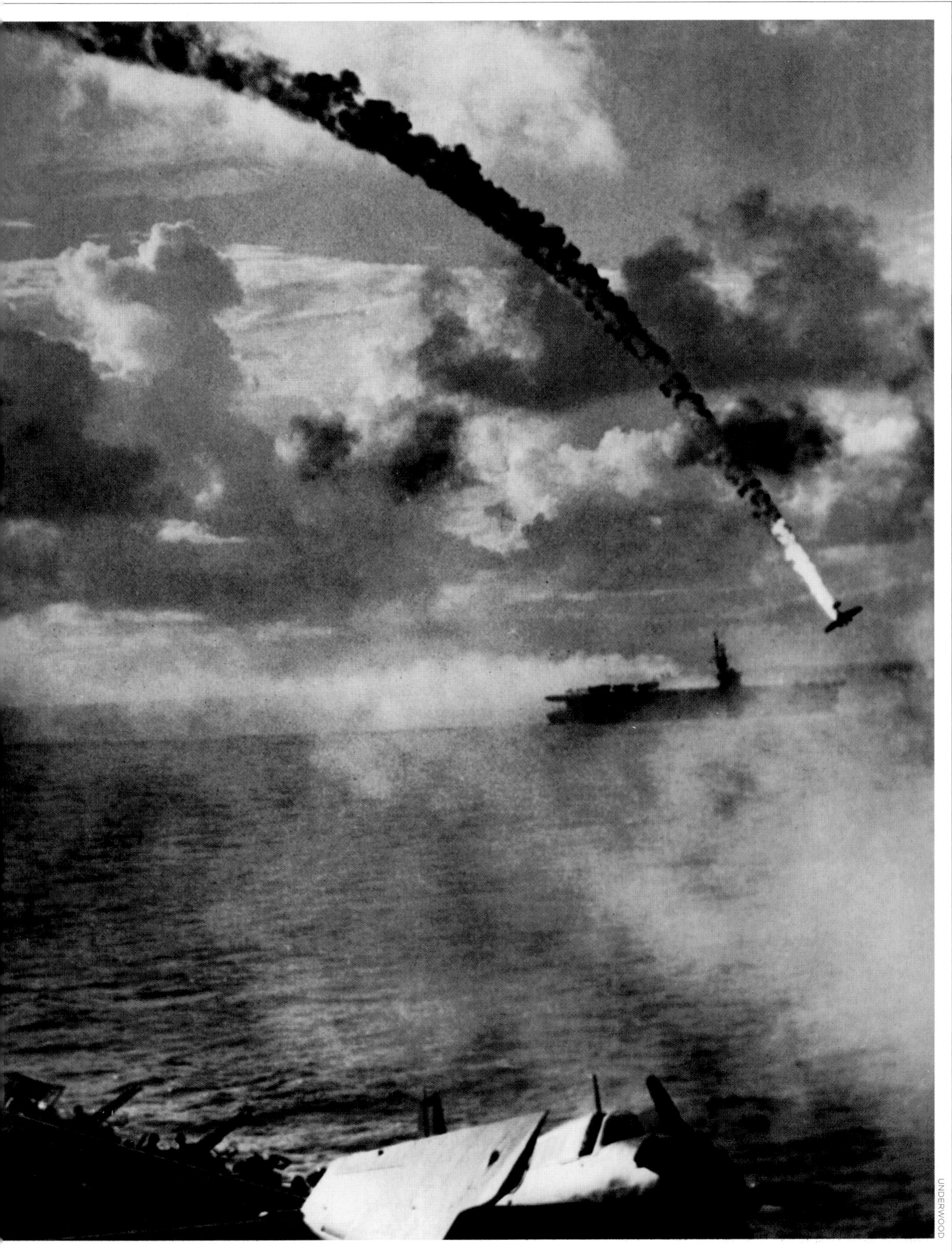

UNDERWOOD

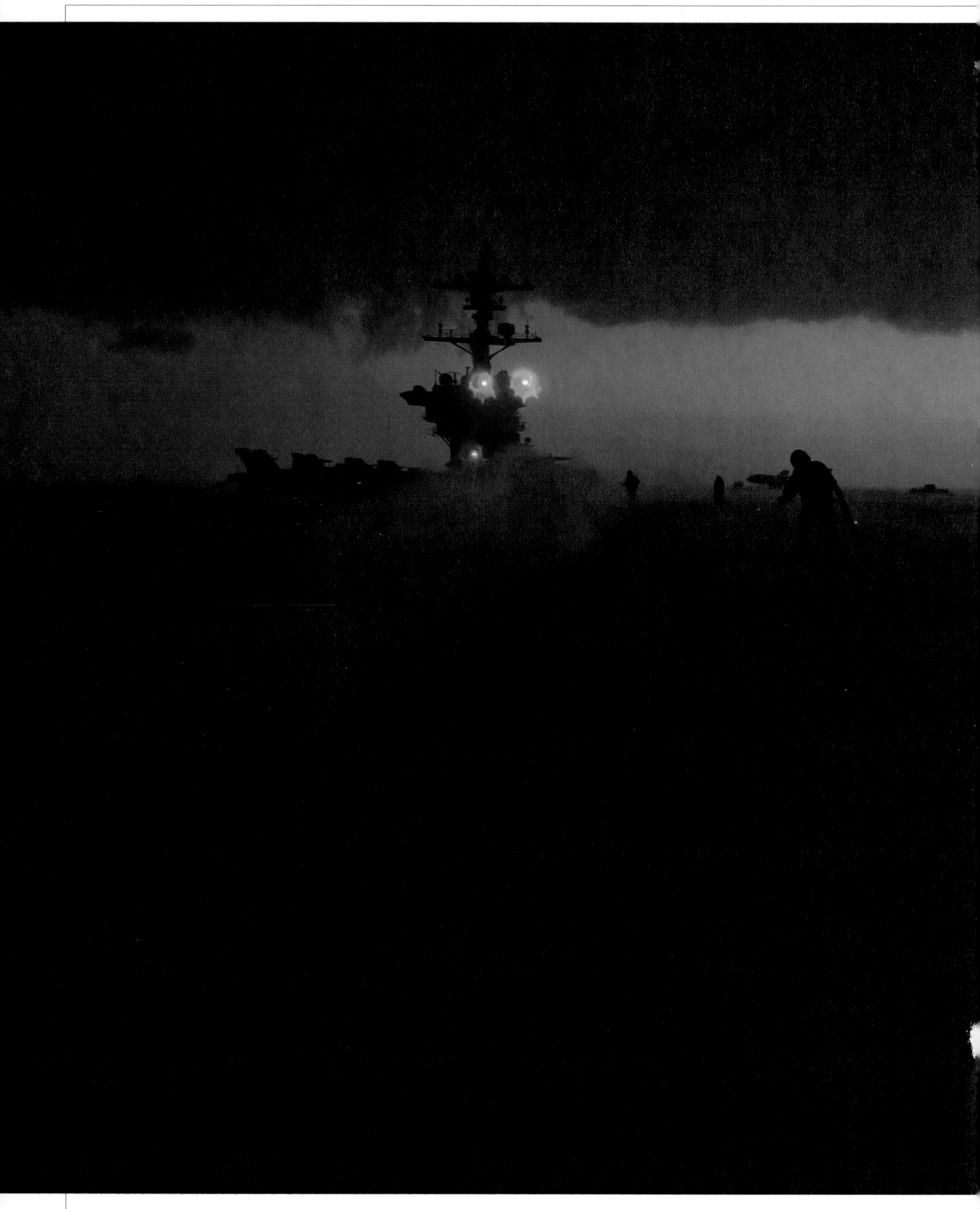

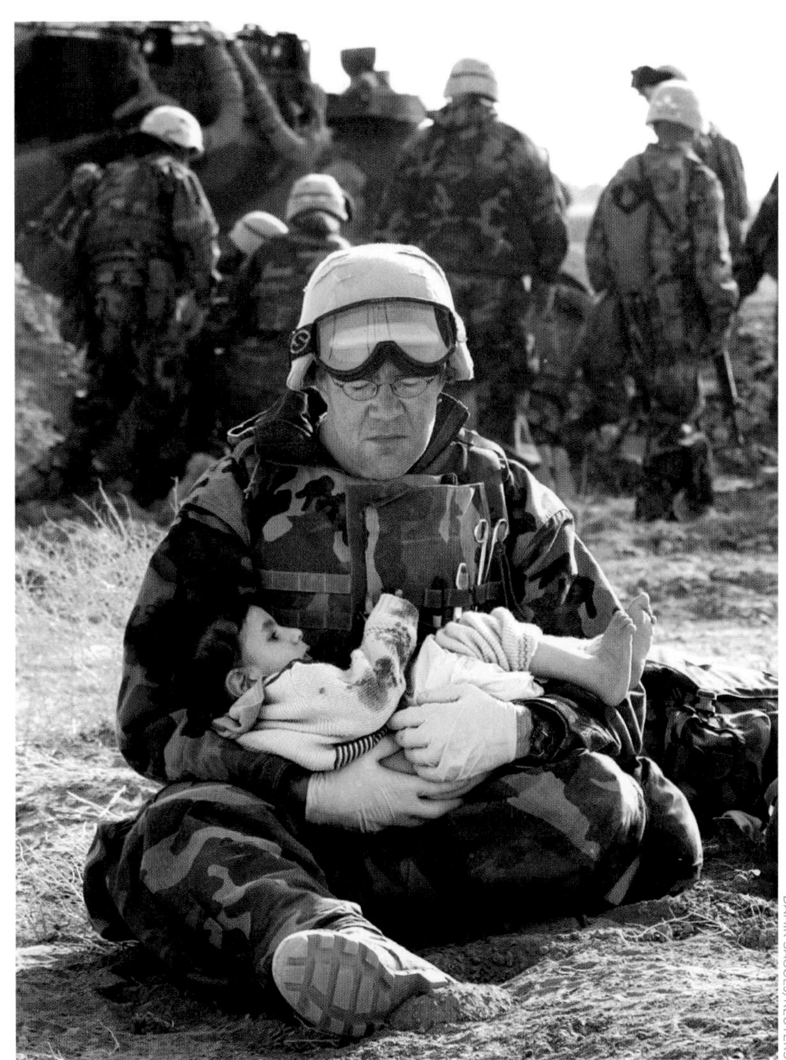

DAMIR SAGOLJ/REUTERS

AT SEA AND ON THE GROUND

As America's involvement in Afghanistan and Iraq escalated, Navy forces were there to assist in ways both traditional and less so. Throughout these wars, the Navy carried out a variety of so-called "irregular warfare and counterterrorism" activities, many of them taking place on shore, with individual sailors assigned to Marine and Army operations, and others serving as part of the Navy Expeditionary Combat Command. By October of 2010, there were 15,000 sailors serving on the ground in Afghanistan, Iraq and the Horn of Africa, and another 12,000 in vessels on nearby seas. At left, sailors work on the deck of the aircraft carrier *Carl Vinson,* part of a strike group under the direction of the Navy's 5th Fleet, as it passes through a storm in the Arabian Sea. Above: Navy Hospital Corpsman Richard Barnett, assigned to the 1st Marine Division, holds an Iraqi child, one member of a family caught in a crossfire in central Iraq.

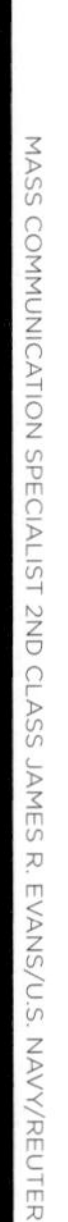

MASS COMMUNICATION SPECIALIST 2ND CLASS JAMES R. EVANS/U.S. NAVY/REUTERS

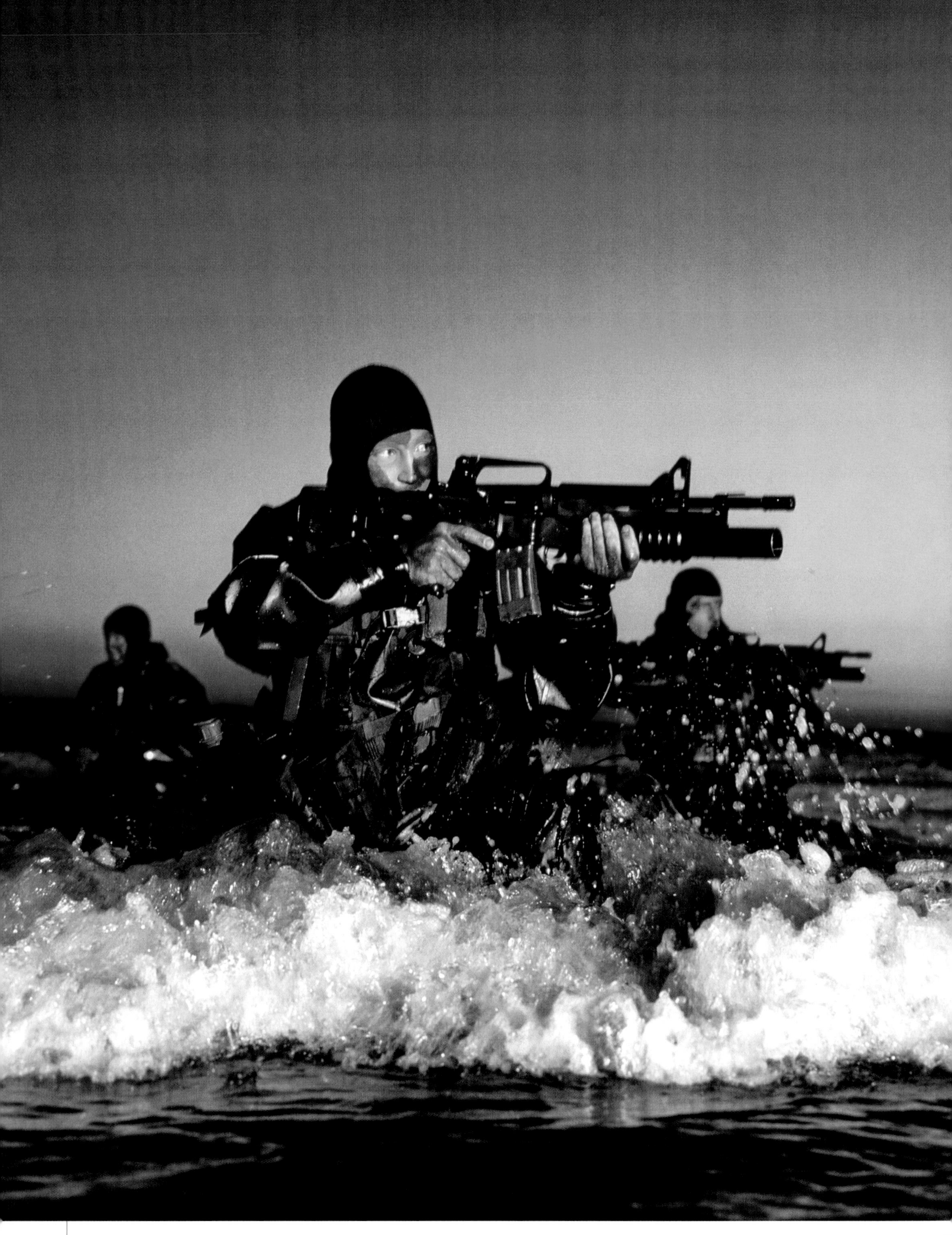

THE MIGHTY SEALS

As the only remaining superpower, America asks much of its Navy—security, yes, but intelligence and peacekeeping missions, too. Also, as has become famously evident in recent years: stealth soirees of almost superhuman courage and sophistication. Meet the Navy Seals (well, you can't really meet them, as their identities are as supersecret as the work they do). These commandoes train to an almost inhuman degree of strength and precision, then execute the most daring assignments, often in the dead of night. All of this came to light in the aftermath of the Seals' greatest hit: the attack on a compound in Abbottabad, Pakistan, and the killing of al-Qaeda leader Osama bin Laden on May 2, 2011. Once the U.S. had developed what it considered sound intelligence that bin Laden was probably in the gated enclave, an operation involving 79 Seals in four helicopters was rehearsed—over and over again—that would allow all of the Americans to get in and out in a half hour. In the event, they needed an extra 10 minutes. The helicopters buzzed in under cover of darkness. One malfunctioned and was forced to "hard land"; it would be useless during getaway. The Seals moved on, and people opposing them were killed. Bin Laden was found on the third floor and was shot in the head and chest; his body was taken to the helicopter and later that morning was buried in the Arabian Sea. Within days if not hours, everyone knew about—and was awed by—the Navy's Seals. Right, above: Part of the damaged helicopter lies near the compound where bin Laden was killed. Right: Navy Seals train in a makeshift compound in preparation for the assault in Abbottabad.

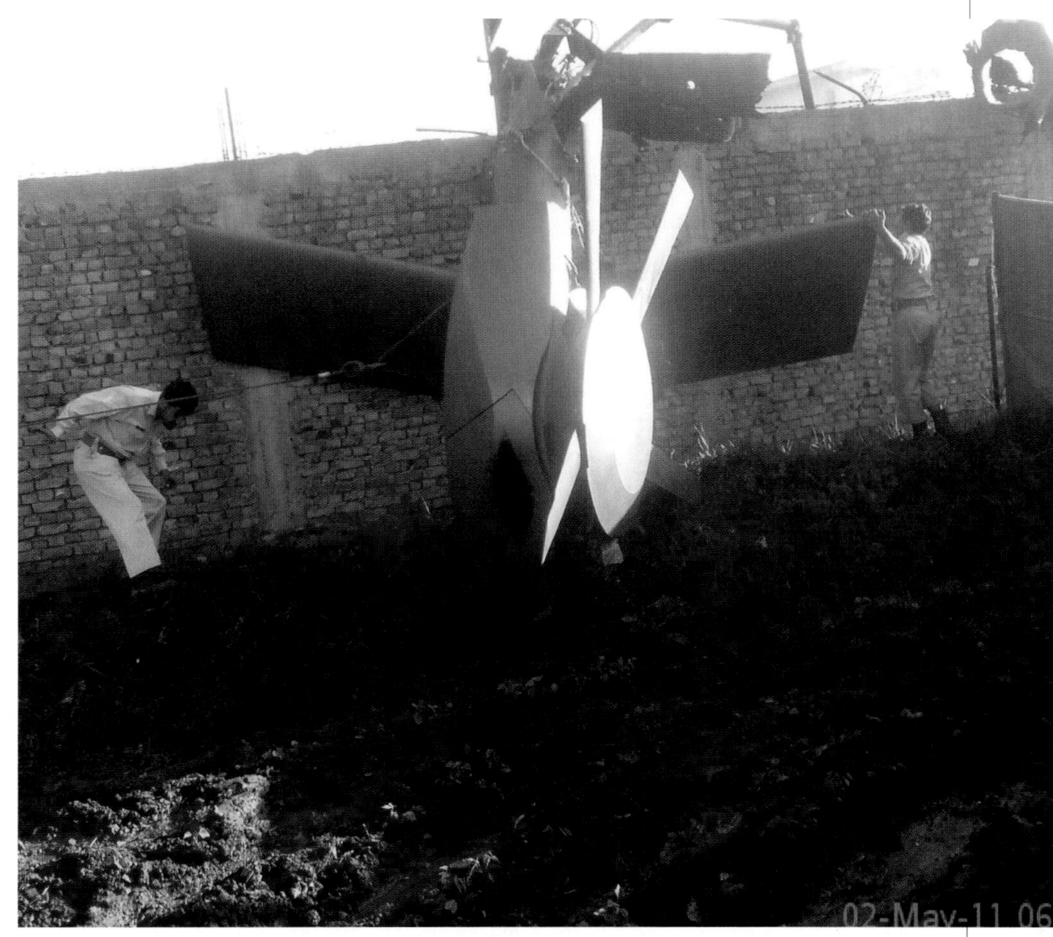

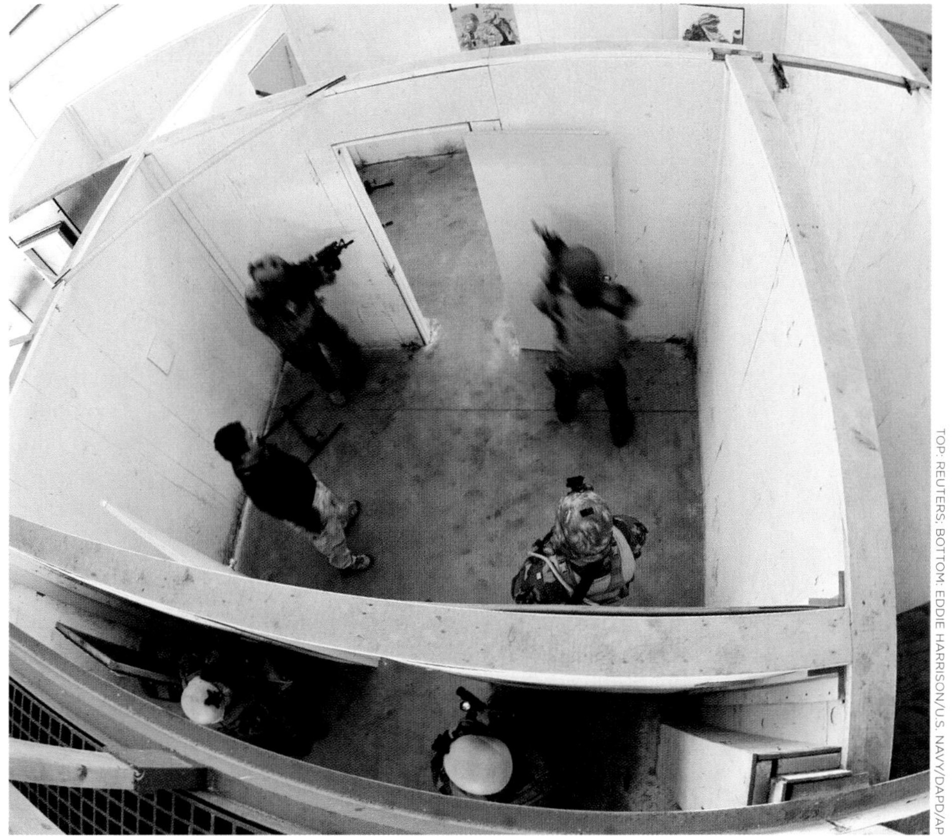

TOP: REUTERS; BOTTOM: EDDIE HARRISON/U.S. NAVY/DAPD/AP

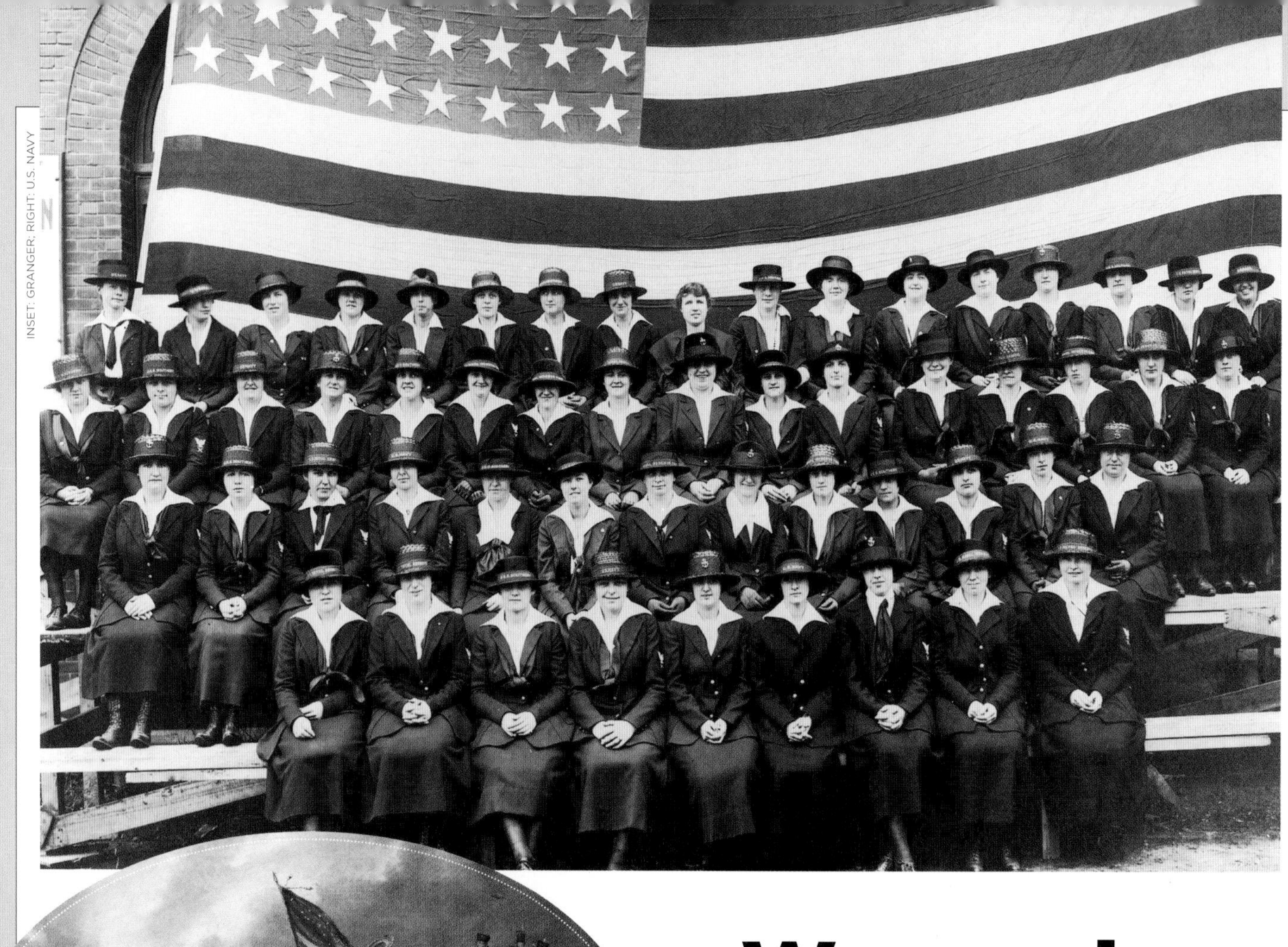

INSET: GRANGER; RIGHT: U.S. NAVY

Women in the Military

Nearly two million women have served in the armed forces. Their contribution has been immense.

THE STORY OF Molly Pitcher is delightful, but as with many legendary figures it has become so embroidered—a cameo by George Washington, who gives her a hatful of gold coins—that it is difficult to tell fact from fiction. Such is not the case, however, with the many other women who have given themselves to their country. In 1778, Deborah Samson of Massachusetts disguised herself as a man for three years in the Revolutionary War. She was wounded twice (once by a sword to the head) and later received a pension and land for her service. In the Civil War, some 250 women in the Confederate army alone may have enlisted as men. In the Spanish-American War, the Army recruited more than a thousand women as nurses, albeit without military status. That inequality began to be righted in WWI when 13,000 women enlisted in the Navy and Marines; they wore a uniform blouse with insignia and had the same status as men. By World War II, women served in every branch and all over the world. Today, one of six members of the armed forces is a woman, and in 2013 Defense Secretary Leon Panetta eliminated the final hurdle when he "officially" cleared them for ground combat roles. Of course, many women had fought or even died for their country already.

Her real name is unknown, but legend has dubbed her Molly Pitcher (inset, in 1778) because she brought water to fighting men. When her husband went down, she took over at the cannon. Top: yeomen at Maine's Portsmouth Navy Yard in 1918. Opposite: a Women's Air Force Service Pilot in 1943.

PETER STACKPOLE

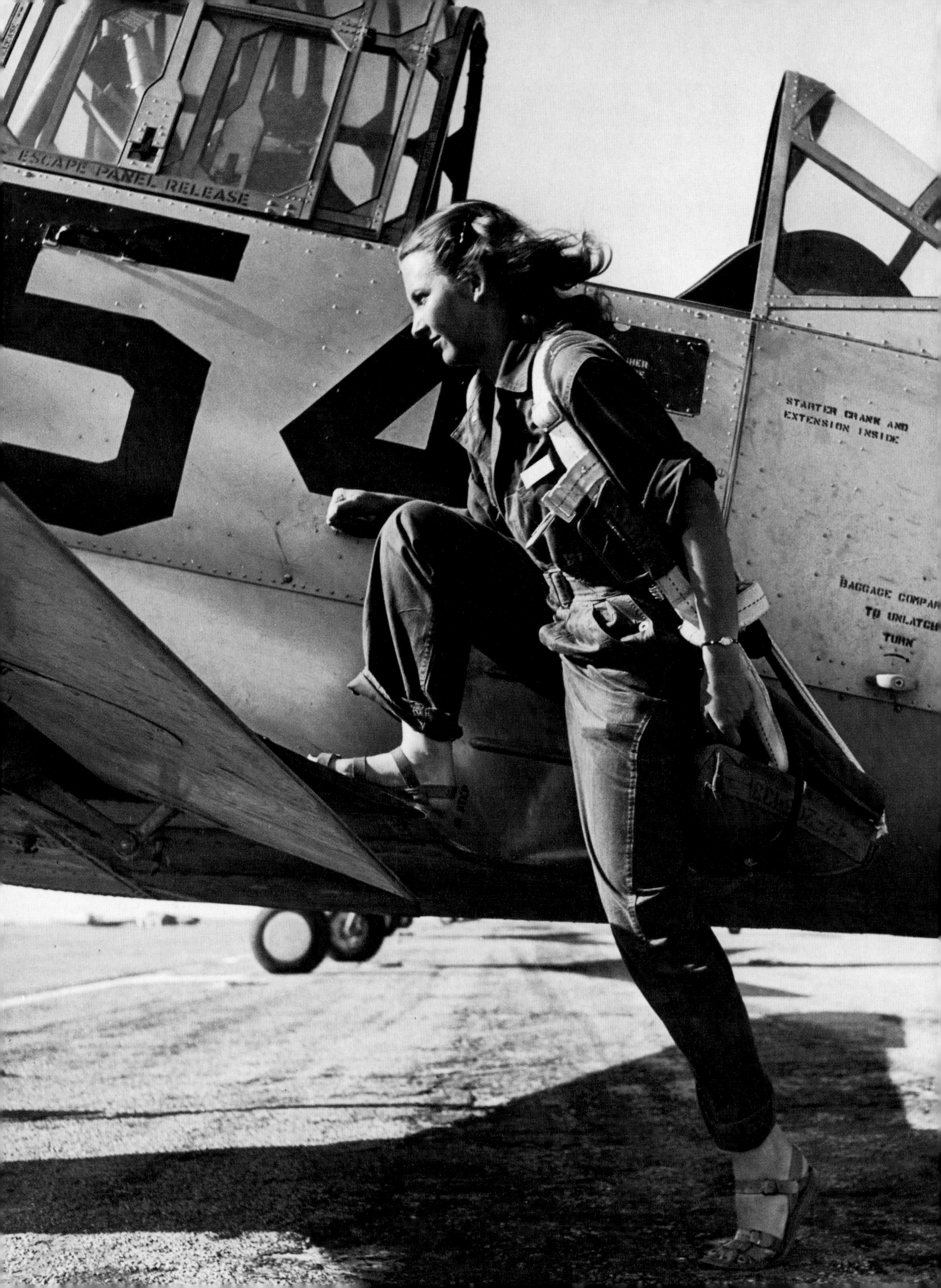
ESCAPE PANEL RELEASE
STARTER CRANK AND
EXTENSION INSIDE
TO UNLATCH
TURN

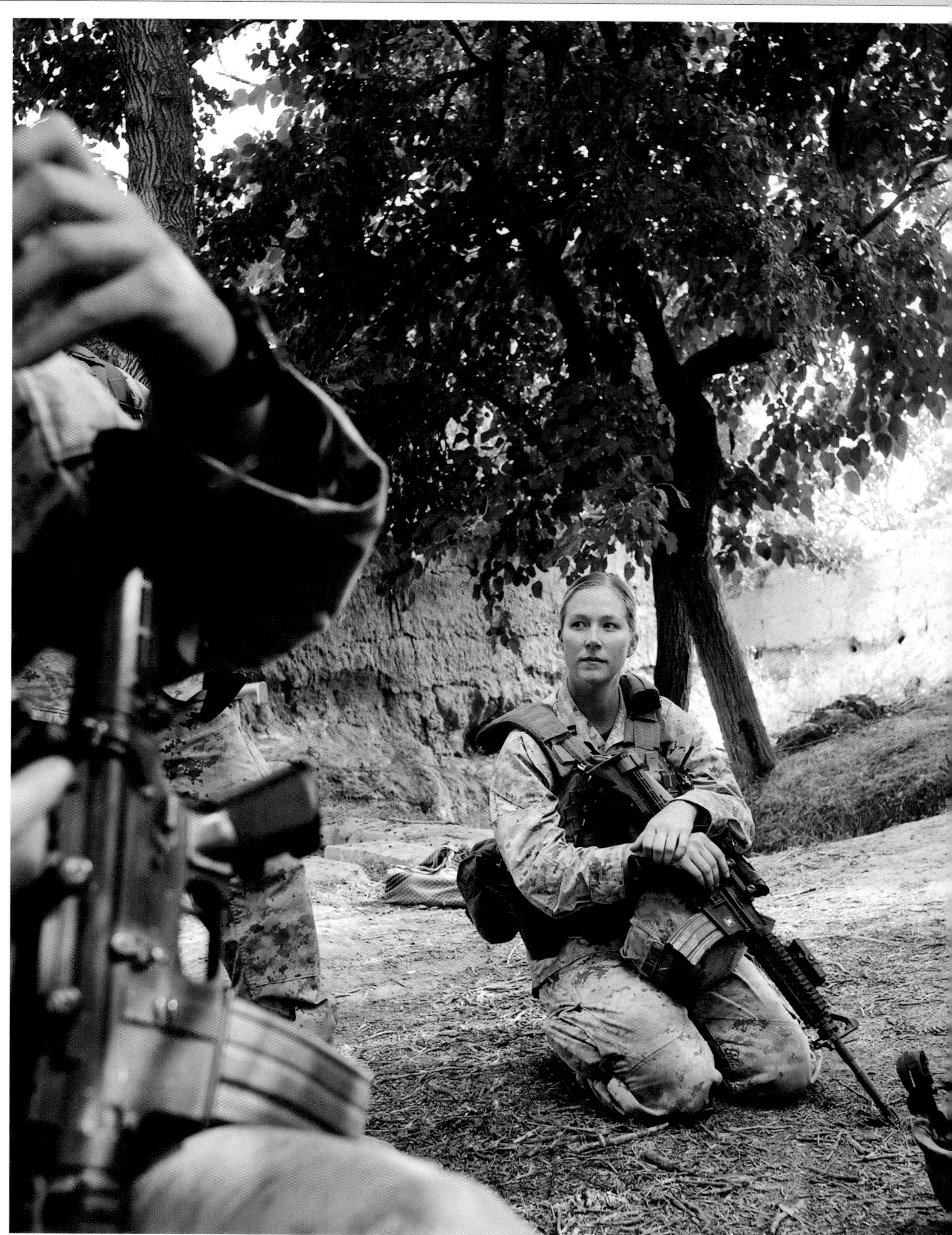

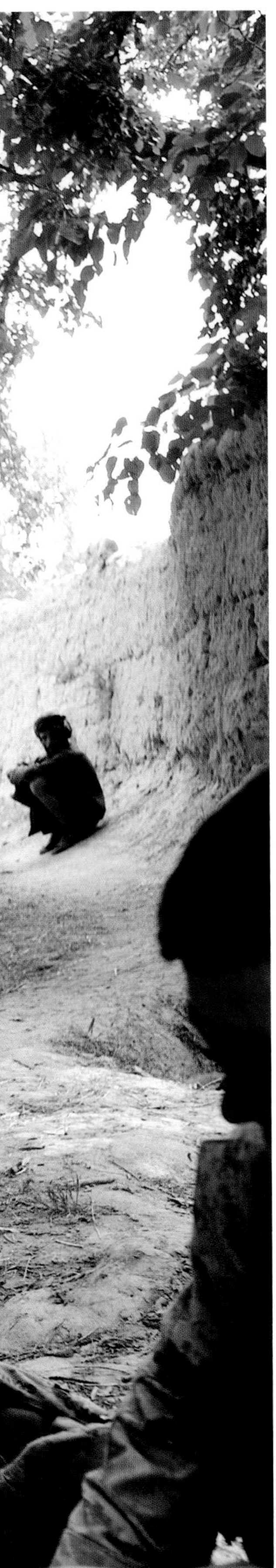
LYNSEY ADDARIO/VII

Left, in 2010, Marine Capt. Emily Naslund pauses during a patrol through the village of Soorkano in Afghanistan along with her male counterparts. Below: Lt. Linda McClory, serving with an Army MASH unit in 1991 near the Gulf War battlefront, tends to a wounded soldier. Right: Air Force reservist Joy Johnson holds her daughter Diana after returning to Charleston, S.C., from a transport mission to the Gulf. This kind of photograph has long been taken of fathers heading off to war. Now, heading into even ground combat assignments, women adopt the same, painful pose.

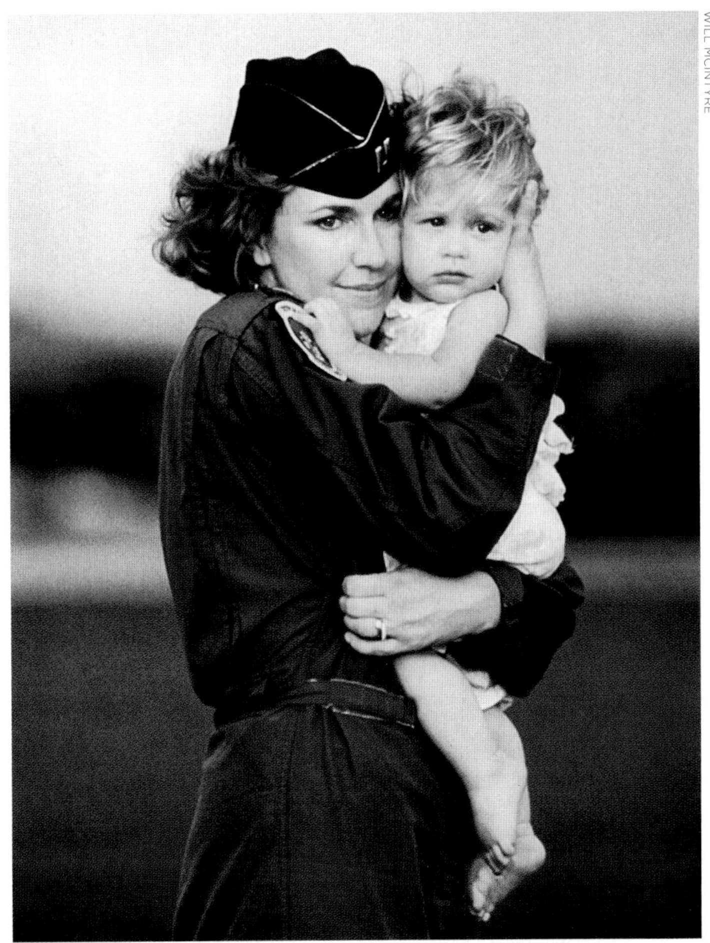
WILL MCINTYRE

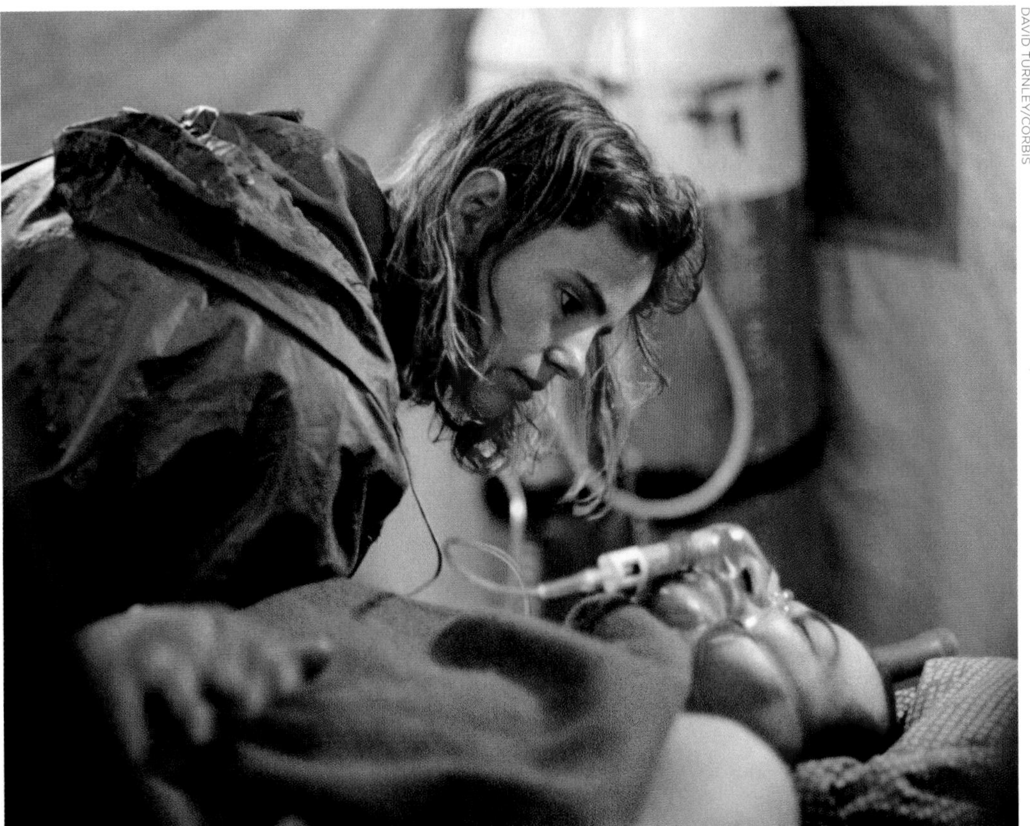
DAVID TURNLEY/CORBIS

THE MARINE CORPS

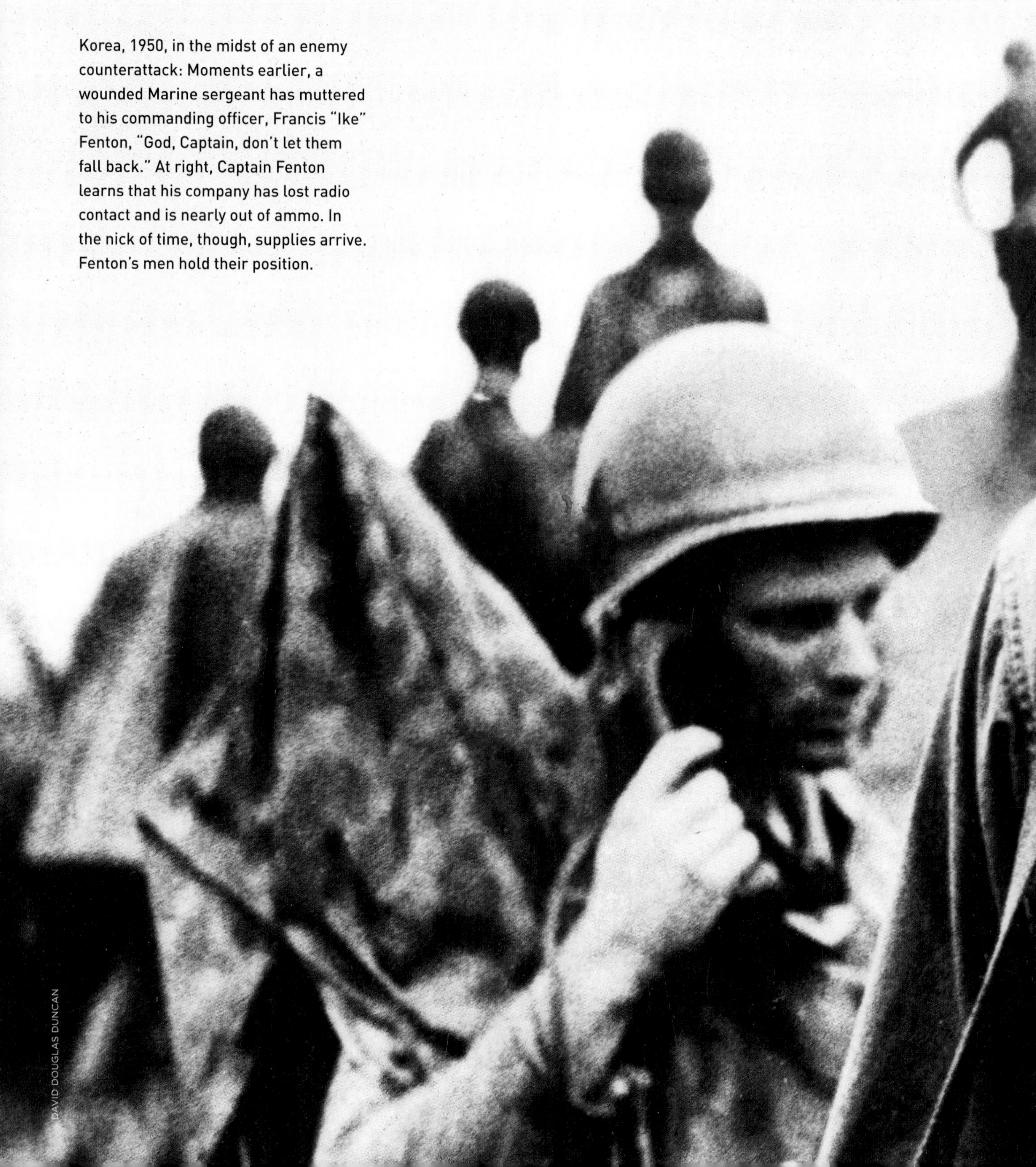

Korea, 1950, in the midst of an enemy counterattack: Moments earlier, a wounded Marine sergeant has muttered to his commanding officer, Francis "Ike" Fenton, "God, Captain, don't let them fall back." At right, Captain Fenton learns that his company has lost radio contact and is nearly out of ammo. In the nick of time, though, supplies arrive. Fenton's men hold their position.

DAVID DOUGLAS DUNCAN

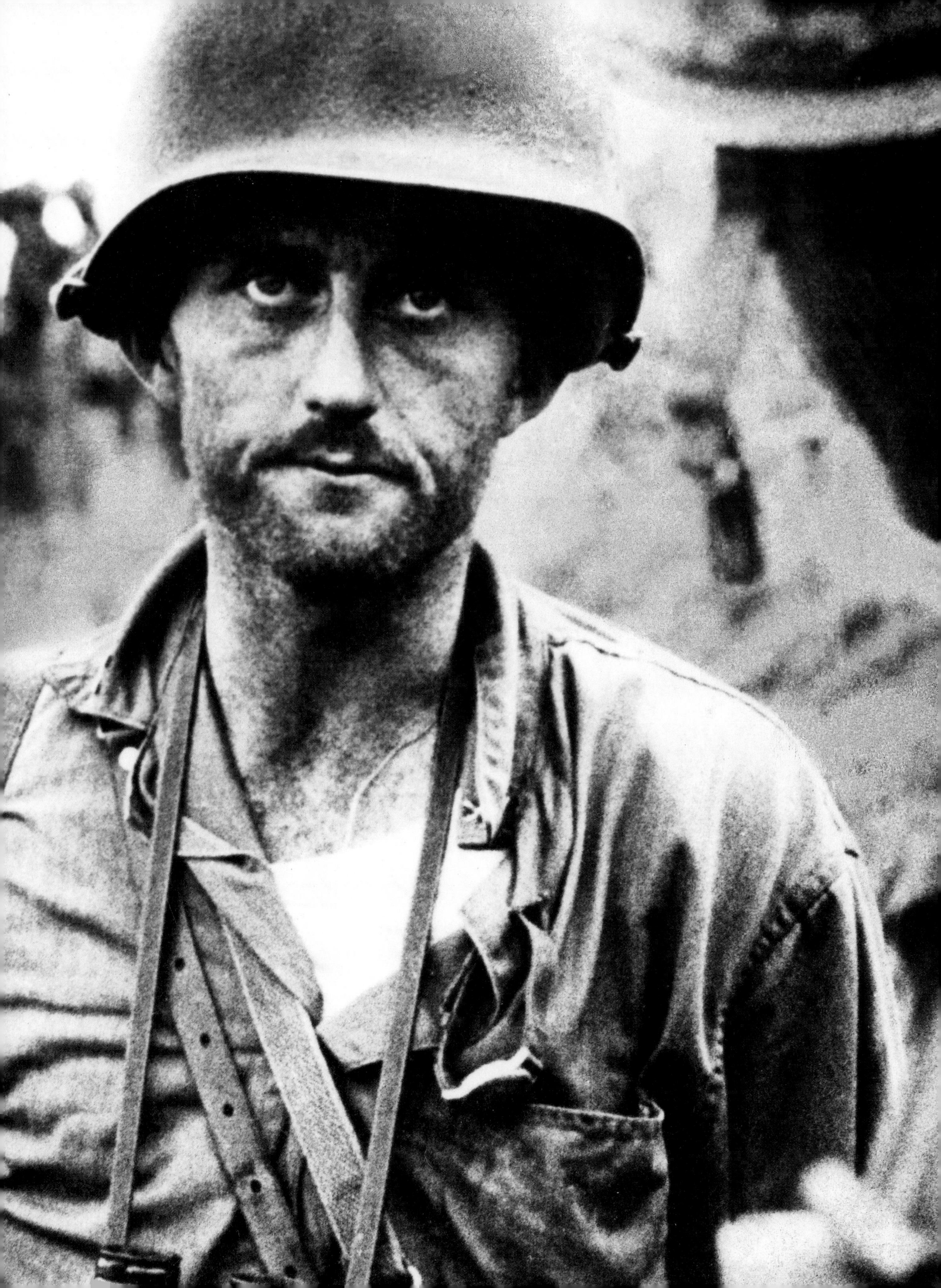

THE MARINE CORPS

"The Marines have landed and have the situation well in hand."

— *Richard Harding Davis*

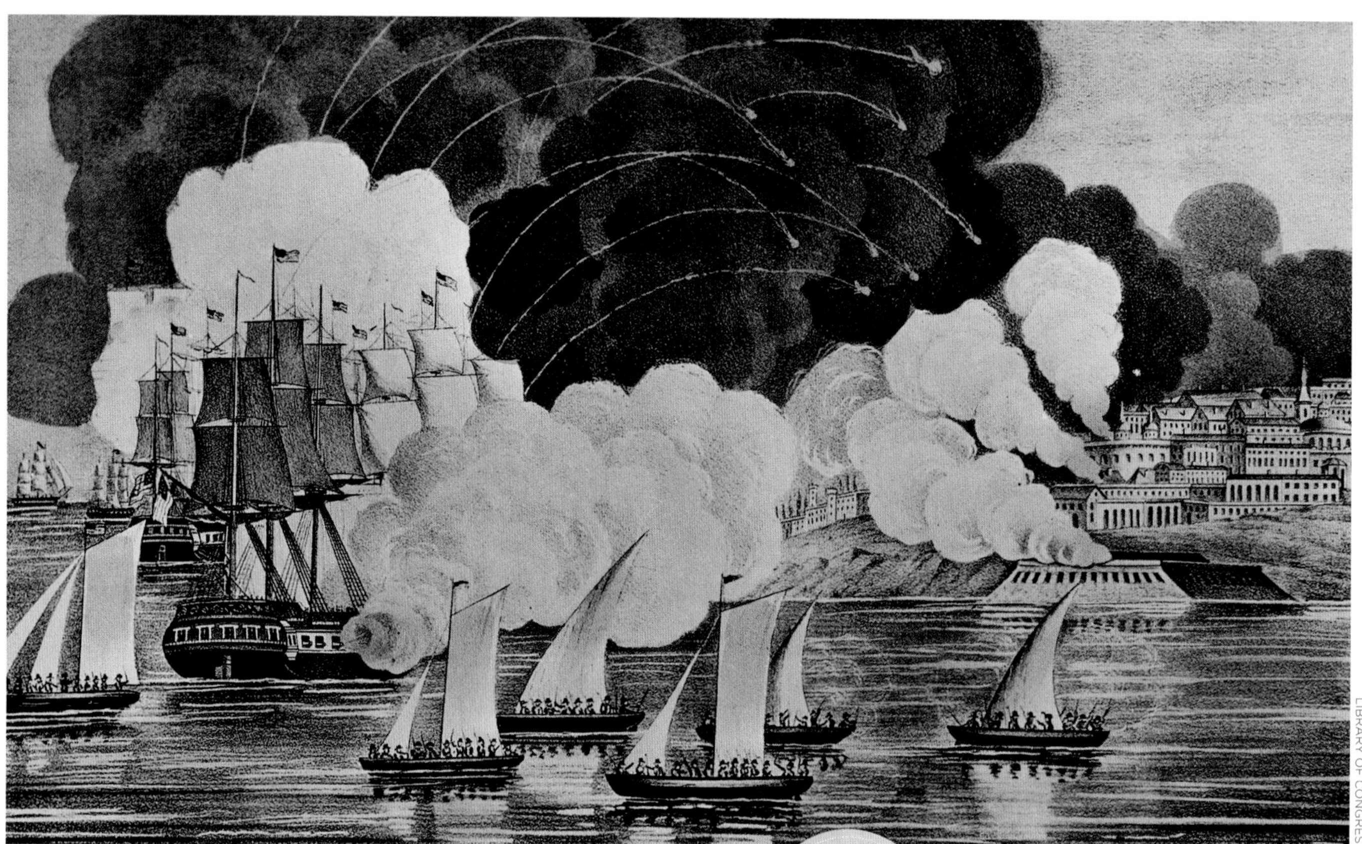

LIBRARY OF CONGRESS

O'Bannon became the first American to raise the flag over an Old World fort when he triumphed in Tripoli in 1805 (above). After a Marine battalion took part in 1848 in the attack on the National Palace during the Mexican War, the anonymous author of "The Marines' Hymn" ignored chronology when he wrote "From the halls of Montezuma to the shores of Tripoli"—the better to rhyme "Tripoli" with "sea."

ON OCTOBER 6, 1922, Earl "Pete" Ellis, a 41-year-old, lean 5'11" American with graying hair and a predilection for drink, suddenly abandoned a hospital bed to embark from Kobe, Japan, aboard the *Kasuga Maru*. Over the course of the next seven months, he would call on coconut plantations in the Mariana, Marshall, Caroline and Palau islands in the western Pacific, all seized from Germany during World War I by Japan, which was then an ally of Britain.

Ellis's passport listed his occupation as "commercial agent" residing in Pratt, Kans., and he said he was a copra buyer working for the Hughes Trading Company in New York City. In truth, Ellis was a Marine lieutenant colonel on a spy mission. But as World War II was to show, he was more than a spy. He was a tormented but strategic genius whose impact on warfare continues to this day.

The concept of using soldiers at sea dates back at least to 480 B.C., when Themistocles stationed archers aboard the Athenian galleys that vanquished the Persian fleet at Salamis. In 1664, King Charles II created what became the Royal Marines.

At the start of the American Revolution, the Continental Congress established "two Battalions of Marines . . . [to be] good seamen, or so acquainted with maritime affairs as to be able to serve to advantage by sea, when required." It was November 10, 1775, a day still celebrated by the successor U.S. Marine Corps as its birthday even though it came into being in 1798.

GRANGER

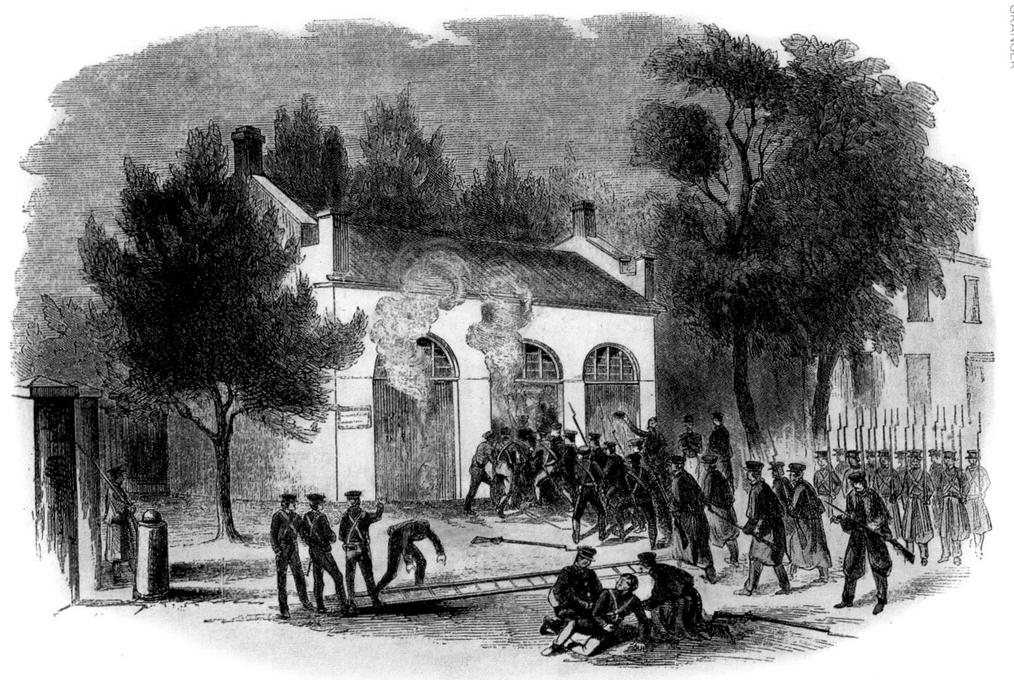

This Corps was to consist of 33 officers and 848 "noncommissioned officers, musicians and privates." They were to serve on Navy ships to enforce discipline among the uniformed sailors, act as sharpshooters in engagements with enemy ships, fire cannons if necessary, lead boarding parties and landings, man coastal defenses and to perform "any other duty on shore, as the President, at his discretion shall direct." The act was ambiguous in that Marines came under Naval Regulations while afloat but the Army Articles of War while ashore. In 1834, Congress ended the confusion by assigning the Marine Corps to the Navy Department, but as a separate service not part of the Navy. The nickname "leatherneck" is said to have come from a black leather collar they wore about the neck to protect the jugular from a slash.

From inception, Marines began to live up to the words of their hymn, "We have fought in every clime and place/Where we could take a gun." In 1805, Lt. Presley O'Bannon led seven Marines and several hundred mercenaries and camels on a 600-mile desert march from Egypt to topple the bey of Tripoli, a leader of the Barbary pirates. In 1848, Marines took part in the final attack on Chapultepec during the Mexican War. By the 1860s Marines had made an appearance or seen action at New Orleans and on lakes Erie and Ontario, in Haiti, Cuba, the Galapagos, the Marquesas, Puerto Rico, Greece, Florida, Sumatra, Panama, Samoa, the Philippines, Antarctica, Nicaragua, Uruguay, Paraguay, the Fiji Islands and China. They accompanied Commodore Matthew Perry to the opening of Japan, and they sailed with the Mediterranean Squadron and the Africa Squadron on antislave patrol.

For much of this time, from 1820 till his death in 1859, Archibald Henderson, a red-haired Virginian, served as Commandant, the longest tenure of any by far. At the outset of the Civil War, the Corps he had bequeathed to the nation—approximately 1,800 officers and men—suffered the loss of almost a third of its force, Henderson's three sons among them, to the Confederate Marines.

In the 19th century, Henderson (below) made the settling of domestic disputes a regular assignment. In 1824, Marines from the Boston Navy Yard quelled a mutiny in the state prison. Above: In 1859, under the command of U.S. Army Col. Robert E. Lee and his aide Lt. Jeb Stuart, 86 Marines end John Brown's uprising at Harpers Ferry. Marine Lt. Israel Greene struck Brown with his sword as he was attempting to reload.

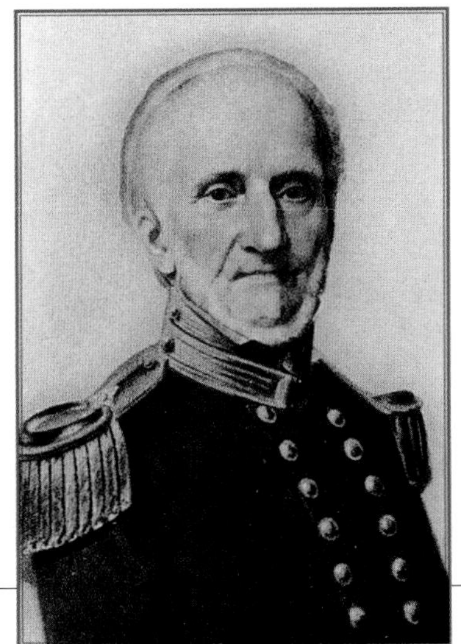

With U.S. Marines never numbering more than 4,000—the Confederate counterpart had 539—"the Corps gained little in the way of reputation," according to Edwin Howard Simmons, a retired brigadier general and former director of the Marine Corps History and Museums Division. "In 1864, there was a Congressional resolution introduced to transfer the Marine Corps to the Army. After debate, the resolution was tabled, but the thought did not go away."

Between the close of the Civil War and the start of the Spanish-American War, the Corps undertook what an old *Guidebook for Marines* quaintly termed "scattered actions," so many, in fact, that Richard Harding Davis came up with that bit about the Marines landing and the situation thus being well in hand. As listed in the book *Soldiers of the Sea* by Col. Robert Debs Heinl Jr., a 1937 Yale graduate (the Corps has long had a strong cast of Ivy League and Southern officers), landings began in Formosa in 1867 and went on to include, sometimes with repeat visits, Korea, Japan, Uruguay, Mexico, Colombia, Hawaii, Samoa, Argentina, Chile, Navassa

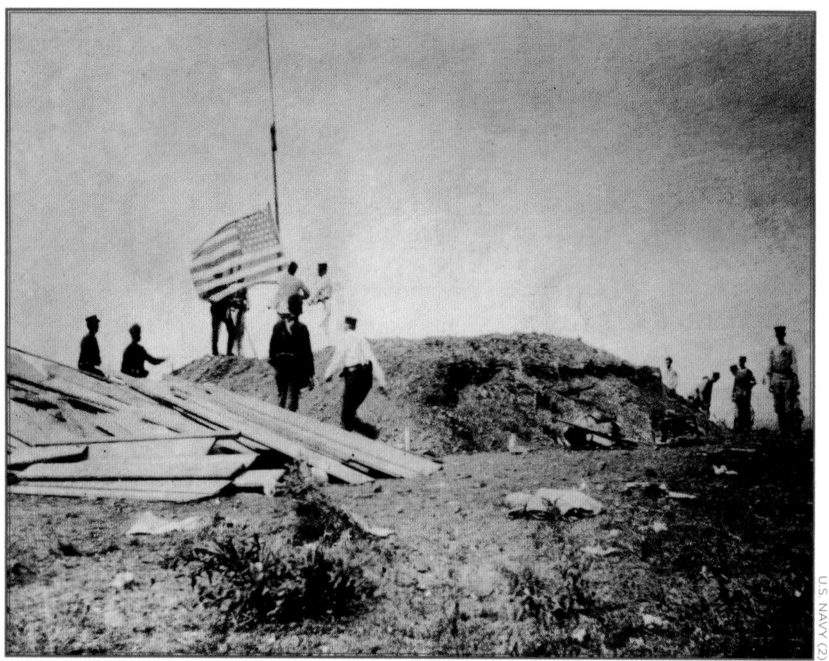

U.S. NAVY (2)

Island, Panama, Nicaragua, China and Egypt.

The first visit to Korea, in 1871, was to avenge insult when forts in the closed "Hermit Kingdom" fired upon a Navy party escorting a U.S. diplomat seeking a treaty of amity and commerce. With no apology forthcoming, Marines took action, with the result of more than 260 Koreans killed or captured; 481 cannons, two dating back to the year 1313, taken or spiked; a huge Korean flag hauled down by a private and a corporal under fire; and six Marines awarded Medals of Honor. That same year, Marines dodged bottles and bricks as they stormed into Brooklyn's Irishtown to allow federal agents to destroy illegal stills.

Having taken Guantánamo, troops commanded by Col. R.W. Huntington (below) raise a flag over Camp McCalla. A few years later President Theodore Roosevelt amended the Monroe Doctrine, allowing Western Hemisphere intervention in the event of "chronic wrongdoing." The unshackled Marines became cops of the Caribbean, engendering great resentment of the United States.

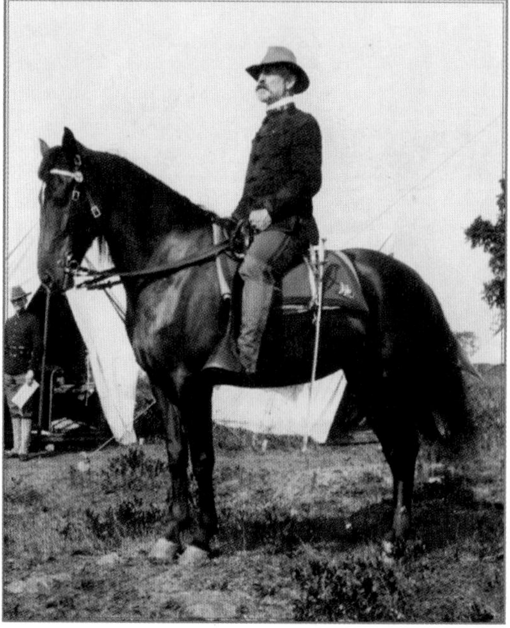

U.S. MARINES

Against Spain in 1898, Marines were the first to land in Cuba, where they seized Guantánamo Bay, for a century the site of a U.S. base; in the Philippines they captured the arsenal at Cavite, later followed by a bloody expedition on the island of Samar against Moro insurrectionists who had ambushed an Army company at breakfast, sliced open several officers and poured jam into their guts. A Marine battalion led by a feisty major from Virginia with the grand name of Littleton Waller Tazewell Waller went after the Moros and, in Waller's words, "drove those devils from point to point," sending them fleeing from their fortress above the Basey River. Upon receiving an Army order to find a telegraph route across the supposedly pacified but unmapped mountainous island, Waller, five officers and 50 men began a trek beset by mutinous bearers, swollen rivers, lost provisions and fever that cost 10 Marines their lives and one his mind. Out of the jungle and convinced that some remaining guides and Filipinos had plotted against his contingent, Waller had 11 of them shot. Returning to Cavite, he drew cheers from the Navy but the charge of murder from the Army. Labeled "the Butcher of Samar" by the press, he was court-martialed. He was acquitted, though the accusation cost him the chance to become Commandant. In tribute to Waller, however, whenever an officer of his battalion appeared at mess, it became custom to offer the toast, "Stand, gentlemen, he served on Samar."

In France in WWI, the 4th Brigade of Marines, composed of the 5th and 6th Regiments and the 6th Machine Gun Battalion, distinguished themselves beyond their numbers at the battles of Belleau Wood, Soissons, St. Mihiel, Blanc Mont and the Meuse-Argonne. In June 1918, as part of the Army's 2nd Division, the two regiments were rushed to the front to face Germans who had broken through a French division near the Paris-Metz road and seemed ready to capture the capital and end the war. The Marines not only stopped the Germans but advanced to take Belleau Wood. In the postwar years, Marines served aboard ships in China, fought anew in Nicaragua and even rode U.S. mail trains to stop an outbreak of robberies.

As an ally of Great Britain during the war, Japan had seized Germany's Pacific island colonies, thus extending her empire halfway across the ocean to Hawaii. In 1919, the Navy began reviewing War Plan Orange, its basic strategy in the event of war with Japan.

Enter Pete Ellis, who had won the Navy Cross in France and had earlier studied and taught at the Naval War College. In Washington in 1920, with War Plan Orange under revision, Ellis wrote a secret 50,000-word paper, "Advanced Base Operations in Micronesia." In it he predicted that Japan would attack the United States, and with that premise he went on to establish the basis for amphibious warfare. Approved in 1921 as Operations Plan 712, it became the blueprint for the American World War II campaign in the Pacific and for Allied landings in North Africa and Europe.

Military thinking had theretofore held that seaborne assault troops could not take a well defended land position, a belief only reinforced by the Allied disaster at Gallipoli in World War I, when the Turks inflicted more than a quarter million casualties and forced the invaders back to sea (and planner Winston Churchill to political exile). Ellis, instead of holding that the Marines' principal mission was to defend advanced bases, called for the creation of an amphibious force that would create new bases for the Navy: "It will be necessary for us to protect our fleet and landing forces across the Pacific and wage war in Japanese waters. To effect this requires that we have sufficient bases to support the fleet, both during its projection and afterwards." In the words of biographers Dirk A. Ballendorf and Merrill L. Bartlett, "he emphasized the value of the element of surprise and rapidity of execution . . . Ellis admonished fleet commanders to approach the amphibious objective area under cover of darkness and to land at daybreak: 'Night landings in force are dangerous unless the coast conditions and the enemy defenses are well known.' His disquisition on tactics concludes with the advice for quick offensive action inland: '[It] confuses the defense in general but the counterattack forces in particular.'"

Ellis then undertook his spy mission to see if the Japanese were violating a treaty by fortifying their newly acquired islands. Tailed by local secret police, the would-be copra buyer spent seven months touring the islands, often boozing it up and acting weirdly. On May 12, 1923, he apparently drank himself to death with two bottles of whiskey the Japanese gave to him. Another school holds that the Japanese poisoned him.

Ellis was gone, but his contribution had been made. In the 1930s, under Commandant John H. Russell, the Marines refined their approach to amphibious warfare. On the lookout for better landing craft, Marine brass were intrigued by a 1937 LIFE photo of an amphibious vehicle in the Everglades. This craft evolved into the "amtrac," which carried initial assault waves to the beaches of the Pacific in WWII. The Marines under Gen. Alexander Vandergrift landed on Guadalcanal in the Solomon Islands in August 1942, in the first of a series of bloody island-takings across the Pacific to the doorstep of Japan.

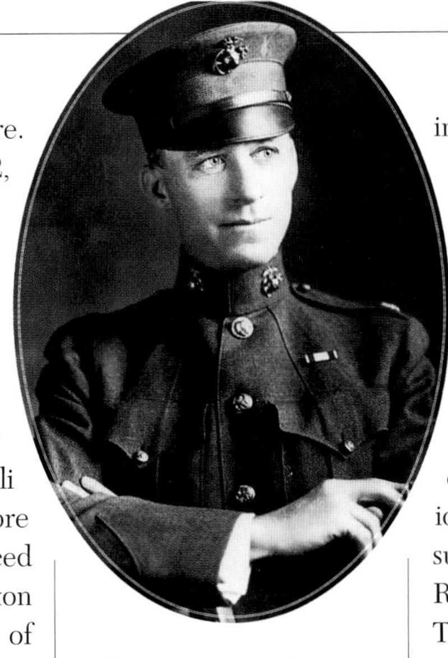

Ellis was a tactical genius and a real piece of work. His fondness for alcohol occasionally led to hospitalization or bizarre behavior. Once, at what he deemed to be a boring dinner with a chaplain, he enlivened the evening by shooting dishes off the table—or so the legend has it. On the island of Palau in the early 1920s, he took a "wife," Metauie, who later recalled that he drank 300 bottles of beer a week. It was alcohol that likely killed him, in 1923, but his legacy of strategic brilliance saved many Allied lives two decades later.

It is not too much to claim that the sum of U.S. Marine, Naval and even Army behavior during WWII, so intrepid and so ultimately successful, is testament to the genius of Ellis, Russell and their fellow Marine strategists. From Tarawa, Saipan, Peleliu, Iwo Jima and Okinawa to the beaches of Normandy, Corps thinking was ever present. In what could be considered as homage to Ellis, Vandergrift wrote after the war, "Despite its outstanding record as a combat force in the past war, the Marine Corps' far greater contribution to victory was doctrinal: that is, the fact that the basic amphibious doctrines which carried Allied troops over every beachhead of World War II had been largely shaped—often in the face of uninterested and doubting military orthodoxy—by U.S. Marines, and mainly between 1922 and 1935."

The Marines continued to contribute in Korea. By September 1950, North Korean troops had overrun most of the peninsula, but following Gen. Douglas MacArthur's strategy, the 1st Marine Division landed at Inchon, at the peninsula's pinched waist, a move that helped send the enemy scurrying back north. Marines entered the fray in Vietnam in 1965 and more than held their own in combat, but drug use, drinking, racial incidents and "fragging" attacks on officers exacerbated a war that historian Allan R. Millett called "the ultimate test of the Corps' survivability." Afterward, reforms were studied, and by 1985 the Corps, notes Millett, "had reached a plateau of excellence in attracting and retaining quality officers and enlisted personnel." During the Gulf War, again it was Marines in first (Gen. Norman Schwarzkopf said of their performance, "If I use words like brilliant, it would really be an under description"), and in Afghanistan and Iraq they joined in pursuing the new enemy. From the halls of Montezuma to the shores of Tripoli—and a thousand other shores—the Marines have covered themselves in glory.

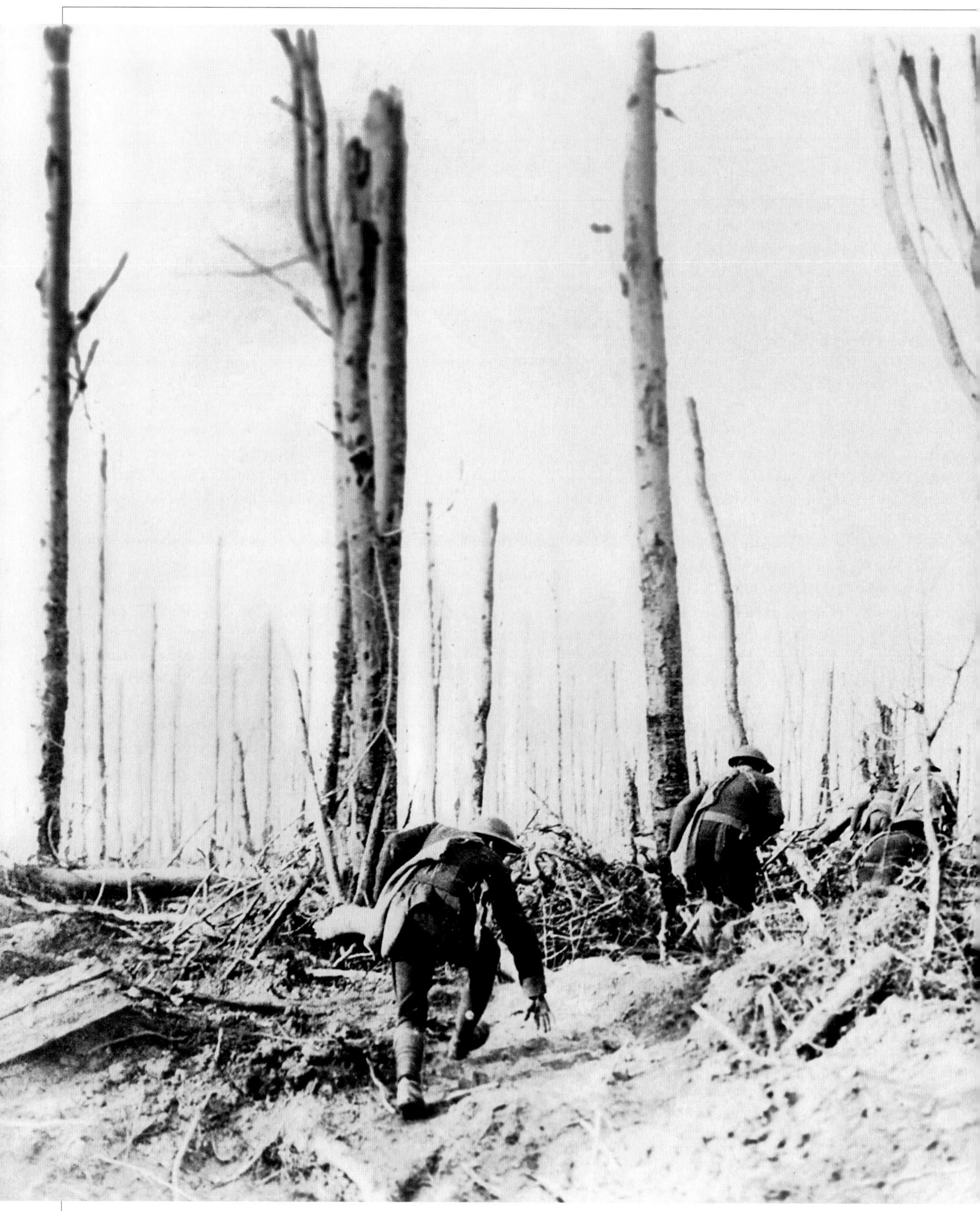

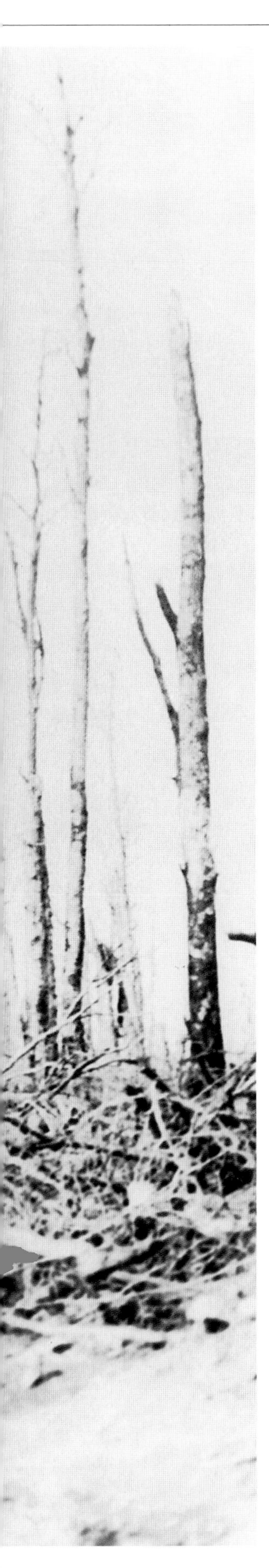

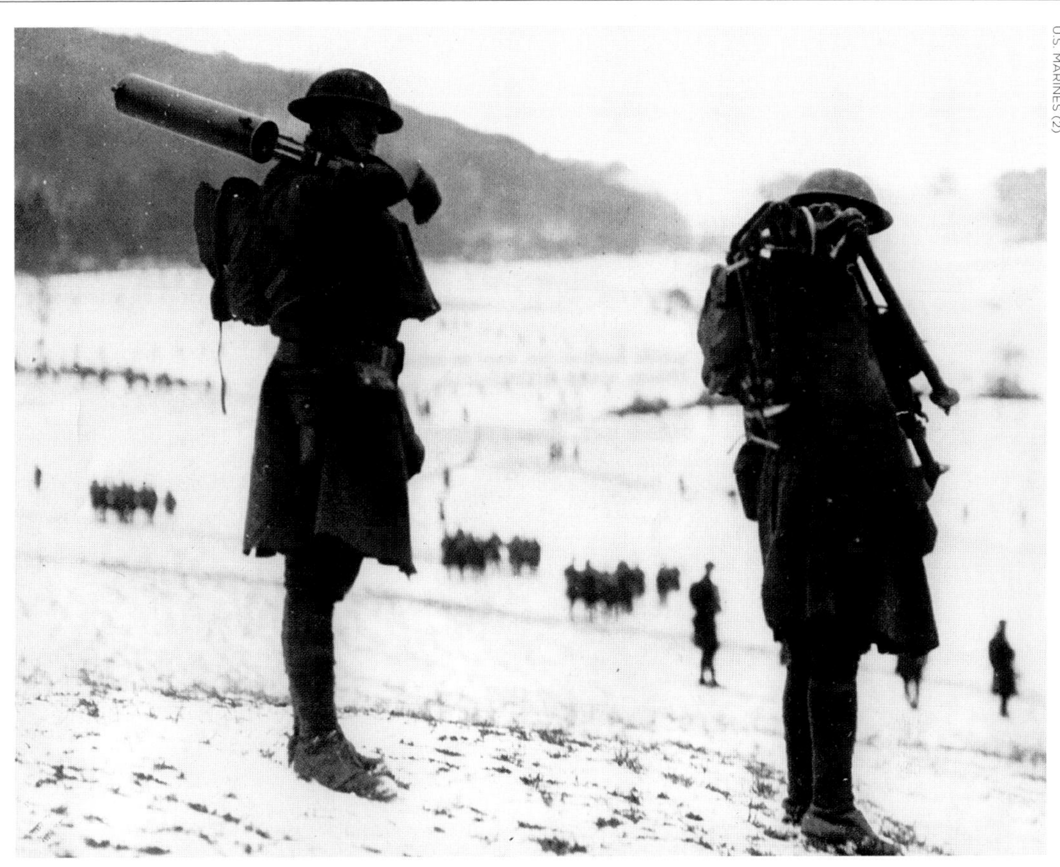

U.S. MARINES (2)

THE BIG SHOW

Although U.S. forces missed most of the grisly trench warfare of World War I, they still saw plenty of action and played a critical role in the war's outcome. Above, a Marine machine-gun crew maneuvers across France in the winter of 1917-18. In June 1918, the French army was on its heels while the Germans had 35 divisions arrayed for a march into Paris. In their way stood the Marines at Belleau Wood (below). After three weeks of grim fighting, Maj. Maurice Shearer signaled: "Woods now entirely—US Marine Corps." Left: Marines ascend the rough terrain of the Meuse-Argonne, the site of the greatest U.S. battle of WWI.

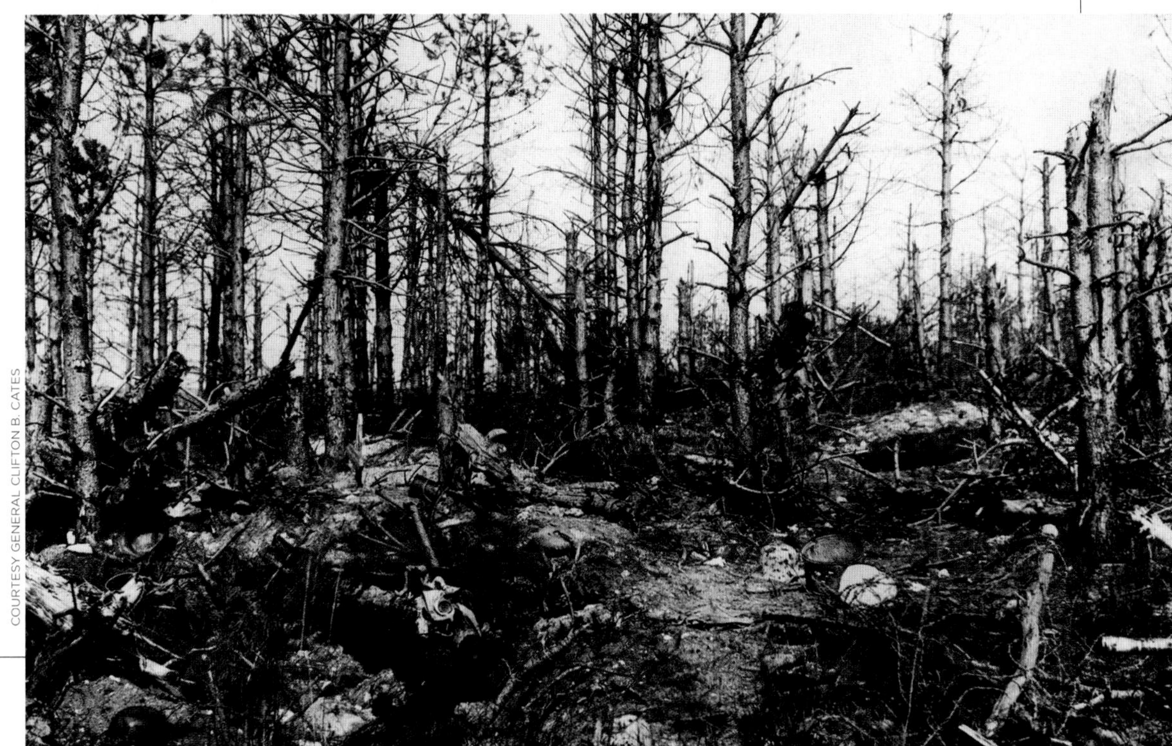

COURTESY GENERAL CLIFTON B. CATES

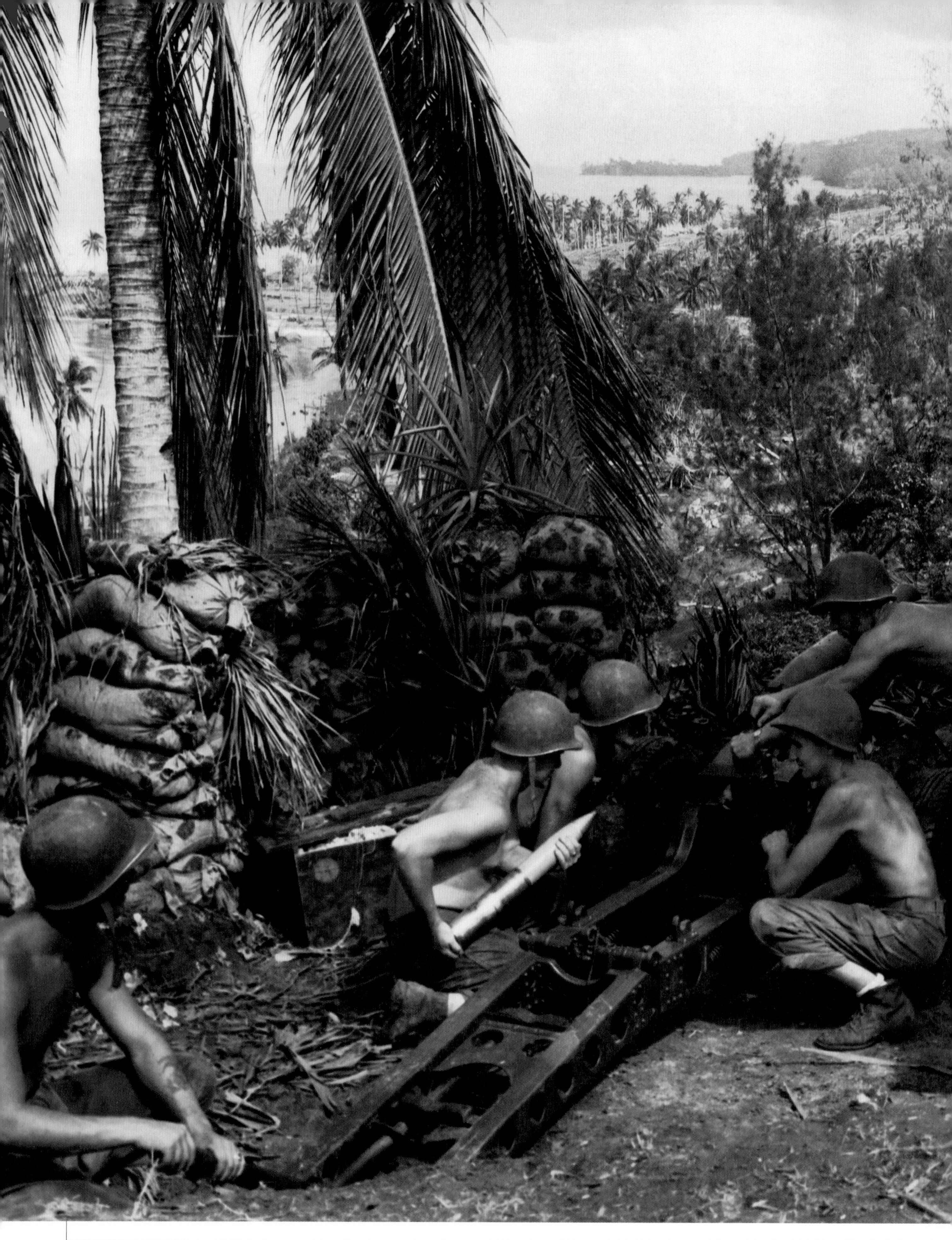

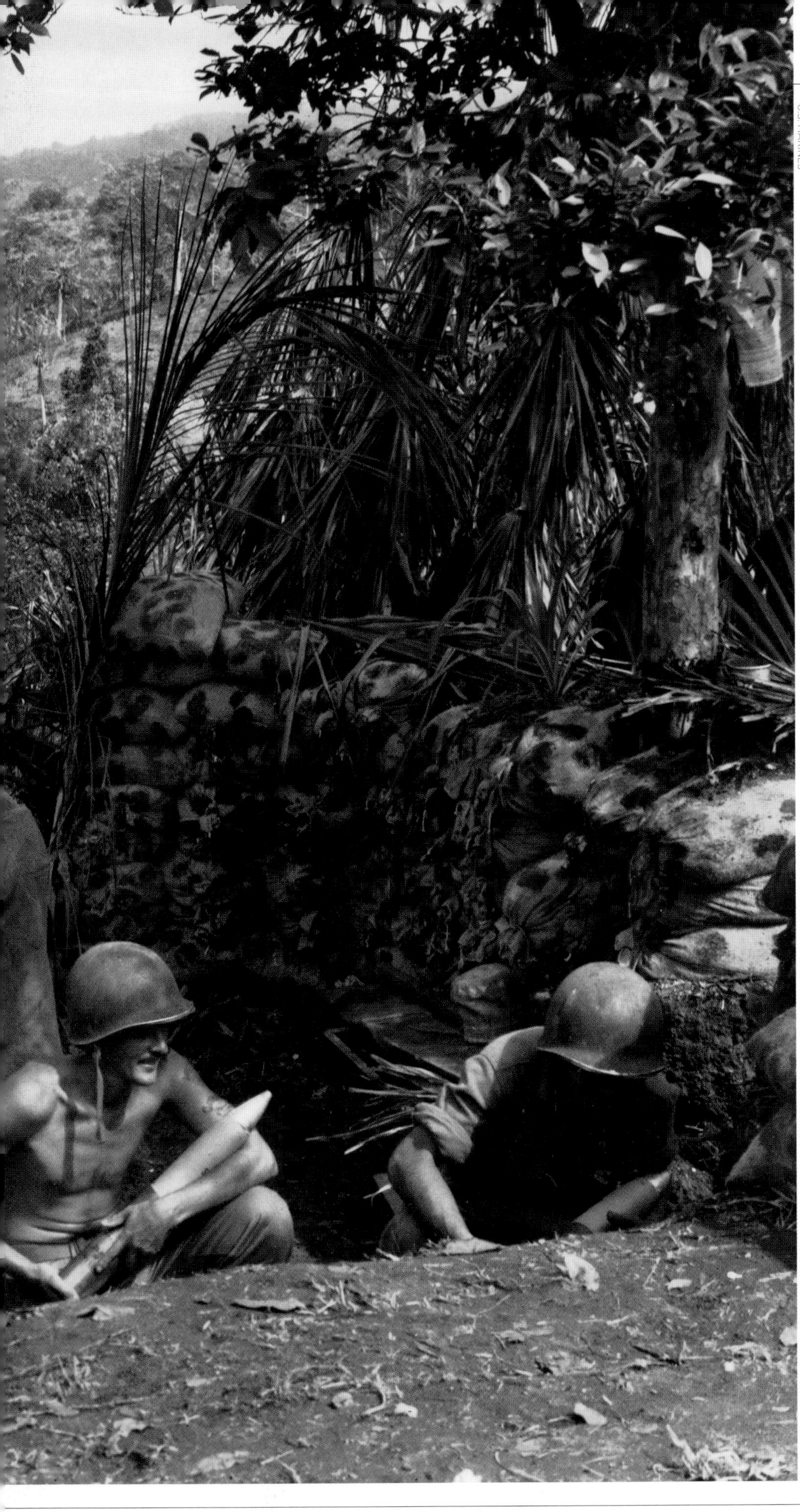

U.S. MARINES

ISLAND FIGHTING BEGINS Guadalcanal, the largest of the Solomon Islands in the Pacific, was a name unfamiliar to most Americans. Then, as would happen with so many other obscure, far-off little places, its name would become all too familiar. The Japanese had begun to build an air base there, from which to harass American ships. The U.S., in turn, wanted the island as a jumping-off point for its drive into Japanese held territories. On August 7, 1942, the Marines invaded Guadalcanal. It was the beginning of a long campaign that was tough every inch of the way. Constant naval bombardment made the island a living hell. Finally, a full half year later, the Japanese evacuated. At left, Marines man a gun emplacement captured from the Japanese.

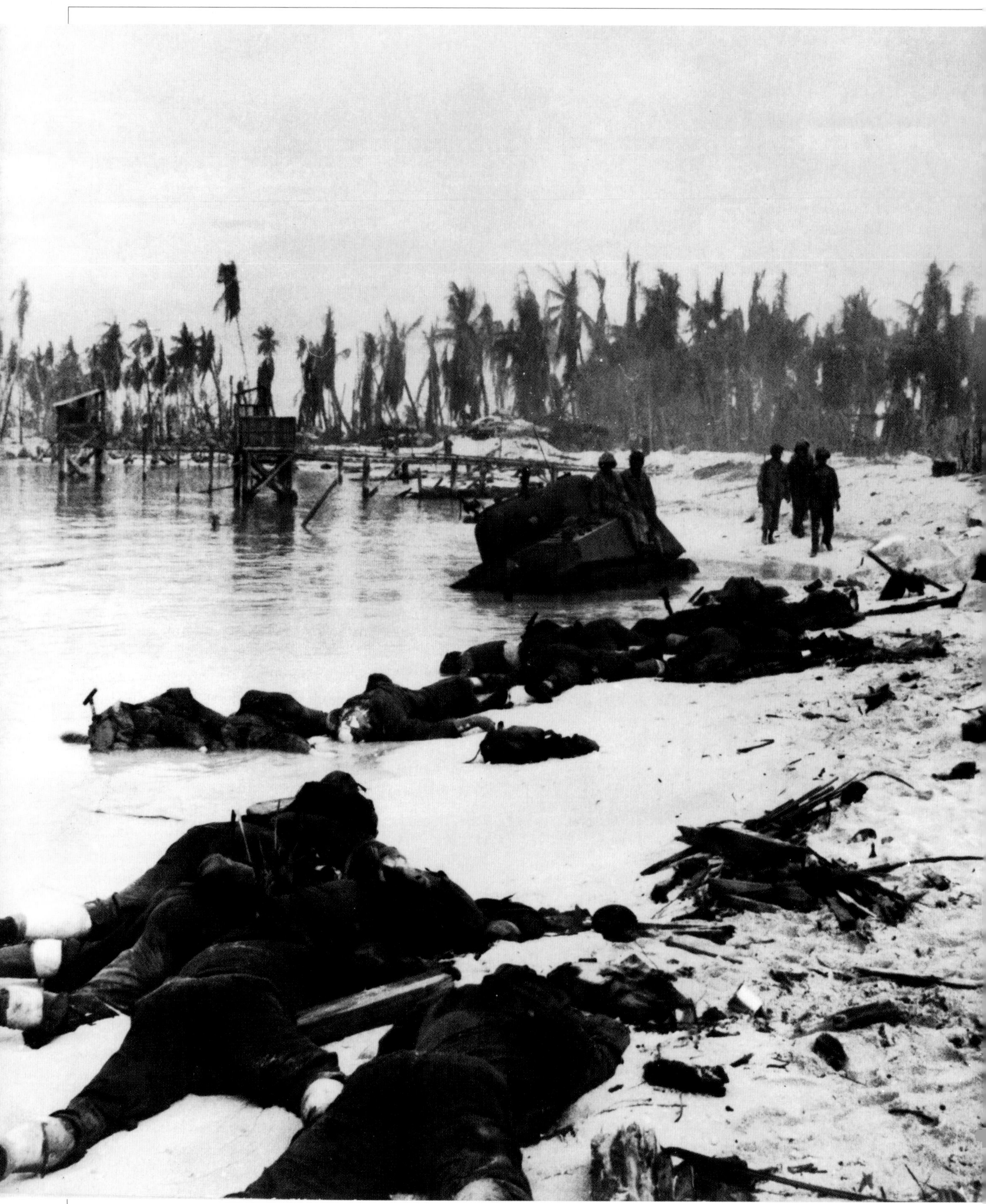

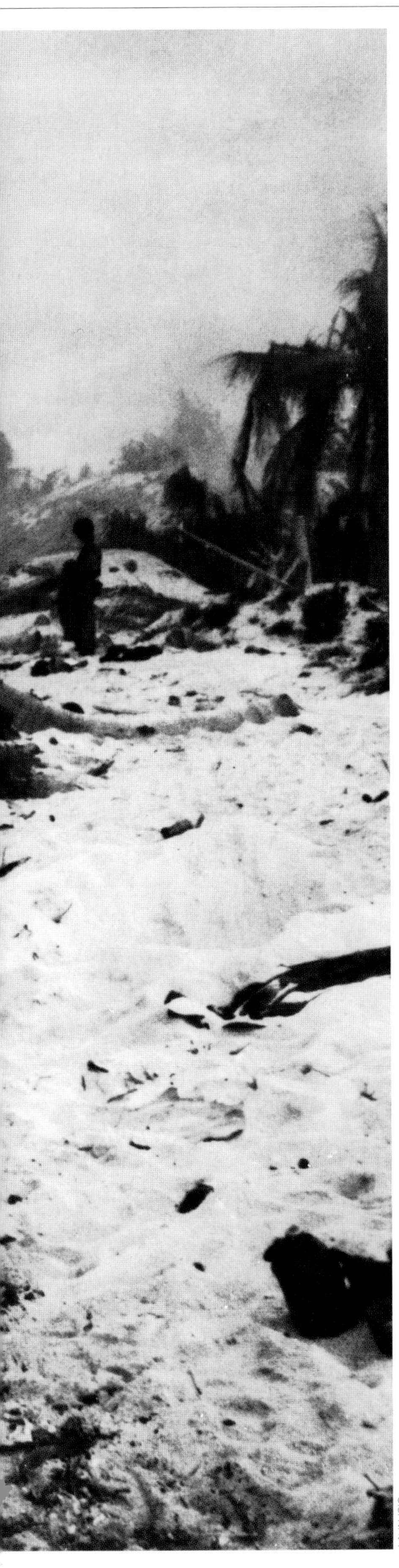

U.S. NAVY

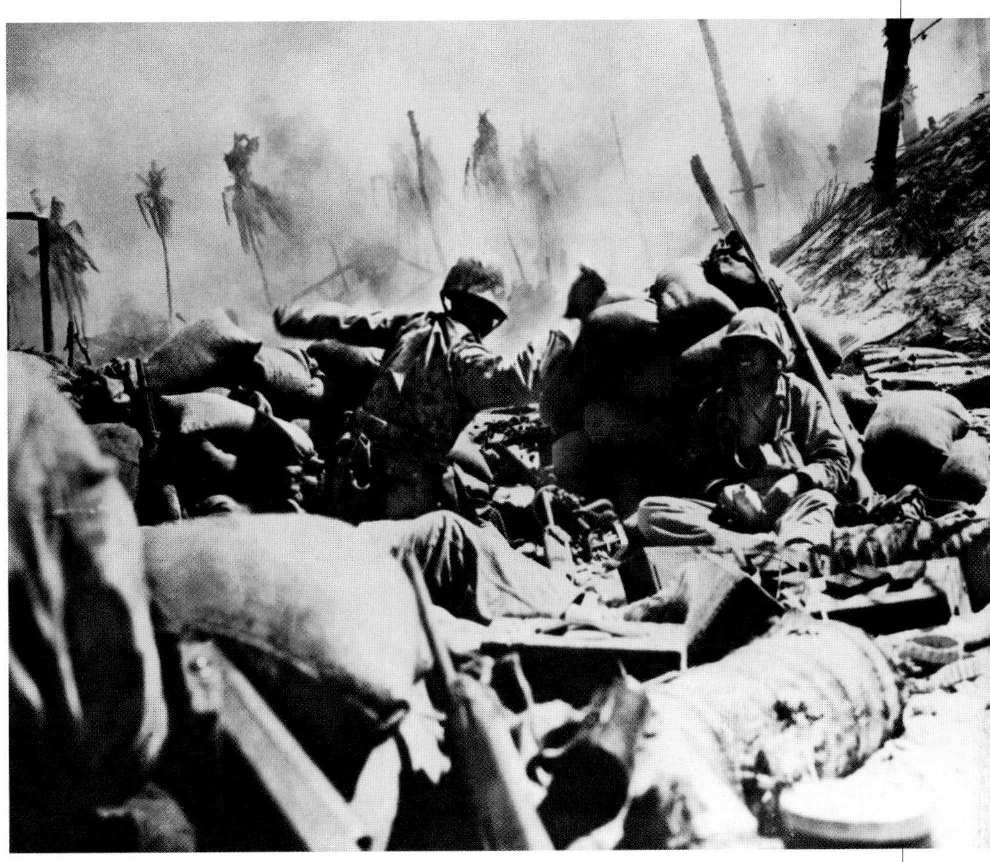

NO QUARTER ASKED, NO QUARTER GIVEN

"A million men and a hundred years." That's what a Japanese admiral said it would take to capture Tarawa, an atoll in the Pacific. The Japanese had spent two years fortifying the strategically placed islands. Guns, bunkers, impediments and wire were ubiquitous. Nevertheless, on November 20, 1943, the Marines began an assault on Tarawa's Betio Island, where the Japanese airstrip lay. Seventy-six hours later, after some of the most harrowing combat of the war, only 17 out of 4,836 Japanese defenders were alive. About a thousand Marines died. Lessons learned at Tarawa would save lives in future landings.

U.S. MARINES

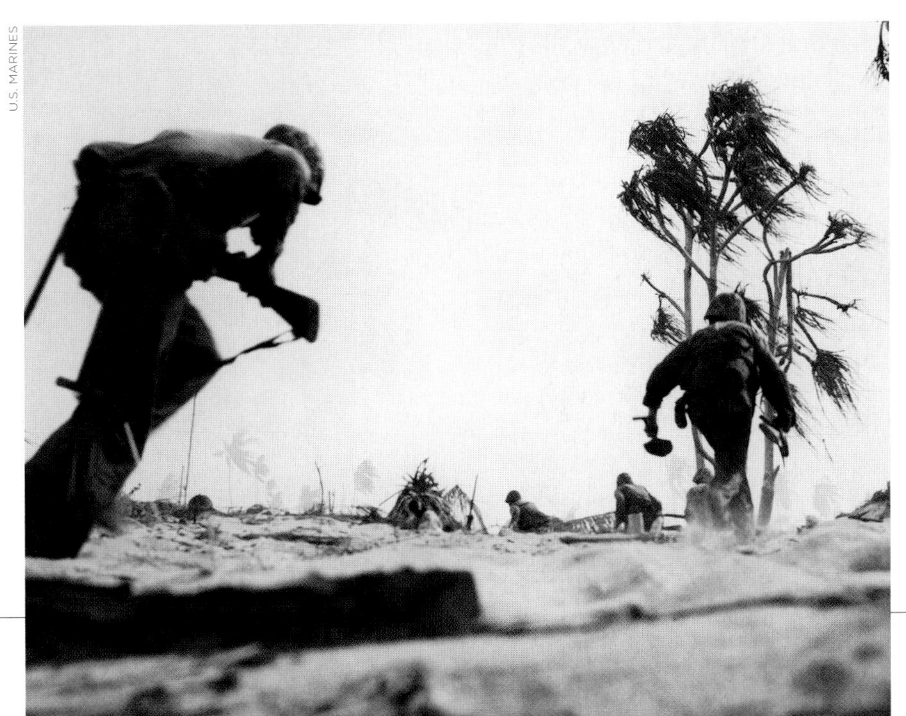

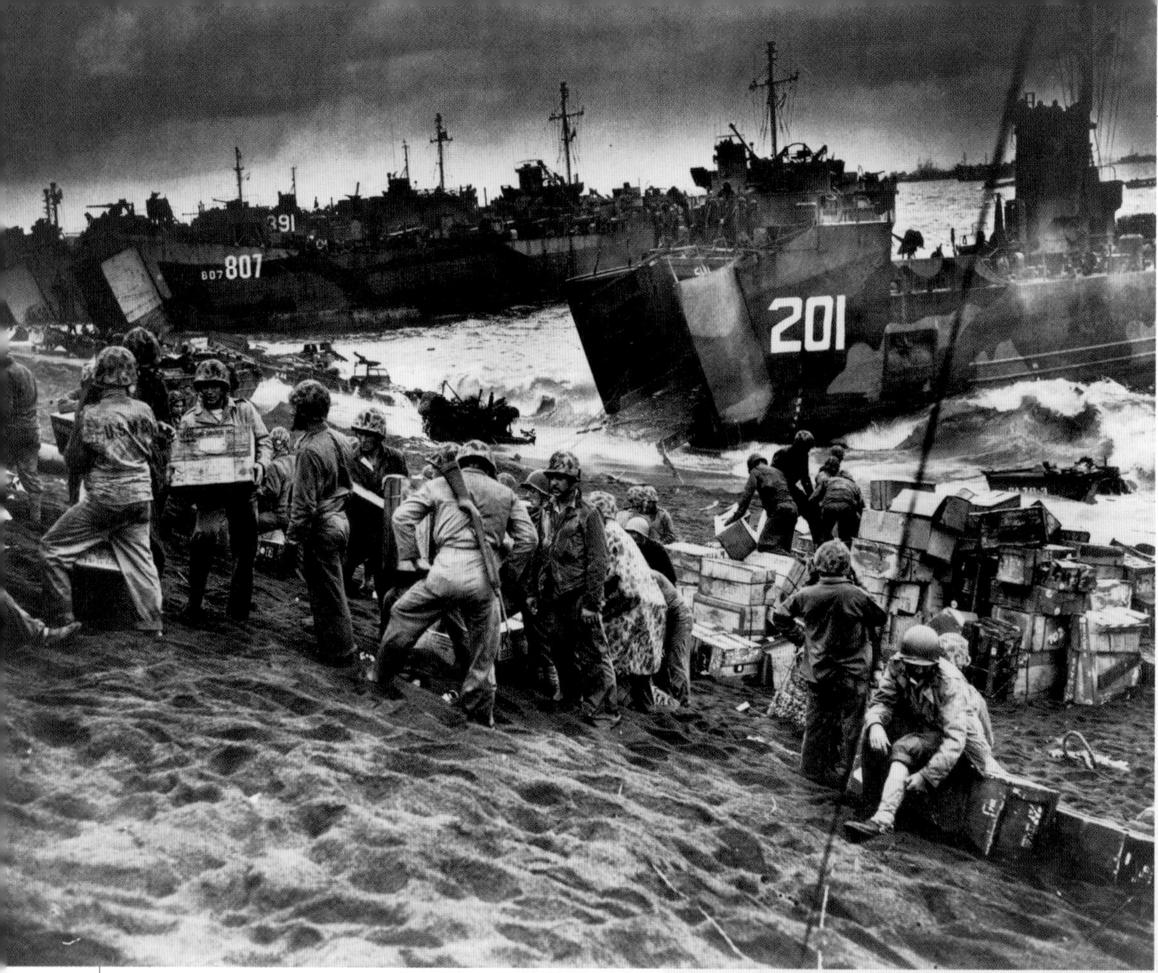

NATIONAL ARCHIVES

UNCOMMON VALOR

Iwo Jima is a small island only 700 miles from Japan, which considered it home ground to be defended at all cost. The Japanese strategy called for 1,500 caves, pillboxes and blockhouses connected by 16 miles of tunnels. The strategy also called for no Japanese survivors. The U.S., which wanted to use the island as a base for bombing runs on Japan, knew that resistance would be ferocious, and the Army and Navy provided the most intensive pre-invasion shelling of any Pacific island during the war. At just after nine a.m. on February 19, 1945, Marines hit the beaches of Iwo Jima. Its name means "Sulfur Island," and the coarse sand made it hard for men and machines to move. Despite the heavy shelling, the Japanese had been well protected in their underground fortresses, and the defensive response was savage. On the 36th day of the courageous assault, after beating back a banzai attack on American troops and air corps personnel near the beaches, the island was secured. Twenty seven Medals of Honor were awarded to Marines and sailors, many posthumously.

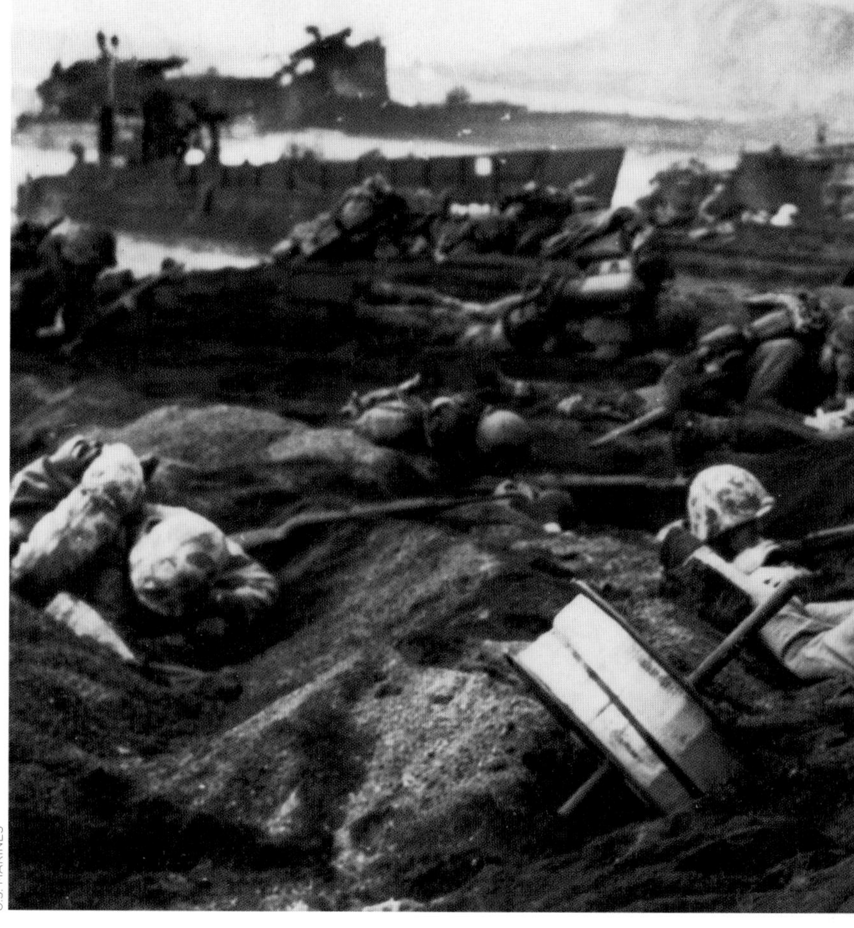

U.S. MARINES

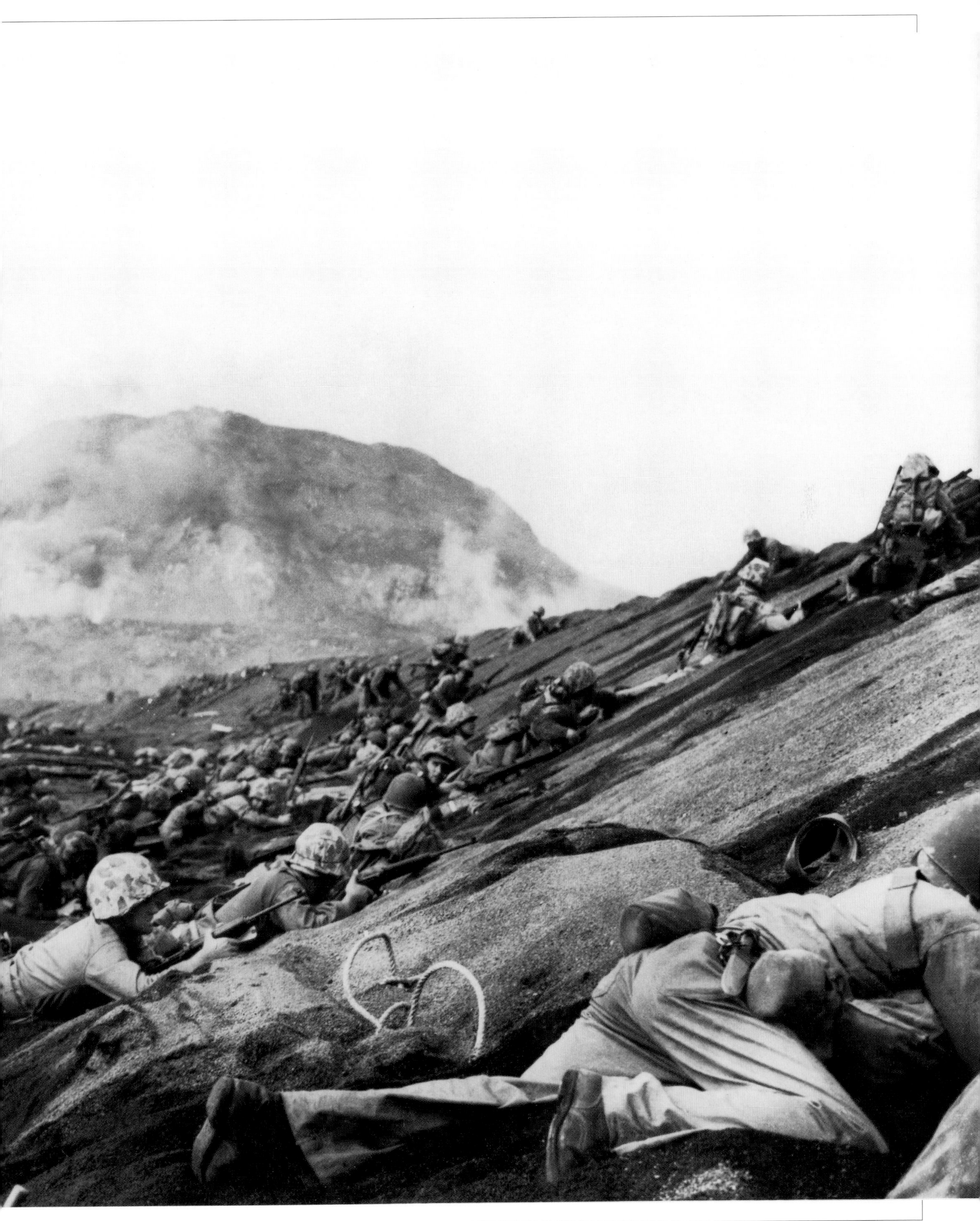

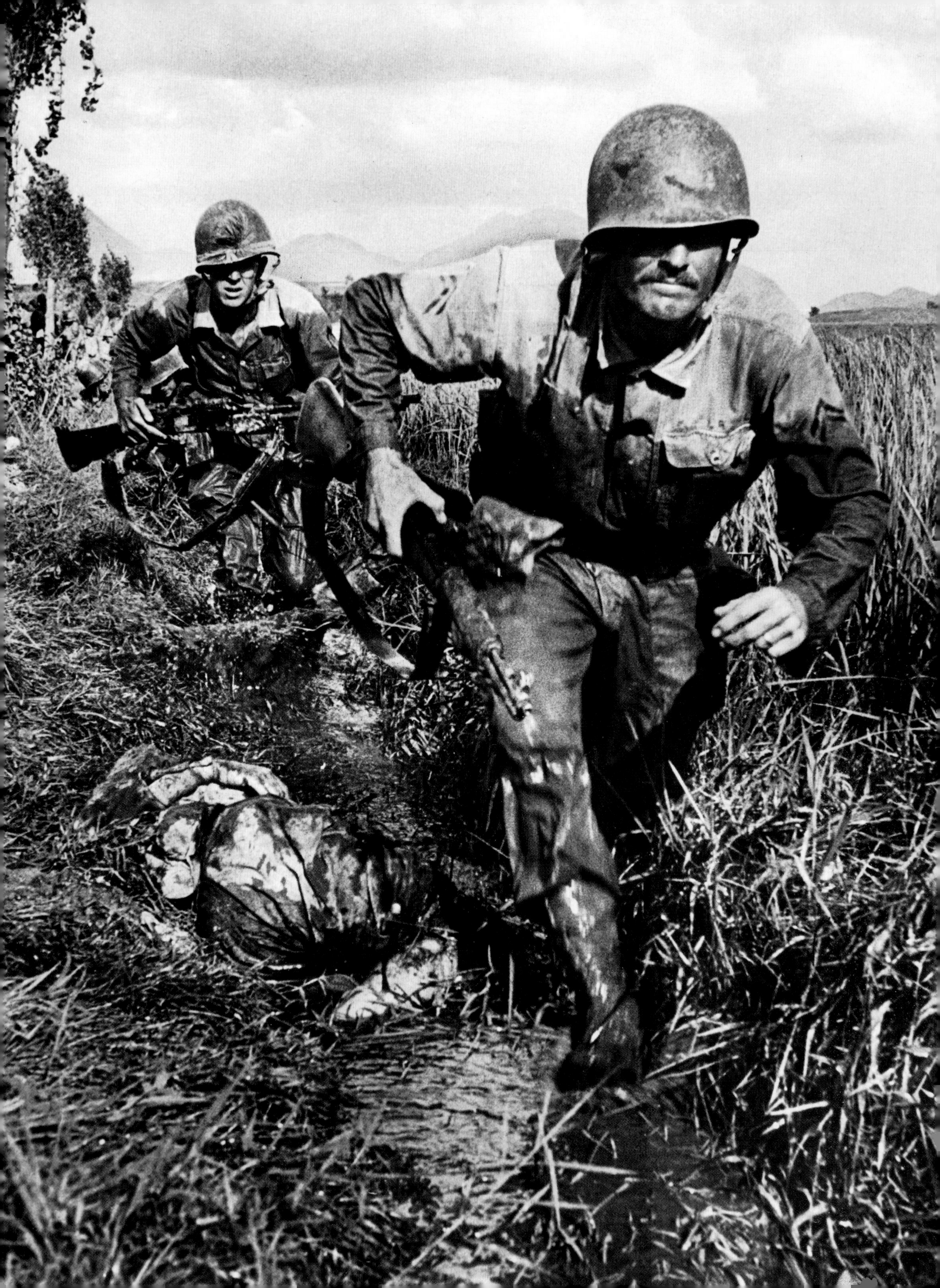

DAVID DOUGLAS DUNCAN (3)

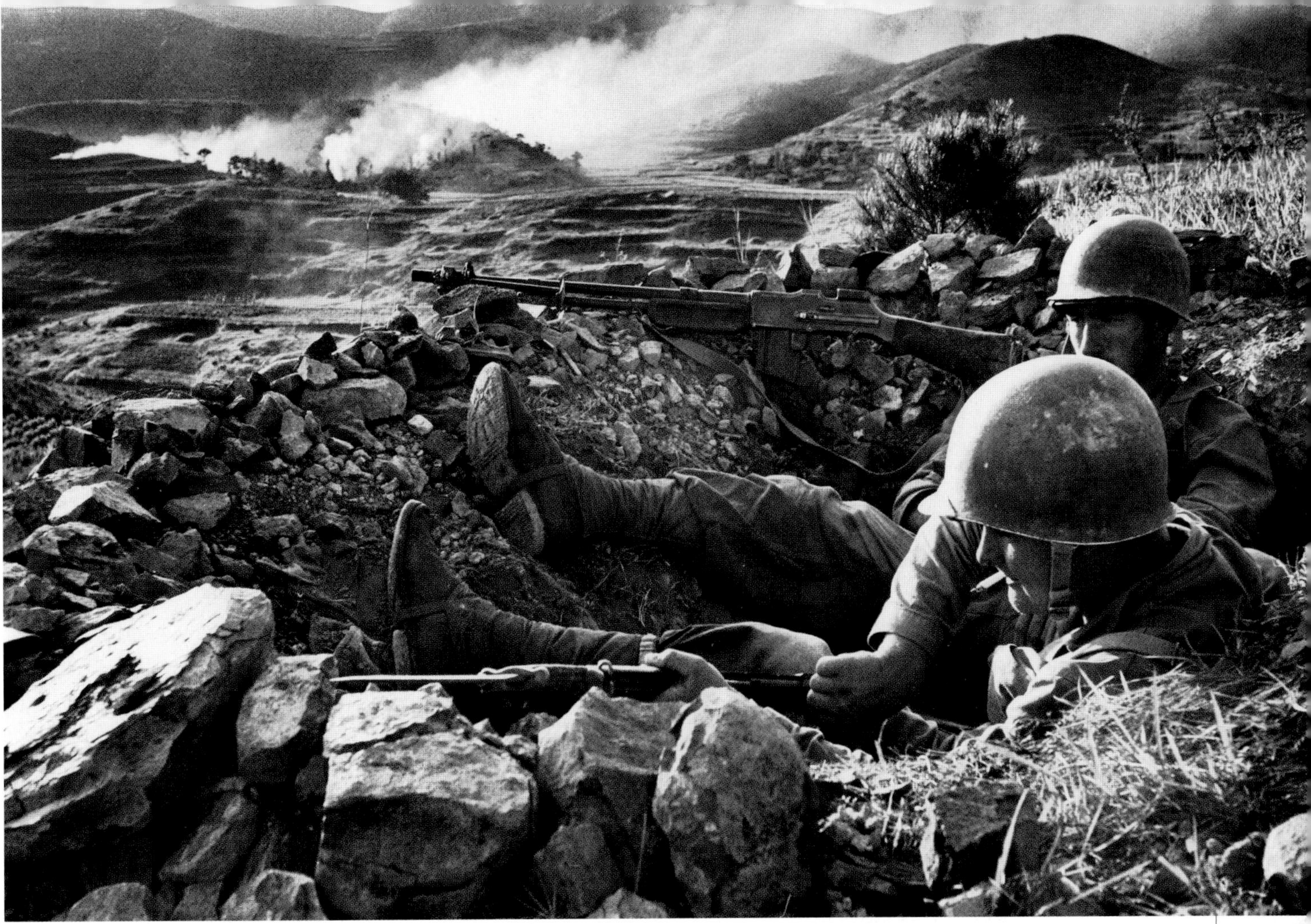

GYRENES IN KOREA

More than 300,000 Marines served in the Korean War, and more than 30,000 were killed or wounded. The Corps typically distinguished itself at Pusan, Inchon, Chosin and countless other arenas of battle. On September 4, 1950, LIFE's David Douglas Duncan, the preeminent photographer of that war, joined the most forward unit of the 1st Marine Brigade, Company B, 5th Regiment, as it fought over the bald, heartless ridges of the western front to drive the North Koreans back across the Naktong River. Above, Marines await a counterattack. Opposite: Advancing leathernecks charge past an enemy corpse. At right, a driver is comforted after his jeep hit a mine.

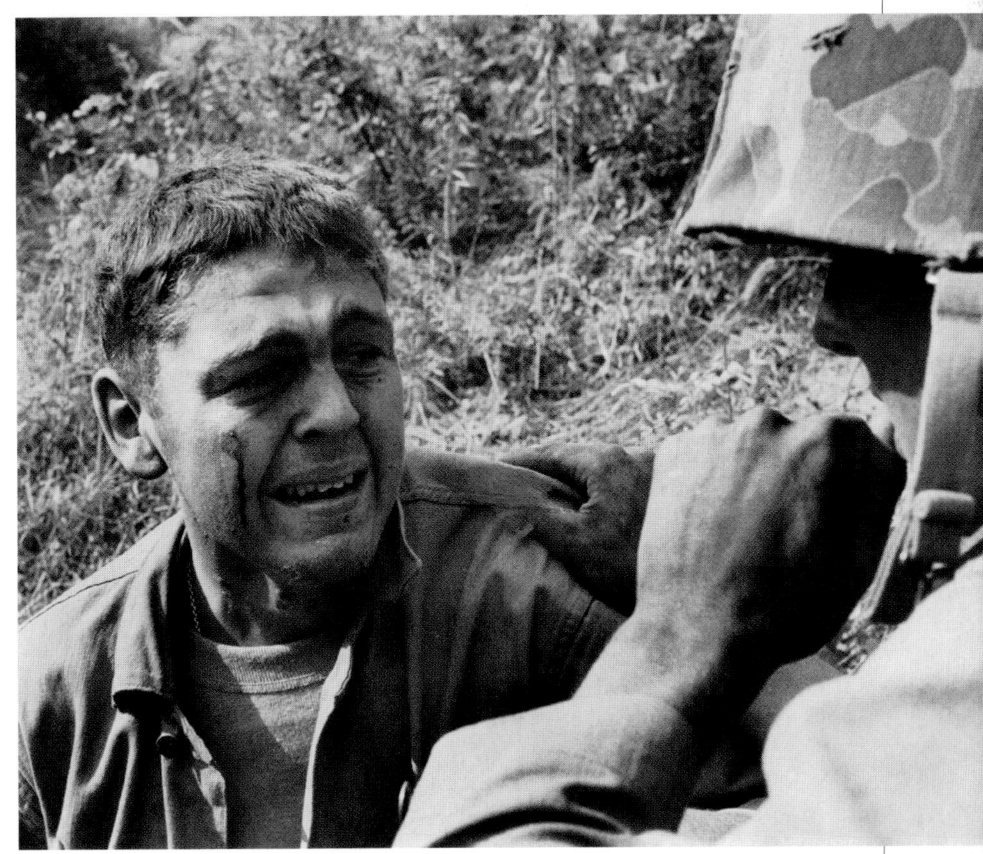

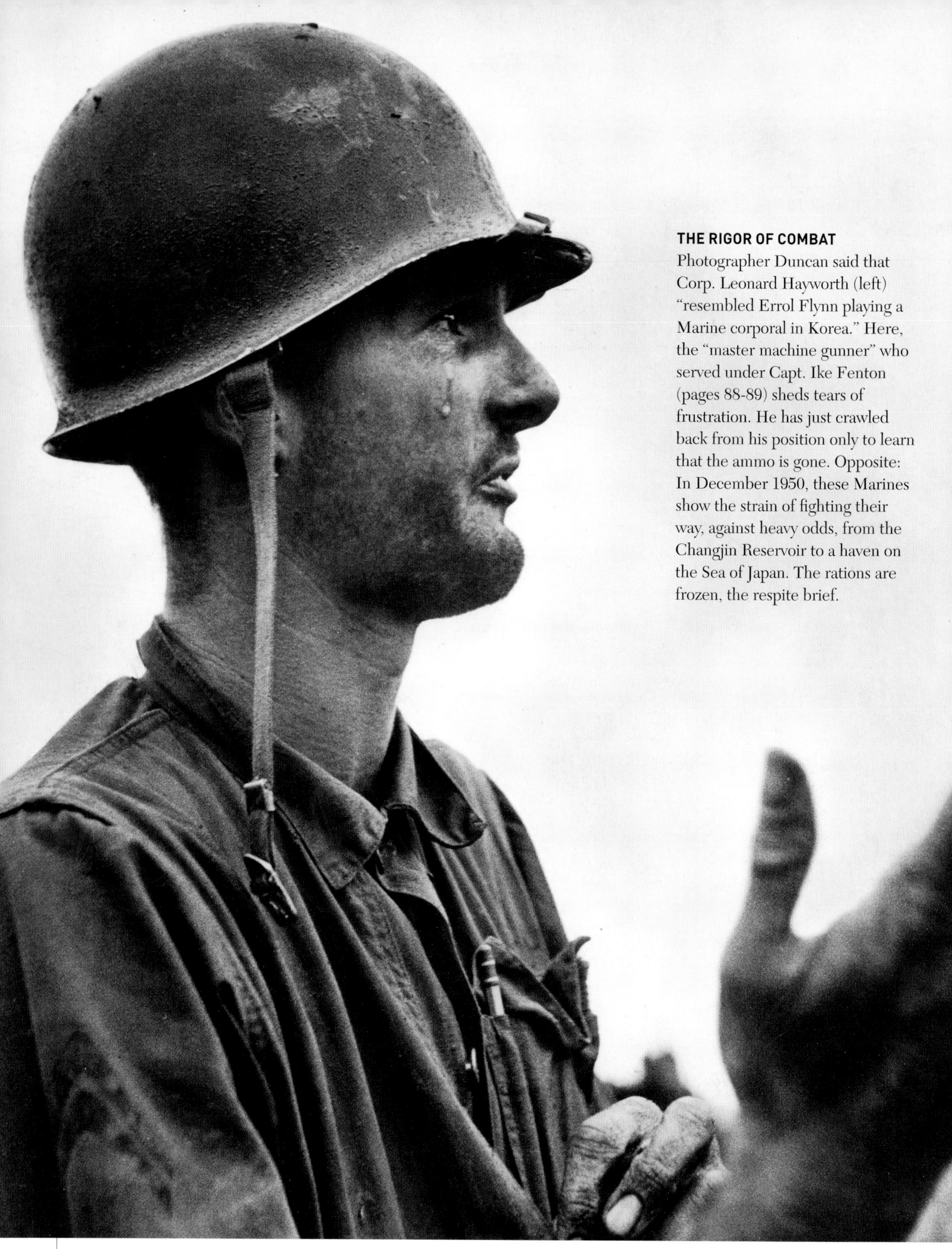

THE RIGOR OF COMBAT
Photographer Duncan said that Corp. Leonard Hayworth (left) "resembled Errol Flynn playing a Marine corporal in Korea." Here, the "master machine gunner" who served under Capt. Ike Fenton (pages 88-89) sheds tears of frustration. He has just crawled back from his position only to learn that the ammo is gone. Opposite: In December 1950, these Marines show the strain of fighting their way, against heavy odds, from the Changjin Reservoir to a haven on the Sea of Japan. The rations are frozen, the respite brief.

DAVID DOUGLAS DUNCAN (5)

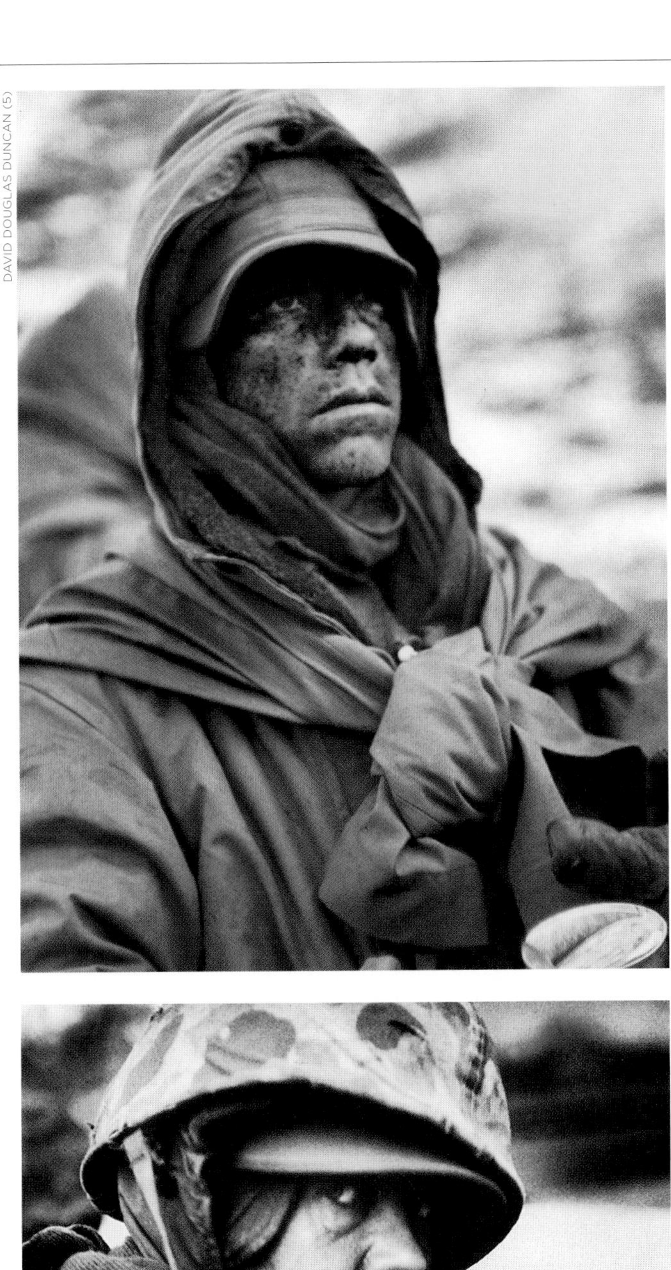

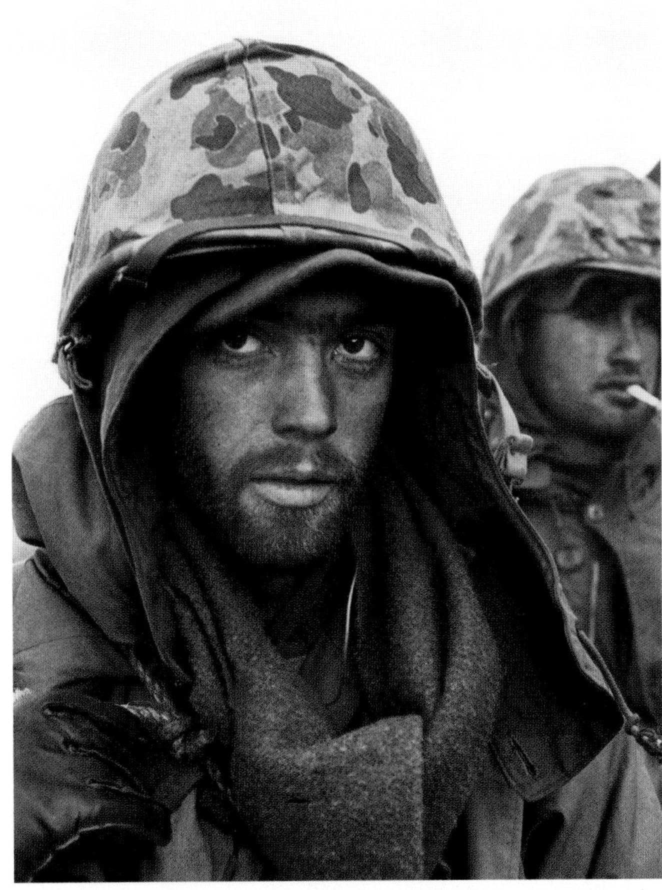

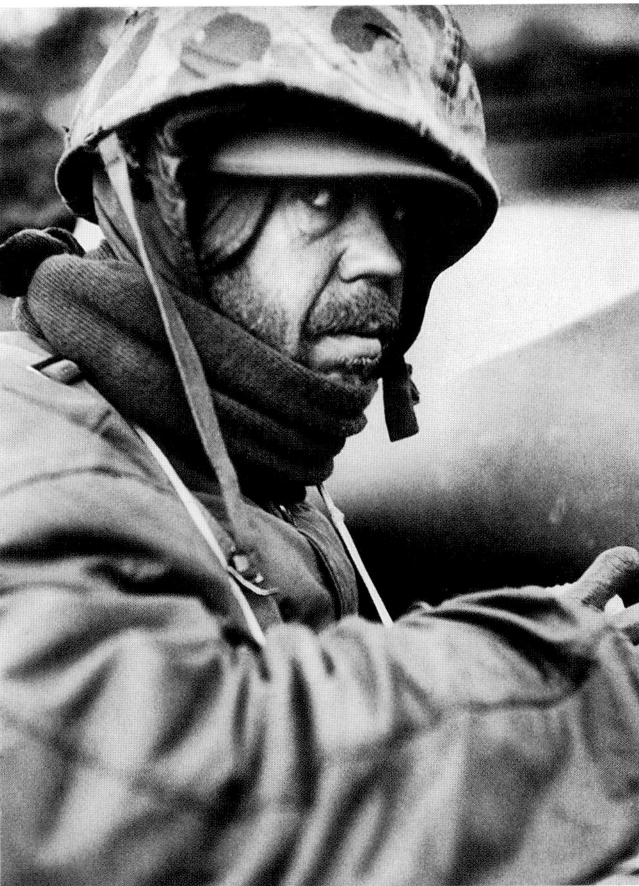

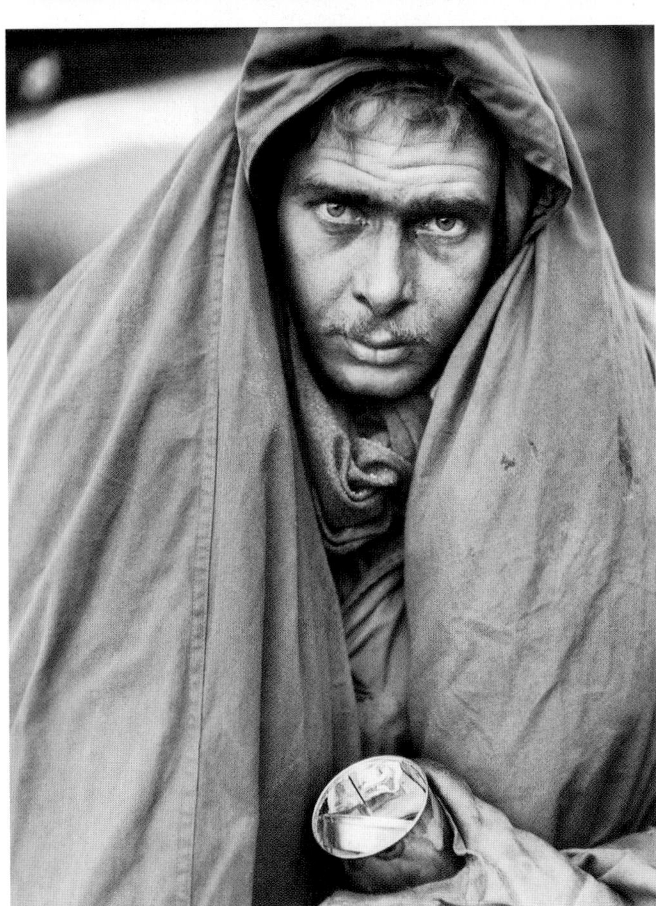

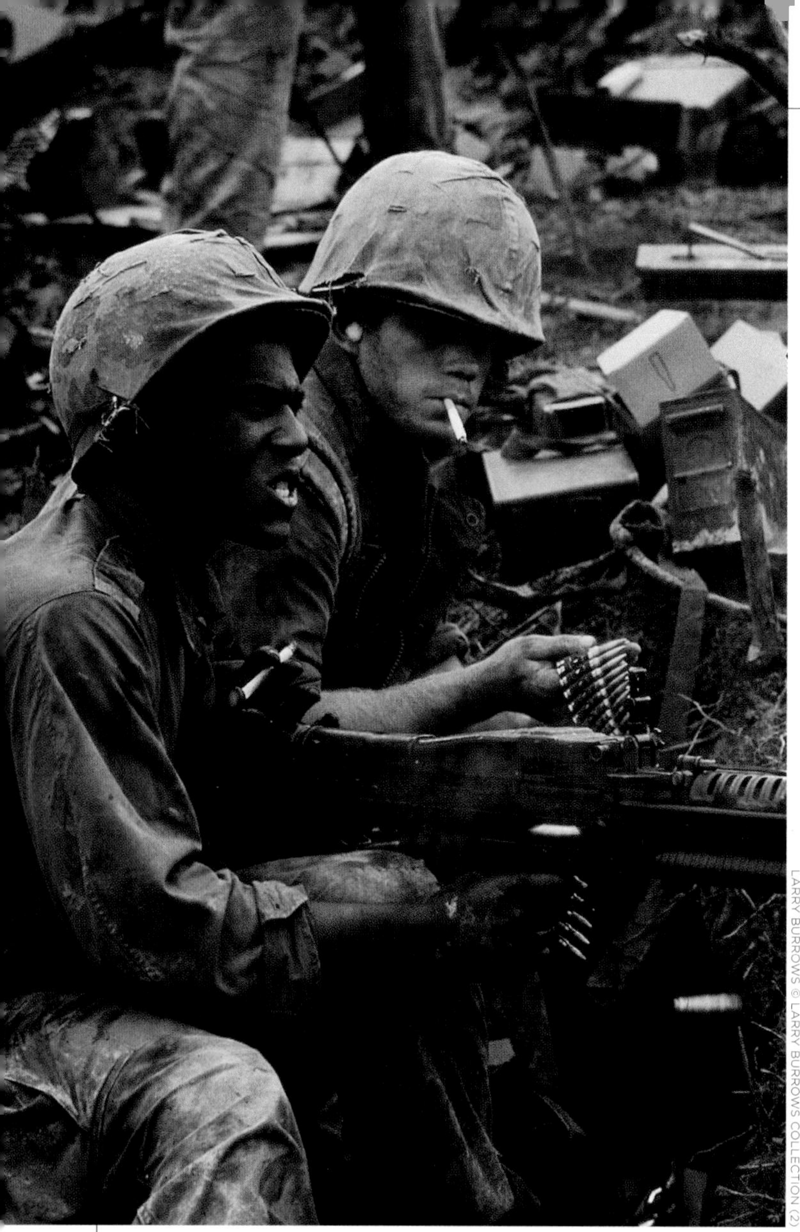

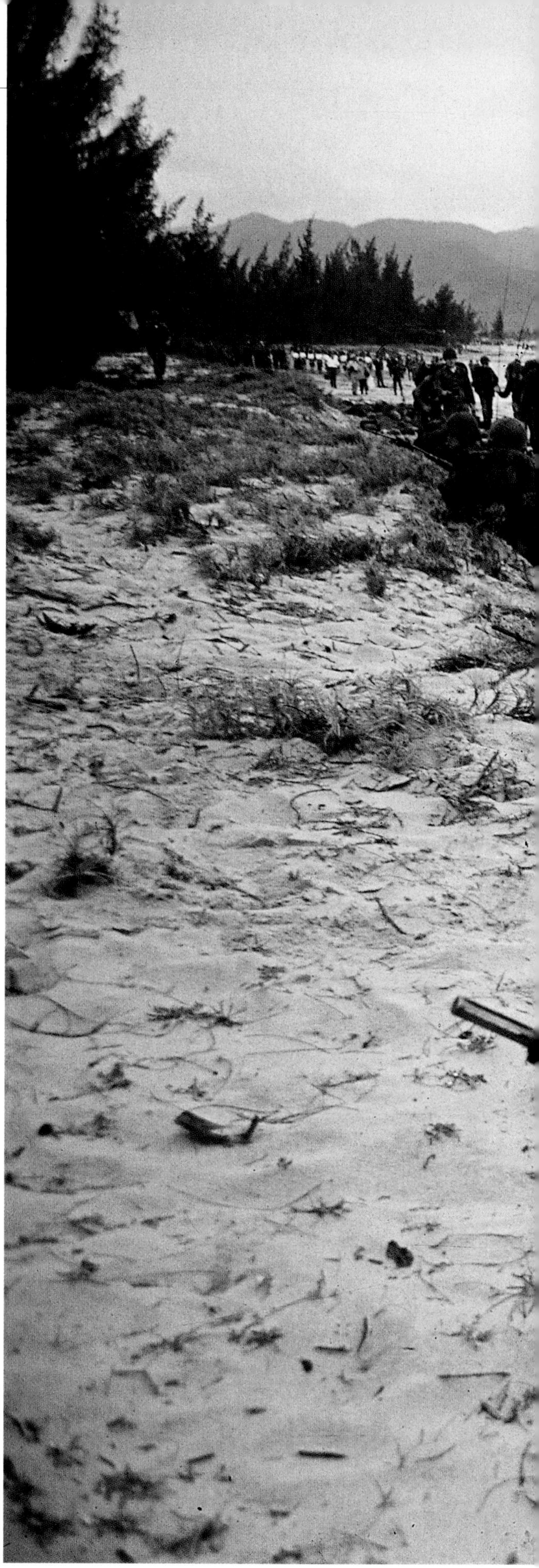

ONCE MORE INTO ASIA

On the order of President Lyndon B. Johnson, the first U.S. combat troops went ashore in Vietnam on March 8, 1965 (right). It was "Red Beach," and they were the Marines of the 3rd Battalion, 9th Regiment. The leathernecks, improbably, were greeted on the shore by young Vietnamese women bearing garlands of flowers, but this was not the prelude to a beach party. These men had landed in order to protect the air base at Da Nang. By the time the Vietnam war finally ground to a halt, 14,838 Marines had lost their lives. The Marines firing the machine gun above are trying to wrest control of Hill 484 during Operation Prairie in the fall of 1966. This campaign was an effort to arrest the flow of North Vietnamese forces across the demilitarized zone. These pictures and those on the following two pages were taken by LIFE's Larry Burrows. The renowned chronicler of Vietnam was killed in Laos in 1971.

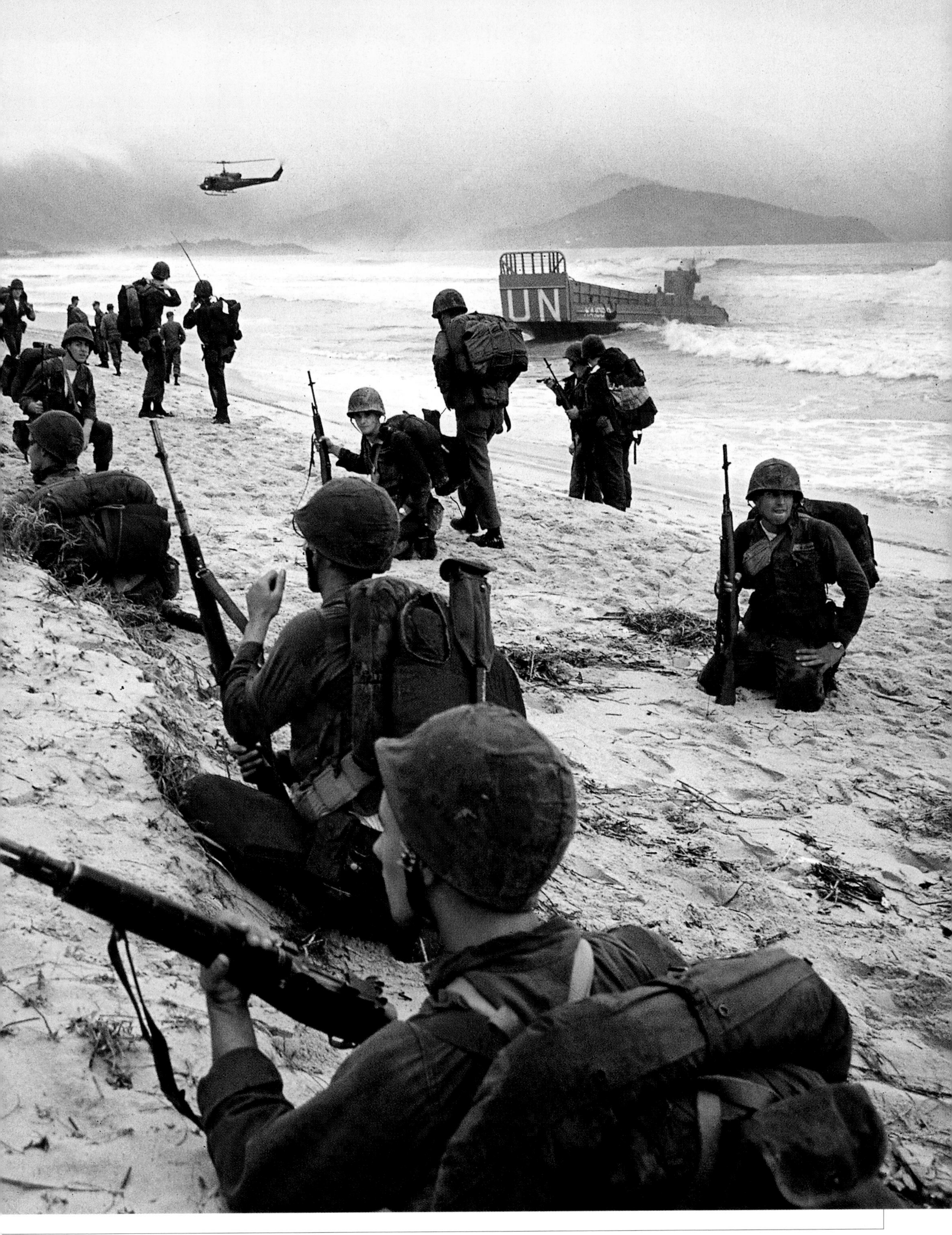
UN

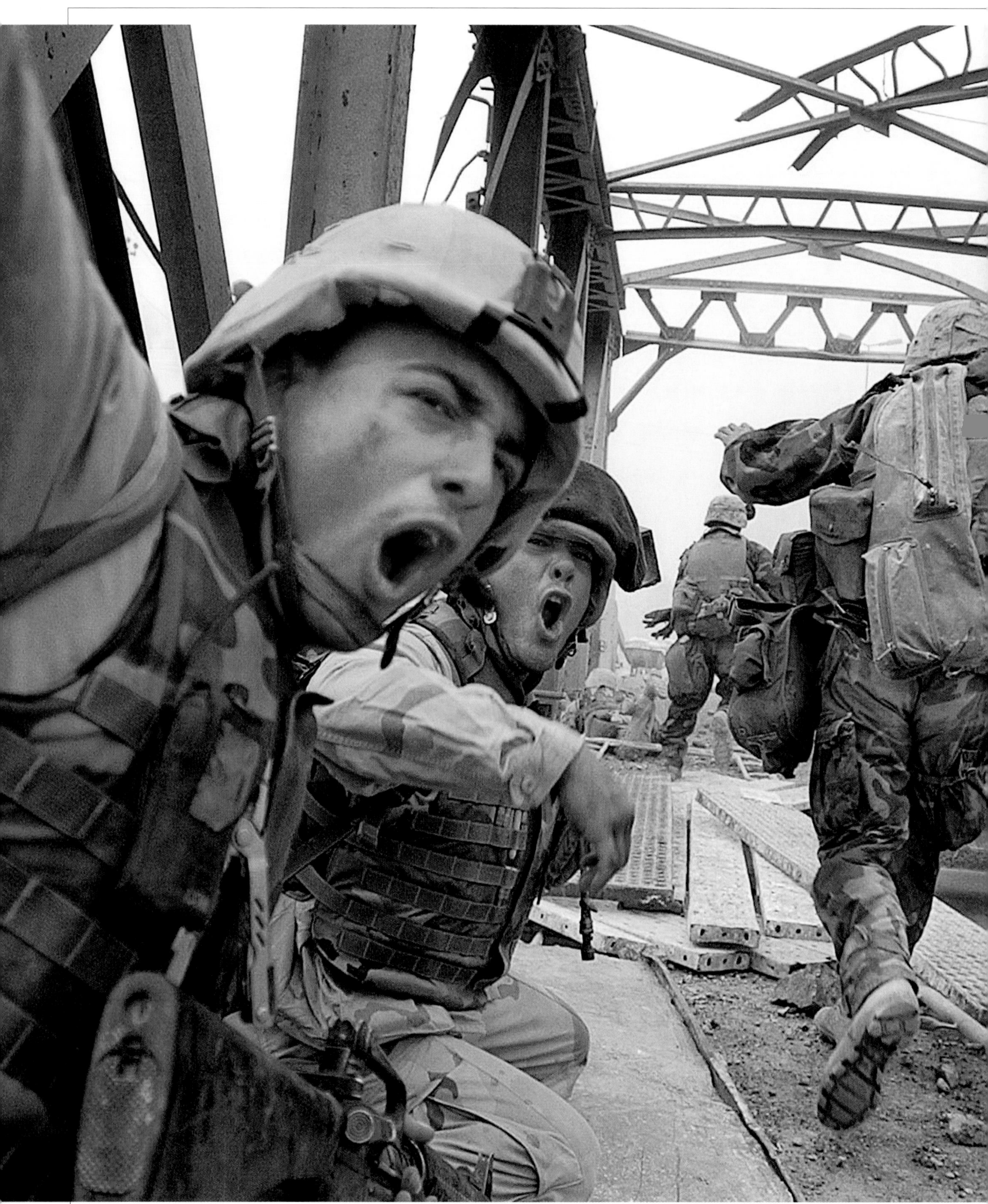

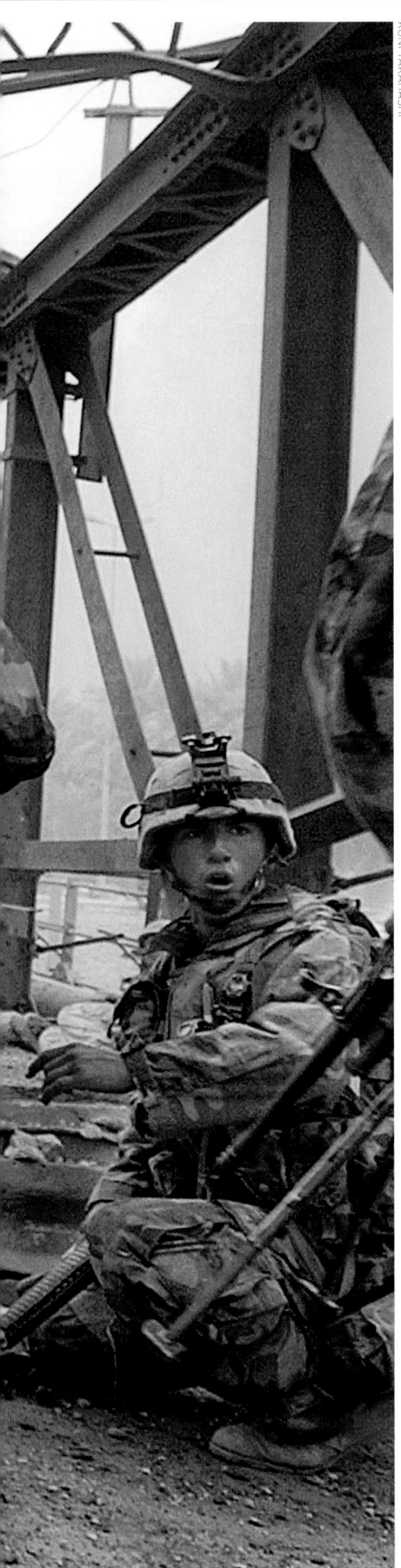
KUNI TAKAHASHI

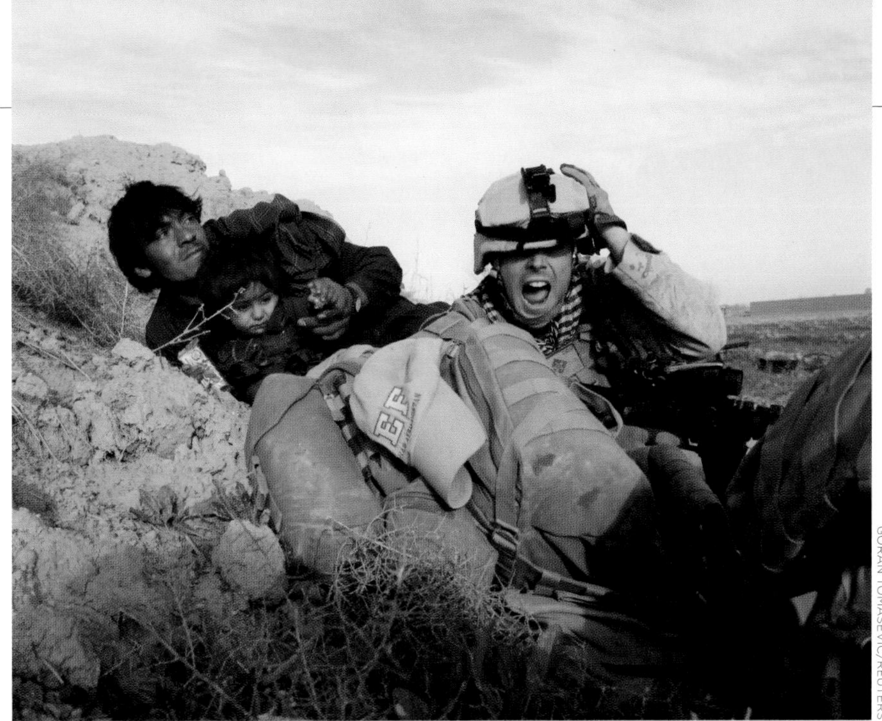
GORAN TOMASEVIC/REUTERS

DIFFERENT CONFLICTS, SAME COMMITMENT

From the beginning of America's protracted conflicts in Iraq and Afghanistan, the Marines were there, as always, in the forefront of the fighting. At left, Marines of the 3rd Battalion, 4th Regiment, under heavy fire in 2003 from Iraqi forces, urge their fellow soldiers to rush across the damaged Baghdad Highway Bridge. Seven years later, Marines faced similar dangers in Afghanistan. Above: Marine Lance Corp. Chris Sanderson shouts as he tries to protect an Afghan man and his child from a Taliban attack in the town of Marjah. Below: Soldiers in Afghanistan share a moment of prayer before heading out into harm's way.

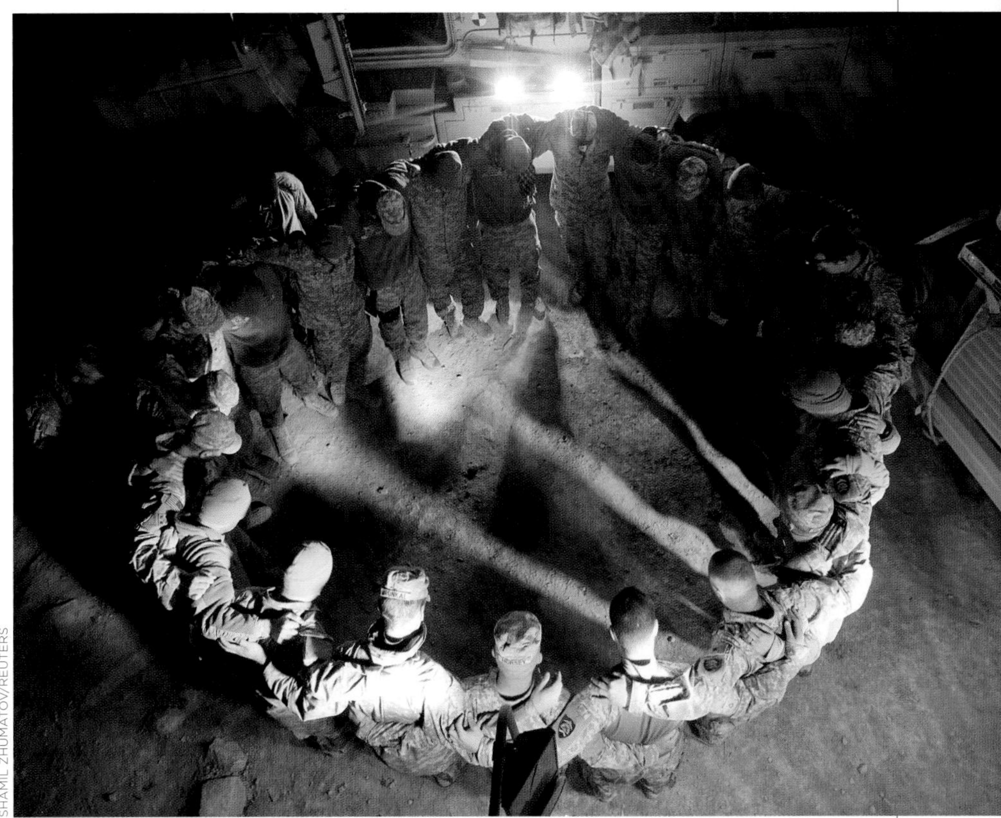
SHAMIL ZHUMATOV/REUTERS

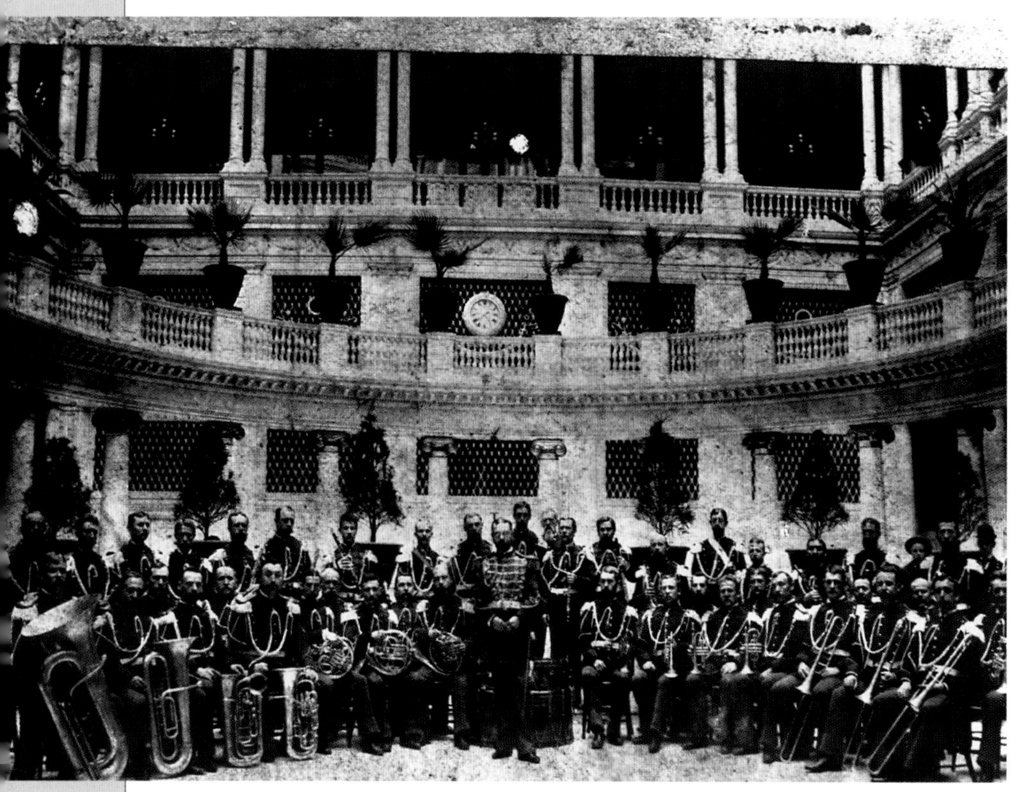

U.S. MARINES

CORBIS

The Marine Band

The service with the tough-as-nails reputation has always had a softer, more lyrical side.

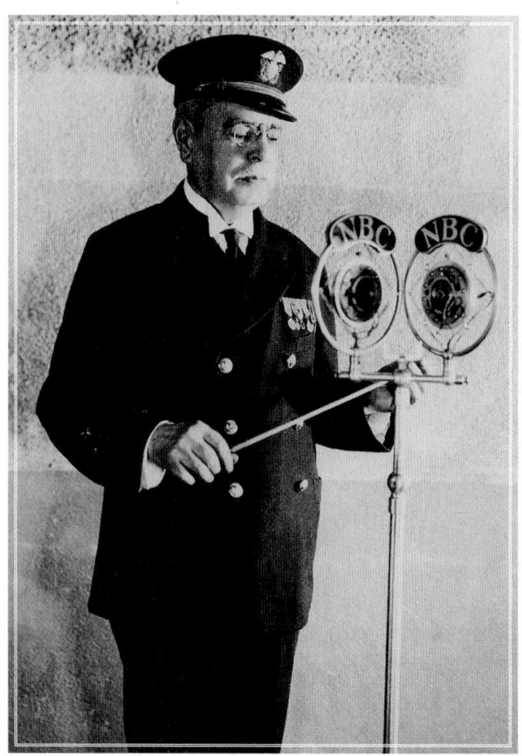

AP

Sousa (left, and with the band in 1892, above) took a unit in disarray and turned it into a crack outfit. When he led the Marine Band on a national tour in 1891 he created a sensation. Today, America's oldest professional music organization plays some 800 gigs a year, in concert halls and on the Mall.

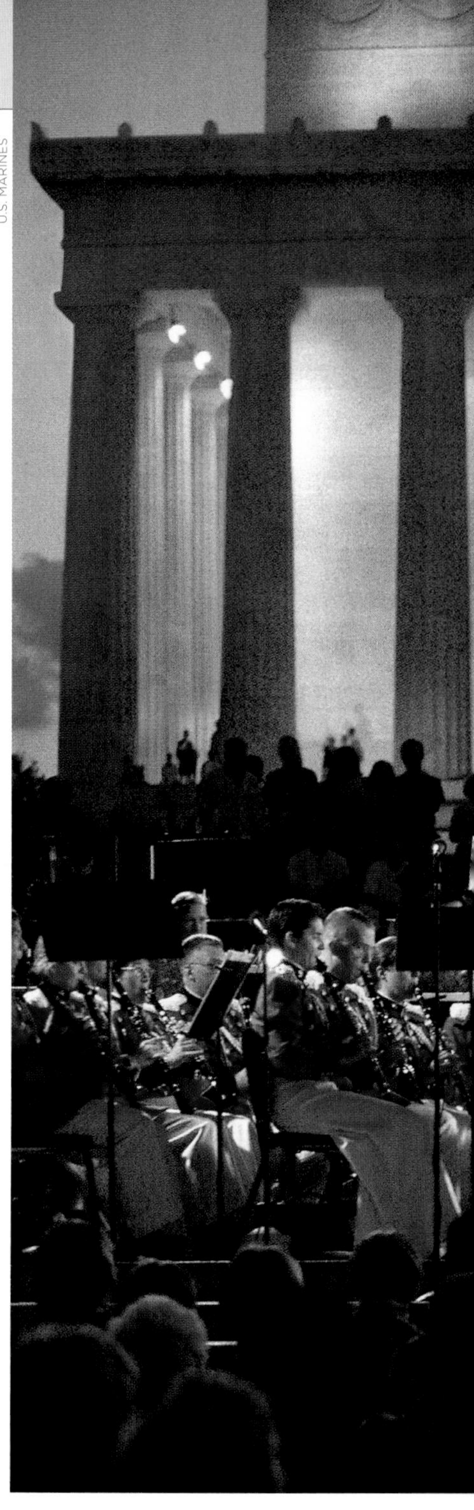

IN 1798, MARINE Maj. William W. Burrows asked for $10 from all colleagues for the purpose of underwriting a band. President John Adams deemed the musicians fine indeed, and asked them to make their White House debut on New Year's Day, 1801. Thomas Jefferson, a musician himself, was even more taken with the band, which performed at his inaugural (as it has at the swearing in of every President since). Jefferson invited the Marine Band

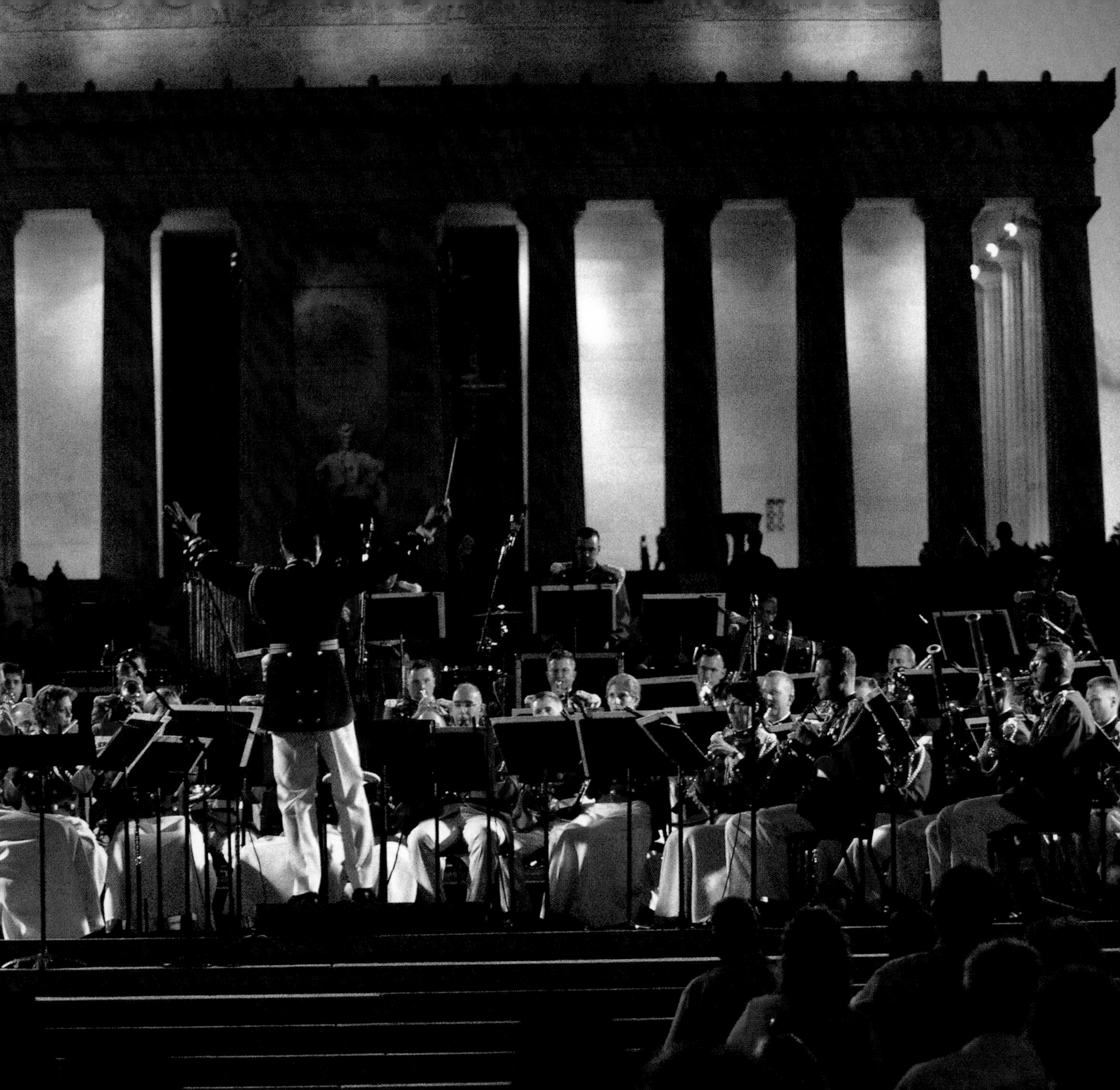

to play at the Executive Mansion regularly, and bestowed upon it a secondary title, "the President's Own." Despite such illustrious beginnings the band went into decline, reaching a nadir under director Louis Schneider, who once garnered this review: "Put a musician in the place of Schneider." Commandant Charles G. McCawley huffed, "The Band gives me more trouble than all the rest of the Corps put together," and sacked Schneider in 1880 as "unfit for service." Schneider's successor, the storied John Philip Sousa, turned the band into the wonderful orchestra it remains today, meantime writing 36 marches for it, including "Semper Fidelis," which means "always faithful" and has been the Corps' motto since 1883. The modern band is staffed by some of the country's finest musicians, who enlist as Marines with but one assignment: melody-making.

THE AIR FORCE

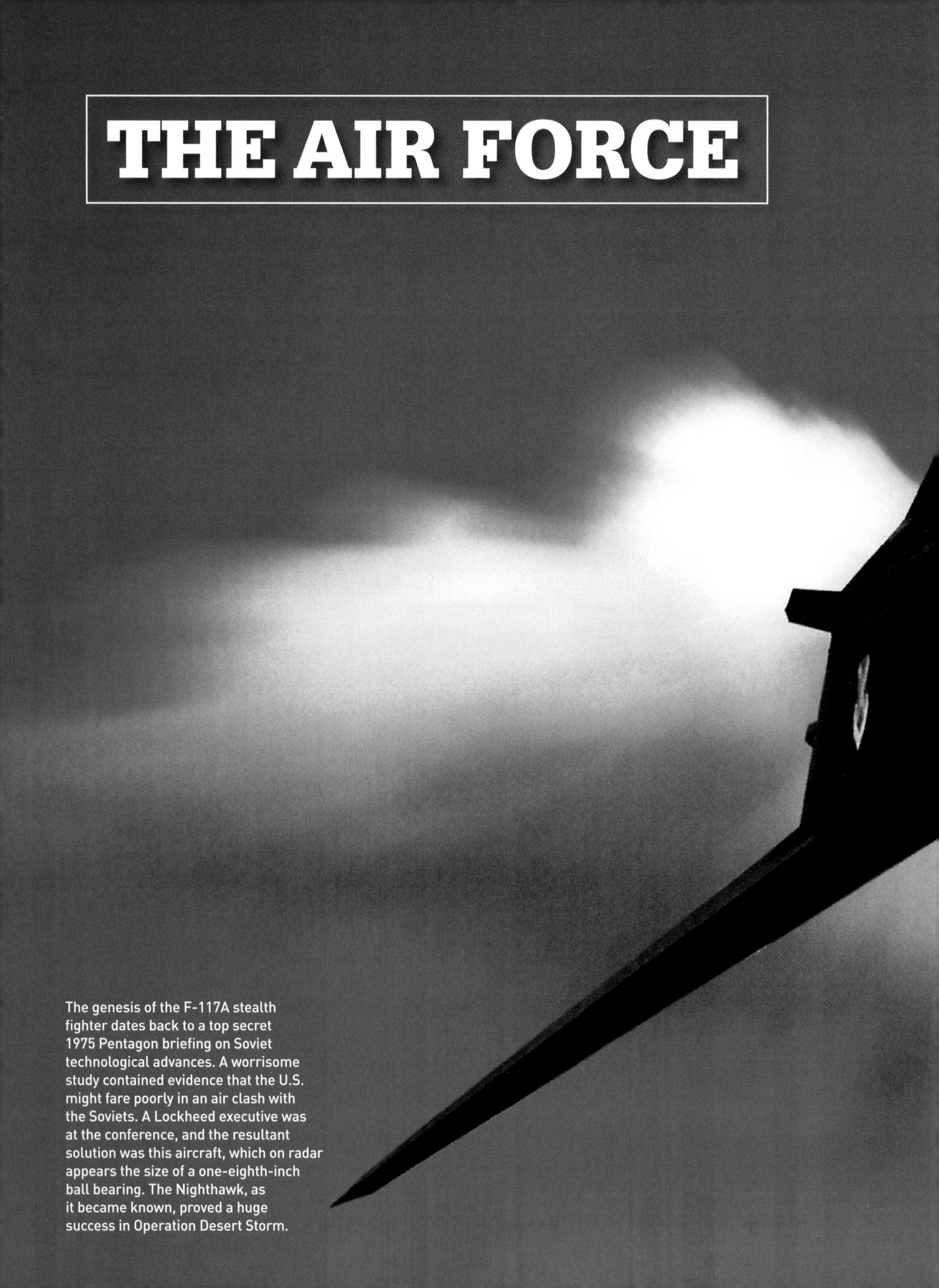

The genesis of the F-117A stealth fighter dates back to a top secret 1975 Pentagon briefing on Soviet technological advances. A worrisome study contained evidence that the U.S. might fare poorly in an air clash with the Soviets. A Lockheed executive was at the conference, and the resultant solution was this aircraft, which on radar appears the size of a one-eighth-inch ball bearing. The Nighthawk, as it became known, proved a huge success in Operation Desert Storm.

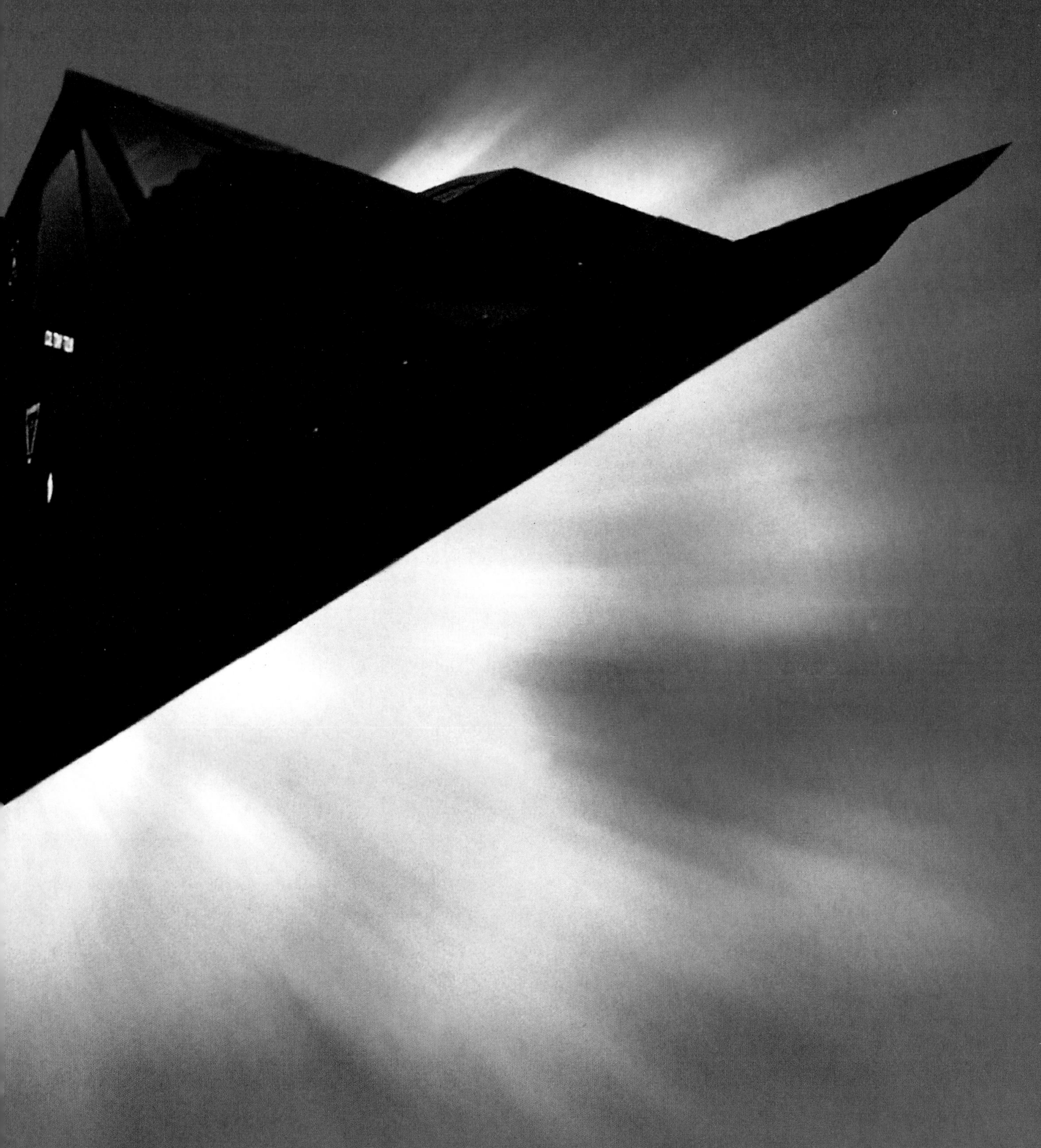

PHILLIP WALLICK PHOTOGRAPHY

THE AIR FORCE

"It is probable that future wars again will be conducted by a special class, the air force, as it was by the armored knights of the Middle Ages."

— *Gen. Billy Mitchell, 1925*

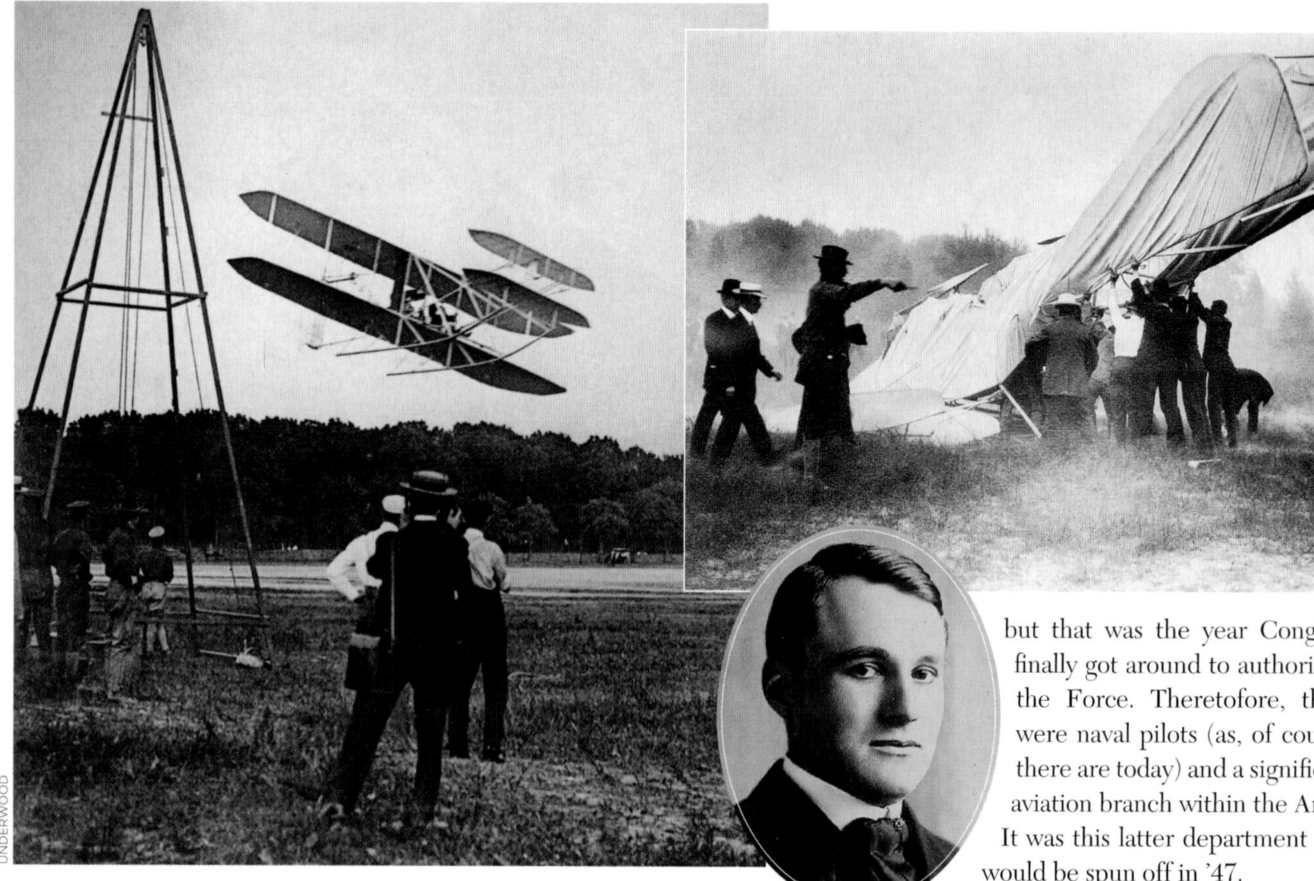

UNDERWOOD

CULVER (3)

In 1904 at Fort Myer, Army personnel observe a Wright brothers trial. Four years later, Orville's plane crashes from 75 feet (top, right). His passenger, Selfridge (above), is killed.

THE EJECTION SEAT. Murphy's Law. *Air Force One*. The U-2. Rolling Thunder. The wild blue yonder. The Air Force is a vital part of the nation's national defense, but it also has a remarkable presence in our domestic culture. And in recent years, when United States air strikes have become the principal—in some cases the only—extension of American military power, the Air Force has come to symbolize our force, will and determination.

All this from a relative stripling of a service: Unlike the centuries-old Army, Navy and Marines, the life of the Air Force can be measured in decades. It's true that American warriors were flying into battle well before 1947, but that was the year Congress finally got around to authorizing the Force. Theretofore, there were naval pilots (as, of course, there are today) and a significant aviation branch within the Army. It was this latter department that would be spun off in '47.

And so, the legendary World War I ace, Eddie Rickenbacker, was, in fact, an Army captain. The commander of the Air Service in that war, the equally renowned Billy Mitchell, was an Army general. His WWII counterpart, Henry H. "Hap" Arnold, was an Army general as well.

We can go much further back than those wars with American military aircraft. The Union deployed balloons to observe Confederate forces during the Civil War, and the U.S. Army did the same in 1898 during the Spanish-American war. The Army's Aeronautical Division was established in 1907 and received its first plane, a customized Wright Flyer, the following year. Its

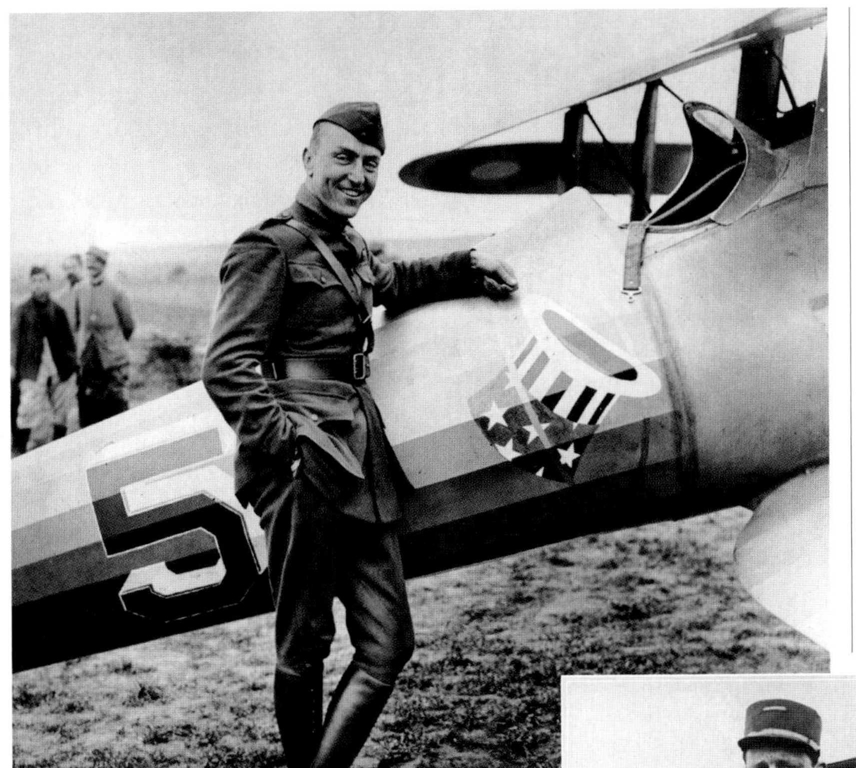

HULTON/GETTY

first two aviators were assigned in 1909 but then reassigned to ground duty; an Army lieutenant, Thomas E. Selfridge, became the first serviceman killed in a plane when a Flyer piloted by none other than Orville Wright crashed on September 17, 1908, at Fort Myer, Va.

The prehistoric Air Force took part in a few skirmishes against Mexican bandits but was hardly ready for big-time action when World War I broke out. This was not a problem, since at the beginning of the war planes were used only for reconnaissance. With the 1915 invention of the Fokker machine gun, however, the airplane was transformed into a formidable weapon. Even before the United States entered the war, in 1917, many American aces were fighting with the French Air Service in a division known as the Lafayette Escadrille. Ultimately, American pilots in the Great War were credited with shooting down 781 enemy planes, along with 72 balloons.

Despite Mitchell's entreaties to build a bigger air force, the Army sector did not grow rapidly between the world wars. There were, nevertheless, significant technological advances in the early '30s, chief among them the development of an all-metal bomber and the huge B-17 Flying Fortress. By the 1940s it had become clear to all that wars could be won or lost in the air, and by the time the U.S. entered the second global conflict, it was with a massive and still-growing air corps. During World War II the Army Air Force flew 2,362,800 sorties and dropped 2,057,244 tons of bombs—ending matters in 1945 with the two atomic devices unleashed on Hiroshima and, then, Nagasaki.

In the aftermath of the war, it became evident to the Army and to policymakers in Washington, D.C., that changing world conditions and rapidly developing technologies called for an independent air combat service. Consequently, as mentioned earlier, the United States Air Force was officially christened in 1947.

Once the U.S. had entered World War I, Rickenbacker (top) and other Yanks were taught to fly by Raoul Lufbery, an American born in France who was a legend with the Lafayette Escadrille. Lufbery, called by Rickenbacker the "ace of aces," had 17 kills to his credit when he himself was shot down in 1918.

In the more than half century that followed, the Air Force would carve out its own slice of American history and lore. It would contribute to American legend a singularly colorful test pilot, Charles E. Yeager, the first man to break the sound barrier. It would perform a near miraculous airlift to Berlin to thwart a Soviet blockade in a signature early confrontation of the cold war. For more than a year beginning in 1948, the Air Force won hearts and smiles in Operation Little Vittles, a humanitarian gesture that involved handkerchiefs full of candy and some 250,000 small parachutes. In all, more than two million tons of treats and food, and needed coal, rained on West Berlin.

The Air Force would supply a pilot, Capt. Francis Gary Powers, whose 1960 capture in a downed U-2 spy plane would result in the cancellation of a summit meeting between President Dwight D. Eisenhower and Soviet Premier Nikita Khrushchev. It would provide the venue for the swearing-in of President Lyndon B. Johnson on a terrible November afternoon in 1963. It would penetrate space, enemy airspace and new frontiers of speed.

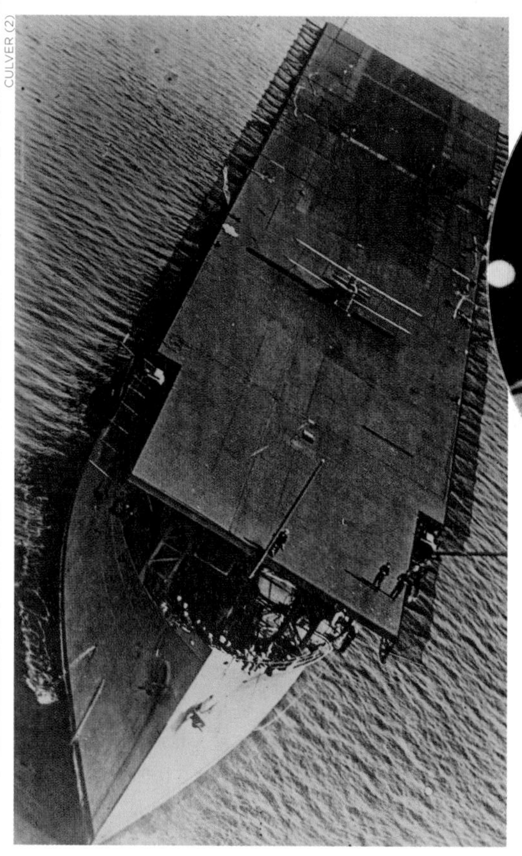

CULVER (2)

And it would bequeath an enduring morsel of American social commentary when, in 1949, Capt. Ed Murphy, an engineer at Wright-Patterson Air Force Base in Ohio working on crash-research testing, was struck with one of the immutable insights of the age: Whatever possibly can go wrong, will.

With its extensive ties to industry, the Air Force became a foremost sponsor of research and, indirectly, one of the great providers of well-paying jobs in the United States. With its breathtaking academy in Colorado Springs, the Air Force developed a rigorous strategic studies program that, today, runs the gamut from geography, weather and aviation physics to the philosophy course War and Morality. With its customized VC-25A aircraft—known to the world as *Air Force One*—the Force became not only an air chauffeur of the President but also the operator of the most famous jetliner in the world, itself a symbol of American might. With figures such as Gen. Curtis E. LeMay, the Strategic Air Command leader from 1948 to 1957, and Gen. Daniel "Chappie" James Jr. of the Tuskegee Airmen, the first African American to win four stars and, later, commander in chief of the North American Air Defense and Aerospace Defense Command, the

BROWN BROTHERS

Billy Mitchell, whose career dated to the Spanish-American War, was a visionary. By the 1920s, when vessels such as the steamship *Langely* were being converted to "aeroplane carriers," Mitchell foresaw a brave new world of air power. But his ideas met with resistance in the Army, and it would be left to Arnold (below) to oversee the transformation of the often ignored Army Air Corps into the not-to-be-denied United States Air Force. Arnold was the only man to be a general in both services.

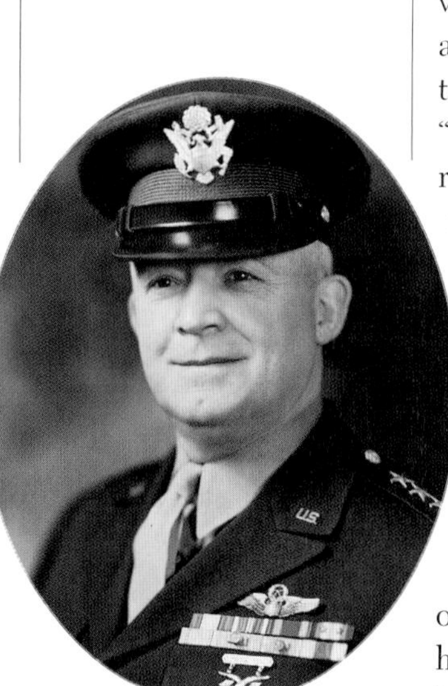

Air Force contributed some of the most vivid characters in American military history. Consider but briefly this testimony from James, who served in World War II, Korea and Vietnam: "I've fought in three wars and three more wouldn't be too many to defend my country. I love America and as she has weaknesses or ills, I'll hold her hand."

In the Korean War, Air Force engagement began as early as the second day of the conflict, June 27, 1950, when four F-82s flying from Itazuke Air Base in Japan shot down seven North Korean YAK aircraft with no American casualties. In the Vietnam era, the Air Force undertook bombing, intelligence and transport operations in missions that eventually also took aviators over Laos and Cambodia. In the Persian Gulf War, relentless Air Force strikes paved the way for a ground campaign that, because of the success from on high, required only 100 hours. In Afghanistan, the Air Force employed fighters, tankers, transports, bombers and command-and-control aircraft, assisted by satellites and the RQ-1 Predator reconnaissance vehicle, a medium-altitude unmanned aerial device that weighs only 950 pounds and is able to fly up to 140 miles an hour.

Air Force aircraft, which could be on the scene in an instant, were often used strategically. Bombing halts, for example, were important elements of diplomatic efforts to end the war in Vietnam. So, too, were their opposites: stepped-up bombing campaigns like the one President Richard M. Nixon undertook in the winter of 1972. ("The North Vietnamese have agreed to go back to the negotiating table on our terms," Nixon told a confidant, Charles Colson. "They can't take the bombing anymore.") In recent years Air Force aviators have enforced no-fly zones in Iraq, conducted another humanitarian airlift, in Bosnia, and provided relief supplies to victims of an earthquake in India, flooding in Africa, wildfires in America's West and hurricanes in Florida. Air Force pilots have flown three Presidents to the Middle East on two separate occasions, in 1981 for the funeral of Egyptian President Anwar Sadat and in 1995 for the funeral of Israeli Prime Minister Yitzhak Rabin. They have taken former Presidents to their new lives as civilians, and to their burial sites.

Over the years, scores of Air Force aircraft have stirred the American imagination. The B-52 was for decades the primary long-range heavy bomber in the United States arsenal. The EC-121D Constellation toted six tons of electronic gear and was used extensively in the Vietnam War. The delta-winged Convair B-58A Hustler was the Air Force's first supersonic operational bomber. The X-15, unveiled in 1959 and carried aloft by a B-52, reached into the lower edge of space when it attained an altitude of 67 miles in 1963. The following year, the SR-71 Blackbird became the world's fastest aircraft—more than 2,200 mph—to take off from the ground. It was able to survey 100,000 square miles of the earth's surface in one hour. The F-117A stealth fighter proved a dramatic success in Operation Desert Storm. Its flat, angular surfaces coated with a secret radar-absorbent material were impervious to detection, permitting the pilot to hug the hills and dales of the desert topography, thereby increasing bombing accuracy. And the Global Hawk is an unmanned drone that can soar to 65,000 feet while securing high resolution images in any weather.

The men and women of the Air Force—proudly, they sing in their anthem, "we live in fame or go down in flame"—have, since the inception of the service, been stalwart exemplars of the American fighting spirit. The Korean War featured the first example of combat between jet aircraft; some air battles involved as many as 150 fighters at one time. In 1967 the Air Force downed 77 North Vietnamese MIGs during Operation Rolling Thunder, while losing 25 of its own planes in air-to-air combat. In Desert Storm, Air Force operations destroyed 60 percent of Iraq's tanks, 60 percent of its artillery and 40 percent of its armored vehicles before any American boots hit the ground running. More recently, we have seen in images from Kabul and Kandahar what the Force has been able to accomplish in Afghanistan.

But the impact of the Air Force hasn't been felt only in war. The service designed the Atlas rocket. Yes, the Atlas was the nation's first intercontinental ballistic missile, and had the ability to deliver a nuclear warhead to any target around the globe. But its greatest role was as the booster propelling American astronauts into space during Project Mercury in the early 1960s. Titan II missiles, the Air Force's most powerful ICBMs until they were retired in 1987, were the boosters that thrust Gemini astronauts into orbit in 1965 and 1966. Today, the Air Force's Global Positioning System, which was vital in directing bombers during the Afghanistan and Iraq conflicts, is indispensable to archaeologists, oceanographers and even vacationers lost in a rental car in Yellowstone National Park.

At the dawn of the new millennium, the Air Force issued "Vision 2020," a statement of its role and goals for the future. "We are warriors," the Air Force said. "We will fight and win wherever our nation needs us. The aerospace realm is our domain, and we are vigilant in our commitment to defend, control and use it in our nation's interest." Off they go, after all these years, into the wild blue yonder, climbing high into the sun.

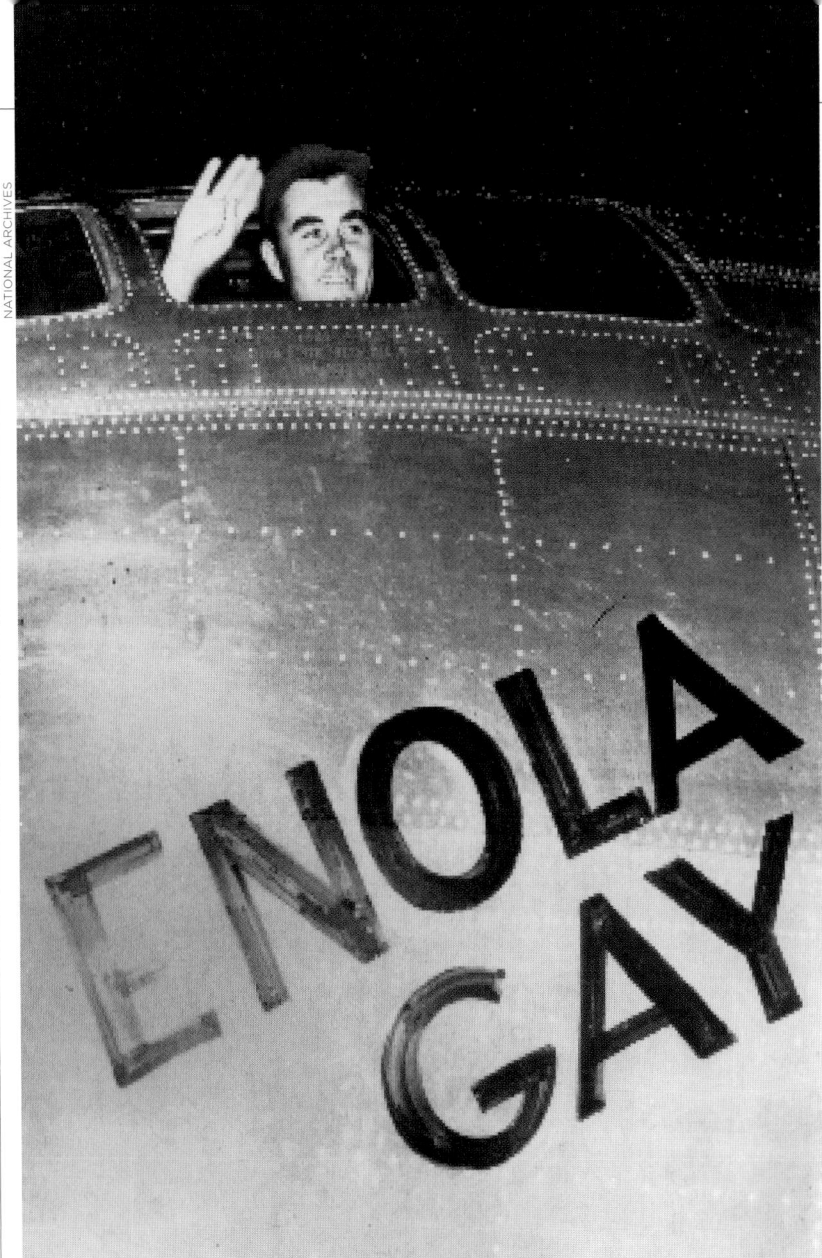

Two final, crucial missions of the Army Air Force came in August 1945. On the sixth, pilot Col. Paul Tibbets Jr. waves from his B-29, the *Enola Gay*, before taking off to drop an atomic bomb on Hiroshima. Three days later a larger bomb hit Nagasaki. On August 14, Japan surrendered.

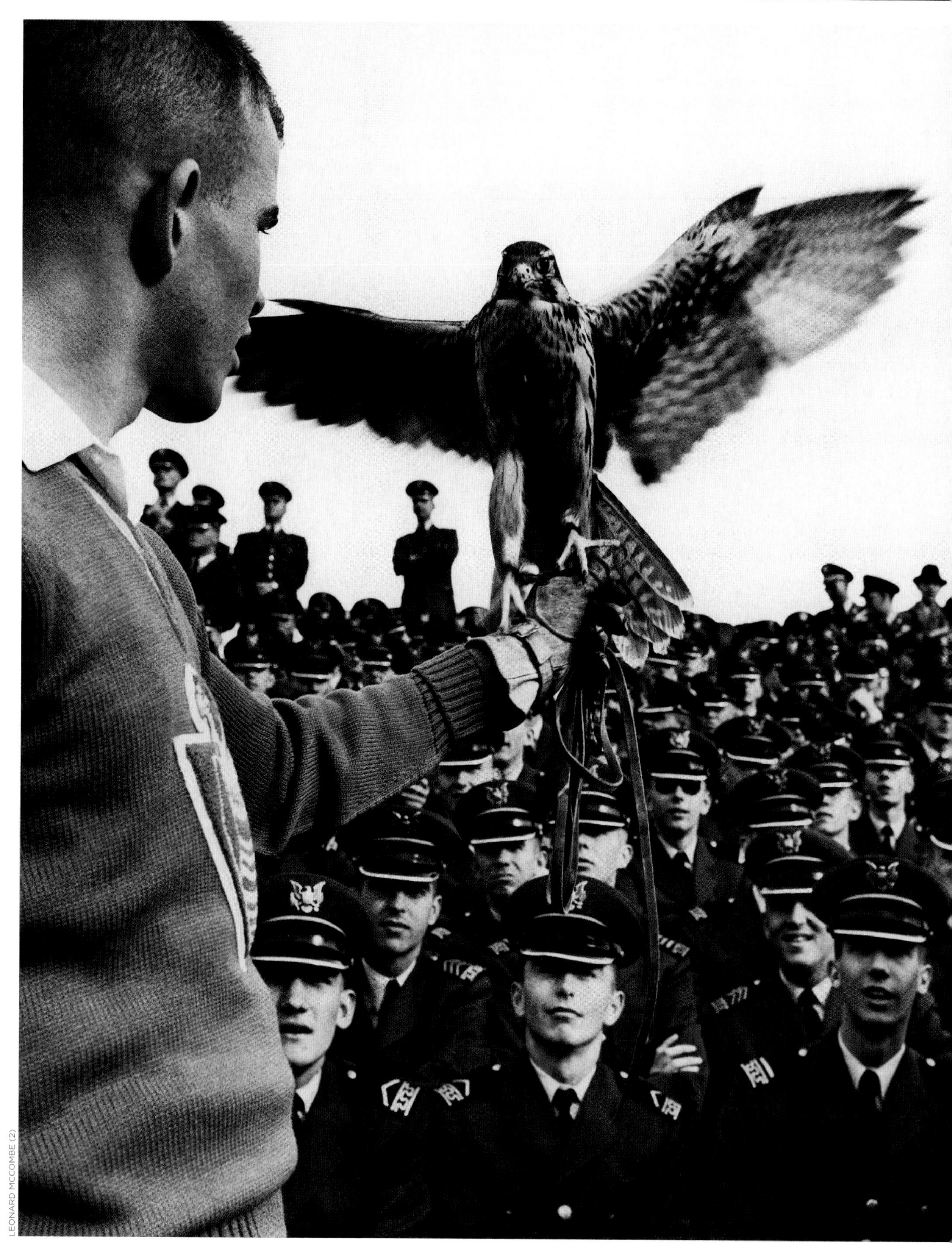

LEONARD MCCOMBE (2)

UNITED STATES AIR FORCE ACADEMY

The last ones in with both a service and a school are, in the modern age, the first ones in during wartime.

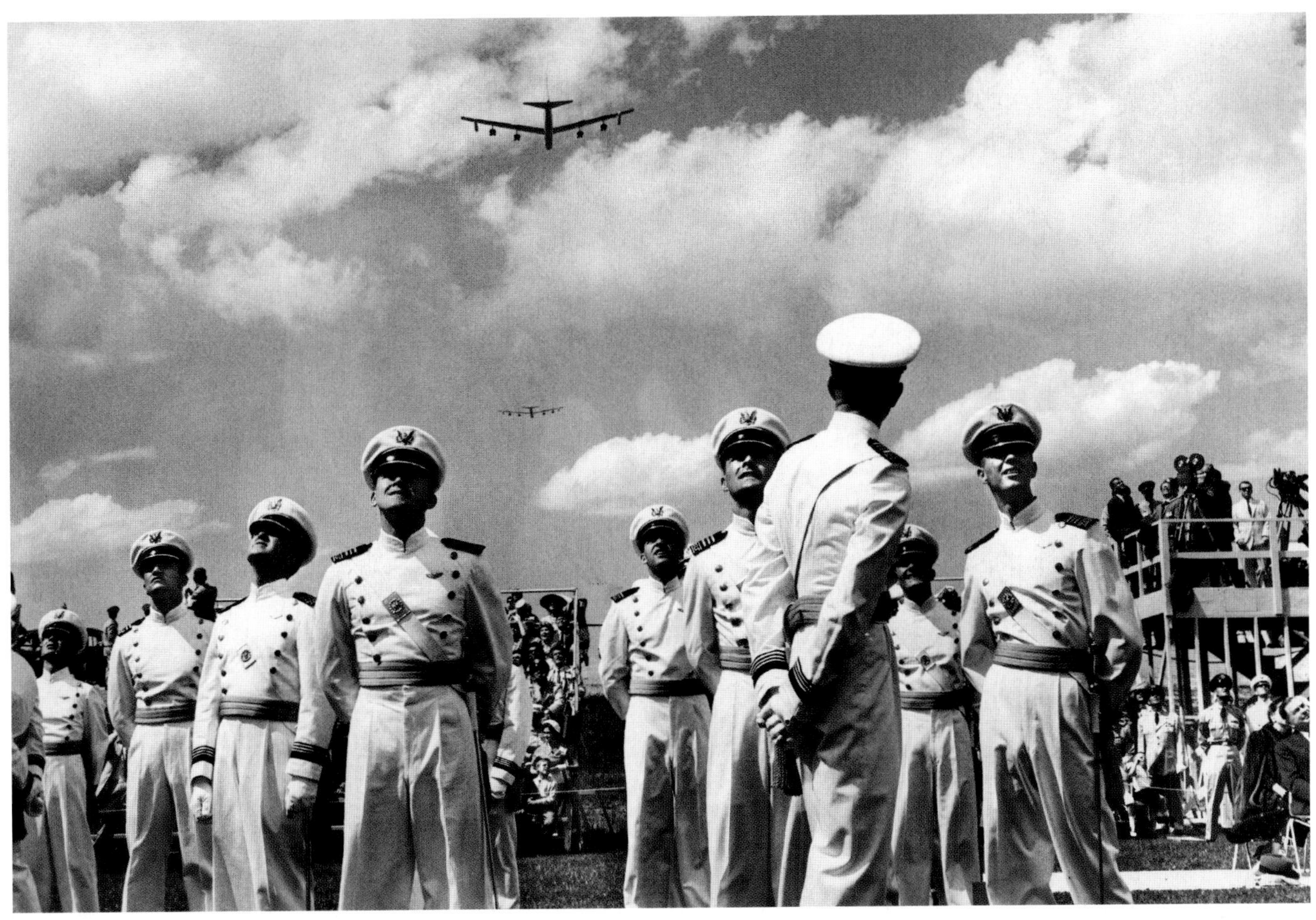

THIS INSTITUTION was yet another brilliant notion of the air service visionary Billy Mitchell. Like most of General Mitchell's other very good ideas—an independent Air Force, increased watchfulness at Pearl Harbor—it was ignored when he first floated it, back in the 1920s. Congress finally got around to authorizing the academy in 1954, and the gleaming 18,000-acre campus in the foothills of the Rockies in Colorado Springs opened four years later. All cadets at the academy were—and are—preparing for careers as Air Force officers, and all of them are required to take courses in the humanities, engineering and military strategies. They also learn the Force's standards for honor and ethics. As at West Point and Annapolis, the hoary tradition of hazing is not what it was in the old days. But much else today remains the same: up at 6:30, taps at 11, a rigorous day in between. There are now some 4,200 cadets on the Air Force Academy campus, and as recent wars have shown, their role in America's defense has become all the more important.

Shortly after the doors opened in Colorado Springs in 1958, LIFE visited America's newest service academy. We found the drill similar to Army's and Navy's, with the suitable addition of a huge western sky. Opposite: A falconer with mascot entertains during a sporting event.

THE AIR FORCE

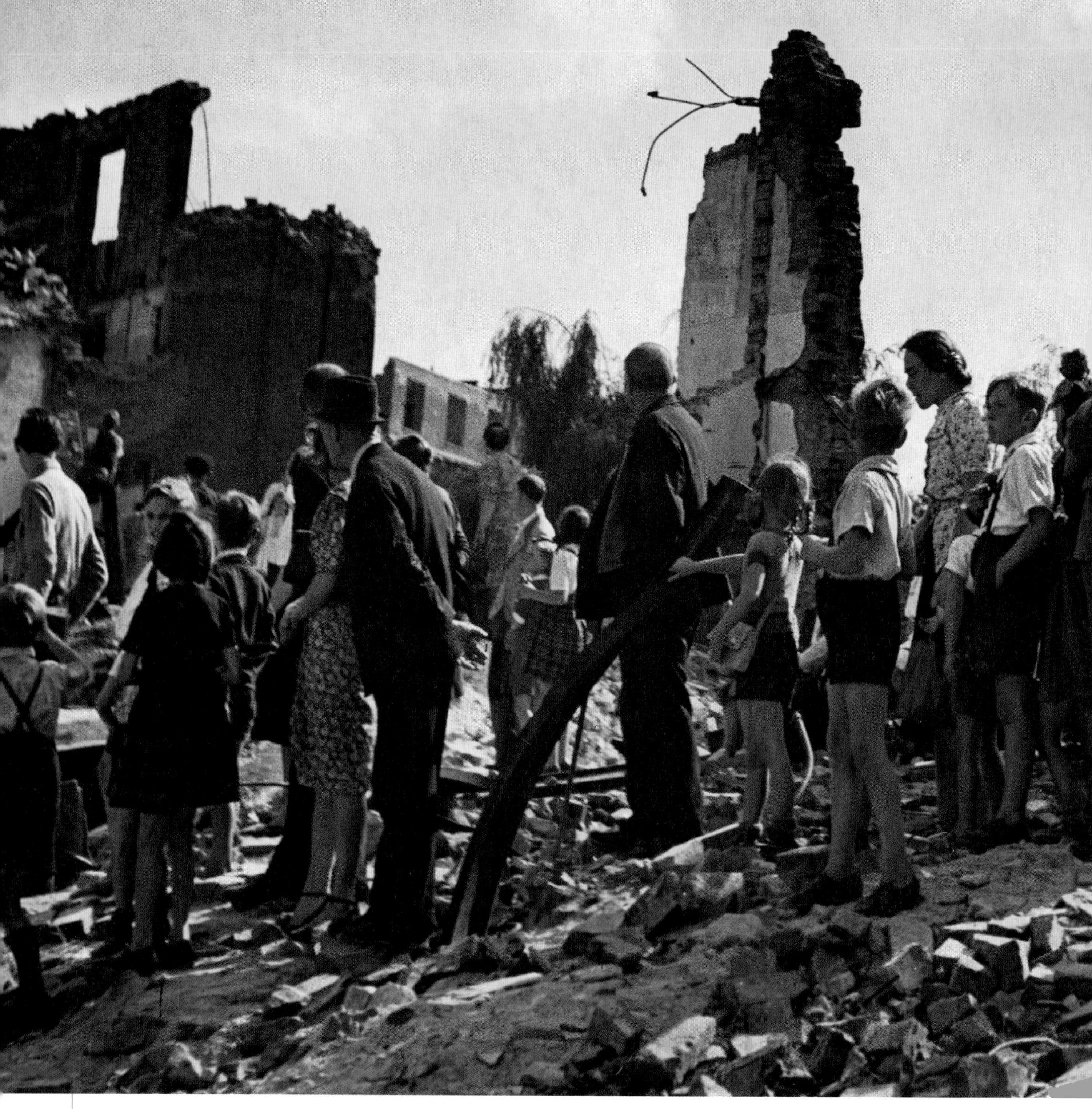

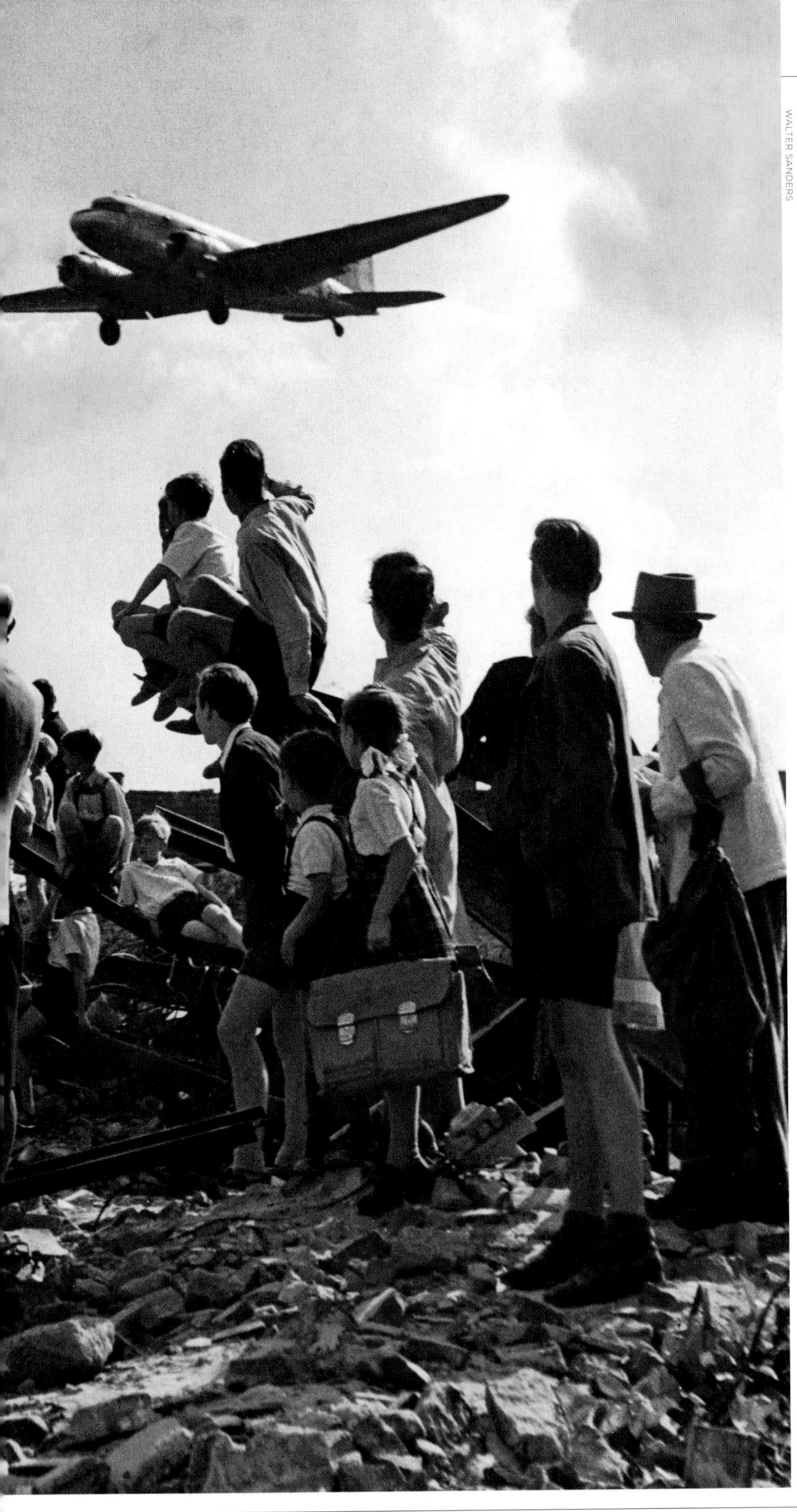

WALTER SANDERS

NOT BOMBS, BUT BREAD
In June 1948, the U.S.S.R. shut down all passages through the Soviet zone into western Berlin—rail, water, roadway. They hoped to drive out Western troops, thereby forcing the residents to accept communism. But one route remained open: the air. On June 26, the U.S. Air Force began to ferry supplies into the city. From then until September 30, 1949, the American and British air forces (and, on a much smaller scale, the U.S. Navy) filled the skies over Berlin. At the height of operations, planes were landing every three minutes. The flights were so synchronized that if one couldn't touch down on schedule, it had to return to base with its load intact. In all, the Berlin Airlift provided an incredible 2,326,406 tons of food, coal and supplies. By comparison, the 1990s multinational airlift into Sarajevo involved 179,910 tons. Here, in July 1948, needy Berliners look skyward as a U.S. C-47 brings in vital cargo.

INSTANT FIREPOWER

When ground troops in Vietnam wanted help in a hurry, they radioed for "Puff," a.k.a. "Puff the Magic Dragon," a.k.a. "Spooky." By any name, it added up to one thing: the workhorse gunship AC-47. This plane, adapted from the DC-3 commercial airliner, was used for transport, towing and the like in World War II and Korea. In Vietnam, however, three sidefiring 7.62mm miniguns were added, each firing 6,000 rounds per minute. The guns were fixed, so the pilot had to tilt the craft to hit the desired target. For this 1966 combat photo, LIFE's Larry Burrows persuaded the Air Force to remove half of the AC-47's rear door. Then he strapped himself in and leaned outside the plane as it circled the Vietcong position.

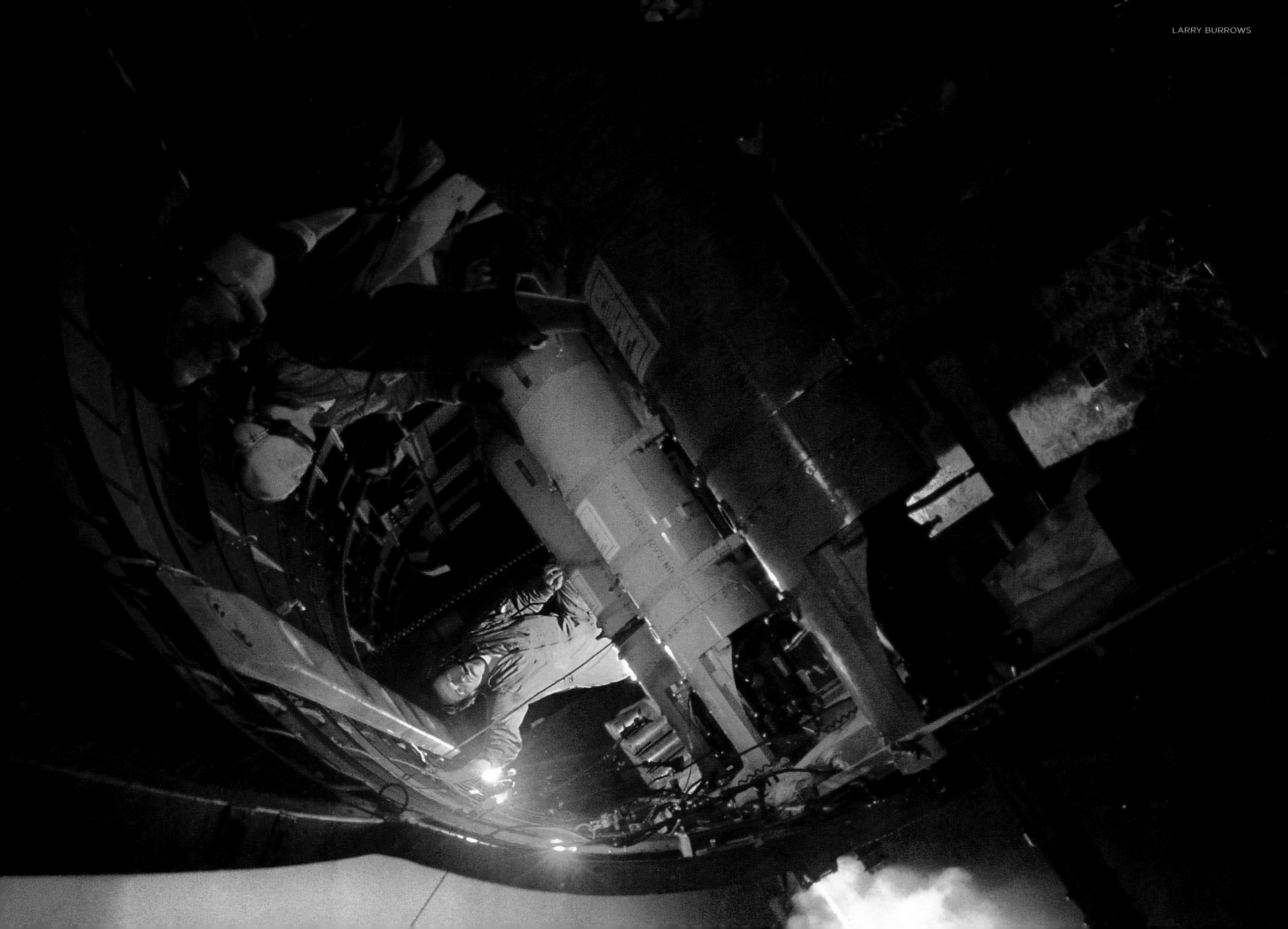

LARRY BURROWS

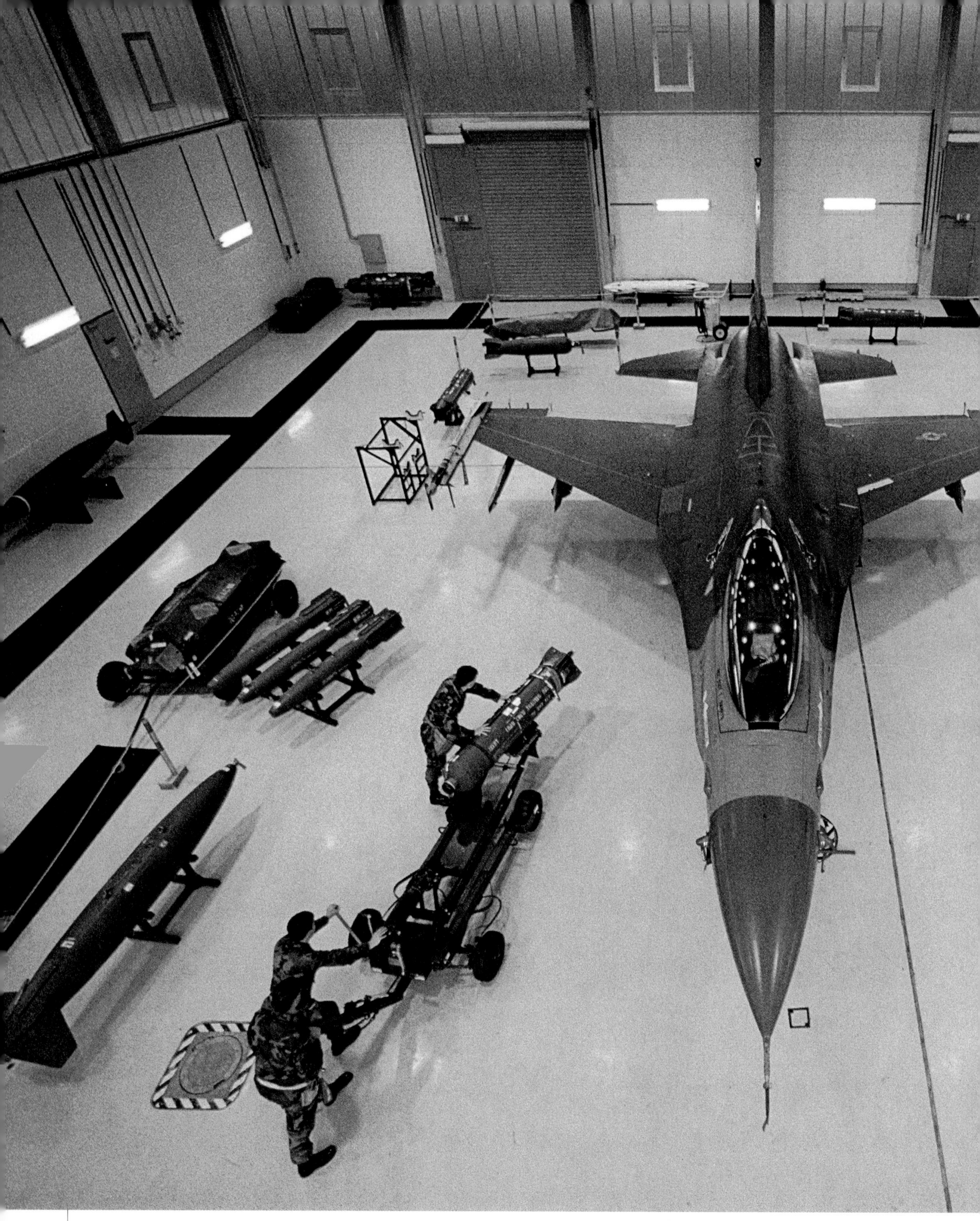

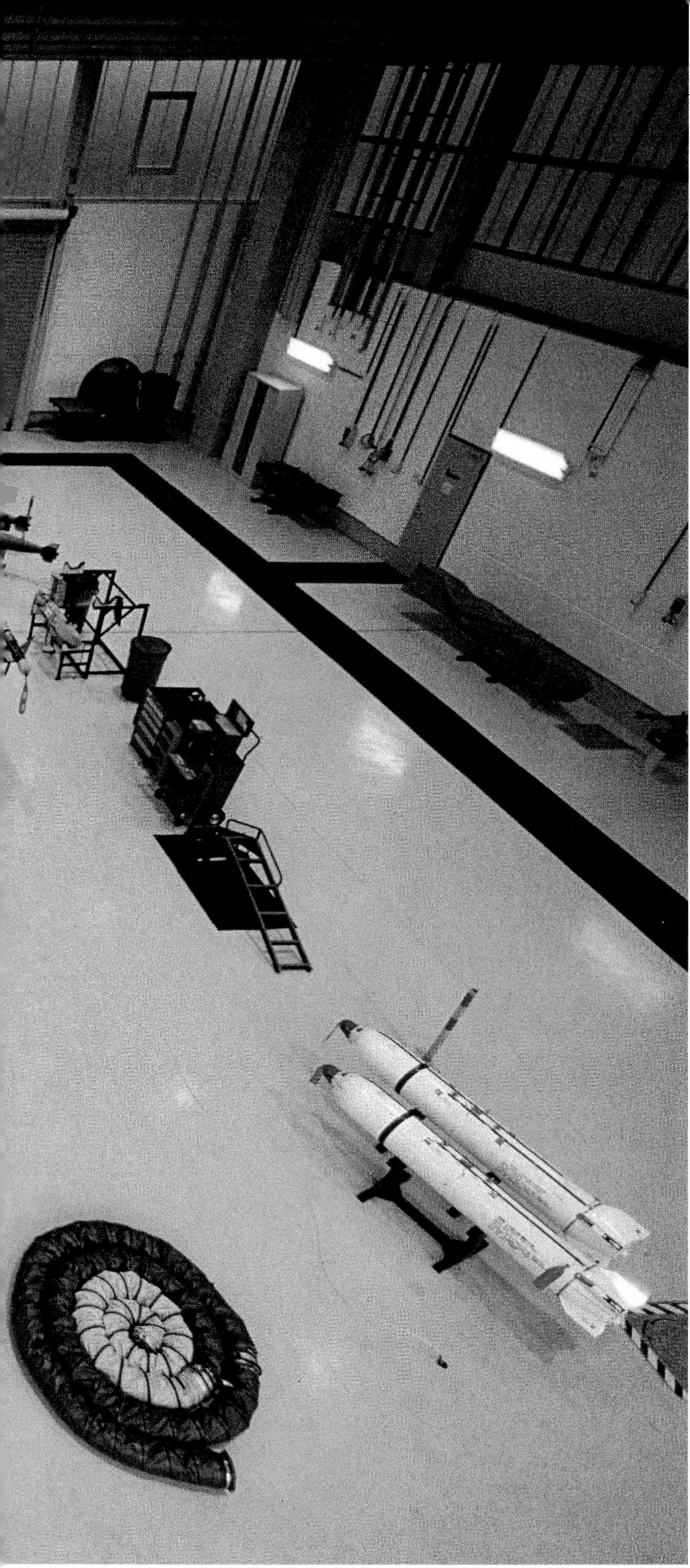

MARK PETERS/DEPARTMENT OF DEFENSE

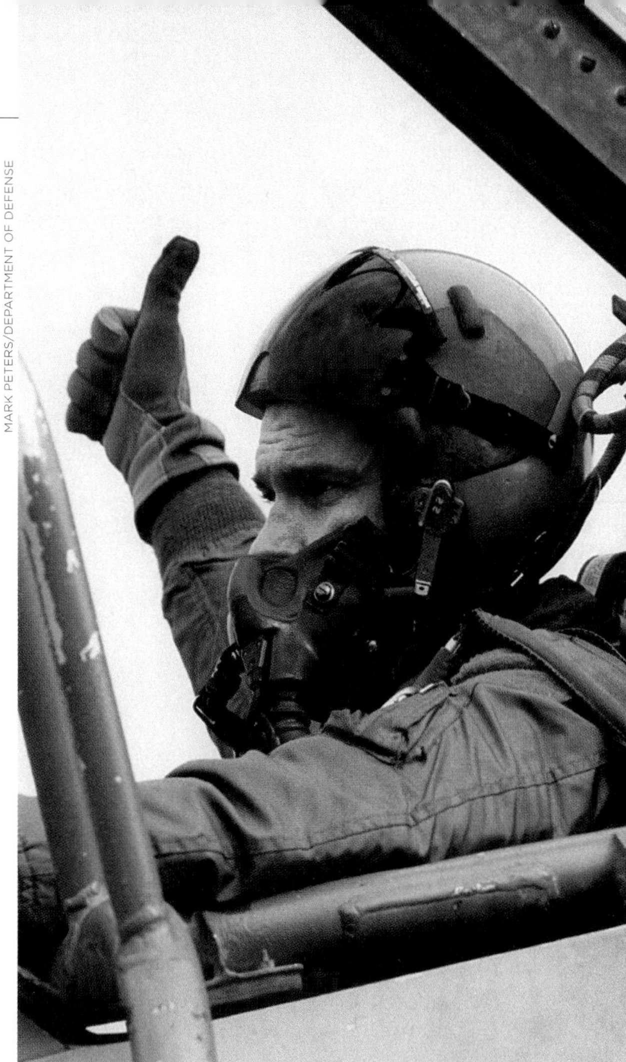

NEIL LEIFER

DESERT STORM DEPLOYMENT
The plane at left is hangared at Ramstein Air Base in Germany in January 1990. It is being fitted for Reforger, a NATO exercise. The plane is an F-16 Fighting Falcon. According to a USAF fact sheet, "the F-16's maneuverability and combat radius (distance it can fly to enter air combat, stay, fight and return) exceed that of all potential threat fighter aircraft." It delivers its weapons accurately in any weather. The Falcon's training and superior qualifications served it in good stead when Operation Desert Storm commenced a year later, on January 16, 1991, at 6:38 p.m. EST. On that day, U.S. warplanes attacked Kuwait, Baghdad and other military targets in Iraq. Six weeks and 69,406 Air Force sorties later, the war was over. The F-16, the backbone of the Air Force, had flown more than any other plane. Above, a pilot returns after a successful mission.

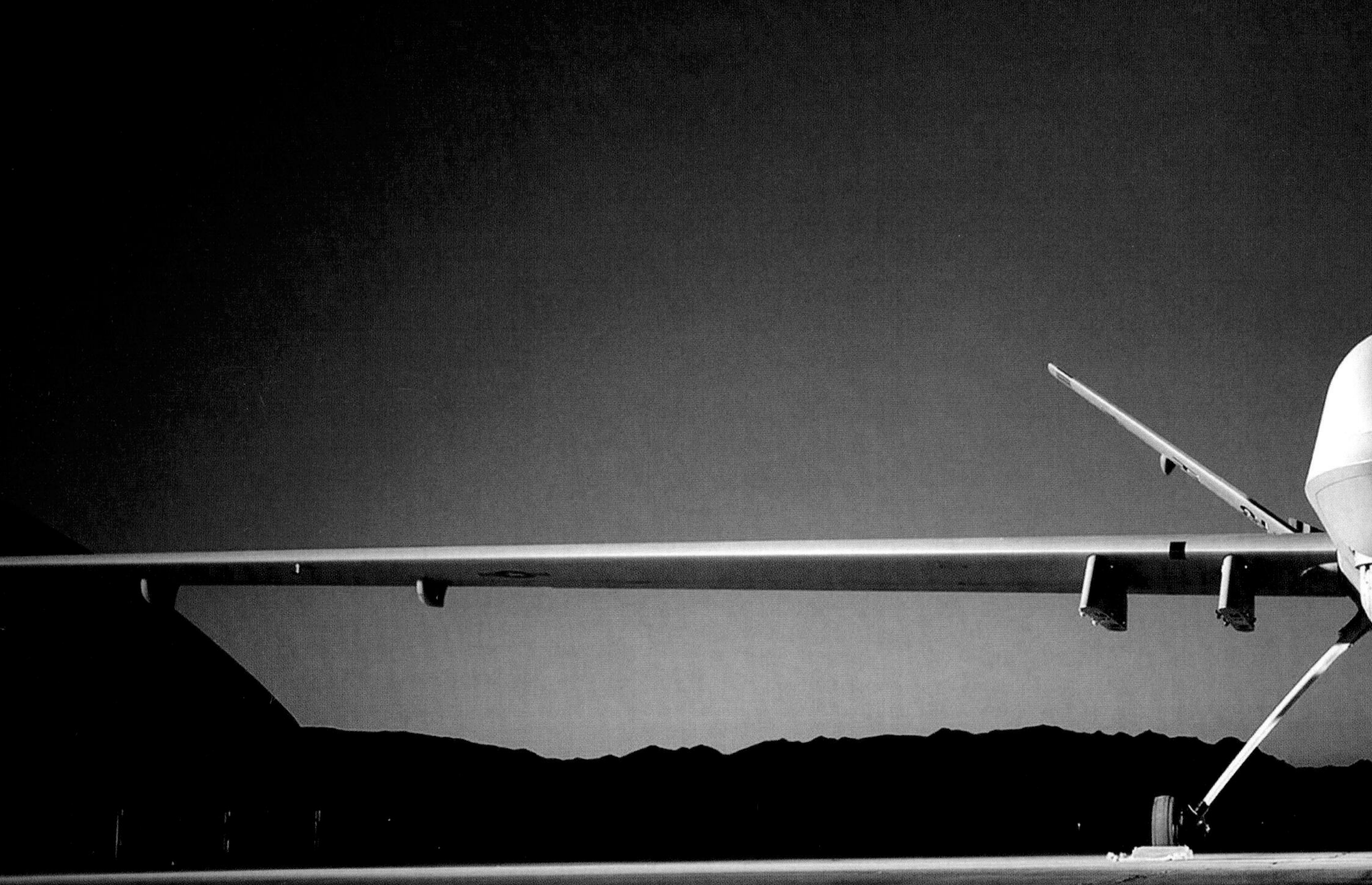

ENLISTING DRONES

Seldom if ever in the history of the U.S. military has such a radical transformation in not only surveillance but combat itself so rapidly changed the way we wage war. It was in 2001, during the initial night of ground fighting in Afghanistan, that the U.S. first ordered a strike utilizing an "unmanned aerial vehicle"—colloquially, a drone: a flying robot that could see things below on the battleground, process the knowledge and, now, attack. *Predator Number 3034,* the drone deployed that night, is now on display in the National Air and Space Museum in Washington, D.C.—a showpiece along with the *Spirit of St. Louis* and Mercury program space capsules. That Predator drone's descendants have multiplied like rabbits, and today a third of all Air Force aircraft are unmanned, while the other services use drones as well (the Navy has a class of submersible drones called SeaFox). It is estimated that in the last decade, remote-controlled drones have killed more than 50 top-level al-Qaeda or Taliban leaders throughout the world, and perhaps 3,000 people in Pakistan alone; nearly 500 drone attacks were launched in 2012 in Afghanistan. There is no question that, despite the military's ability to home in on targets, there has been collateral damage. Estimates of civilian casualties in Pakistan in the past decade have ranged from around 300 to nearly 900, and the debate over the ethics of using this powerful tactic continues, even as it seems clear that drones are here to stay.

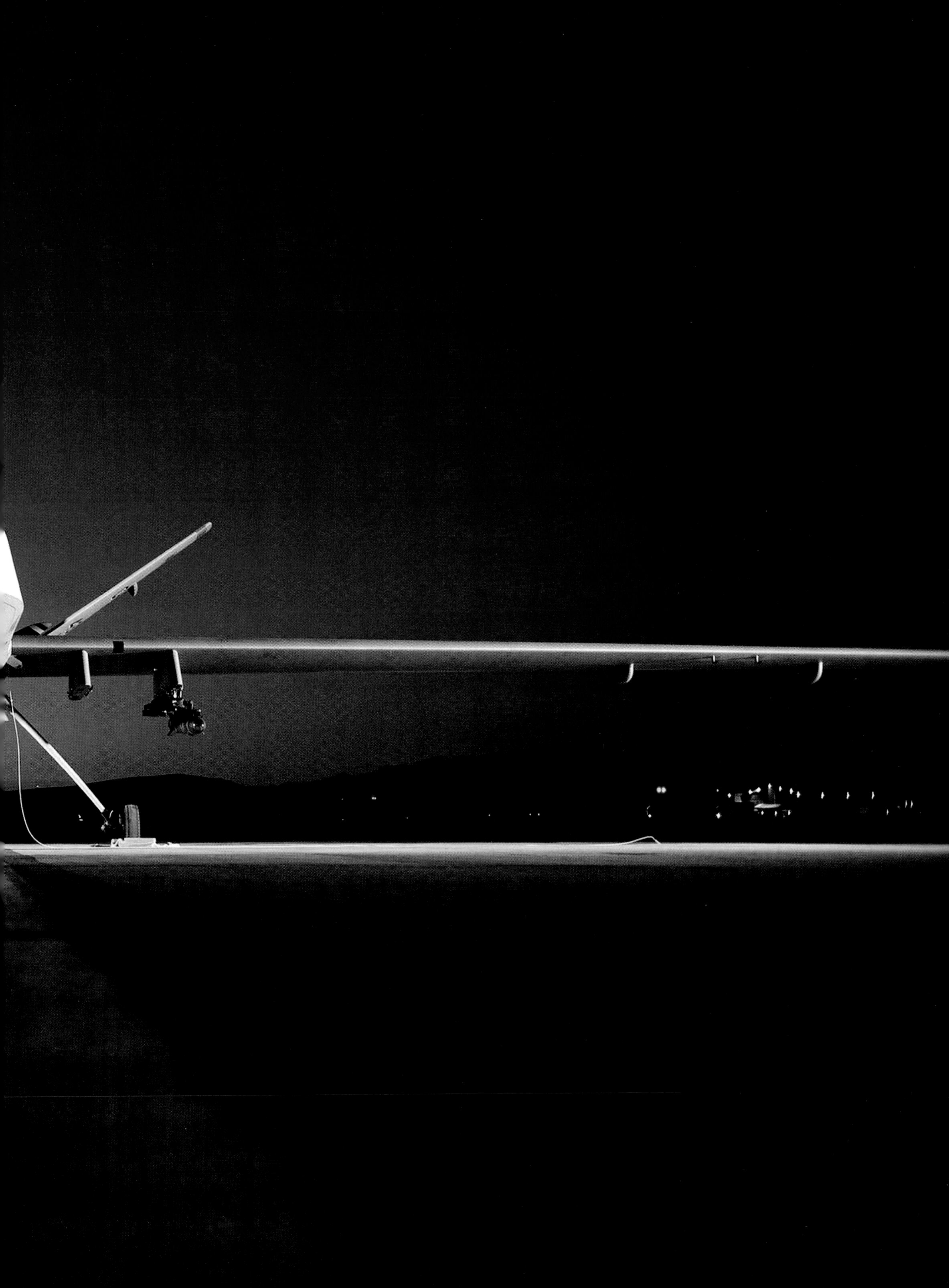

THE ULTIMATE SACRIFICE

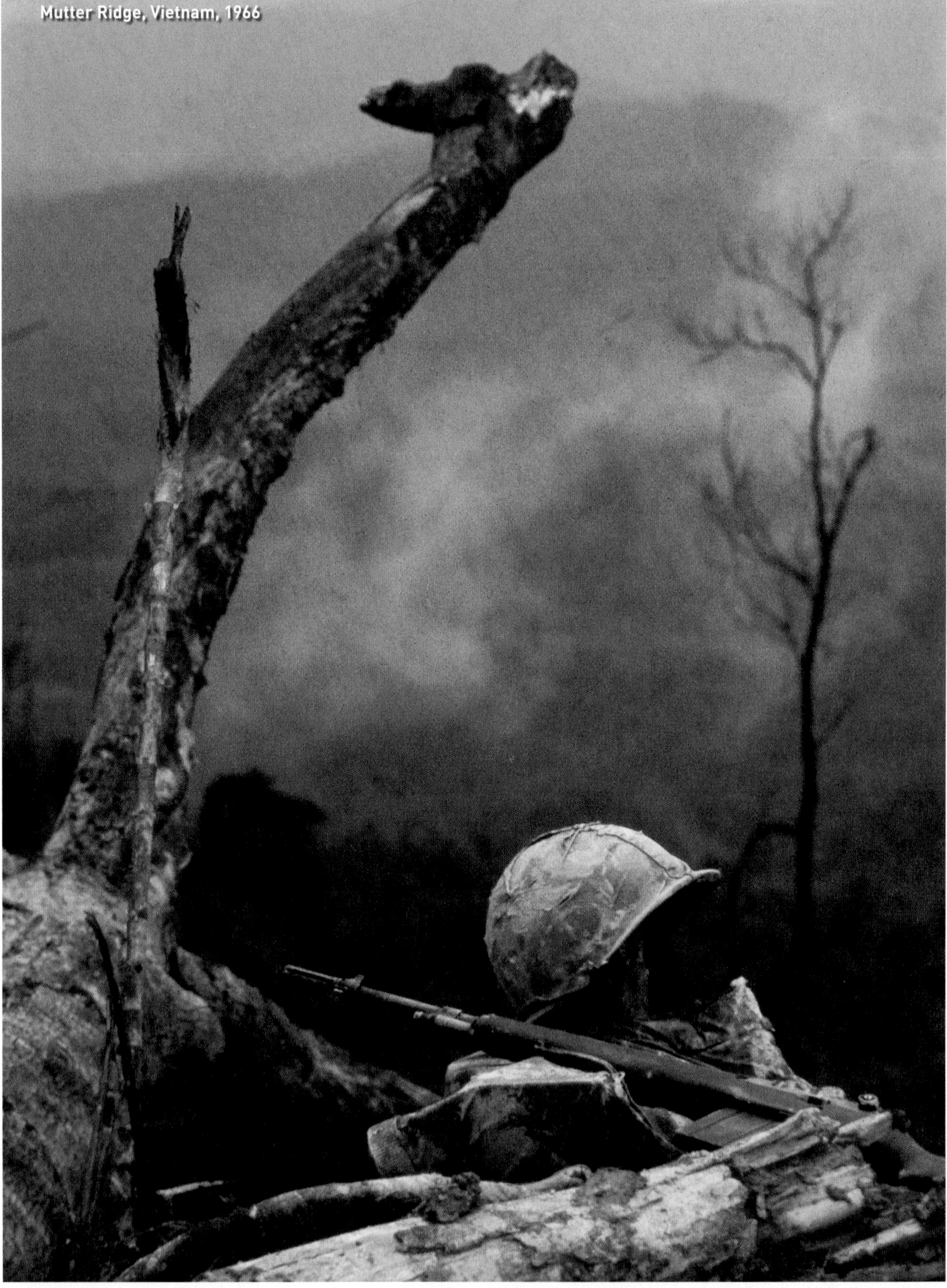

Mutter Ridge, Vietnam, 1966